Commodities and Commodity Derivatives

For other titles in the Wiley Finance Series
please see *www.wiley.com/finance*

Commodities and commodity derivatives

"The book, written by a leading expert in mathematical finance, is long overdue. It is one of the preciously few to succeed in providing a unified analytical approach to commodity markets. Hélyette Geman superbly combines her academic depth, theoretical insights, pedagogical talent, and unique practical experience acquired during many years as advisor to major financial and large commodity trading companies, to give an excellent exposé of the most interesting and pressing issues in the world of commodities. The breadth of the book is remarkable. I recommend it to anyone interested in theory and practice of commodity derivatives."

Alexander Eydeland, Executive Director, Commodities, Morgan Stanley

"The first scientific compendium ever written on the intricacies linked to the physical nature of commodities and the pathologies encountered in their derivatives. Enjoy this impressive book and the tour of the exciting world of commodities."

Nassim Taleb, Founder and CEO, Empirica

"Professor Geman has accomplished the rarest of feats in this book. She has presented material in a way which is innovative, educational and highly insightful. This volume is written with clarity and deep understanding of commodities markets. It is a brilliant synthesis, and a must read for the educated layperson as well as the professional. Commodities markets have now taken center stage, and no credible investment manager can afford to ignore them."

Bernard Oppetit, Founder and CEO, Centaurus Capital

About the author

HELYETTE GEMAN is a Professor of Finance at the University Paris Dauphine and ESSEC Graduate Business School. She is a graduate of Ecole Normale Superieure in mathematics, holds a Masters degree in theoretical physics and a PhD in mathematics from the University Pierre et Marie Curie and a PhD in Finance from the University Pantheon Sorbonne. Professor Geman has been a scientific advisor to a number of major energy companies for the last decade, covering the spectrum of oil, natural gas and electricity as well as agricultural commodities origination and trading. She was previously the head of Research and Development at Caisse des Depots. She has published more than 60 papers in major finance journals including the *Journal of Finance, Mathematical Finance, Journal of Financial Economics, Journal of Banking and Finance* and *Journal of Business*. She has also written a book entitled *Insurance and Weather Derivatives* and is a Member of Honor of the French Society of Actuaries. Professor Geman's research includes asset price modeling using jump-diffusions and Lévy processes, commodity forward curve modeling and exotic option pricing for which she won the first prize of the Merrill Lynch Awards. She was named in 2004 in the Hall of Fame of Energy Risk.

Commodities and Commodity Derivatives

Modeling and Pricing for Agriculturals, Metals and Energy

Hélyette Geman

John Wiley & Sons, Ltd

Published by   John Wiley & Sons Ltd, The Atrium, Southern Gate, Chichester,
West Sussex PO19 8SQ, England
Telephone (+44) 1243 779777

Email (for orders and customer service enquiries): cs-books@wiley.co.uk
Visit our Home Page on www.wiley.com

Other Wiley Editorial Offices

John Wiley & Sons Inc., 111 River Street, Hoboken, NJ 07030, USA

Jossey-Bass, 989 Market Street, San Francisco, CA 94103-1741, USA

Wiley-VCH Verlag GmbH, Boschstr. 12, D-69469 Weinheim, Germany

John Wiley & Sons Australia Ltd, 33 Park Road, Milton, Queensland 4064, Australia

John Wiley & Sons (Asia) Pte Ltd, 2 Clementi Loop #02-01, Jin Xing Distripark, Singapore 129809

John Wiley & Sons Canada Ltd, 22 Worcester Road, Etobicoke, Ontario, Canada M9W 1L1

Wiley also publishes its books in a variety of electronic formats. Some content that appears
in print may not be available in electronic books.

Library of Congress Cataloging-in-Publication Data

Geman, Hélyette.
Commodities and commodity derivatives : modeling and pricing for
agriculturals, metals, and energy / Hélyette Geman.
    p. cm.
Includes bibliographical references and index.
ISBN 0-470-01218-8 (cloth : alk. paper)
1. Commodity futures.   I. Title.
HG6046.G46 2005
332.63'28 – dc22   2004027082

British Library Cataloguing in Publication Data

A catalogue record for this book is available from the British Library

ISBN 978-0-470-01218-5

Project management by Originator, Gt Yarmouth, Norfolk (typeset in 10/12pt Times)

To Arnaud, Laure, Nathanaël and Don
To the memory of my parents

Contents

Foreword

NASSIM NICHOLAS TALEB

It is a great honor to find myself writing this foreword for my thesis director's book – although once someone's student always her student, it feels awkward to comment on one's supervisor's work. I was also pleased to find myself among its first readers, and benefit from its contents, as this work contains the first scientific compendium ever written on the intricacies linked to the physical nature of commodities.

Commodity options are not just interesting; they harbor all the pathologies encountered in the practice of derivatives, to the point of perhaps teaching us how to value derivatives with a different, deeper approach. Methodologists consider that, to understand a phenomenon, there are two routes. The first consists in examining the regular, the ordinary and the well-behaved, and excluding the unusual. The other consists in examining pathologies, the abnormal cases, then closing in on the ordinary as the exception. Economists, alas, have traditionally tended to use the first method, by pushing the exceptions under the rug – while physicists and other hard scientists tend to resort to the second as a way to satisfy their curiosity about the world.

Why are commodity options the most interesting, and the least misunderstood, of all derivatives? And why are they the exception that would teach us about derivatives? I will attempt here to make a short list and show how we can generalize into the wrinkles of *all* options, including the generally perceived theory-friendly financial ones.

First, the temporal dimension. The action of borrowing and lending is hardly predictable in commodities. They are heavily grounded in their physical nature. We have been taught that securities are derived by arbitrage arguments that allow us to seamlessly borrow and lend, in order to move the asset and liability across the temporal dimension. This makes the passage from the spot to the forward (or future) seamless, smooth and direct. In the arbitrage relationship, the forward equals the spot times some function of the differential between the yield r_1 and the cost of carry r_2. Accordingly, the forward contract is a mere extension of the spot, with stochasticity entering on occasion with one or both of the rates r_1 and r_2 being nondeterministic.

Now consider that you are trading in products that are not transferable into the future. Arbitrage becomes hardly possible – and, with it, the arbitrage argument. You may be dealing with a perishable commodity, like, say, an agricultural product. Storage can cause shrinkage in quantity, as with, say, electricity. The forward might not be born yet, as in the case of cattle. Forward oil may still be in the ground and might cost no carry to the producer, whereas the arbitrageur would have to bear onerous storage costs. The relationship might hold, owing to the activities of the producer, but for arbitrage reasons.

How do you deal with it? Clearly, you need to treat every expiration like a separate underlying security. And you need to be careful about any arbitrage involving physical delivery. How does it apply to the other derivatives? Consider currency options. Currencies, I was told when I started trading two decades ago, were "clean". No worry, you just satisfy a forward obligation by buying spot and lending it, or vice versa. But every crisis, all except for one currency, the now defunct deutschmark, started behaving like commodities. They become impossible to borrow, sometimes, as was the case of the Irish punt, in 1992, commanding as high as several thousand percent interest rates. The Canadian dollar, the New Zealand and Australian currencies, all behaved unexpectedly outside the textbook. Emerging market currencies almost always behave like commodities.

Had I been trained in commodities I would not have been squeezed on the occasion; I would have considered such possibility unlikely but a present risk. And every underlying security bears that risk, with no exception: bonds become impossible to find to satisfy a delivery obligation; stocks with heavy short interest become unavailable for the borrower. The only products that seem to escape such problem are options on Futures.

The second point is the geographic limitation. While a security that you borrow is an abstract item, a mere balance sheet entry, commodities present location specificity that can make arbitrages arduous. You can own all the oil you need in Rotterdam; but, if your delivery is in New York tomorrow, you will have a problem. In electricity, shortage in one part of a continent can rarely be compensated with excess elsewhere.

How does it apply to other derivatives? Consider the "safe" currencies again. Say that you have the currencies available in a Brazilian bank but that you have an offshore delivery obligation. The bank calls you to explain that the government forced exchange controls and that delivery will not be possible. You will have an immediate need to find offshore Brazilian currencies. There have been similar pressures with pricing differentials problems with almost all currencies.

The third point is the intricacy of storage. Commodities are "heavy", unlike financial products. If you are expecting delivery and do not line up a warehouse you will be in trouble. Environmental agencies will not even let you dump your oil in the ocean. Cows are expensive to feed.

Do we have equivalent problems with cleaner derivatives? Of course: consider bonds that may be costly to own relative to your cost of carry, particularly when you have to borrow at a prohibitive short rate to fund them.

Fourth, the meat of the problem: dynamic hedging. Clearly, it is not possible to dynamically hedge a security that you cannot short, sometimes cannot easily own and that can be severely illiquid. Transaction costs can be monstrous. Fat tails and gaps thwart the argument that an option is a redundant security because it is safely replicated with a stream of dynamic hedges. We have enough evidence of large deviations to realize that dynamic hedging is not attainable in practice.

Then how do people value options? Clearly, options trade and we still manage to price them using risk-neutral probabilities. How do we do it? We practitioners consider an option as simply the expected value of its pay-off under some probability distribution, but not necessarily using dynamic hedging arguments.

As President of the Bachelier Finance Society, Professor Geman organized an international conference in Louis Bachelier's honor in the summer of 2000 which featured, among others, such prominent speakers as Paul Samuelson, Robert Merton, Henri McKean and Steve Ross. Reading this book, I come to realize that we have finally vindicated Louis Bachelier: Commodities are teaching us that we do not dynamically hedge.

Enjoy this impressive book and the exciting discovery of the world of commodities.

Preface

"The world is hungry for commodities", was the headline of the April 2004 issue of a widely read economic publication. And, indeed, there is no day when daily financial newspapers do not dedicate many columns to commodity-related issues, from cotton to nickel, coffee and freight while an unprecedented rise in oil prices has inflamed all markets.

How to define a commodity? An economist would say that it is a consumption asset whose *scarcity*, whether in the form of exhausting underground reserves or depleted stocks, has a major impact on the world and country-specific economic development. A banker would observe that it is not a financial security, giving rise to a stream of cash flows and priced by net present value arguments. An ecologist would suggest that it is a natural good whose original integrity should be preserved. An academic would argue that, given the current volatility of all currencies, including the most established ones, a commodity is an exemplary *numéraire* with respect to which portfolio values should be measured. Indeed, oil-producing countries concerned with the decline of the dollar and uncertain about the long-term health of the euro recently proposed that a barrel of oil be priced against an average of the dollar and the euro (*Financial Times*, February 2004). A valid suggestion would be to go the other way around and suggest a barrel of oil or a million Btus of natural gas as a "universal numéraire" relative to which all currencies would be expressed (the role gold used to play decades ago).

Commodities constitute the only spot markets which have existed nearly throughout the history of humankind. Over the centuries, even millennia, the scope of commodities available for human existence has grown from essential agricultural commodities to include metals and energy. The nature of trading has evolved from *barter* organized on town marketplaces in the absence of any monetary vehicle, to more elaborate *forward contracting* between producers and merchants, then to organized Futures markets with clearing houses guaranteeing the creditworthiness of transactions. The specification of contracts has evolved from "plain-vanilla" forwards to exotic options and structured products allowing originators and intermediaries to hedge away the risks residing outside the domain of their primary expertise.

Some key properties of commodity markets contrasting them with stock and bond markets include the following:

- Commodity spot prices are defined by the intersections of *supply and demand* curves in a given location, as opposed to the net present value of receivable cash flows.

- Demand for commodities is generally inelastic to prices, given the indispensable nature of the good. *Inventories* when they exist in sufficient volumes allow a smooth balance of supply and demand over time to be created. Hence, their importance in the discussion conducted in the economic literature for decades.
- Physical transactions – which were the only ones prior to the introduction of financial trades – still have a crucial importance today. Among other virtues, they provide a reference spot price or index against which derivative transactions are financially settled.
- Supply is defined by production and inventory. But, in the case of energy commodities, underground *reserves* also play a role since they have an impact on long-term prices.
- Financial transactions (forwards, Futures, options) represent today a huge volume. They involve prices closely related to spot prices in particular because physical delivery is a choice that is left to the buyer. Consequently, the understanding of spot markets and their characteristics is a necessary step in the analysis of commodities and commodity derivatives.
- For most energy commodities, the balancing of supply and demand now takes place both at the regional level and at the world level. This explains the explosion of shipping and freight markets and the emergence of new trading strategies such as the rerouting of an LNG (Liquid Natural Gas) tanker to countries where gas prices exhibit a momentary spike.
- Commodities represent today a new asset class in its own right. Many institutional investors and funds are increasingly turning to it for diversification benefits *and* for the returns generated.

The goal of the book is to present the three fundamental groups of commodities: agriculturals, metals and energy, with a particular emphasis on the third one in the context of deregulation of gas and electricity markets worldwide. However, the importance of the first two groups should not be dismissed: today, soybean exports from the US to China are bigger than the exports of airplanes while, in the case of Brazil, soybeans represent one-third of the shipments to China. The technical discussions will systematically emphasize the differences (or similarities), with the corresponding properties of stocks and bond markets. For instance, a crucial difference between securities and commodities is the *physical delivery* attached to spot, forward contracts and Futures positions not closed prior to maturity and translates into good transfer, with the corresponding constraints for both parties in terms of shipping arrangements, warehousing and so forth. The famous Sugar Quay in London gets its name from the fact that buyers of forward contracts used to be called on the phone to look out of the window and contemplate the product of their sugar transaction sitting in a barge on the Thames. At the other end of the commodity spectrum, sellers of forward contracts and options on electricity learned the hard way what physical delivery means during the crisis of June 1998: the combination of a lengthy heatwave and transmission disruption drove electricity prices up to thousands of dollars in the Midwestern part of the United States, and sent to bankruptcy firms which had sold power options without fully envisioning their unique features.

Another key difference between security and commodity markets is the existence, in the latter case, of *quantity risk*. Investors owning stocks or bonds are only concerned by equity markets going down or interest rates going up (i.e., by the *price risk* attached to the instruments they are holding). Coffee producers and power generators know that their revenues are not only affected by random moves in the spot price of coffee or electricity, but also by the *variability of demand* due to changes in consumption, in growth development worldwide and in weather conditions.

This explains why the variety of exotic options which are now familiar in securities markets, such as Asian, exchange or spread, are the most appropriate options in commodity markets. In the latter case, moreover, contracts quasi-unknown in financial markets, such as "take or pay" or "swing", are playing a key role since they are designed to provide a hedge against *volumetric risk*. These options trade today as individual financial instruments, after having been included at no cost in contracts signed for decades between gas and electricity producers and end-users. Lastly, these options naturally appear in the so-called "real options approach" to the valuation of power plants, gas storage facilities or pipelines, as will be discussed at the end of the book.

We will try to cover a variety of theoretical and practical issues related to Futures and options markets, ranging from the mechanics of Futures trading to the discussion of equilibrium relationships between Futures and options prices, on the one hand, and spot prices, on the other hand, under some equilibrium (e.g., no-arbitrage) assumption.

The guiding thread, beyond the qualitative properties and knowledge of fundamental trading rules prevailing, respectively, in agricultural, metals and commodity markets, is to try to bring together the fundamental results from economic theory, the constraints of physical delivery and the lessons learned in modern finance and option pricing. The mathematics are kept to a minimal admissible level of formalism in order not to obscure the economic message. Readers should also get some insights about "weather to buy or sell" coffee or sugar Futures contracts, looking at the climate pattern – late frost versus warm and dry weather – prevailing across Brazil in August. Or they may wisely conclude to never plan a trip to Florida without first scrutinizing the frozen Orange Juice Futures prices posted on the New York Cotton Exchange.

Acknowledgements

First and foremost, I want to express my gratitude to Sophie Lémann, my Assistant in the Finance Department at ESSEC. Her editing talent and relentless optimism have allowed this work to move forward across oceans, airports and power conferences.

Then, I would like to thank those who helped me in various ways, including Philippe van den Abeele, Omar Alami, Martine Azara, Nilgon Baykara, Carole Boussiba, Naïma Esskali, Raj Gupta, Benjamin Geman, Aymeric Khalife, Stelios Kuruvakalis, George Martin, Jean-Pierre Mateille, Alessandro Moro, Julien Mutin, Steve Ohana, Patrick Perfetti, Patrick Slama, Jean Winghart.

Last but not least, I wish to thank Etienne Amic and Chris Harris, each of whom I invited to write chapters in his domain of unique expertise, oil and metals respectively. It is my admiration for them which explains why, throughout the book, the brilliant trader is referred to as "he", instead of the more politically correct "she".

1

Fundamentals of Commodity Spot and Futures Markets: Instruments, Exchanges and Strategies

1.1 THE IMPORTANCE OF COMMODITY SPOT TRADING

Commodity price risk is an important element of the world physionomy at this date, as it has an impact on the economy of both developed and developing countries: in a rough approximation, one can state that the latter include most commodity producing countries, the former being originators, marketers and manufacturers. All parties are still involved in activities of spot trading with physical delivery while the formidable development of liquid derivative markets – forward, Futures contracts and options – has paved the way for risk management and optimal design of supply and demand contracts.

Every commodity is traded on a spot market. In the old days, buyers and sellers used to meet on the marketplace where transactions led to immediate delivery. In the 18th and 19th centuries, potato growers in the state of Maine started selling their crops at the time of planting in order to finance the production process. In a parallel manner, numerous forward transactions were taking place in Chicago for cereals and agricultural products and in London for metals. A need for standardization in terms of quantity, quality, delivery date emerged and led to the establishment of the New York Cotton Exchange (NYCE) in 1842 and the Chicago Board Of Trade (CBOT) in 1848. The clearing house, unique counterparty for buyers and sellers of Futures contracts was the effective signal that the Exchange was operating. As of today, some of these clearing houses are owned by independent shareholders, others are primarily owned by market participants as in the case of the London Metal Exchange (LME) and the International Petroleum Exchange (IPE). Different qualities of the same commodity may be traded on different exchanges. The most famous examples include: coffee which in its "arabica" variety is traded on the New York Coffee, Sugar and Cocoa Exchange (CSCE), while the "robusta" type is traded on the London International Financial Futures Exchange (LIFFE); and oil which is traded on the New York Mercantile Exchange (NYMEX) as Western Texas Intermediate (WTI) and on the IPE in its Brent variety.

Let us observe that the fact that any transaction on commodities may be physical (delivery of the commodity) or financial (a cash flow from one party to the other at maturity and no exchange of the underlying good) is in sharp contrast to bonds and stock markets where all trades are financial. However, physical and financial commodity markets are, as expected, strongly related. Price and volatility observed in "paper" transactions are correlated to the analogous quantities in the physical market, both because of the physical delivery that may take place at maturity of a Futures contract and the existence of spot forward relationships that will be discussed throughout the book.

Lastly, let us note that the last two decades have experienced dramatic changes in world commodity markets. Political upheavals in some countries, economic mutation, new environmental regulation, a huge rise in the consumption of commodities in countries such as China and other structural changes have contributed to increase the volatility of supply and prices. This has made hedging activities (through forwards, Futures and options) indispensable for many sectors of the economy, the airline industry in particular being an important example.

As mantioned before, we call spot trading any transaction where delivery either takes place immediately (which is rarely the case in practice) or if there is a minimum lag, due to technical constraints, between the trade and delivery. Beyond that minimal lag, the trade becomes a forward agreement between the two parties and is properly documented by a written contract which specifies, among other things, who among the buyer and seller is responsible for shipping, unloading the goods and other transportation-related issues.

Consider a standard situation where the seller is a producer (e.g., of copper) and the buyer a manufacturer: in general, they never meet and, even if they did, would rarely agree on prices, timing and so forth. Hence the existence of intermediaries who play the role of go-between, are prepared to take delivery of goods that may not resell immediately and organize the storage and shipping.

We can represent the different phases of the physical execution of a trade as:

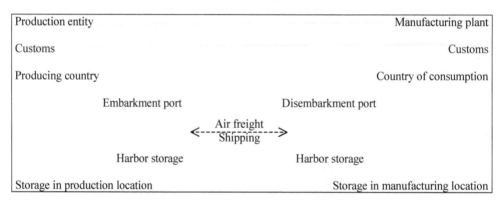

The document that represents the ownership of the good is called a *bill of lading*. It is issued either by the captain of the transportation ship or by the transporter in charge. That transportation contract may eventually be traded. It can bear the label "shipped" or "to be shipped"; the latter terminology indicates that the merchandise has been embarked, leading to the qualification *clean on board.*

Responsibility for commercial execution

It may lie in the hands of the seller, or the buyer, or the intermediary (since, in practice, many intermediaries will play a role, in particular because of the lags in the timing of different operations).

The responsibility will take different forms:

- For the exporter, sale Free On Board (FOB).
- For the commercial intermediary, purchase FOB out of the dock or in warehouse.
- For the importer, purchase on the dock or in warehouse.

Note that the commercial responsibility may be fragmented in the course of contract execution. For instance, a manufacturer who buys metals under a FOB specification is responsible for organizing the shipping but the armator is in charge of managing the shipping and holds the corresponding risk.

Major risks in commodity spot transaction

Four major types of risk may be identified in commodity spot markets:

- *Price risk*, which will be discussed throughout the book and for which the first examples of hedging strategies are presented in Section 1.2.
- *Transportation risk*, which is described below.
- *Delivery risk*, which concerns the quality of the commodity that is delivered and for which there is no financial hedge that may be put in place. The only coverage is provided by a very customized contract or by a solid long-term relationship with the originator.
- *Credit risk*, which is present all along until the final completion of the trade.

Risk attached to the transportation of commodities

1. The first category of risks concerns the deterioration, partial or total, of goods during transportation. Two types of risks are usually recognized in this category:

   o "ordinary" risks;
   o "extraordinary" risks such as wars, riots and strikes.

   The expeditor of the goods or the FOB buyer directly holds the transportation risk, unless they purchase an insurance contract to be covered. Different companies specialized in freight insurance (such as the famous Lloyds of London) propose various types of contracts. We need to keep in mind that transportation risk is an important one as it includes the entire community – the tanker that sank in Alaska being a sad example. If no specific insurance coverage has been purchased, the company that bears the liability must put in place some kind of *self-insurance* process as do some major oil companies today.

2. Cost of transportation risk: All Futures exchanges around the world quote FOB prices. Consequently, if a trade (e.g., on sugar) is settled for delivery 12 months later with the CIF price as a reference, the seller needs to hedge his position not only against a decline in sugar prices by, say, selling Futures on the New York Coffee, Cocoa and Sugar Exchange, but also against changes in the shipping cost. The latter risk will be hedged by entering into a Forward Freight Agreement (described in Section 1.5). Consequently, the two components of the CIF price will get hedged in totally different exchanges.

1.2 FORWARD AND FUTURES CONTRACTS

A forward contract may be generically described as an agreement struck at date 0 between two parties to exchange at some fixed future date a given quantity of a commodity for an amount of dollars defined at date 0. A Futures contract has the same general features as a forward contract but is transacted through a Futures exchange. The clearing house standing behind that exchange essentially takes away any credit risk from the positions of the two participants engaged in the transaction. This default risk is almost reduced to zero through margin deposits or initial margins that need to be made before entering into any contract, as well as the daily margin calls required to keep a contract alive if its market value has declined from the previous day.

Futures contracts serve many purposes. Their first role has been to facilitate the trading of various commodities as financial instruments. But they have from the start been providing a hedging vehicle against *price risk*: a farmer selling his crops in January through a Futures contract maturing at time T of the harvest (say, September) for a price $F^T(0)$ defined on 1 January has secured at the beginning of the year this amount of revenue. Hence, he may allocate the proceeds to be received to the acquisition of new machinery or storage facilities and, more generally, design his investment plans for the year independently of any news of corn oversupply possibly occurring over the 9-month period.

It is noticeable in many markets, ranging from agricultural commodities to electricity, that Futures contracts are used as a substitute for the spot market by hedge funds, Commodity Trading Advisors (CTAs) or any class of investors wishing to take a position in commodities, both because it takes away the physical constraints of spot trading and provides the flexibility of short and long positions, hence the choice of positive or negative exposure to a rise in prices. This will be discussed in detail in Chapter 14.

What follows describes in detail the mechanisms of forward and Futures contracts with their various characteristics as well as the way exchanges operate. The different classes of participants, the mechanism of *price discovery* and the crucial relationships, if they exist, between spot prices and Futures prices under some form of equilibrium assumptions are described in detail.

Forward contracts

A forward contract is an agreement signed between two parties A and B at time 0, according to which party A has the obligation of delivering at a fixed future date T an underlying asset and party B the obligation of paying at that date an amount fixed at date 0, denoted $F^T(0)$ and called the forward price for date T for the asset. Note that this price is not a price in the sense of the price of a stock, but rather a reference value in the contractual transaction. If the underlying asset is traded in a liquid market, the no-arbitrage condition between spot and forward markets at maturity implies that:

$$S(T) = F^T(T)$$

If the value at date T of the Futures contract maturing at that date was different from the spot price, an arbitrage opportunity would be realized by buying in one market and selling immediately in the other.

Keeping in mind that the buyer of the forward contract may immediately sell at maturity in the spot market at the price S_T the commodity which was delivered to him against the payment of $F^T(0)$ dollars, the respective Profit and Loss (P&L) of party A (called long forward) and party B (called short forward) are depicted by the following graphs:

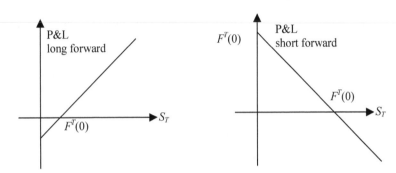

Obviously, the contract is a zero-sum game between the buyer and the seller. Note also that, by definition, both P&Ls are expressed in dollars at date T.

For practical purposes, party A represents an economic agent who wants to hedge against a possible rise in the price of the underlying asset between dates 0 and T and locks in at date 0 a purchase price equal to $F^T(0)$. Party B, conversely, fears a collapse of this price or expects to profit from a rise. The price $F^T(0)$ represents their estimation at date 0 of how much the underlying asset S will be worth at date T together with the risk premium they are willing to pay (or receive). We will come back to this discussion in Chapter 2.

Should parties A and B enter into this T maturity contract at a future date t in the interval $(0, T)$, the price $F^T(t)$ on which they will agree is likely to be different from $F^T(0)$ and translates the changes between dates 0 and t in the expectations perceived by the market of the commodity future spot price $S(T)$.

Futures contracts

They are analogous to forward contracts in terms of their definition but present some key differences from them:

- They are "standardized" in terms of their characteristics (maturity, quantity of the underlying commodity, quality or variety).
- They are traded on an exchange, such as NYMEX or the IPE; hence, they carry no counterparty risk since both the buyer and the seller of the Futures deal with the clearing house of the exchange which is in principle fully trustworthy.
- They require the payment of margin deposits in order to be able to start placing orders on the exchange.
- They are marked-to-market daily and the participants have to adjust their positions: for instance, if a participant has a long position in a Futures contract acquired at the price $F^T(0)$ and if the price $F^T(\text{day } 1)$ is lower, then this participant has experienced a loss between days 0 and 1 equal to $F^T(\text{day } 1) - F^T(0)$. In order to keep his

position, he has to adjust it by adding at the end of day 1 a cash amount equal to his loss.

Forward and Futures prices on the same underlying asset with the same time to expiry are different because of taxes, transaction costs and other important elements, such as the impact of credit risk on the one hand and stochastic interest rates on the other hand. In practice, they remain very close to each other since the fluctuations of the underlying commodity represent the most important explanatory factor. Except when stated otherwise, we will view the two prices as the same in a first-order approximation.

We can recap the similarities and differences between the fundamental types of transactions prevailing in commodity markets as depicted in the following diagram:

Spot trading	Forward contracts	Futures contracts
◆ *commercial contract* ◆ flexible covenants	◆ *bilateral agreement* ◆ flexible covenants	◆ *standardized instrument* ◆ necessity of a physical delivery or termination of the position before maturity
◆ juridical commitments of the buyer and seller until execution of the contract	◆ replace spot transactions on many occasions (e.g., in the case of a non-storable commodity such as electricity)	◆ buyer and seller only refer to the clearing house
⇩	⇩	⇩
◆ long transaction ◆ illiquid and discontinuous market ◆ allows the transfer of goods in conditions suiting the demand	◆ form of contracting totally appropriate for commodities ◆ credit risk fully present ◆ flexibility regarding the optimal transfer of goods	◆ central clearing mechanism generating "market prices" ◆ price transparency ◆ liquidity ◆ low transaction costs

1.3   THE ACTORS IN FUTURES MARKETS

Hedgers

Futures markets were originally set up to meet the needs of hedgers, namely farmers who wanted to lock in advance a fixed price for their harvests. Commodity Futures are still widely used by producers and users of commodities for hedging purposes. Suppose that the date of analysis is January and company XYZ knows that it will have to buy on 25 September (date T) of the same year one million tons of fuel. In order to hedge against the possible increase in fuel price between January and the end of September, airline company XYZ will buy (equivalently, *enter a long position in*) Futures contracts written on fuel, maturity September and in an amount corresponding to the necessary quantity of fuel. By doing so, the airline company has locked in at the beginning of the year the price $F^T(0)$ it will pay in September and has done so with no cash flow payment at the beginning of the year.

Another possible hedge (as we will see later) would be to buy options – again in the appropriate quantity – written on the fuel as the underlying, with maturity T and strike price $k = F^T(0)$ for example.[1] In this case, the resulting cost of fuel in September for company XYZ will be either $F^T(0)$ or, strictly, less if the market spot price is very low. This alternative is strictly superior for the hedger at maturity, but at inception of the option contract in January company XYZ will have to pay the premium of the options involved in the hedge.

Returning to Futures contracts, *basic risk* refers to the risk remaining after the hedge has been put in place and essentially represents the difference between the Futures price – should the Futures position be closed prematurely – and the spot price. It also includes other components such as:

- The price of cleaning the local grade of the commodity into a grade deliverable in a Futures contract (or the premium for a superior grade).
- The price of transportation to or from the delivery point in the Futures contract.
- The physical cost of storage, including insurance, between the time of the harvest and the delivery date of the Futures contract.

Speculators

While hedgers want to avoid exposure to adverse movements of the price of a commodity which is part of their manufacturing process in the economy, speculators wish to get exposure to commodity price moves (i.e., take risks in order to make profits). Using the same example as before, a bank ABC which has no "natural" exposure to the price of fuel may decide to take a position either in a Futures contract on fuel or in an option written on fuel and, by doing so, will create for itself exposure to the fuel price; obviously, the nature of the position – long or short in either instrument – will be determined by the "view" that bank ABC has on the subsequent moves of the fuel price. It is in fact "betting" that this price will go up or will go down and counting on the corresponding profits the bank will generate. Unsurprisingly, commodities are becoming increasingly attractive to investors and hedge fund managers who view them as an *alternative asset class* allowing one to reduce the overall risk of a financial portfolio and enhance the return as well. Futures are the obvious instrument – because of their liquidity, because of the low transaction costs on the exchange, because of the absence of credit risk – to take positions reflecting an anticipation of a price rise by purchasing Futures or a decline by selling Futures. Most of the liquidity is generated by the combined activity of speculators and hedgers.

Arbitragers

Arbitragers represent a third important – but smaller in size – group of participants in futures and options markets. An arbitrage is a *riskless* profit realized by simultaneously

---

[1] For practical purposes, this will be the strike most often chosen when hedging with an option since everyone has the forward position in mind as the alternative hedge.

entering into several transactions in two or more markets. Arbitrage opportunities are very desirable but not easy to uncover and they do not last for long. If a given instrument is underpriced, buying activity will cause the price to rise up to a value which is viewed by the market as the "fair" price and at which there will be no more excess demand.

In this book, as in the fundamental models of option pricing, the values of Futures and options contracts will be based on the assumption of no-arbitrage opportunities. Given the importance of this concept, we are going to propose several definitions of what is called in daily language "no free lunch".

Definition 1 A portfolio P is called an "arbitrage portfolio" if it satisfies simultaneously the following conditions:

$$\begin{cases} V_p(0) = 0 \\ V_p(H) \geq 0 \quad \text{in all states of the world at date } H \\ V_p(H) > 0 \quad \text{in some states of the world} \end{cases}$$

where H is a date later than date 0.

Definition 2 A market is said to be arbitrage-free if there exists no arbitrage opportunity; in other words, for any portfolio P:

$$\begin{cases} V_p(0) = 0 \\ \text{and} \qquad\qquad\qquad\qquad\qquad\qquad \Rightarrow V_p(H) = 0 \quad \text{in all states of the world} \\ V_p(H) \geq 0 \quad \text{in all states of the world} \\ \qquad\qquad \text{at date } H > 0 \end{cases}$$

In other words, if a portfolio *requires a null investment* and is *riskless* (there is no possible loss at the horizon H), then its terminal value at date H has to be zero. These are the various expressions of the no free lunch property: if you start with no money and *take no risk*, your final wealth will be zero. In the above statements, the assumption of "riskless" is crucial: if you have no money, you can always borrow from your banker and invest the proceeds in a hedge fund. Your final wealth may be quite large or very negative once you have repaid your loan, but rarely equal to zero.

Comments

For practical purposes, traders searching for arbitrage opportunities are realistically looking, in fact, for "quasi-riskless" strategies generating profits. Such a strategy should be as simple as possible and, hence, involve only spot and forward positions which have *linear payoffs and P&Ls* in the underlying price, making the nullification of risk possible by the resolution of a *single* equation in the price S of the underlying commodity. When we move to positions involving options, we will see that the convexity (or concavity) of the P&L (i.e., the gamma of the option), together with the sensitivity to volatility (i.e., the vega), make this "quasi-riskless" feature much more problematic. Hence, it is indeed in Futures markets that the fundamental concept of arbitrage finds its origin, since *fungibility* between the underlying commodity and the derivative is highest. This property will be lost, however, in the case of electricity because of the specificities of this commodity (see Chapter 11) and this loss is certainly a significant part of the complexity of electricity markets. It allows us at the same time to measure the value of the spot–forward relationship when it exists, even if it holds in a temporal window because of some necessary assumptions on the convenience yield, as discussed in Chapter 2.

1.4   THE STRUCTURE OF FUTURES MARKETS

While some trading of Futures contracts may be traced back centuries ago in Europe and Japan, the modern form of Futures markets appeared in the 19th century in the American midwest. In fact, over the second half of the 19th century, more than 1,600 exchanges were established across the United States, often in the vicinity of harbors or railroad crossings. Most of them are gone today and there are only six exchanges in the United States where more that 600 million Futures contracts are traded every year (mostly softs in Chicago, energy in New York). The CBOT, established in 1848, was from the start an active exchange for agricultural commodities, especially corn and wheat. It set its General Rules in 1865. Shortly after, the New York Cotton Exchange organized cotton Futures trading. Futures trading in many other agricultural commodities followed.

The Grain Futures Act in 1922 defined the regulation of Futures exchanges; the Commodity Futures Trading Act of 1974 established the Commodity Futures Trading Commission (CFTC) as the new independent regulatory commission in charge of Futures markets. In the 1970s Futures contracts on stocks, equity indexes, bonds, foreign currencies as well as Futures on options were introduced. Active financial Futures markets have been introduced in different countries worldwide, such as Japan, the UK, France, Hong Kong and so on. Lower transaction costs, increased trading volume, expanded trading hours, electronic trading and international inter-market links contribute to make the Futures markets of today an efficient globalized trading network.

The classical structure of a Futures market is represented in the diagram below:

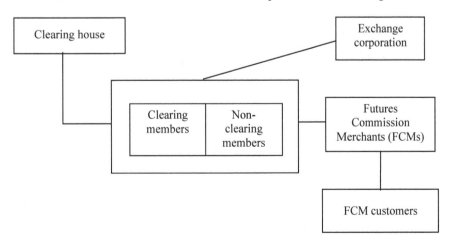

Most Futures exchanges are incorporated as membership associations and operated for the benefit of their members who are generally engaged in their own businesses related to Futures trading. The first purpose of an exchange is to provide an organized marketplace, with uniform rules and standardized contracts. Like any corporation, a Futures exchange has shareholders, a board of directors and executive officers. An exchange may operate markets for spot commodities, options and other financial securities in addition to Futures contracts and provide other services to the public (in particular, *price discovery* which will be discussed in Chapter 2). An exchange funds its activities by membership dues and by transaction fees paid on the contracts traded on the exchange.

EXCHANGE MEMBERS

Although membership is limited to individuals, these individual members often act on behalf of firms, such as brokerage houses, investment banks, or commodity dealers and producers. The total number of members of an exchange is limited; memberships are available for sale on the floor of an exchange. The value of membership lies mainly in the possibility it grants for trading contracts directly on the floor of the exchange. Those members, nominees of members and other individuals who actually use floor-trading privileges are traders. Although floor brokers sometimes trade on their own accounts, their basic role is to allow the public at large to buy or sell contracts. Collectively, they meet a critical need for *liquidity*, namely the ability of the market to act as a reliable and efficient mechanism for quickly taking or offsetting contract positions.

Major Futures exchanges

Chicago Board of Trade

CBOT used to be exclusively dedicated to agricultural commodities. Today, it trades Futures and options on corn, soybean, soy meal, wheat, rice as well as precious metals (gold and silver). Corn, soybean and wheat are, in this order, the most traded underlyings.

Chicago Mercantile Exchange

CME is the biggest Futures exchange in the US and the second in the world. It trades pork bellies, beef, dairy products and lumber. Founded in 1898 as a non-profit entity, it rapidly became a world platform for trading Futures.

New York Mercantile Exchange

NYMEX was founded in 1872 under the name "Butter and Cheese Exchange of New York". It merged in 1994 with the Commodity Exchange (COMEX), itself resulting from a merger in 1933 of four smaller commodity exchanges. Today, NYMEX is the biggest exchange for commodity Futures; in particular, crude oil (WTI), gas, copper, aluminum and precious metals.

Regarding energy commodities, NYMEX trades Futures and options on crude oil, natural gas, domestic fuel, unleaded gasoline and propane. Oil Futures contracts were introduced in 1983 and are the most active contracts in the world (see Tables 1.1 and 1.2).

Futures and options on gold, silver, copper and aluminium are traded on COMEX. The gold Futures contract, launched in 1974, is a world reference today.

New York Board of Trade

NYBOT regroups the two oldest commodity exchanges in New York: the Coffee, Sugar and Cocoa Exchange (CSCE) and the New York Cotton Exchange (NYCE). The first contracts on coffee, sugar and coca were respectively introduced in 1882, 1914 and 1925 on the CSCE; those on cotton and orange juice in 1870 and 1966 on the NYCE. NYBOT also controls the New York Futures Exchange (NYFE).

International Petroleum Exchange

IPE was founded in 1980 by a consortium of energy companies. The first contract, written on gas oil, was launched one year later. In June 1988, the successful Brent contract started trading and another on natural gas was quoted as of 1997.

London International Financial Futures Exchange

LIFFE was established in 1982 and started trading agricultural commodity Futures in 1996, after it merged with the London Commodity Exchange (LCE). Futures and options on cocoa, barley, robusta coffee, sugar and potatoes are traded on LIFFE.

London Metal Exchange

LME came to existence in 1877 to serve the needs created by the industrial revolution in the United Kingdom. It specializes in non-ferrous metals: aluminum (pure or alloy), copper, nickel, tin, lead and silver. LME is where metals are traded: producers trade with speculators and hedgers, e.g., a company producing copper wires and wishing to hedge its revenues against a rise in the price of copper.

Le Marché à Terme International de France

Created in 1986 and first dedicated to bond Futures, MATIF introduced commodity Futures two years later. Today Futures on corn and Futures and options on colza and wheat are traded.

It is interesting to observe that most US Futures exchanges still function today as *open outcry trading*. Many exchanges around the world now operate with an electronic platform, as do some divisions of the NYMEX and the whole EUREX system existing in Europe and recently established in Chicago.

More precisely, energy trading is conducted on NYMEX in open outcry from 10.05 a.m. until 2.30 p.m. After hours Futures trading is conducted via the NYMEX

Table 1.1 The currently most active commodity Futures exchanges in the US and worldwide

Traded commodities	Exchange	Abbreviation
Wheat, corn, soybeans, silver	Chicago Board of Trade (One Chicago) *www.cbt.com*	CBOT
Hogs, pork bellies, lumber, gold, weather	Chicago Mercantile Exchange (One Chicago) *www.cme.com*	CME
Cotton, rice	Chicago Rice and Cotton Exchange	CRCE
Cocoa, sugar, coffee	Coffee, Sugar and Cocoa Exchange	CSCE
Wheat, corn syrup, orange juice	Minneapolis Grain Exchange *www.mgex.com*	MGE
	New York Cotton Exchange	NYCE
	New York Mercantile Exchange *www.nymex.com*	NYMEX
Oil, crude oil, heating gasoline, propane gas	New York Mercantile Exchange	NYMEX
	Hong Kong Futures Exchange *www.hkfe.com*	HKEX
	Philadelphia Board of Trade	PBOT
	International Petrol Exchange *www.ipe.uk.com*	IPE
Metals	New York Mercantile Exchange	NYMEX
	London Metal Exchange *www.lme.co.uk*	LME
	Commodity Exchange *www.comex.com*	COMEX
Electricity	New York Mercantile Exchange (delisted in 2002)	NYMEX
	Minnesota Grain Exchange	MGEX
	Nordic Power Exchange	NORDPOOL
	European Energy Exchange	EEX
	Amsterdam Power Exchange	APX
	Paris Power Exchange	POWERNEXT

access Internet-based trading platform beginning at 3.15 p.m. on Mondays through Thursdays and concluding at 9.30 a.m. the following day. On Sundays, the session begins at 7 p.m.

On the metals front, CBOT unveiled in August 2004 details of a plan to challenge NYMEX's grip on trading of gold and silver Futures by offering them on an electronic basis on 6 October 2004. NYMEX announced in September that it would introduce on the same day a new system called "Neon" that will automatically send a customer's order to NYMEX gold and silver open outcry trading pits; currently, customers typically talk to floor clerks by phone. The Neon system should be extended to energy trading pits later. NYMEX – the largest energy futures and gold and silver Futures exchange – wants, however, to keep its practice of open outcry, which it views as a unique source of liquidity. It is interesting to observe how various exchanges are incorporating electronic trading while aiming at preserving their own specificity.

Returning to Futures contracts, trade can occur for delivery at different maturity dates in the future. The contract design also includes position limits, daily price limits

Table 1.2   Commodity Futures contracts

Commodity group	Commodity type
Grains	Corn
	Oats
	Rice
	Wheat
Oil and meal	Soybean
Livestock	Pork
	Beef
Foodstuffs	Cocoa
	Coffee
	Orange juice
	Potatoes
	Sugar
Textiles	Cotton
Forest products	Lumber
	Pulp
Metals	Gold
	Silver
	Platinum
	Palladium
	Copper
	Aluminum
Energy	Crude oil
	Heating oil
	Gasoline
	Natural gas
	Propane gas
	Electricity

and quotation conventions and attempts to reduce to the greatest extent any ambiguities as to the nature of a physically settled contract. Although an extremely small fraction of contracts purchased or sold are actually held until delivery, possible residual uncertainty as to the terms of the contract would reduce the quality of the hedge it provides and, in turn, its popularity. The details of delivery are fully specified by the exchange, namely: the quantity – number of bushels or tons per contract, number of cubic feet for natural gas; the type – robusta versus arabica for coffee; the location – which in general has nothing to do with the exchange (a NYMEX WTI contract is delivered at Cushing in Oklahoma). Sometimes, a choice is given to the seller with respect to one of these items, including the time window of delivery: this *option to deliver* (analogous to the one that exists for bond notional Futures regarding the specific bond that is delivered) has a positive value that can be computed in terms of the type of flexibility and this value is obviously negative for the buyer of the Futures contract.

Basis risk

1. Understanding basis risk is fundamental to hedging. *Basis* is defined as:

$$\text{Basis}_{t,T} = \text{Spot price}_t - F^T(t)$$

is usually quoted as a premium or discount: the cash price as a premium or discount to the Future price.

The basis is said to be one dollar "over" Futures if the spot price is one dollar higher than the Futures price.

2. There are several types of basis risk:

   (a) In the case of a trading desk which needs to cut at date t (e.g., to avoid negative margin calls[2]) – a position in Futures which was meant to hedge a position in the spot commodity – the basis risk is represented by the quantity defined above.
   (b) More generally, basis risk exists when Futures and spot prices do not change by the same amount over time and, possibly, will not converge at maturity T:
       - because the Futures contracts were written on an underlying similar but not identical to the source of risk, such as an airline company hedging exposure to a rise in jet fuel prices with NYMEX heating oil Futures contracts;
       - because of the optionalities left to the seller at maturity in the physical settlement of the Futures contract: grade of the commodity, location, chemical attributes.

Today, market participants analyze their risk in a mark-to-market perspective at date t (and not only at date T). Consequently, basis risk is often defined as the *variance of the basis*:

$$\sigma^2(S_t - F^T(t)) = \sigma^2(S_t) + \sigma^2(F^T(t)) - 2\rho\sigma(S_t)\sigma(F^T(t))$$

where ρ is the correlation coefficient between the Futures and spot price series.

This equation shows that basis risk is zero when variances between the Futures and spot prices are identical *and* the correlation coefficient ρ between spot and Futures prices is equal to one. In practice, the second condition is the most stringent one and the magnitude of basis risk depends mainly on the degree of correlation between cash and Futures prices.

Since hedgers are trying to eliminate price risk, the classical measure of the effectiveness of hedging a spot position with Futures contracts is defined by:

$$h = 1 - \frac{\sigma^2(\text{basis})}{\sigma^2(S_t)}$$

The closer h is to one, the more effective the hedge. To return to the airline example, if crude oil contracts and heating oil contracts are available to hedge its exposure to jet fuel price risk, it will choose the solution leading to the higher number h. Remembering

---

[2] One needs to keep in mind that the major bankruptcies of hedge funds occurred because of funds' inabilities to face the margin calls related to existing positions.

that the position in the hedging of Futures may need to be cut at any time, one wants to be left with as small a basis as possible.

Returning to the different optionalities attached to delivery of the physical commodity, they have been the subject of a vast body of literature since both the seller and buyer of the Futures contract are quite aware of their financial value (see, e.g., Gay and Manaster, 1986).

Some commodity contracts, like most financial Futures, are based on cash delivery rather than physical delivery. In this case, the holder of a long contract receives at maturity the last marginal call, positive or negative, corresponding to the change of the Future price over the last trading day, since his gain or loss over the period has been incorporated daily in his account at the exchange.

In summary, a Future position may be terminated essentially in three ways:

1. By taking prior to maturity a symmetric position in an equal number of contracts in order to nullify the position and avoid the cumbersome and expensive procedure of physical delivery.
2. Roughly 1% of the Futures contracts go into physical delivery at maturity. The benefit of the existence of physical delivery is that it implies the convergence of spot and Futures prices at maturity of the contract; hence, the consistency in the moves of these two quantities over time. The constraining part, however, is that the clearing house needs to fully specify the delivery location, the delivery period – which usually covers the delivery month for monthly Futures contracts on commodities, in contrast to financial Futures on bonds, for instance, which result in a unique delivery of the bond – as well as the delivery rate. Lastly, the grade of the commodity needs to be made clear as well as the optionalities left to the seller (respectively, buyer) in the delivery procedure. When the grade specification is left open, the seller will choose *the cheapest to deliver*; a vast literature exists on this issue in the case of bond Futures contracts.
3. By entering into an Exchange For Physical (EFP) agreement.

Exchange For Physical

An EFP is an agreement between a party holding a long Futures position and a party with an equal size short position to enter a bilateral contract specifying the terms of physical delivery (location and price). The two parties notify the clearing house of the quantity and price negotiated between them and both futures positions are then terminated under the terms of the EFP. In grain markets, this type of transaction is called "ex pit".

Alternative Delivery Procedure

An ADP is available to buyers and sellers who have been matched by the exchange subsequent to the termination of trading in the spot month contract. If buyer and seller agree to achieve delivery under terms different from those prescribed in the contract specifications, they may proceed on that basis after submitting a notice of their intention to the exchange.

1.5 SHIPPING AND FREIGHT: SPOT AND FORWARD MARKETS

The current issues in the booming freight market

A recent jump in ocean-shipping rates to their highest levels in decades is adding upward pressure on already rising commodity prices that could increase further the cost of imported goods in the US, in China, in Europe and worldwide. The demand for sea-faring vessels is far outstripping supply and the cost of shipping iron ore, soybeans and other commodities used in the manufacture of a wide range of goods nearly tripled in 2003. The Baltic Dry Index (BDI), the key industry indicator published in London and representative of loose goods transportation (cereals, minerals, coal) kept rising sharply, showing no signs of relief on the horizon in terms of lower prices or additional supply of vessels. The Baltic Panama Index (BPI), essentially dedicated to cereals, follows the same pattern. A similar trend, at an even larger scale, is observed in the cost of oil tankers where the price of insurance for tankers coming from the Middle East adds to the other rising components.

China's surging economy is creating a huge demand for ships to import the basic raw materials the country needs to build infrastructure, supply its massive manufacturing sector and satisfy a growing consumer market. As more ships go to China, fewer are available to ferry goods between other parts of the world, causing a supply shortage and price rises. Compounding the problem, shrinking mining industries in the Americas and Europe have increased these regions' imports of coal. Besides these structural elements, events like the summer 2003 drought in Europe that boosted grain shipments from the US contribute to the price pressure.

Clarksons, a large London-based ship broker which has kept records on shipping rates for about 30 years, observed that the end of 2003 was the highest rate market of all times. Obviously, the impact on the world economy comes with some lag in the form of higher prices on goods made of steel, aluminum and other metals. For countries like China, the US and the European Community, which import more that they export, this may translate into inflationary pressure. The increase in the shipping cost is particularly clear for products like textiles and metals since they are heavier and bulkier (the situation being quite different for electronic equipment, for instance). In September 2003, copper was trading on the LME at $2.083 per ton, a 6-year high point. The cost for alumina, the basic ingredient to produce aluminum, nearly doubled in 2003 and cotton prices were trading at 5-year highs of about 84 cents a pound, in part because of increased demand from China and India.

The growing use of world freight is greatly explained by the rising demand in China which, for instance, in 2003 increased its imports of iron ore (the basic material to make steel) by nearly 40 million tons, or 33%. Meanwhile, imports by Europe of coal from China, Indonesia and Australia rose by 35%. On another register, Brazil – a major producer of soybeans (as we will see in Chapter 7) – shipped greater quantities of them to China where they are used for animal feed and human food products, such as soybean oil.

Higher freight rates are mainly hitting bulk-shipping vessels, specialized carriers that transport commodities in their raw form and that account for about one-third of all commercial ocean-going trade. More that 30% of all bulk ships carry iron ore and coal.

The other classes of freight ships are: container vessels that carry semifinished and finished goods, such as electronic devices and appliances; and tankers that are used for oil and, more recently, natural gas. Although ships come in different sizes and shapes, the spot cost to rent a typical bulk to ferry coal or iron ore was about $75,000 a day at the end of 2003, according to traders and ship brokers – quite different from the $20,000 to $28,000 a day prevailing in January 2003. About 40% of goods are transported in ships hired on the spot market. As a comparison, companies that had bought forward contracts on freight back in 2001 or 2002 for "delivery" of freight in 2003 had locked in a forward price which was only around $30,000 a day.

At the same time, the shipbuilding business, centered in South Korea, Japan and China, is backed up with orders and the lead times for taking new deliveries are almost twice as long as normal. One of the reasons for the delays is the fact that the world's shipbuilders are busy building new oil tankers to satisfy the more stringent safety requirements called for by European regulators. Hence, previous orders for new container ships have pushed any new orders for bulk ships to the back of the line; a new ship that used to take 18 months to 2 years for completion now requires as much as 3 years for delivery.

Spot and Forward Freight Markets

Freight contracts can be transacted either in the spot market or in the Forward Freight Agreement (FFA) market, since Futures exchanges no longer trade them today. The Baltic International Freight Future Exchange (BIFFEX) offered Futures contracts between May 1985 and April 2002; the underlying asset was a basket index comprising the seven routes of the BPI. This index, as it stands today, is presented in Table 1.3.

Table 1.3 Baltic Panama Index (BPI) weighting

Routes	Route description	Cargo	Weight in the BPI (%)
1	US Gulf of Mexico to ARA (Antwerp–Rotterdam–Amsterdam)	Light grain	10
2	Transatlantic round of 45–60 days	Time charter contracts	20
3	US Gulf to South Japan	Heavy grain, soybean, sorghum	12.5
4	Gibraltar to the Far East via Gulf of Mexico (duration 50–60 days)	Time charter contracts	12.5
5	US North Pacific port to South Japan	HSS	10
6	Transpacific round of 35–50 days	TCC	20
7	US West Coast or British Columbia to Japan/South Korea	TCC	15

Since April 2002, only FFAs have been traded. They mostly trade on specific routes rather than on the entire index.

The aim of the introduction in 1992 of forward contracts, besides the BIFFEX Futures contracts, was to provide another way of hedging freight rate risk in the dry-bulk and wet-bulk sectors of the shipping industry. FFA contracts are principal-to-principal contracts to settle a freight or hire rate for a specified quantity of cargo or type of vessel for usually one (or a combination) of the major trade routes. The reason for the success of FFA contracts over BIFFEX ones is primarily related to the high basis risk remaining after hedging with a contract written on an index. Most market agents in the shipping industry operate in some defined regions of the world and, therefore, demand route-specific derivatives contracts.

Typically, a shipowner or a charterer feeling that the freight market in a given route and a specific vessel/cargo size might move against him would approach an approved broker to buy or sell FFA contracts. This broker would find another charterer or another broker with a client with opposite expectations in order to fix the FFA contract. The major FFA brokers are those on the panel of shipbrokers of the Forward Freight Agreement Brokers Association (FFABA) created in 1997. They include Clarksons Securities Ltd, Lynch Flynn & Associates, Yamamizu Shipping. The city of London has established itself as the major FFA market.

Each member shipbroker of the FFABA submits to the Baltic Exchange its daily review of the rate on each constituent route of the Baltic indices. The Baltic Exchange excludes the highest and lowest assessments of the day and takes an arithmetic average of the remainder. The average rate of each route is then multiplied by the weighting factor to return the contribution of each route to the index; finally, by adding all the route contributions together, an overall average index is created (i.e., the daily BPI):

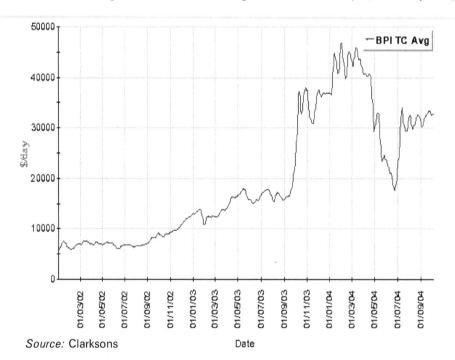

Source: Clarksons

Currently, FFA contracts have the BHMI, BCI and BITR as underlying asset spot freight rates in routes of the BPI. As an example, consider a charterer who, on 10 June 2004, is interested in transporting Heavy grain, Soya and Sorghum (HSS) from the US Gulf to Japan under a voyage charter party two months later (31 August). In order to avoid adverse freight-rate movements between 10 June and 30 August (day of the spot fixture), the charterer will approach a broker and define the following contract specifications: route US Gulf–Japan; cargo size 80,000 tons HSS, contract date 31 August 2004. The broker will search for another broker with a client, typically a shipowner, having the same contract characteristics in mind, but with opposite expectations on evolution of the freight rate.

The FFA market is a private market; hence, transactions and their nature are not made public. According to reliable sources, the total FFA volume went from 2,000 contracts in 2000 to 2,500 contracts in 2001 and more than 3,000 contracts in 2002. In practice, most of the trading concentrates in the nearby (1-month) and 2-month contracts, with much lower volumes in 3-month contracts. According to Kavussanos and Nomikos (2001), new information disseminates faster in the FFA market than in the spot market. Hence, it seems that FFA prices in all routes contain useful information about subsequent spot prices and can be used as price discovery vehicles for decision-making. Kavussanos and Nomikos (2001) investigate the relationship in daily returns and volatilities between spot and FFA price series on the major transatlantic and transpacific freight routes. Not only do they show that prices and volatilities in the spot and forward freight markets are "co-integrated" in the sense that they move together over long time periods,[3] but, by going through a lead–lag analysis, they also exhibit that it is the *forward market that leads the spot market*, as is the case in all commodity markets. They conclude that FFA prices in all routes contain information about future freight spot prices and, therefore, can be used as price discovery vehicles.

1.6 VOLUME, LIQUIDITY AND OPEN INTEREST IN FUTURES MARKETS

Table 1.4 displays the average daily volumes of Futures contracts traded on major exchanges in January 2004. Underlyings are divided into broad categories and ranked according to decreasing volumes. Unsurprisingly, oil products are by far the most traded: more than 200,000 transactions on crude oil take place every day on NYMEX and 100,000 on the IPE Brent. Gas immediately follows oil, showing the growing importance of this commodity. Agricultural products come after the energy group, starting with cereals. Among all commodities, corn has the second largest volume of trades after crude oil. Corn volume is higher than that for soybean, but not that of soybean and soybean complex. Outside cereals, it is coffee which has the highest volume. Aluminum and copper are the most traded among the industrial metals, while gold and silver are the most traded among the precious metals.

---

[3] Two processes (X_t) and (Y_t) are said to be co-integrated if there exists a linear combination $(aX_t + bY_t)_{t \geq 0}$ of the two processes that is a stationary process.

Table 1.4   Average daily volumes on various commodity Futures during January 2004

Exchange	CBOT	CME	NYMEX	COMEX	NYBOT	IPE	LME	MATIF
Energy								
Crude oil WTI			216,728					
Brent						97,801		
Natural gas			61,165			2,377		
Heating fuel			60,728					
Unleaded gasoline			50,320					
Gasoil			·			44,177		
PJM electricity index			322					
Propane			149					
Agriculturals								
Corn	101,286							161
Soybean	75,485							
Soymeal	32,435							
Wheat	32,844							373
Sugar					27,030			
Coffee					20,519			
Cotton					14,366			
Cocoa					9,194			
Oatmeals	1,687							
Rice	891							
Colza								647
Metals								
Aluminum				496			106,830	
Copper				11,239			85,235	
Zinc							44,211	
Lead							18,369	
Nickel							14,751	
Tin							5,061	
Gold				83,227				
Silver				20,266				
Platinum				860				
Palladium				806				
Agriculturals								
Beef		18,115						
Pork bellies		10,621						
Milk		893						
Lumber		896						

An important feature shared by all commodity Futures is that the highest liquidity is observed for short maturities, of the order of a few months. As an example, Figure 1.1 depicts the average daily volume observed in January 2004 on a Brent Future contract as a function of its maturity; volume gets divided by 10 when the time to maturity is 4 months instead of 1 month. This makes the establishment of reliable statistics difficult for the prices of Futures with medium- to long-term maturities.

Even though liquidity modeling is one of the topics on which financial theory needs more findings even in the context of classical instruments such as bonds and stocks, some qualitative concepts have emerged that can be extended to commodity markets:

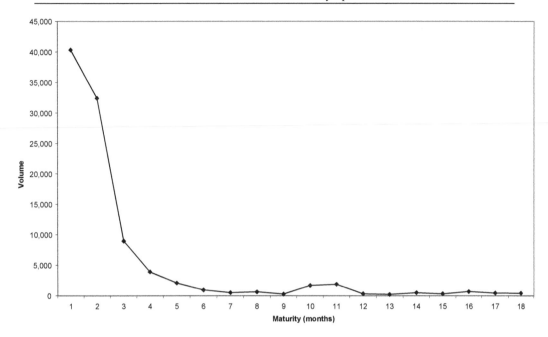

Figure 1.1 January 2004 average daily volume on the IPE Brent Future contract as a function of its maturity.

- Liquidity may be measured by the size of the trade it takes to move the market.
- *Market depth* may be measured by the time it takes for an order of a standard size to be executed.

Open interest in Futures market

Open interest refers to the number of futures contracts outstanding at a particular moment, i.e., the number of contracts that have not been canceled by an offsetting trade. Official figures on open interest are released by the exchange in a daily manner for the day before. One needs to keep in mind that it represents the total number of contracts held by buyers *or* sold short by sellers since these two numbers are always equal. The size of the open interest reflects the determination of the two groups, longs and shorts, to hold to their positions. It is a major indicator for technical analysts who derive buy-and-sell rules from the combined effect of an upward or downward trend with a rising or falling open interest.

Conclusion

Commodities and commodity markets have undergone dramatic changes over the last few years, with the deregulation of gas and electricity markets, the boom in South American production of soybean and the arrival of new actors in the coffee market. Countries like China are absorbing an increasing percentage of world commodity production and shifting up demand figures. Liquidity has increased in all Futures contracts, in particular for energy commodities which represent today the highest volume of traded Futures. This translates into higher volatility and price risk in all markets; hence, more hedging activities become necessary in all sectors of the economy, from the agrifood business to airline companies.

2

Equilibrium Relationships between Spot Prices and Forward Prices

2.1 PRICE DISCOVERY IN FUTURES MARKETS

One of the benefits of Futures markets, which has been identified for a long time, is to provide *price discovery*. As observed in Chapter 1, the wide variety of market partici- pants brings the key property of liquidity together with price transparency; moreover, the presence of arbitragers tends to absorb fairly quickly price abnormalities between spot and forward prices. Whether one looks at the oil market, which has been a liquid world market for more than a decade, or at newly deregulated energy markets, such as electricity, in all cases forward prices provide an indication of where the price of a barrel of oil or a megawatt-hour of power is heading to. This explains why the forward curve, i.e., the set of available forward prices as a function of their maturity, is the subject of intense scrutiny on the part of participants in any commodity market. This forward curve also allows companies to *mark-to-market* a book of existing positions, without relying on the view of a specific trader in the firm. Moreover, all the difficulties attached to physical transactions (delivery procedure involving transportation, storage, insur- ance and so forth) explain why portfolio managers wishing to diversify their invest- ments into commodities choose to intervene in the Futures markets, bringing further liquidity. Accordingly, Commodity Trading Advisors (CTAs) represent another class of major players in commodity markets.

All these economic agents are particularly interested in the relationship between current prices, both spot and Futures, and available inventory. The forecasting power of forward and Futures prices to predict future spot prices is part of the social utility that may be attached to Futures markets.

Futures markets provide highly visible prices against which the current cash prices of dealers can be compared, any difference being explained by the transportation costs involved in moving the commodity or the storage costs implied in a cash and carry relationship. All cash prices, therefore, will somehow reflect the centralization of the supply and demand for a commodity brought by trading on a Futures exchange. The uniformity and accuracy of current cash prices in reflecting current aggregate supply and demand for a commodity is socially beneficial because it permits individual con- sumers to avoid costly searches in order to pay fair prices.

Regarding Futures prices, they are the result of open and competitive trading on the floors of exchanges and, as such, translate the underlying supply and demand or, rather, their expected values at various points in the future. Information about expected future spot prices is valuable for several reasons:

1. In the case of storable commodities, these prices determine the storage decisions of commercial firms; higher Futures prices signal the need for greater storage and lower Futures prices point to a reduction in current inventory.
2. Reflecting expectations about future supply and demand, Futures prices trigger decisions about storage, production and consumption that reallocate the supply and demand for a commodity over time. Social welfare is increased by the avoidance of disruption in the flow of goods and services.

Many theorists working on Futures markets emphasize the informational content of Futures prices and their role in price discovery. In an influential article, Grossman (1977) proposes that Futures markets serve principally as a marketplace for the exchange of information, arguing that there is an incentive to trade Futures contracts because some traders have information about the future that others do not. Futures prices, according to Grossman, reveal to uninformed traders informed traders' expectations about the next period spot price. This feature of publicly transmitted prices is what Grossman calls the *informational role* of Futures markets.

At the same time, the arrival of news every day has a major impact on Futures prices. For agricultural markets, weather conditions represent a key piece of information. The *Wall Street Journal* sometimes ends its page on weather with an insert titled "Weather to buy or sell"; for instance, on 10 August 2004, a dry and warm weather pattern was shown to cover the Brazil sugarcane areas, with the comment "Harvesting and planting of sugarcane in south-central Brazil will benefit from warm, dry weather."

Back in 1939, the great economist Kaldor had emphasized that "in the case of agricultural crops, the supply curve is much less elastic and subject to frequent and unpredictable shifts due to weather. It is impossible to foretell the size of the crop a year ahead, and it is not possible to say when prices will return to normal."

2.2   THEORY OF STORAGE, INVENTORY AND CONVENIENCE YIELD

The theory of storage aims at explaining the differences between spot and Futures prices by analyzing the reasons why agents hold inventories. The models proposed over the last 50 years for price determination of storable commodities have emphasized the importance of the knowledge of quantities produced and stored for the derivation of testable predictions about price trajectories.

Initiated by famous economists in the 1930s and 1940s, the theory of storage illuminates the benefit of holding the physical commodity: inventories have a productive value since they allow us to meet unexpected demand, avoid the cost of frequent revisions in the production schedule and eliminate manufacturing disruption. For instance, owning aluminum is a sure way to avoid disruption in production in the case of a crisis arising in a major producing country of the raw commodity. In order to represent the advantages attached to the ownership of the physical good, Kaldor (1939) and Working (1948, 1949) define the notion of convenience yield as a benefit that "accrues to the owner of the physical commodity but not to the holder of a forward contract." Note that, in the same spirit, the dividend yield is paid to the owner of a stock but not to the holder of a derivative contract written on the stock. Brennan (1958) and Telser (1958) view the convenience yield as an "embedded timing option attached to the commodity" since inventory (e.g., a gas storage facility) allows us to put the commodity on the market when prices are high and hold it when prices are low. It also avoids the costs of manufacturing disruption or the nuisance of revisions of the production schedule.

In order to keep the analogy with the stock market and the option pricing formulas attached to dividend-paying stocks, the convenience yield y used throughout the book will be:

1. Expressed as a rate, meaning that the benefit in dollar amount for the holder of the commodity will be equal to $S(t) \cdot y \cdot dt$ over the interval $(t, t + dt)$, if $S(t)$ is the spot price of the commodity at time t.
2. Defined as the difference between the positive gain attached to the physical commodity *minus the cost of storage*. Hence, the convenience yield y we will be discussing may be positive or negative, depending on the period, the type of commodity and the corresponding level of inventory. The different values of y, in particular compared with interest rates, will explain the different shapes of forward curves, from backwardation to contango, which will be discussed in Section 2.4.
3. Not inclusive of the cost of financing the purchase of the physical commodity.

A substantial amount of recent research on commodities has chosen to model the convenience yield as a random quantity, allowing explanation of the various shapes of forward curves observed over time. Some authors (e.g.,Gibson and Schwartz, 1990) view the convenience yield as an exogenous random variable. In contrast, Routledge et al. (2000) propose an equilibrium model for storable commodities in which the convenience yield appears as an inventory-dependent endogenous variable and allows one to make predictions about the volatilities of forward prices at different horizons.

A third approach directly analyzes the role of inventory in explaining commodity spot price volatility. A statistical study performed by Fama and French (1987) on a number of commodity Futures including metals, wood and animals shows that the variance of prices decreases with inventory levels. Williams and Wright (1991) analyze a quarterly model with a yearly production of the commodity and identify that price volatility regularly increases after harvest time until the next one. Geman and Nguyen (2002) reconstruct a world monthly database of soybean inventory over a 10-year period and show that volatility can be written as an exact inverse function of inventory. Regarding energy markets, the property is the same and widely discussed in actuality: whenever there is a downward adjustment of the estimated oil reserves in the US or another region, the volatility of oil prices increases sharply (and prices as well).

Figure 2.1 depicts the evolution of inventories together with prices over the period October 1995 to March 2003 in the case of six important metals: aluminum, copper, lead, nickel, tin and zinc. In nearly all cases, low inventories coincide with high prices, and using the data series we can show that there exists a high correlation between commodity prices and inverse inventories as was discussed above in the case of soybeans. For instance, we can observe a collapse in the aluminum inventory over the last two years together with a sharp rise in prices, while the reverse situation prevails for zinc.

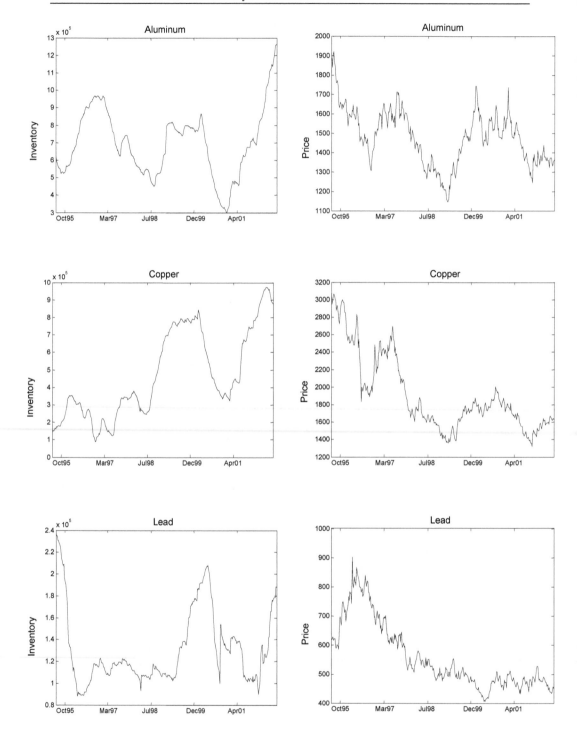

Figure 2.1   Inventories (in tons) and prices (in $/ton).

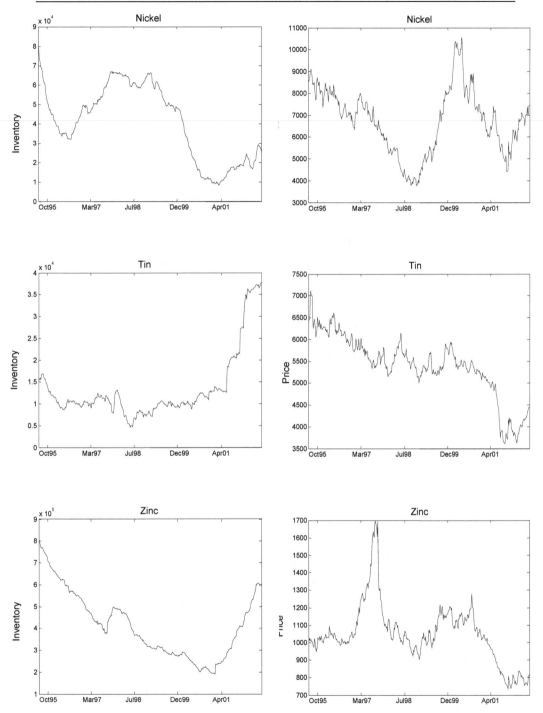

Hence, the important implications of theory of storage may be summarized as follows:

- The volatility of a commodity tends to be inversely related to the level of global stocks. In case of a stock outage, spot prices change dramatically in response to stocks in supply and demand since inventories are not there to provide a buffering effect.
- The price of a commodity and its volatility are positively correlated since both of them are negatively related to the inventory level. This is in sharp contrast to the situation of equity markets where volatility rises sharply when stock prices collapse. This feature was called the "leverage effect' by Black (1992) in the case of stocks and reflected in the prices of options written on these stocks. We will call the *inverse leverage effect* the negative relationship between commodity prices and their volatility. Exploiting the dependence between the current price and the expectation of future prices at a given inventory level, Deaton and Laroque (1992) find that the conditional variance of prices increases with current price. As long as the current price is a decreasing function of available inventory, their model implies that price volatility decreases with higher stocks.
- The volatility of forward prices tends, everything else being equal, to decrease with their maturity. This property is called the "Samuelson effect" (see Samuelson, 1965) and is explained by the fact that the arrival of news (e.g., on inventories or reserves) will have an immediate impact on short-term forward prices, while long-term contract prices tend to remain unchanged since production adjustment is likely to take place before the contracts come to delivery at maturity. The Samuelson effect is especially pronounced in the case of energy contracts, with a particularly steep increase in volatility occurring in the last six months of the life of the contract.
- An inventory-dependent convenience yield has become in the recent literature a popular-state variable for the explanation of the different shapes of forward curves.

2.3   SCARCITY, RESERVES AND PRICE VOLATILITY

One feature shared by most commodities is the high volatility of prices. We mentioned before the considerable effect of weather events. Other additional factors may be the deterioration of agricultural products, such as soybeans or oats, the fact that some commodities are not continuously produced or the cost of storage in the case of metals. We would like in this section to reflect on the issue of volatility in different commodity markets and compare commodities with other assets, such as stock prices.

A vast body of the financial literature over the last 40 years has been dedicated to the analysis of the relationship between the arrival of news, trading activity, price changes and volatility. Various authors have converged on a number of empirical results, the most important ones being:

- The arrival of news generates higher trading activity.
- A larger number of trades leads to an increase in volatility.
- Both a higher volume or more numerous individual trades create unexpected changes in volatility (i.e., stochastic volatility).

Geman and Yor (1993) demonstrate that the use of a "transaction clock" allows us to transform stochastic volatility into constant volatility by adequately "bending" the time. Geman and Ané (1996) show that the number of trades in stock markets is a better driver of the stochastic clock than volume, in the perspective of generating interesting mathematical properties of stock prices, such as normality of returns.

Returning to commodities, a number of authors have argued that the knowledge of quantities produced and existing inventories are key elements in the derivation of testable predictions about commodity prices. Regarding the *volatility* of these prices, the role of inventories has been brought forward in much research (see Deaton and Laroque, 1992; Williams and Wright, 1991). In the case of soybeans, Geman and Nguyen (2002) exhibit a quasi-perfect inverse affine relationship between price volatility and world inventory reconstructed by adding the inventory numbers of the United States, Brazil and Argentina. Taking a proxy for the inventory expressed as a Futures spread, Fama and French (1988) conclude that, in the case of metals, spot prices are more variable than Futures prices. Ng and Pirrong (1994) also analyze metal prices, use the same proxy and find that spot and forward return variances increase with low inventory.

Considering the recent outlook of commodity markets, we can observe that not only do inventories matter in explaining price spikes and volatilities, but also *reserves*, particularly in commodity markets where exhaustion of the commodity may take place within a few decades. If we analyze coffee, for instance, estimated demand is compared with the supply provided by the addition of current crops and existing inventory (of non-perished beans). Both components of the supply are going to impact the supply/demand equilibrium price, the volatility being primarily driven by the level of inventory. The following year the problem is posed in the same terms, taking into account the possible stocks carried over from the previous year.

Let us now turn to oil or natural gas, where existing inventories are quite crucial. In these markets, however, the arrival of news about reserves – which are finite and may be depleted one day – is another source of shocks to prices and volatility. At the level of a single company, this adjustment of reserves may have an important impact on the market price of the shares, as shown by the example of Royal Dutch Shell share price over the year 2004: in January 2004, Shell announced that its reserves were overestimated by 20%. Between January and May 2004, this number was further reduced by 15%. Note that, according to the Securities and Exchange Commission (SEC), *proven* oil and gas *reserves* are the estimated quantities of crude oil, natural gas and natural gas liquids which geological and engineering data demonstrate with *reasonable certainty* to be recoverable in future years from known reservoirs under existing economic and operating conditions. These reserves do not include oil and gas whose recovery is subject to reasonable doubt because of uncertainty as to geology, extraction technology, reservoir characteristics or economic factors.

The Royal Dutch Shell share price (in euros) over the period 1 January to 12 February 2004 is shown in the following diagram:

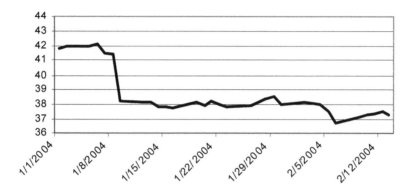

The IPE Brent index (in US$) between January and October 2004 had the following trajectory:

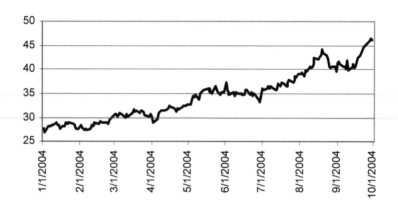

The oil company Total's share price (in euros) between January and October 2004 exhibited a fairly similar path:

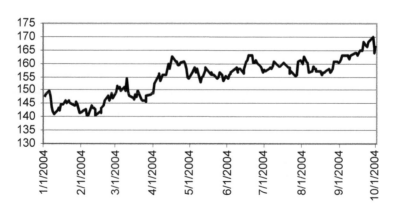

The Royal Dutch Shell share price between January and October 2004 displayed sharp upward and downward moves:

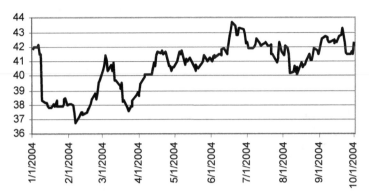

Along the same lines, we can observe that, within a 2-day period in September 2004, crude oil prices went up by 5.9% – a move which is definitely a jump by finance standards. The catalyst was two pieces of news that came out simultaneously: a warning issued by the company Yukos about its ability to continue its operations with more bank accounts frozen by the Russian government; and a report from the US Energy Department about lower oil inventories than expected.

Let us conclude this section by observing that, today more than ever, the origins of volatility spikes in the oil and gas markets have become increasingly numerous since, besides inventory, proven reserves, reserves identified "with reasonable certainty" and unexpected revisions of these numbers, we are facing the volatility generated by the trading activity of commodity-related funds. The identification of the *transaction clock* driven by the market activity has become quite complex indeed.

2.4 FUTURES PRICES AND EXPECTATIONS OF FUTURE SPOT PRICES

Decades ago, as well as in the recent past, famous economists, such as Keynes and Lucas, have analyzed in the context of interest rates the validity of the *Rational Expectations Hypothesis*, expressing that the current forward rate prevailing for a future time interval is the best estimator of the future rate attached to this interval. This "hypothesis" has been tested by many authors and was either rejected or accepted, depending on the period under scrutiny. Our goal here is not to discuss the results obtained on interest rates in detail, but to focus on the similar issue in the case of commodities.

At date t, participants in a given commodity market observe the Futures price $F^T(t)$ for delivery at a date $T > t$, a quantity we may also denote as $F^{\text{market}}_{t,T}$. The natural question that springs to mind is the following: Given that the spot price at time T is a random quantity $S(T)$ viewed from date t, is the Futures price prevailing at date t the best representation of this quantity? Or, in mathematical terms, can we state that:

$$F^T(t) = E[S(T)/\mathcal{F}_t] \qquad (2.1)$$

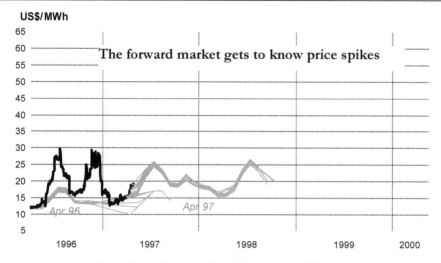

Figure 2.2   Electricity Palo Verde (hub NYMEX).

where, throughout the book, the letter E will denote the expectation operator and $\mathcal{F}_t$ represents the information available at date t, conditional on which expectation is computed. Equation (2.1) expresses that the current Futures price is a *non-biased predictor* of the unknown future spot price and that, indeed, a quasi-perfect price discovery is provided by Futures markets. The information $\mathcal{F}_t$ will cover in the case of an energy market, such as electricity, all available knowledge about producing units, maintenance outage, transmission availability and, obviously, demand, since spot prices will be obtained as the intersection of the supply and demand curves.

Figures 2.2 and 2.3 depict how, both before and during the development of the California crisis, electricity forward prices – the darker curves – remarkably anticipated

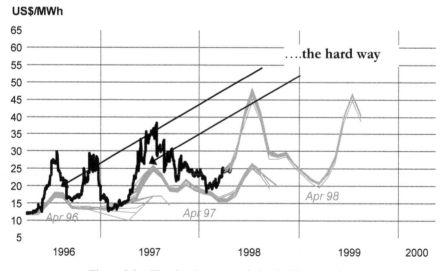

Figure 2.3   The development of the California crisis.

the future spikes in spot prices – the lighter curves – due in particular to a structural situation of under-capacity that existed in California prior to the beginning of the problems. The details regarding the painful experience of electricity deregulation in California are described in Chapter 11.

Returning to equation (2.1), we cannot "prove' it in a mathematical sense under some assumption, such as the no-arbitrage assumption; however, it can be statistically tested. Unsurprisingly, most tests lead to reject it (except in a coincidental manner), but the relevance of the question is central in all commodity markets and has been studied in much research.

When the equality does not hold, the Futures price $F^T(t)$ is a biased estimator of the future spot price $S(T)$. When $F^T(t)$ is an upward-biased estimate, it means that risk aversion among market participants is such that buyers are willing to pay more than the expected spot price in order to secure access to the commodity at a future date T – an obvious example being the oil market during political tensions worldwide. On the contrary, if $F^T(t)$ is smaller than the expected spot price at date T, this may reflect a perception of excess supply for that horizon.

The *theory of normal backwardation* states that Futures prices are, in general, downward-biased estimates of future spot prices. This is what induces speculators to take on the risk of a position in Futures contracts. Keynes (1930) argues that "the spot price must exceed the forward price by the amount which the producer is ready to sacrifice in order to hedge himself, i.e., to avoid the risk of price fluctuations during his production period. Thus in normal conditions the spot price exceeds the forward price, i.e., there is a backwardation."

The speculator earns a premium for bearing this risk because Futures prices are lower than the estimates of spot prices that will rule in the future.

We can represent in our terminology the theory of normal backwardation in the following diagram:

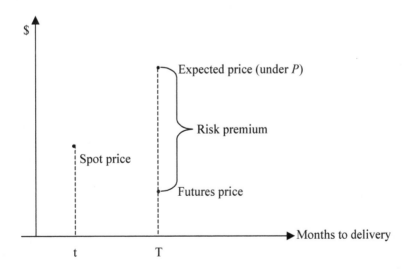

By the 1960s, economists such as Telser (1960) had already stated they found no bias in Futures prices for large markets, such as wheat, cotton and corn. Indeed, at the crux of the theory of normal backwardation is the *assumption* that hedgers are net short as a group. In our view, there are many commodity markets where participants have such a variety of motivations that this assumption is not appropriate, and the theory of normal backwardation may be somewhat obsolete (see below the discussion of electricity), as has been for the last 18 years the theory of "preferred habitat" for interest-rate markets. We will develop the discussion of the rational expectations hypothesis versus normal backwardation versus neither of the two in the case of different commodity markets throughout the book. A key message to keep in mind in all cases is that the price of a Futures contract $F^T(t)$ will always reflect the combination of two elements:

- The forecast of the future spot price of the commodity (i.e., its expectation) as made by the economic actors.
- *Risk aversion* of market participants and the premium they are possibly willing to pay (or expect to receive) to secure a fixed price today for future delivery of the commodity.

These two key pieces will be present for the other large family of derivatives, namely plain-vanilla and exotic options.

We need to add the important following observations:

1. In our view, the sign of the "risk premium" (and the existence of "normal backwardation") depends on the specific commodity under analysis and, in particular, the level of available inventory.
2. In contrast to Futures markets in Keynes' days, market participants today face a whole forward curve and, at the very least, a few maturities with good liquidity. Our claim is that in some markets the sign of the difference (forward price minus expected future spot price) has no reason to be independent of maturity T. For instance, given the extreme volatility of spot prices and the non-existence of storage (other than hydroelectric power) in electricity markets, the forward price is an upward-biased estimator of the spot price for short maturities. Geman and Vasicek (2001) analyze a database of PJM (Pennsylvania–New Jersey–Maryland) spot forward prices and exhibit that for small values of $(T - t)$, the probability distribution of the differences $F^T(t) - S(T)$ is clearly skewed to the right. Indeed, market participants are willing to pay a higher number than their expectation of future spot prices in order to secure short-term delivery because of the high volatility of electricity spot prices. In the long term, on the contrary, utilities owning power plants need to secure revenues for the repayment of the long-term financing of their physical assets and are prepared to sell long-term Futures contracts at prices $F^T(t)$ which may be lower than expected spot prices (this is particularly true in the case of nuclear plants).
3. Disentangling the two components of $F^T(t)$ mentioned earlier is impossible *ex ante* since, by definition, the estimated future price is not known with certainty. *Ex post*, this estimation can be made, using an average over time as a proxy for the true expectation prevailing at date t.
4. Another view we can have, as developed in Chapter 5, is to incorporate the risk premium in the probability measure used to compute expectations and derive an

elegant property for the Futures price under the "risk-adjusted" probability measure.

2.5 SPOT–FORWARD RELATIONSHIP IN COMMODITY MARKETS UNDER NO-ARBITRAGE

It is important to observe that the analysis of Section 2.4 was conducted in the absence of any economic or financial assumption about the market structure. Unsurprisingly, no *exact* relationship between current forward prices and expected Futures spot prices was established, but the issue of identifying an estimator of the future spot price in the current Futures price deserved to be discussed since it is present in the minds of all actors in the market.

In this section, the perspective and the results will be indifferent; we will assume that the commodity market under analysis is *arbitrage-free*, in the sense already mentioned: if we have no initial wealth and take no risk, then our terminal wealth will be surely null. Under this assumption, we are going to show that the forward price for maturity T and denoted as $f^T(t)$ is related to the *spot price at date* t by the fundamental relationship:

$$f^T(t) = S(t)\, e^{(r-y)(T-t)} \qquad (2.2)$$

where r is the continuously compound[1] interest rate prevailing at date t for maturity T and y is *convenience yield* on the commodity.

We need, before moving on to the proof, to observe that both r and y are supposed to be constant over the period and that the existence of y does make sense (i.e., that the commodity is *storable*). In order to have a better perception of the notion of convenience yield in the context of forward prices, we will start by proving the analogous relationship successively in the case of a non-dividend paying stock, and then in the case of a continuous stream of dividend paid on a stock.

(A) Spot–forward relationship for a non-dividend paying stock

In the case of a non-dividend paying stock and assuming no-arbitrage, the spot price $S(t)$ is related to the T forward price $f^T(t)$ by the relationship:

$$f^T(t) = S(t)\, e^{r(T-t)} \qquad (2.3)$$

where r denotes the continuously compounded rate prevailing at date t for maturity T. The proof will simply come from application of the no-arbitrage assumption to a well-chosen portfolio. Let us construct at date t the following position P and keep it unchanged up to date T:

---

[1] Starting with \$1 at date t and investing it in a riskless investment at the continuously compounded rate r, we denote $V(t)$ as the wealth obtained at date t. If we now look at this wealth at date $t+dt$, $V(t+dt) = V(t) + r\, dV(t)$, the second term representing the accrued interest on the capital $V(t)$ over the interval $(t, t+dt)$. We recognize here an *ordinary differential equation* whose unique solution taking the value 1 at date 0 is $V(t) = e^{rt}$.

	t	T
Buy the stock S	$-S(t)$	Delivery
Borrow to finance the purchase	$+S(t)$	$-S(t)\,e^{r(T-t)}$
Sell a forward contract, written S, for maturity T	$-$	$+f^T(t)$ ◀

Some comments are in order at this point:

1. The position P does not give rise to any cash flow between t and T since the stock pays no dividend and the *forward contract* (in contrast to a Futures contract) does not necessitate any margin calls.
2. By construction, the algebraic sum of cash flows involved in building the position at date t is zero. At maturity T, the stock is delivered to the buyer of the forward contract who pays the promised amount $f^T(t)$. Lastly, the loan is repaid together with accrued interest, which amounts to $S(t)\,e^{r(T-t)}$.
3. The most important property to observe is that cash flows generated by the position at maturity are quantities which do not involve $S(T)$ and, hence, are fully known at date t. Therefore, the position P deserves the qualification of being *riskless* over the time interval (t, T). Since its initial value at date t was zero, by *no-arbitrage*, its final value has to be zero at maturity: no investment and no risk lead to a null terminal wealth. Hence:

$$f^T(t) = S(t)\,e^{r(T-t)}$$

(B)   Spot–forward relationship for a dividend-paying stock

If we now suppose that the stock pays a continuous dividend at rate g, intermediate cash flows appear in the previous position: the owner of the stock bought at date t receives the dividend $gS(t)\,dt$ over the time interval $(t, t + dt)$. In order to find ourselves in the previous setting, we may decide that these dividends get immediately reinvested in the purchase of an extra quantity $g\,dt$ of the stock, which leads to a total growth of $e^{g(T-t)}$ over the period in the quantity of stock S detained.

Consequently, we will start with a number $e^{-g(T-t)}$ of shares of stock S at date t that will grow to one share at date T and follow the same reasoning:

	t		T
Buy $e^{-g(T-t)}$ shares of S	$-e^{-g(T-t)}S(t)$	Continuously reinvest the dividend payments in S	Get one share of stock
Borrow to finance the purchase	$+e^{-g(T-t)}S(t)$		$-e^{-(r-g)(T-t)}S(t)$
Sell a T forward contract on one share S			$+f^T(t)$ ◀

The same arguments as the ones developed above on this riskless position built at date t allow us to conclude that the sum of cash flows at date T is zero, hence:

$$F^T(t) = S(t) e^{(r-g)(T-t)}$$

(C)   Spot–forward relationship for a storable commodity

When going to a *storable* commodity, we have argued that the convenience yield y plays the role of the continuous dividend rate g and the spot–forward relationship becomes:

$$f^T(t) = S(t) e^{(r-y)(T-t)} \qquad (2.4)$$

Note that in the case of linear rates, this relationship takes the form:

$$f^T(t) = S(t)[1 + (r - y)(T - t)]$$

Lastly, if we decompose y into two components:

$$y = \underbrace{y_1}_{\text{Benefit from the physical commodity}} - \underbrace{c}_{\text{Storage cost}}$$

We can write:

$$f^T(t) = S(t)[1 + \underbrace{r(T - t)}_{\substack{\text{Cost of financing} \\ \text{the purchase of } S}} + \underbrace{c(T - t)}_{\substack{\text{Cost of storage} \\ \text{during } (t,T)}} - \underbrace{y_1(T - t)}_{\substack{\text{Pure "benefit" from holding} \\ \text{the physical commodity}}} \qquad (2.5)$$

This relationship is the one which is the most familiar to market participants: if the current forward price $f^T(t)$ was greater than the right-hand side of equation (2.6), one would sell the forward contract, buy the commodity through a loan, pay the cost of storage, benefit from holding the physical commodity over the interval (t, T) and realize at maturity T a *cash and carry* arbitrage. Conversely, if $f^T(t)$ was strictly smaller than the left-hand side of equation (2.6), a *reverse cash and carry* arbitrage would be possible. If such arbitrage opportunities are excluded (and, indeed, the presence of arbitragers in Futures markets makes these opportunities very limited in time and size), equation (2.6) has to prevail. We can observe that y_1 appears in equation (2.6) with a minus sign since the holder of the forward contract does not benefit from the physical commodity over the time interval (t, T), therefore, should not pay for the yield it provides.

Note that in the case of a *non-storable* commodity, such as electricity, the cash and carry and reverse cash and carry arguments vanish since there is no possibility of "carrying" the commodity during the time period (t, T). Hence, as first argued by Eydeland and Geman (1998), there is a collapse of the spot–forward relationship for electricity, which is one of the unique difficulties presented by electricity markets (these issues will be discussed in Chapter 11).

The merit of formulas (2.4) and (2.5), as long as we remain within a time period reasonably limited in order to be consistent with the assumption of r and y constant, deserves to be emphasized: *the spot and forward commodities are redundant assets* and one or the other may equivalently be used in a hedging strategy or any position. Liquidity will be the only decisive criterion.

Fundamental properties

1. We just stated that, from equation (2.4), the spot commodity and any forward contract are redundant assets, because of the deterministic relationship between them. Moreover, the *linearity* of the forward price as a function of the spot price allows us to focus, say, on the latter quantity $S(t)$ when risk-managing a book of Futures contracts.

    This is in sharp contrast to the situation we will face with a book of options: in this case convexity, i.e., the second derivative with respect to the spot price $S(t)$, which can be positive or negative, will play a key role; as well as the vega, partial derivative with respect to the volatility that explicitly appears in the option price. For our present discussion, note that *the forward price does not depend explicitly on the volatility of the spot price, as is the case with an option (plain-vanilla or exotic) price.*

2. Moreover, when t approaches T, there is smooth convergence of $f^T(t)$ with the spot price $S(T)$ and, close to maturity, the spot commodity and the forward contract become perfectly *fungible*.

3. If the spot price is not taken into account – which is often the case in commodity markets – it suffices to have some liquidity in two forward contracts F^{T_1} and F^{T_2} to be able to derive the values of $S(t)$ and convenience yield y (since the interest rate is observed).

4. Knowledge of $S(t)$ and y then leads to the whole *forward curve*, since for any maturity T:

$$f^T(t) = S(t)\, e^{(r-y)(T-t)} = S(t)\, e^{(r+c-y_1)(T-t)}$$

We observe that in the case where $(r-y)$ is negative, this forward curve is a decreasing function of maturity and we obtain the situation of *backwardation*:

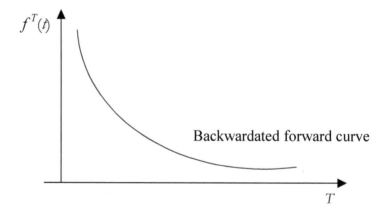

This happens when $r + c < y$ (i.e., when interest rates are low – as well as storage costs – and the benefit of holding the physical commodity high). In the recent past, with the perception of insufficient availability of oil, convenience yields have been positive and quite high, and oil forward curves have been backwardated.

Conversely, when the difference $(r - y)$ is positive, the forward curve is an increasing function of maturity and we obtain the situation of contango:

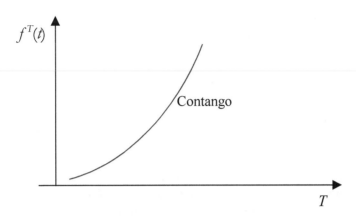

Note that, given its smoothness, this forward curve allows us to obtain an $f^{T_1}(t)$ with good accuracy if T_1 is comprised between two liquid maturities T_2 and T_3. In all markets, however, it is difficult to extend it to maturities T of the order of 20 or 30 years. Keeping the proof of the spot–forward relationship in mind, we see that the assumption of a constant convenience yield over (t, T) becomes quite unrealistic; we will show in Section 2.8 that the formula can, on the contrary, be extended to stochastic interest rates. This is the reason why we will be proposing in Chapter 3 models for the forward curve involving a *stochastic convenience yield*.

Beyond any mathematical consideration, we need to keep in mind that, for storable commodities, the convenience yield is in one-to-one relationship with the *shape of* the forward curve, the value of the spot price (or nearby Future), thus indicating whether the whole curve is located at a high or low level. Anticipation of a change in the shape of the forward curve will lead a market participant to change his or her holdings in short- and long-dated maturities Futures, i.e., to change the range of maturities of his position. This is why financial economists and oil traders converge in recognizing a *time spread option* in the convenience yield.

2.6   PRICE OF A FUTURES CONTRACT AND MARKET VALUE OF A FUTURES POSITION

This section aims at discussing a subtle but important issue, namely the difference between the price of a Futures contract, i.e., the price at which we can buy or sell this contract today, and the value of a position built in the past and containing this contract.

In what follows, we consider a well-defined Futures contract, with a fixed maturity T, for instance 31 December 2005, and a designated underlying (e.g., a number of barrels of crude oil). The price $F^T(0)$ of this contract at date 0 is defined as the dollar amount the buyer of the contract agrees to pay at date 0 in order to take delivery of the oil from the seller at a future date T. A day later (denoted as t_1), the price of this same contract is denoted by $F^T(t_1)$ and has every chance of being different from $F^T(0)$ because of the arrival of information (on weather conditions, new technologies and so forth) between the dates 0 and t_1.

If this number is smaller than $F^T(0)$, the buyer, also called the long position, of the contract is facing a loss equal to $F^T(t_1) - F^T(0)$ and needs to pay a *margin call* equal to this amount in order not to see his position closed by the clearing house. Assuming for clarity that the buyer does not close his position before maturity T, his algebraic gain may be written, assuming the business days are denoted by $t_1, t_2, \ldots, t_n = T$:

$$F^T(T) - F^T(0) = \underbrace{F^T(T) - F^T(t_{n-1})}_{\text{margin call on last day}} + \cdots + \underbrace{F^T(t_1) - F^t(0)}_{\text{margin call on day 1}} \qquad (2.6)$$

(Note that the margin call is indeed a "collect" when the difference is positive.)

The left-hand side represents the Profit and Loss (P&L) of the long position P initiated in the Futures contract at date 0. Denoting by $V_p(t)$ the market value of this position at any date t between 0 and T, we can observe that $V_p(0) = 0$ since the transaction is a fair game between the buyer and the seller. Immediately afterwards, this market value will differ from 0 and reflect the positive or negative arrival of news about the coming harvest or metal production.

Moreover, at maturity T:

$$F^T(T) = S(T)$$

since it is equivalent to buying the commodity in the spot market or as a Futures contract maturing immediately (no spot/Futures arbitrage).

Consequently, we obtain the following representation for the P&L at date T of a long position in a Futures contract initiated at date 0, in terms of the value $S(T)$ of the underlying commodity:

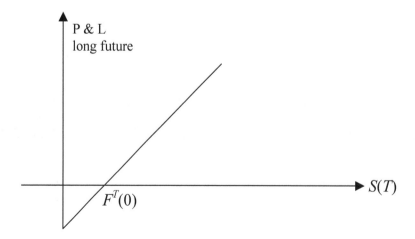

Since we have a zero-sum gain between the buyer and the seller of the contract, we obtain accordingly the P&L of a short position:

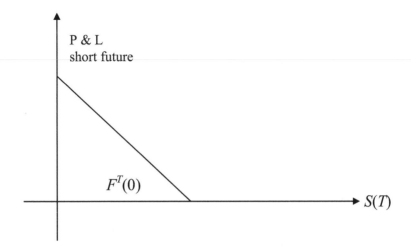

Both P&Ls are zero ("breakeven" situation) in the remarkably rare circumstance where the underlying commodity S has a spot price at maturity precisely equal to $F^T(0)$, the price at date 0 of the Futures contract. In this case, the (Futures) market had perfect anticipation at date 0, probably just by chance, of the spot price at maturity.

As mentioned earlier, the daily resettlement procedure of the position through margin calls allows the clearing house to preserve the integrity of the exchange.

Market value of a forward contract after inception

We consider the position P consisting of the purchase at date 0 of a forward contract for maturity T: this will lead to payment at date T of $F^T(0)$ dollars against delivery of the commodity.

We wish to find the market value $V_p(t)$ of this position at date t. In this order, we introduce at date t a new position P' consisting of the sale of a forward contract with the same maturity, ending with delivery of the commodity T against the payment of $F^T(t)$ dollars.

Let us denote the aggregation of these two positions as $P'' = P + P'$ and examine what it leads to at date T: obviously, the two deliveries offset each other and the cash flows are the following:

P	$-F^T(0)$
P'	$+F^T(t)$
P''	$F^T(t) - F^T(0)$

Consequently, $V_p(T) = F^T(t) - F^T(0)$ and P'' is *riskless* at date t since its value at date t is known with no uncertainty (we assume no credit risk in this argument). By assumption of no-arbitrage, the value of P'' at date t is the value at date T discounted by the risk-free rate:

$$V_{p''}(t) = e^{-r(T-t)}[F^T(t) - F^T(0)]$$

Lastly, we need to observe that $V_{p''}(t) = V_p(t) + V_{p'}(t)$ and that $V_{p'}(t) = 0$ since t is the date of inception of the position P'. We have thus demonstrated that:

$$V_p(t) = e^{-r(T-t)}[F^T(t) - F^T(0)]$$

Some remarks are in order at this point:

1. This number is also the P&L between dates 0 and t of position P since $V_p(0) = 0$.
2. This result is fundamental in order to *mark-to-market* at the current date t a book of forward contracts that have been signed at various dates and to compute by aggregation the P&L on the book.

   Note that, since $F^T(t)$ is linear in $S(t)$ (as was established in Section 2.4), the P&L of the book is *linear* in the value of the underlying. Hence, only the sensitivity $\partial V_p(t)/\partial S(t)$ needs to be monitored over time – and nullified if we want no exposure to the underlying commodity price S.

   We will see that, in the case of a book of options, the gamma (second partial derivative in S) and the vega (partial derivative with respect to volatility) need to be managed as well, which will be obviously more complex. This linearity of the forward contract value in S makes this instrument the most *fungible* with the underlying.
3. As will be shown in Section 2.6, Futures and forward prices are equal if we make the assumption of non-stochastic interest rates and absence of credit risk. Hence, all the previous results hold as well for a Futures position.

Note that we tried as much as possible to use the exact terminology, forwards versus Futures, when presenting their various properties.

2.7   RELATIONSHIP BETWEEN FORWARD AND FUTURES PRICES

So far, we have discussed forward and Futures prices in their respective contexts, but without establishing the possible relationship between them. In this section we are going to establish a fundamental result:

Under non-stochastic interest rates, forward and Futures prices for the same underlying and maturity are equal (assuming no credit risk in the forward contract transaction).

We denote the forward price $f^T(t)$ and the Futures price $F^T(t)$ as before and, for simplicity, assume that the underlying is a non-dividend paying stock. We start with the following result:

Under deterministic or stochastic interest rates, the spot-forward relationship for a storable commodity can be written as:

$$f^T(t) = \frac{S(t)}{B(t, T)} \tag{2.7}$$

where $B(t, T)$ is the price at date t of a zero-coupon bond maturing at date T.

We observe that, under constant interest rates, $B(t, T) = e^{-r(T-t)})$ and equation (2.7) reduces to (2.2). In the general case of stochastic interest rates, it suffices to observe that one dollar borrowed at date t is repaid as $1/B(t, T)$ at date T; equivalently, investing the amount $B(t, T)$ (smaller than 1) at date t gives a final payment of one dollar.

(A) In order to analyze the specific situation of Futures contracts and the effect on their prices of daily margin calls, we split the period $[t, T]$ into daily sub-periods and consider the following sequence of investments:

- At date t, take a long position in a quantity of $1/B(t, t+1)$ Futures contracts with maturity T on the commodity. This position will be closed at date $(t+1)$ and the algebraic profit $1/B(t, t+1)[F^T(t+1) - F^T(t)]$ invested on a daily basis until date T will provide a final wealth of:

$$1/B(t, t+1)[F^T(t+1) - F^T(t)] \cdot 1/B(t+1, t+2) \cdots 1/B((T-1), T)$$

- At date $(t+1)$, take a long position in $1/B(t, t+1)B(t+1, t+2)$ Futures contracts. Close the position after one day and invest the profits in a roll-over of one day lending which yields the final wealth:

$$1/B(t, t+1)B(t+1, t+2)[F^T(t+2) - F^T(t+1)] \cdot 1/B(t+2, t+3) \cdots 1/B(T-1, T)$$

Repeating that operation until date $(T-1)$ provides at date T the aggregate position:

$$\frac{1}{B(t, t+1) \cdots B(T-1, T)}[F^T(T) - F^T(T-1) + \cdots - F^T(t)]$$

$$= \frac{F^T(T) - F^T(t)}{B(t, t+1) \cdots B(T-1, T)}$$

Lastly, we add to this sequence an investment of $F^T(t)$ dollars in a roll-over of one day lending up to time T, which provides at maturity a wealth equal to:

$$\frac{1}{B(t, t+1) \cdots B(T-1, T)} F^T(t)$$

By addition, this global position P_1 has a terminal value equal to:

$$\frac{1}{B(t, t+1) \cdots B(T-1, T)} F^T(T) \tag{2.8}$$

and required an initial wealth of $F^T(t)$, since there is no payment to be made when entering a Futures contract (we ignore margin deposits which may be bonds or other collateral). In the case of deterministic interest rates, all quantities:

$$B(t, t+1), B(t+1, t+2), \ldots, B(T-1, T)$$

are known at date t and, again, through no-arbitrage, the following relationship prevails:

$$B(t, T) = B(t, t+1) \dots B(T-1, T) \tag{2.9}$$

(since there is no uncertainty in future values of interest rates, a long-term investment or a roll-over of short-term investments should lead to the same wealth; otherwise, an arbitrage opportunity would arise).

Remembering that $F^T(T) = S(T)$, the final value of P_1 can also be written as $S(T)/B(t, T)$ and required an initial investment of $F^T(t)$ at date t.

(B) Consider now the simple position P_2 consisting in buying at date t a number $1/B(t, T)$ of shares of a non-dividend paying stock and keeping them until T. This position P_2, which required an investment of $S(t)/B(t, T)$ dollars at date t, has $S(T)/B(t, T)$ as its terminal value.

The positions P_1 and P_2 have the same value at date T in all *states of the world*. By means of no-arbitrage, it has to be the case that they have the same value at date t and:

$$f^T(t) = F^T(t) \tag{2.10}$$

Under deterministic interest rates and in absence of credit risk, forward and Futures prices with the same maturity are equal.

In the case of stochastic interest rates, it is no longer true that:

$$B(t, T) = B(t, t+1) \cdots B(T-1, T)$$

and the price of the Futures contract at date t is not necessarily equal to the price of the forward contract.

Turning to storable commodities, and *assuming a constant convenience yield*, the spot–forward relationship becomes:

$$f(t, T) = S(t)\, e^{-y(T-t)}/B(t, T) \tag{2.11}$$

The reader interested in analogous issues for non-storable commodities may read the paper by Geman and Vasicek (2001).

Let us focus on some final important comments:

(a) When analyzing forward and Futures contracts on oil, electricity and other commodities, interest-rate risk is of secondary importance and may be viewed as negligible. That's why traders and market participants speak indifferently of forward and Futures prices.

(b) Even when interest rates are stochastic, the exact equality holds as long as the covariance[2] between changes in commodity price and interest rates is zero, the situation most encountered in practice. The question may be posed in the case of oil if one views that a rise in oil prices may impact inflation and, in turn, nominal interest rates.

---

[2] This covariance must be computed under the pricing measure Q, as will be discussed in Chapter 5.

(c) This property no longer holds if the credit risk involved in the forward contract is itself non-negligible since the *forward price* should reflect the comparative rating of the two counterparties.

2.8 THE BENEFITS OF INDEXES IN COMMODITY MARKETS

Indexes represent key instruments in commodity markets and their benefits may be classified in four categories:

1. They provide the wider public with the price of a commodity either worldwide, or at a given location in the case of fragmented regional markets.
   Since commodity prices enter in the computation of the consumption price index or consensus forecasts of economic growth, knowledge of their exact values is indispensable.
2. They allow for new players to enter the scene, since *opacity* of prices (and traded volumes) is a serious disincentive in any market and they render *price manipulation* difficult by those who have a dominant position at a regional level or even world-wide.
3. They make possible the existence of derivatives contracts, Futures and options, since many of them are financially settled and an index is the benchmark for the under-lying at maturity. The *convergence* at maturity of the Futures price to the spot price may only take place if there is a spot price.
4. They may be investment vehicles for market participants who wish to be exposed to commodity prices without dealing with the physical commodity.

The last point will be extensively developed in Chapter 14. The issue of the settlement of derivatives contracts is discussed throughout the book. The second point regarding the modeling of liquidity and existence of large player(s) is crucial in commodity markets. It is a challenging subject for which the answers are fairly limited at this point – in particular, in financial theory.

Indicators such as market depth, volume and open interest provide descriptive elements of market liquidity that were described in Chapter 1. Hence, we analyze here the second point.

Market concentration index

In energy markets prior to deregulation, vertically integrated utilities providing electricity used to have a monopolistic – or oligopolistic – situation. Interestingly, this situation has not changed after restructuring of the power industry which is, in Europe for instance, more concentrated than ever.

In economic theory, a popular index, the so-called Herfindahl index, is meant to give an indication of market concentration.

Definition The *Herfindahl Index* (HHI) is defined as:

$$\text{HHI} = \sum_{i=1}^{n} (\% \text{ market share of firm } i)^2$$

when n denotes the number of firms operating in the industry under analysis.

Comment If there are many participants in the market, n is large and each of them holds roughly a market share $1/n$. Then it is easy to show that HHI $\approx n/n^2$ and, hence, is close to zero.

At the other end of the spectrum, we have the situation of a monopoly: $n = 1$ and HHI $= 1$.

In general, the closer HHI is to zero, the less likely is the market not to face the possible bad effects of monopolies or oligopolies and the possible existence of *market power*.

Returning to the indexes reflecting the prices currently prevailing in commodity markets, the main sources are:

- *Major publications* – such as the UK-based *Platts* for oil, *Natural Gas Daily* in the US for natural gas; *McCloskey Coal Report*, *Energy Argus Coal Daily* in the US and *South African Coal Report* for coal; *Heren* for gas and electricity.
- *Information providers* – Dow Jones produces the DG–AIG index (discussed in detail in Chapter 14) which is a key element in commodity-related investments. Dow Jones also brings its contribution to the definition of the Swiss Electricity Price Index (SWEP). Reuters and Bloomberg are also major sources of information.
- *Exchanges* – The New York Mercantile Exchange (NYMEX) has a number of reference energy indexes which are the underlyings of its Futures contracts, ranging from the Crude Oil and Heating Oil indexes to the Central Appalachian coal index.

  The Natural Gas Exchange (NGX) in Calgary, Canada, which provides electronic trading of natural gas to buyers and sellers in Alberta, has acquired the Alberta Gas Price Indices from a statistical energy company, Canadian Enerdata.

  Nordpool has posted since 1993 the Nordpool electricity index; the European Energy Exchange (EEX) ties its newly introduced Futures contracts to the EEX (Leipzig) indexes. Powernext in Paris quotes on-peak and off-peak electricity indexes.

  The US Intercontinental Exchange posts electronic trading data on gas every day at 1 : 00 p.m. Central Time. The indexes represent an average of physical fixed price natural gas for delivery the day after, weighted by volume. The indexes relate to five major delivery points, including Henri Hub and Southern California Border.
- *Hubs* – Natural Gas Henri Hub (Gulf of Mexico) is the most famous hub index; Zeebrugge (in Belgium) is becoming an important natural gas hub index for Western Europe.
- *Major energy brokers* – The London Energy Brokers Association's (LEBA) electricity index is viewed today as the best representation of UK power prices. The broker Tradition Financial Services (TFS) is responsible for the international coal

indexes TFS API[3] #2, 3, 4 compiled from information provided by the *McCloskey Coal Report* and *South African Coal Report*. Another Europe-based broker, Spectron, provides online gas and gas swap prices in the UK as well as day-ahead indices for Dutch and French baseload and on-peak electricity prices.

Indexation methodology

Commodity index providers assert they follow some fundamental principles, such as:

- Computing the index from actual physical trades with transaction prices suitably verified.
- Surveying an equal number of buyers and sellers.
- Discarding "outliers", such as the lowest bid estimate if it is 2% below the next lowest and the highest bid estimate if it is 2% above the next highest offer estimate.
- Excluding paper trades from the survey.

Index averaging and weighting

Whether one looks at an index reflecting the average price of electricity at a given location or a basket of commodities in which to invest (see Chapter 14), at least three types of questions arise immediately:

1. The idea of computing the index as an average is certainly beneficiary in markets where there are missing data, some form of opacity or spikes that may be transient. The virtues of averaging being established, the question now is to choose between the two averages popular in financial markets – namely, the arithmetic average and the geometric average. The arithmetic average has the merit of being the one that springs to mind immediately; the geometric average is appropriate when we think in terms of *return* on a strategy related to the index.
   Remembering that the return over the period $(t - 1, t)$ is defined by:

$$\ln \frac{S_t}{S_{t-1}} \approx \frac{S_t - S_{t-1}}{S_{t-1}}$$

then, the formula:

$$\sqrt[n]{\ln(r_1, r_2, \ldots, r_n)} = \frac{1}{n} \sum_j \ln r_j$$

provides the average compound return over n subperiods.
   Unsurprisingly, both types of averages are used in the world of commodities, the arithmetic average being more popular (as will be illustrated by the various indexes described in the book). Note that the same problem is posed in equity markets where most indexes are computed as arithmetic averages. However, the Value Line index, which has existed for decades, is a geometric average of a basket of stock prices.
2. Besides the type of average, the second issue when constructing an index relates to *weights*. One possibility is to have all weights equal to 1; for instance, by considering

---

[3] API stands for American Petroleum Institute, the association based in Washington, DC that standardizes the industry's equipment and procedures.

in an index the average of 24-hourly prices of electricity at a given location as representative of the base cost for industrial and residential customers.

In the stock market, all famous equity indexes (e.g., Dow Jones, S&P, Eurostoxx 50, Nikkei) are averages of stock prices on a given day weighted by the *market capitalization* of the corresponding firm. In the case of commodities, the equivalent of market capitalization that comes to mind is:

- either the world *production* (possibly with the addition of *inventory*) of the commodity, since it reflects the importance of that specific commodity relative to the others in terms of output. However, this choice may give an excessive weight to fast-perishing commodities, such as livestock, relative to gold (as discussed in Chapter 14); or
- the *volume* of transactions on that commodity, which translates its importance for consumption, hedging and investment purposes; or
- both.

A deep analysis of theses issues is worthwhile, whether one wants to create an index to best reflect prices in a given country or region, or produce an index that investors would try to track because of the superior investment it provides.

3. We mention throughout the book the *mean-reversion* properties of commodity prices, a property certainly not exhibited by stock prices. Hence, the question: Should this mean-reversion be translated in the way the commodity index is constructed and how should this be done? The DBLCI-MR Deutsche Bank Liquid Commodity Index-Mean Reversion (described in Chapter 14) conveys in its name that "mean-reversion" is incorporated in the index; details regarding the method and its potential merits are unsurprisingly not included in the documentation provided by the bank not to disclose the strategy behind it.

Stochastic Modeling of Commodity Price Processes

3.1 RANDOMNESS AND COMMODITY PRICES

The goal of this chapter is to discuss *modeling* of the dynamics of commodity spot prices and forward curves in detail. The situation is the following: today, the spot price of a given commodity is observed – assuming there exists a reliable and liquid index, hence the importance of the existence of such an object. The forward curve is also available, with liquid maturities varying from 1 month to a few years depending on the underlying commodity. Current spot and forward prices should be used in order to *mark-to-market* a book of physical and/or financial contracts. The forward curve also provides information about the market perception of future spot prices. However, the numbers observed today are in no way sufficient to make decisions about future activity (e.g., in terms of generation), nor to decide on the current exercise of swing options or injection of gas in a storage facility.

Regarding the future, spot and forward prices are *random*; hence, need to be modeled. The perspective of this chapter is not to provide *forecasting* recipes but to discuss the fundamental *models* that have been investigated for stock and interest rates over the last 30 years and see how they can be adjusted to the specific properties of commodity prices (in other words, as in all sciences, we build on existing knowledge to move forward).

To take the simple case of a single commodity spot price S, its values over time from now on constitute a stochastic process $S(t)$; if not otherwise specified the current date is denoted as t. Our concern is threefold:

1. To find the most appropriate mathematical structure for S, i.e., the type of process: geometric Brownian motion versus jump diffusion or any other structure, using the properties observed in the historical database of S – with possible adjustment for economic growth or technological change. The choice of this stochastic process $(S(t))$ should:

   - lead to a probability distribution for the random variable $S(T)$ $(T > t)$ that agrees in particular with the *empirical moments* and other known features of this distribution;
   - be consistent with the observed *dynamics*, i.e., the properties involved in the change of S between two dates t' and t''.

2. Once we have chosen the "backbone" of $S(t)$, there will be parameters attached to this stochastic process. These parameters will be *estimated* from market data. Hence, we need liquid markets and "clean" data to make the right decision about the choice

of the stochastic process $(S(t))$, i.e., to have the necessary information from which to extract the parameters. Note that if a model involves, say, three parameters and 10 items of data are currently available, methods such as least squares or maximum likelihood will lead to more reliable values for the parameters than if we only had three items of data to obtain the desired parameters. The rule is to always use all the information provided by the market.

Comments   A few other remarks are appropriate at this point in order to bring some clarity to the existing terminology:

1. Many authors in the commodity and financial literature call models that are directly specified in a mathematical form "reduced-form models", as opposed to being derived from some general equilibrium setting, such as Pareto efficiency. Even though economic arguments are constantly in mind in this book, our models will indeed be probabilistic, hence "reduced".
2. However, our view is that model parameters have to be found in *current* market prices that contain messages about the market perception of where prices are heading *and* about current risk aversion – leading to a willingness to pay a premium in order to buy the commodity, e.g., oil during the conflict in Iraq. Hence, our models may deserve the denomination of *hybrid*, sometimes used in the commodity literature.
3. Any model will result from a compromise between being very complex – in the hope of being more accurate – and *parsimonious* in terms of the number of parameters involved. It is the latter perspective that we will adopt.
4. A model should be *robust*, in the sense that the parameters should not move wildly from one day to the next, leading to a complete change in a hedging portfolio. Were this the case, we would be better off reformulating the model to capture properties in the *mathematical structure* that, possibly, were not properly taken into account previously.
5. In order for a model to be accepted, it must be satisfactory:

   • from a *trajectorial* standpoint – the trajectories generated, e.g., by the Monte Carlo methods described in Chapter 5, must on average look like the observed ones;
   • from a *statistical* standpoint – the *moments* of the distribution of $S(T)$ (for $T > t$) must coincide with empirical moments, at least for the first four (i.e., mean, variance, skewness, kurtosis), as will be discussed in Section 3.2.

6. On another register, more economic and financial, we need to make a distinction between:

   • the probability of the price of oil $S(T)$ in January 2006 being comprised between $65 and $70. This number (comprised between 0 and 1, of course) represents the probability p of that event $\mathcal{E}$ under the real (or statistical) probability measure, denoted as P throughout the book;
   • the price $C(t)$ market participants are willing to pay today to receive $1 (or $1m) at date $T = 1$ January 2006 *if* the market price of oil on that day is comprised between $65 and $70. Ignoring, for the sake of simplicity, discounting between

dates t and T, the number $C(t)$ (which is in fact the *price of a digital option*) is also comprised between 0 and 1 but has no reason to be equal to p. We will refer to this number as the probability of the event $\mathcal{E}$ under the *pricing measure Q*. This probability Q will be discussed in detail in Chapter 5, but we can already understand why both probability measures P and Q will necessarily come into play in any commodity-related issue. The head of energy trading in a bank is certainly interested in the probability of electricity prices going over \$500 per megawatt-hour in Boston during July 2005 and this number will be estimated using the real probability measure P. But, since he is wondering now whether to purchase for July 2005 a *virtual power plant* located near Boston, i.e., getting the electricity without owning or running the plant, he is interested in the probability of the same event measured under the pricing measure Q. The first number only involves statistical data, in particular, weather-related data; the second number also includes the risk aversion component as well as human judgement about how much the market, or a *representative agent*, is willing to pay to secure today electricity generation for July 2005.

As we see, all these elements lead to a non-elementary problem that we will try to address by building one block after another. Keeping the global picture in mind, it is worth observing that all the discussion conducted so far about the spot price of the commodity $(S(t))_{t\geq 0}$ needs to be extended to the forward curve $\{F^T(t), T > t\}_{t\geq 0}$. The latter is, by definition, more complex since we have an infinite number of points: $T = 1$ month, 3 months, 1 year, etc. which evolve randomly over time. However, this *randomness* can be organized under some mathematical representation of its dynamics, as argued above. But, it also has to be *structured under the economic constraint of no-arbitrage*: if there was an obvious arbitrage opportunity between two forward prices $F^{T_1}(t)$ and $F^{T_2}(t)$, there are enough players in most commodity markets today to intervene in order to benefit from it. By doing so, they bring prices back to their "fair" values within a short period of time.

This last point does not make things simpler; on the contrary. When one builds a model, this model should be *arbitrage-free*. Whatever the state of efficiency reached by the commodity market under analysis, there will at any time exist at least one market participant to take advantage of the arbitrage opportunities that a firm is leaving open through an inappropriate model.

The goal of this chapter is to describe the stochastic processes commonly used in the representation of commodity prices and to compare/contrast them with their counterparts for stock prices or interest rates. As discussed in Chapter 4, the choice of a given stochastic process for the underlying has a crucial impact on the type of pricing formula one obtains for European call and put options – together with the very existence of a closed-form expression for these derivatives. When such an expression exists, it will be easy to incorporate it in any computer as a software program; but, just as importantly, all the sensibilities (Greeks) are obtained with the same precision and can be used in the design of risk management strategies as well as Value-at-Risk computations. Lastly, the choice of a given model to deal with the uncertainty of the future will impact strategic decisions in terms of output scheduling, storage injections and so forth.

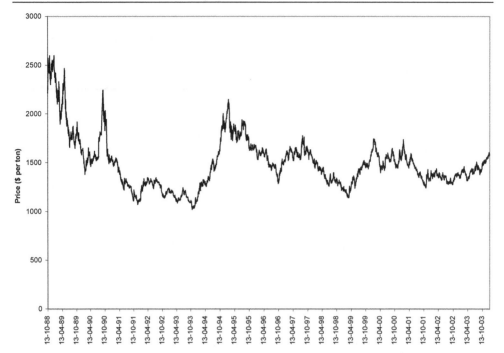

Figure 3.1 Aluminum nearby Futures price on the London Metal Exchange from October 1988 to December 2003.

3.2 THE DISTRIBUTION OF COMMODITY PRICES AND THEIR FIRST FOUR MOMENTS

In contrast to stock prices which grow on average – since the investor is rewarded for the time value of his money augmented by a risk premium – commodity prices do not generally exhibit trends over long periods;[1] we may want to leave aside in this statement the particular situation of oil at the present time. Taking markets as different as the UK natural gas (energy), corn (agriculture) and aluminum (metals), the behavior of prices over time is fairly similar: Figure 3.1 depicts the evolution of the aluminum nearby Futures price on the London Metal Exchange (LME) for the period October 1988 to January 2004; and Figures 3.2–3.8 exhibit the behavior of various metal spot prices between July 1993 and July 2002. Even if sharp rises are observed during short periods for specific events, such as the weather or political conditions in producing countries, commodity prices tend to revert to "normal levels" over a long period. This may be viewed as unsurprising: if demand is constant or slightly increasing over time as in the case of coffee and if supply adjusts to this pattern, prices should stay roughly the same on average. The resulting properties of commodity prices are a consequence of the general behavior of *mean-reversion* combined with spikes in prices caused by shocks

---

[1] The discussion is in fact more complex. If one believes in economy cycles – and many celebrated economists do – there is indeed a trend. A number of experts recognize the current period as the beginning of a bull market for commodities. Readers should decide for themselves. At any rate, model 3, as proposed in Section 3.6, provides mean-reversion around an upward (or downward) trend.

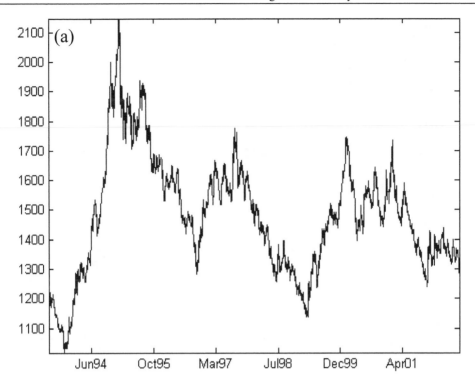

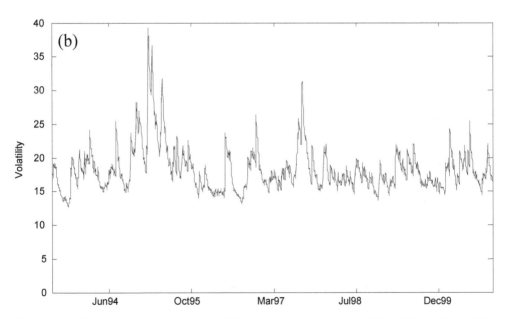

Figure 3.2 (a) Aluminum cash price (USD/ton) over the period July 1993 to July 2002. (b) Aluminum volatility (%) over the period July 1993 to November 2000.

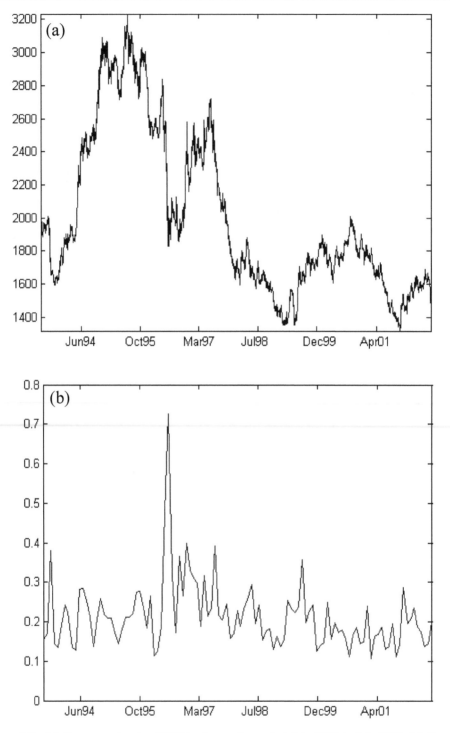

Figure 3.3 (a) Copper cash price (USD/ton) over the period July 1993 to July 2002. (b) Copper cash volatility over the period July 1993 to July 2002.

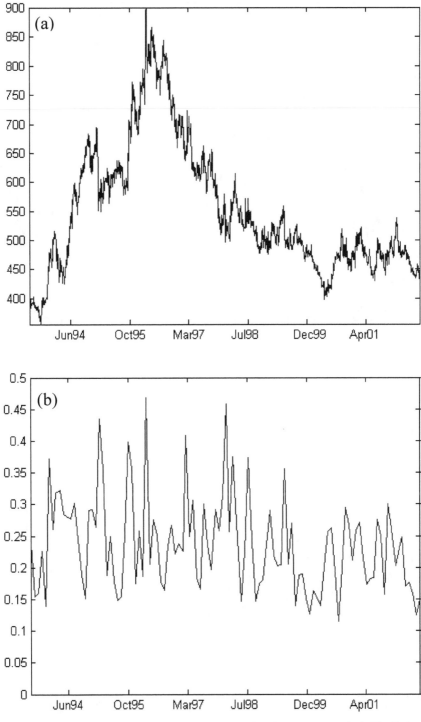

Figure 3.4   (a) Lead cash price (USD/ton) over the period July 1993 to July 2002. (b) Lead cash volatility over the period July 1993 to July 2002.

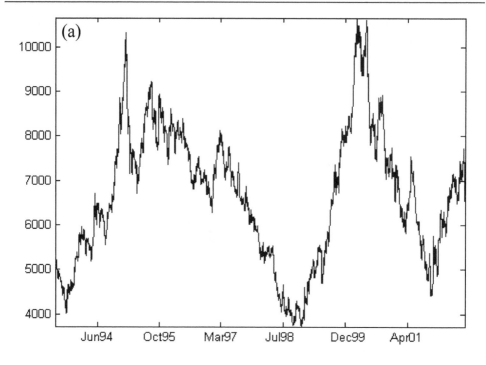

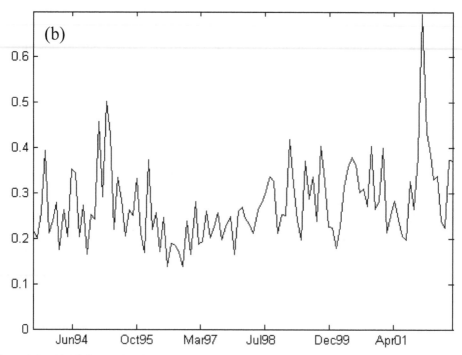

Figure 3.5   (a) Nickel cash price (USD/ton) over the period July 1993 to July 2002. (b) Nickel cash volatility over the period July 1993 to July 2002.

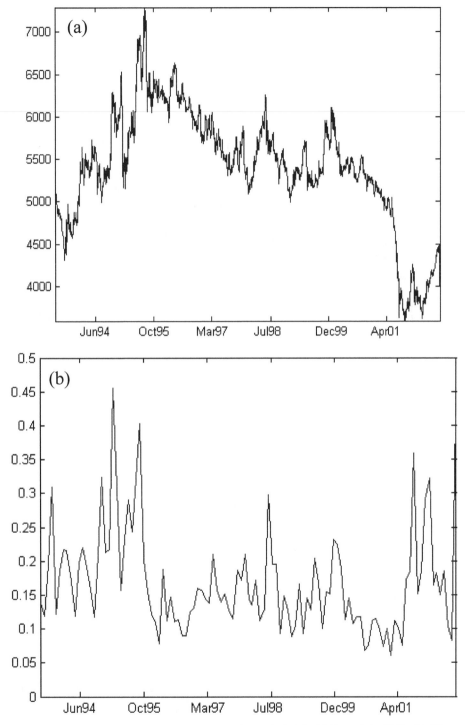

Figure 3.6 (a) Tin cash price (USD/ton) over the period July 1993 to July 2002. (b) Tin cash volatility over the period July 1993 to July 2002.

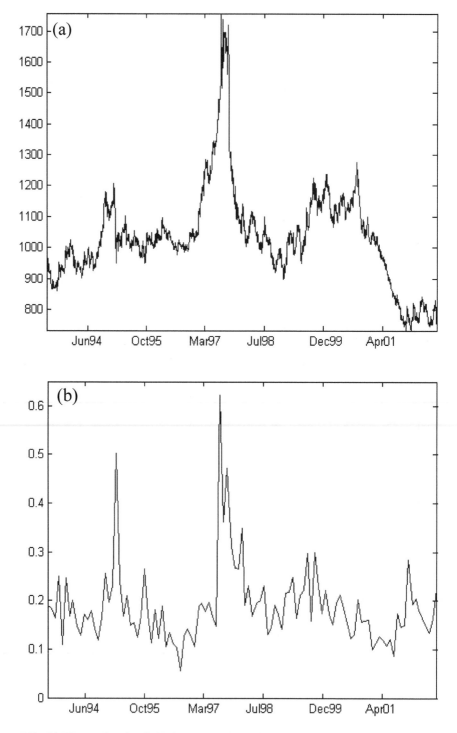

Figure 3.7 (a) Zinc cash price (USD/ton) over the period July 1993 to July 2002. (b) Zinc cash volatility over the period July 1993 to July 2002.

Table 3.1   First four moments of commodity price returns over the period July 1993–November 2000

Commodity	Underlying	Source	Mean	Standard deviation	Skewness	Kurtosis
Crude oil	Nearby Futures	NYMEX	0.0794	0.3507	0.0832	6.2057
Brent	Nearby Futures	IPE	0.0803	0.3325	−0.1647	6.0807
Natural gas	Nearby Futures	NYMEX	0.1197	0.666	−1.0125	30.7429
Heating fuel	Nearby Futures	NYMEX	0.0789	0.3457	−0.9507	11.1104
Unleaded gasoline	Nearby Futures	NYMEX	0.0654	0.3412	−0.3282	4.7057
Corn	Nearby Futures	CBOT	−0.0136	0.2599	−2.9179	51.2049
Soybeans	Nearby Futures	CBOT	−0.0451	0.2261	−1.2871	19.0947
Soymeal	Nearby Futures	CBOT	−0.0232	0.2571	−1.116	15.782
Soy oil	Nearby Futures	CBOT	−0.0643	0.2053	−0.0798	5.0402
Wheat	Nearby Futures	CBOT	−0.0141	0.3072	−0.7754	59.6257
Oats	Nearby Futures	CBOT	−0.0396	0.3292	0.3196	23.5515
Coffee	Nearby Futures	CSCE	0.026	0.4806	0.4458	10.1014
Aluminum	Spot	LME	0.0239	0.1854	−0.1132	6.0372
Copper	Spot	LME	−0.0066	0.2442	−0.3599	7.5366
Zinc	Spot	LME	0.0236	0.2161	−0.8367	12.4078
Nickel	Spot	LME	0.0476	0.2831	−0.0768	5.3854
Tin	Spot	LME	0.0037	0.1849	−0.3114	6.7626
Lead	Spot	LME	0.0277	0.2607	0.125	6.0316

in the supply/demand balance. Moreover, as discussed in the light of the theory of storage, shocks in demand in the context of scarce inventories also result in spikes in volatility. These different features are depicted in Figures 3.1–3.9 and expressed in the first four moments listed in Table 3.1.

Table 3.1 provides the first four moments computed on an annualized basis of daily returns for a number of commodity prices, where, as in finance, the return at date t is defined by:

$$R_t = \ln \frac{S_t}{S_{t-1}} \approx \frac{S_t - S_{t-1}}{S_{t-1}}$$

and S_t denotes either the spot price of the commodity at date t or the price of the first nearby Futures contract. Given a time series $R_1, R_2, \ldots, R_T$ of length T, the mean $\bar{R}$ is classically computed as:

$$\bar{R} = \frac{R_1 + R_2 + \cdots + R_T}{T}$$

and the variance as:

$$\sigma_T^2 = \frac{1}{T-1} \sum_{i=1}^{T} [(Ri - \bar{R})^2]$$

The square root of the variance is the standard deviation referred to as *volatility* in finance.

The length of the time interval $(0, T)$ is computed as a fraction of the year. Hence, the volatility σ_T must be transformed into its annual equivalent through the formula:

$$\sigma = \sigma_T \sqrt{\frac{250}{T}}$$

It is this annualized volatility[2] that appears in Section 3.3 in the representation of the commodity price process (S_t) by a geometric Brownian motion and that will be compared with the volatility *implied* in option prices in Chapters 4 and 5.

Note that, compared with the interest-rate market where volatility is of the order of 10% and the stock market where ordinary volatility is of the order of 15–18%, this volatility is higher for all commodities. Natural gas volatility – 66.87% on an annual basis – is the highest (note that electricity is not included in this panel) followed by the 48.25% volatility of coffee. The high volatility of gas may be explained by the limited number and cost of storage facilities, the regional nature of the gas market which, unlike the oil market, is not yet today a world market, and its strong relationship with electricity, the most volatile commodity. In the case of coffee, high volatility is explained by the high risk related to weather conditions.

Another observation is that metals in general are less volatile than other commodities. One obvious reason is that metals are easier to store and that inventories allow shocks in supply and demand to be absorbed, as already mentioned. Returning to Table 3.1, we observe that skewness is different across commodities, but kurtosis is greater than 3 in all cases. Hence, the distribution has fatter tails than the normal distribution, indicating a higher occurrence of extreme events: kurtosis is 59 for wheat, 51 for gas and 19 for soybeans. These high values of kurtosis should be properly represented when conducting stress-testing scenarios of a portfolio of supply contracts or a position in derivatives written on the commodity under analysis. We recall that the kurtosis of a random variable X with mean m and variance σ^2 is defined by:

$$\kappa = \frac{E[(X - m)^4]}{\sigma^4}$$

and is equal to 3 if X is normally distributed. When kurtosis is much greater than 3, it means that the density in the tails – which makes an important contribution to a high-order moment such as $E[(X - m)^4]$ – is higher than that which prevails for a Gaussian distribution; hence the names "fat tails" or "leptokurtosicity".

3.3 THE GEOMETRIC BROWNIAN MOTION AS A CENTRAL MODEL IN FINANCE

(A) Arithmetic Brownian motion

We recall that a process X is called "a Brownian motion with drift" (or an arithmetic Brownian motion) if it satisfies the stochastic differential equation:

$$dX_t = \alpha\, dt + \sigma\, dW_t \tag{3.1}$$

---

[2] In the case of electricity, the number of "business days" in the year is viewed as 360 instead of 250.

where:

- α and σ are real numbers, σ being strictly positive;
- dX_t represents the change in X over an infinitesimal time interval dt ($dt = 1$ day, in practice); put in a different way:

$$dX_t = X(t + dt) - X(t)$$

$$= \text{Difference between the values of } X \text{ at dates } t \text{ and } t + dt$$

- dW_t represents the differential of Brownian motion (W_t) (i.e., $dW_t = W(t + dt) - W(t)$) and follows a normal distribution with mean 0 and standard deviation $\sqrt{dt}$.

Among many properties, equation (3.1) implies that $E(dX_t) = \alpha\, dt + \sigma \cdot 0$. Hence, $\alpha = (1/dt)E(dX_t)$ represents the expected change in X per unit of time and is called the "drift of arithmetic Brownian motion" whereas:

$$\text{Var}(dX_t) = \sigma^2 \, \text{Var} \, dW_t$$

(since a non-random quantity makes no contribution to the variance):

$$\text{Var}(dX_t) = \sigma^2 \, dt \tag{3.2}$$

Hence, dispersion of the change in X around its expected mean $\alpha\, dt$ increases with σ, the fundamental *volatility* parameter. Dispersion also increases with the length of the time interval dt over which the change in X is measured, a property which agrees with our intuition. Another consequence of equation (3.1) is that the price changes dX_t are:

- Independent (knowledge of the change between Monday and Tuesday has no impact on the change from Thursday to Friday).
- Stationary (the change in X over one day has the same distribution over time).

The distribution of the price change dX_t depends on the length of the interval $(t, t + dt)$, but not on its origin t. As we will see, many commodities exhibit seasonality features which contradict this property; however, the introduction of a seasonal deterministic component in α can take care of this feature at a very low cost in terms of complexity.

Note that equation (3.1) may also be written as:

$$X(t + dt) = X(t) + \alpha\, dt + \sigma\, dW_t$$

A first observation is that the expression of $X(t + dt)$ – which represents the price tomorrow – depends on $X(t)$ but does not depend on any value of X prior to date t. This means that, assuming equation (3.1) is a valid model for the process $(X(t))$, the distribution of X at a future date $(t + dt)$ *only* depends on the current value $X(t)$. This fundamental property is called the "Markov property" and will play a key role in the founding models of option pricing. It is not present in the practice of *technical analysis* where, on the contrary, the whole history of prices is supposed to provide buying or selling signals. Trading strategies involving "head and shoulders" or the comparison of short-term and long-term moving averages are very popular among Commodity

Trading Advisors (CTAs). But, CTAs are not option traders, and different models are adapted to different management styles.

Analyzing the right-hand side at time t, we also see that it is an affine function of dW_t (since $X(t) + \alpha\, dt$ is a real number) and, hence, it also follows a normal distribution. As a normal variable, $X(t + dt)$ may take *negative values*.

Equation (3.1) was proposed by the mathematician Louis Bachelier in 1900[3] who was the first to introduce a mathematical definition of an option as well as a pricing method-ology for options on stocks. These possible negative values for the stock price, which contradict the principle of limited liability attached to a stock (whose market price cannot go below 0), represent the main limitation of this otherwise remarkable model.

Besides its relationship to the geometric Brownian motion described below, it is important to keep in mind that the arithmetic Brownian motion is a very popular way of representing a quantity which may be positive as well as negative. In particular, for our purposes in this book, spreads between two commodities or two types of crude oil, when one price has no reason to be consistently higher than the other, may be valuably represented by an arithmetic Brownian motion. In Chapter 12 we will provide a calculated example of the valuation of an option on a commodity spread; it will be shown that the computations of expectations involved in this valuation are particularly simple in the case of the arithmetic Brownian motion.

Lastly, let us observe an important particular case of equation (3.1) – namely, the case $\alpha = 0$. Now:

$$E(dX_t) = \sigma E(dW_t) = 0$$

On average, the value X_t does not change over time and the process (X_t) is a continuous version of a *random walk* – that of a particle moving with the same probability to the right or left along an axis, but staying at the starting point $X(0)$ on average. This representation will be appropriate to represent the spread between two commodities whose price differences remain on average the same over time.

(B)   Geometric Brownian motion

Aware of the properties of Bachelier's model, Paul Samuelson introduced in 1965 a revised version of the former's model, where the *return* and not the stock price follows an arithmetic Brownian motion; obviously, negative values are admissible for returns.

The equation specifying the dynamics of the stock price:

$$\frac{dS_t}{S_t} = \mu\, dt + \sigma\, dW_t \tag{3.3}$$

has been used as a fundamental assumption many times after Samuelson's seminal paper; in particular, by Black and Scholes (1973) and Merton (1973) when they pro-posed their celebrated pricing formula for options on stocks.

In equation (3.3), the left-hand side represents the change in values of S over the time interval $(t, t + dt)$ divided by the initial price of S at date t. We recognize in this ratio

---

[3] It is interesting to note that, in 1827, the botanist R. Brown had noted some properties exhibited by random movements of pollen particles at the surface of a liquid. Bachelier (1900) makes the same assumptions for the random evolution of stocks in his option pricing model. In 1917, Einstein observes the same behavior when analyzing the moves of gas molecules. The botanist, the financial scientist and the physicist had uncovered the same mathematical structure and its beautiful properties which led to the definition in 1923 of the *Brownian motion* $W(t)$ by the mathematician Wiener.

the *return* obtained by investing in the stock for the period $(t, t + dt)$: in the case of no dividend payment, the return is solely generated by the price change. Moreover, the quantity $(\mu\, dt + \sigma\, dW_t)$ is a normal variable, as mentioned in Section 3.2(A). Hence, in the Black–Scholes model, *returns are normally distributed*; conversely, if returns on a given asset present clear deviations from normality, the use of the Black–Scholes formula should be carefully questioned.

Lastly, using Itô's lemma, we obtain that the process (U_t) defined by:

$$U_t \equiv \ln S_t, \qquad \forall t \geq 0$$

satisfies the equation:

$$dU_t = \left(\mu - \frac{\sigma^2}{2} \right) dt + \sigma\, dW_t \tag{3.4}$$

Hence, (U_t) is an arithmetic Brownian motion. Since $S_t \equiv \exp U_t$, the process $(S_t)_{t \geq 0}$ is the exponential of an arithmetic Brownian motion and called a "geometric Brownian motion".

Let us now turn to the interpretation of the parameters μ and σ. If we compute the expectations of both sides of equation (3.3), we obtain:

$$\mu = \frac{1}{dt} E\left(\frac{dS_t}{S_t} \right) \tag{3.5}$$

and the constant parameter μ (also called the "drift") is the expected *return per unit of time*.

Lastly, if we compute the variance of the two sides of equation (3.3), we obtain:

$$\frac{1}{dt} \mathrm{Var}\left(\frac{dS_t}{S_t} \right) = \sigma^2 \tag{3.6}$$

and the square of the volatility appears as the *variance of the return per unit of time*.

Coming back to equation (3.5), it is crucial to emphasize that the sign of μ is typically perceived as positive since no investor would buy a stock offering a negative expected return. More precisely, the Capital Asset Pricing Model (CAPM) states that, under some equilibrium conditions, the expected return on a risky stock is equal to the risk-free rate r plus a risk premium (involving the beta of the stock and the expected excess of performance of the market portfolio over the risk-free rate).[4] Hence, in the case of a share price driven by equation (3.3), the drift μ is usually higher than the risk-free rate, and positive.

This has a fundamental consequence that needs to be kept in mind: besides normality of returns, a key mathematical assumption on which the Black–Scholes model is established implies that the *stock price grows on average over time*. If we do not believe this property is true for commodity prices, the Black–Scholes formula in its original form should not be used to price options written on the spot prices of commodities.

---

[4] $E(\tilde{r}) = r_f + \beta(E(\tilde{r}_m) - r_f)$ where the left-hand side is the expected return on the stock; r_f is the risk-free rate; $\tilde{r}_m$ is the market return; and $\beta = \mathrm{Cov}(\tilde{r}, \tilde{r}_m)/\mathrm{Var}\,\tilde{r}_m$.

Another key feature implied by equation (3.3) is the following: the expression of S at date $t + dt$ is given by:

$$\frac{S(t + dt) - S(t)}{S(t)} = \mu \, dt + \sigma \, dW_t$$

or $S(t + dt) = S(t)[1 + \mu \, dt + \sigma \, dW_t]$

Hence, the representation of $S(t + dt)$ only involves $S(t)$ and *no prior values of S*. Like the arithmetic Brownian motion, the geometric Brownian motion is a Markov process.

Lastly, the assumption of constant volatility σ is obviously not consistent with the behavior of commodity prices. This volatility may be changed to a deterministic function of time at a low mathematical cost. It may be made stochastic either through the introduction of stochastic volatility or by adding a jump component to the model (see Section 3.5).

Figures 3.1–3.9 show that soybean volatility exhibits seasonality, natural gas volatility presents spikes and that there is no particular pattern in aluminum volatility.

3.4 MEAN-REVERSION IN FINANCIAL MODELING: FROM INTEREST RATES TO COMMODITIES

In 1977 Vasicek introduced the first continuous time model to represent the random evolution of interest rates and proposed representing term structure moves through changes in the spot rate $r(t)$.

To prevent the large windings of the arithmetic Brownian motion described in equation (3.1) (which may go to infinity positively and negatively and is inappropriate for interest rates that move in a narrow band of the type $[0; 0.20]$); and to avoid the growth over time of the geometric Brownian motion contained in equation (3.3) obviously unsuited for interest rates, Vasicek introduced the so-called Ornstein–Uhlenbeck process to describe the short-term rate dynamics:

$$dr(t) = a(b - r(t)) \, dt + \sigma \, dW_t \tag{3.7}$$

where a, b, σ are positive constants.

A key feature of this process is obtained by looking, from date t, at the expected change $dr(t)$; this is represented by the first term, since $E(dW_t) = 0$, and $r(t)$ is observed at date t:

$$E[dr(t)/F_t] = a(b - r(t)) \, dt$$

Hence, if $r(t)$ is smaller than b, the expected change is positive; if $r(t)$ is greater than b, the expected change is negative and this creates a property of *mean-reversion* towards the level b

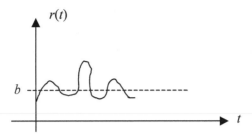

Commodity prices neither grow nor decline on average over time; they tend to mean-revert to a level which may be viewed as the marginal cost of production. This has been evidenced a number of times in the literature (see, for instance, Geman and Nguyen, 2002, for the case of agricultural commodities; and Pindyck, 2000, for energy commodities). Hence, mean-reversion is one of the main properties that has been systematically incorporated in the recent literature on commodity price modeling.

Equation (3.7) provides the following expression of $r(t + dt)$:

$$r(t + dt) = r(t) + a(b - r(t)) \, dt + \sigma \, dW_t$$

which, at date t, is an affine function of dW_t. Hence, $r(t + dt)$ is, like dW_t, normally distributed and may take negative values, which is obviously an undesirable feature for prices. Consequently, some transformation is desirable.

Mean-reversion and positivity

A popular model used for modeling energy and agricultural commodities aims at resembling the geometric Brownian motion while introducing mean-reversion to a long-term value θ in the drift term:

$$\frac{dS_t}{S_t} = k(\theta - \ln S_t) \, dt + \sigma \, dW_t \tag{3.8}$$

where k is the force of mean-reversion. Besides mean-reversion, this model has the merit of precluding negative values. Moreover, if we change the variables:

$$Z_t = \ln S_t$$

the use of Itô's lemma leads to:

$$dZ_t = k\left(\theta - \frac{\sigma^2}{2k} - Z_t\right) dt + \sigma \, dW_t$$

Now, introduce the variable $X_t = e^{kt} Z_t$ and use Itô's lemma again to obtain:

$$dX_t = e^{kt} \, dZ_t + k \, e^{kt} Z_t \, dt$$

$$dX_t = k\left(\theta - \frac{\sigma^2}{2k}\right) e^{kt} \, dt + \sigma \, e^{kt} \, dW_t$$

Integrating this equation between dates t and T (where $T > t$) provides:

$$X(T) = X(t) + \left(\theta - \frac{\sigma^2}{2k}\right)(e^{kT} - e^{kt}) + \sigma\sqrt{\frac{e^{2kT} - e^{2kt}}{2k}}W(T - t) \qquad (3.9)$$

At date t, $X(t)$ is observed and $X(T)$ is an affine function of the normal variable $W(T - t)$. Hence:

$$\mathcal{L}[X(T)/F_t] = \mathcal{N}\left(X(t) + \left(\theta - \frac{\sigma^2}{2k}\right)(e^{kT} - e^{kt}); \sigma\sqrt{\frac{e^{2kT} - e^{2kt}}{2k}}\right)$$

and the law of $Z(T) = e^{-kT}X(T)$ is immediately derived as a normal variable with an adjustment of the mean and variance parameters of $X(T)$:

$$\mathcal{L}(Z(T)/F_t) = \mathcal{N}\left(e^{-k(T-t)}Z_t + \left(\theta - \frac{\sigma^2}{2k}\right)(1 - e^{-k(T-t)}); \sigma\sqrt{\frac{1 - e^{-2k(T-t)}}{2k}}\right)$$

Forward prices $F(t, T)$ are obtained by writing $F(t, T) = E[S(T)/F_t]$ if we assume that the rational expectations hypothesis holds or that the computations were, from the start, conducted under the pricing measure Q (discussed in detail in Chapter 5):

$$F(t, T) = \exp\left\{e^{-k(T-t)}\ln S_t + (1 - e^{-k(T-t)})\left(L - \frac{\sigma^2}{2k}\right) + \frac{\sigma^2}{4k}(1 - e^{2k(T-t)})\right\} \qquad (3.10)$$

The sensitivity of the Futures price to different values of the speed of mean-reversion is depicted below:

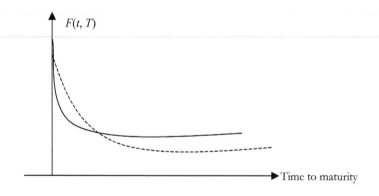

When T goes to infinity, the only remaining quantity comes from the second term:

$$F(t, +\infty) = \exp\left\{L - \frac{\sigma^2}{2k}\right\} \qquad (3.11)$$

Lastly, differentiating equation (3.10) provides the volatility of $F(t, T)$:

$$\sigma_F(t, T) = \sigma e^{-k(T-t)} \qquad (3.12)$$

We see that in this single-factor model the evolution of the only source of risk (S_t) was described in equation (3.8); still, we can introduce different volatilities for different maturity contracts, a feature which is reflected by the prices of options written on

Futures and observed in all markets. Moreover, equation (3.12) implies that forward contract volatility decreases for long maturities, which is in agreement with the *Samuelson effect*. However, this volatility goes to zero for long times to maturity, a property which is clearly a limit of the model since this is not observed in practice. This illuminates the benefit of the introduction of several factors to explain the dynamics of forward prices or, alternatively, jumps or stochastic volatility in order to better capture the properties of the forward curve.

Mean-reversion and seasonality

Many commodities, such as agriculturals or natural gas, exhibit seasonality in prices, due to harvest cycles in the former case and changing consumption as a result of weather patterns in the latter case depicted in Figures 3.8 and 3.9 below. In order to translate that seasonal feature while keeping the virtues of mean-reversion to account for the return of prices to the marginal cost of production, a simple and popular model for commodity spot prices under the real probability measure P may be written as follows:

$$\ln S(t) = f(t) + X(t)$$

where $f(t)$ is a deterministic component accounting for the seasonality of prices:

$$dX(t) = (\alpha - \beta X(t))\, dt + \sigma\, dW_t \tag{3.13}$$

The use of the log price guarantees positive values while benefiting from the tractability of the Ornstein–Uhlenbeck process driving the component $(X(t))$.

The deterministic function $f(t)$ – which is usually expressed as a sin or cos with annual or semi-annual periodicity – as well as the parameters α, β and σ are derived from a database of spot prices.

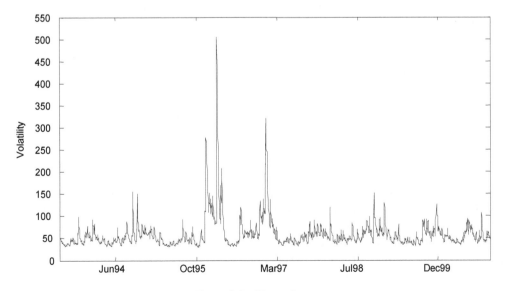

Figure 3.8   Natural gas.

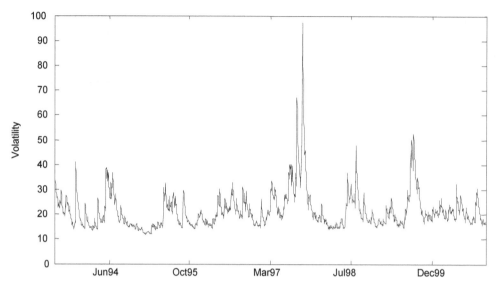

Figure 3.9   Soybeans.

3.5   INTRODUCING STOCHASTIC VOLATILITY AND JUMPS IN PRICE TRAJECTORIES

For the last 30 years the geometric Brownian motion has been the reference model for stock prices (particularly, because of its role in the central Black–Scholes model discussed in Chapter 4). However, continuity of the trajectories it produces is contradicted by violent downward movements of the stock market (e.g., the crash of 1987) or, on the contrary, a sharp upward rise generated by the arrival of positive news on a company or sector.

To take these effects into account, Merton introduced in 1976 the famous "jump–diffusion model", where a jump component is added to the diffusion term. Specifically, the spot price dynamics are described by the stochastic differential equation:

$$\frac{dS(t)}{S(t)} = \mu \, dt + \sigma \, dW_t + U_t \, dN_t \qquad (3.14)$$

where:

- (N_t) denotes a Poisson process with intensity λ accounting for the arrival of jumps.
- U_t is a real valued random variable (e.g., normally distributed), since the jump size may be positive or negative.
- μ and σ are parameters of the diffusion term that accounts for changes in commodity price return during "ordinary" days.

A trajectory generated by equation (3.14) has the following shape:

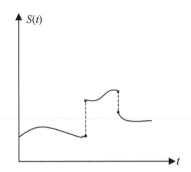

Obviously, this representation may be appropriate for representing such spot prices as oil prices where the arrival of news about a change in Russian politics or an update on the reserves of a major oil company may generate a spike. Conversely, any upward change in estimated world inventories is generally followed by a collapse of the corresponding commodity price. In both cases, prices generally continue to diffuse gently after the jump. Electricity is a particular situation which will be discussed in Chapter 11 together with the general issues involved in the calibration of processes including jumps.

3.6 STATE VARIABLE MODELS FOR COMMODITY PRICES

Besides improvements to the price process dynamics brought by mean-reversion or the jumps discussed in previous sections, another way to increase the quality of modeling is not to be limited to a single-state variable (namely, the spot price), but to enrich the representation by the introduction of one extra – or several – state variables. From the discussion conducted in previous chapters, it appears that these potential state variables may be the convenience yield, the long-term value of mean-reversion and stochastic volatility.

1 A stochastic convenience yield model for oil prices

Gibson and Schwartz (1990) note that the convenience yield has been shown to be, in theoretical and empirical research, a key factor driving the relationship between spot and Futures prices. Gabillon (1991) also comments that the shapes of backwardation and contango successively displayed over time by oil forward curves are inconsistent with a constant convenience yield. Hence, the following two-state variable model for oil-contingent claim pricing was proposed by Gibson and Schwartz (1990):

$$
\begin{cases}
\dfrac{dS(t)}{S(t)} = \mu \, dt + \sigma_1 \, dW^1(t) \\[2mm]
dy(t) = k(\alpha - y(t)) \, dt + \sigma_2 \, dW^2(t) \\[2mm]
dW^1(t) \cdot dW^2(t) = \rho \, dt
\end{cases}
\tag{3.15}
$$

The first equation describes a classical geometric Brownian motion for the oil spot price. The second equation defines the Ornstein–Uhlenbeck process driving the convenience yield and leading to positive and negative values, since, as observed in Chapter 2, dependent on the period and commodity, the convenience yield may have a different sign.

2   A stochastic volatility model for commodity prices

Eydeland and Geman (1998) propose extending the Heston (1993) stochastic volatility model to gas or electricity prices by introducing mean-reversion in the spot price and writing the following two-state variable model:

$$
\begin{cases}
dS_t = k(a - \ln S_t)S_t \, dt + \sigma(t)S(t) \, dW^1(t) \\
d\sum(t) = b(c - \sum(t)) + e\sqrt{\sum(t)} \, dW^2(t) \\
dW^1(t) \cdot dW^2(t) = \rho \, dt
\end{cases}
\tag{3.16}
$$

where:

- $\sum(t) = [\sigma(t)]^2$;
- the parameters k, a, b, c, e are all positive;
- the correlation coefficient ρ is in general negative since, in contrast to stock prices, the volatility of commodity prices tends to increase with prices – the *inverse leverage effect* which leads in option prices to a volatility smile "skewed" to the right as discussed in Chapter 5.

All parameters involved in the dynamics of $S(t)$ under the real probability measure P need to be estimated by methods, such as maximum likelihood, from a database of commodity spot prices. We can observe that, in contrast to the second equation in (3.15) where the convenience yield may be negative, the presence of $\sqrt{\sum(t)}$ in the coefficient of $dW^2(t)$ in equation (3.16) ensures that $\sum(t)$, the square of stochastic volatility $\sigma(t)$, remains positive. The parameter a represents the equilibrium/cost of production value of the commodity under analysis. The process $(\sum(t))_{t \geq 0}$ which is different from that described in equation (3.8) is referred to in finance as the CIR process since it was used for the first time by Cox, Ingersoll and Ross (1985) in order to introduce positivity in the mean-reverting Vasicek model. Mathematically, it is a much more complex process, since the quantity $\sum(t)$ is no longer normally distributed. The process $(\sum(t))$ belongs to the family of Bessel processes and represents today the most popular stochastic volatility model used in financial institutions (see Geman and Yor, 1993 for a mathematical discussion of this model).

Note that the addition of a jump component to the first equation of (3.16) would lead to a model where random changes in the total volatility of $S(t)$ arise because of the arrival of jumps *and* because of the random moves of $\sigma(t)$ in the diffusion component.

3   A three-state variable for oil prices

If we consider oil at the present time or any commodity at the beginning of a bull cycle, which seems to many economists to be the current situation, the mean-reversion feature is no longer so clear, at least toward a fixed level a as described in the above subsection. A valid model (see Geman, 2000), if we do not wish to introduce jumps in trajectories, may be one of the following form:

$$\begin{cases} dS_t = k(L_t - \ln S_t)S_t + \sigma(t)S_t\, dW_t^1 \\[2mm] \dfrac{dL_t}{L_t} = \mu\, dt + \sigma_2\, dW_t^2 \\[2mm] d\sum(t) = b(c - \sum(t))\, dt + e\sqrt{\sum(t)}\, dW_t^3 \end{cases} \qquad (3.17)$$

where:

- $\sum(t) = [\sigma(t)]^2$;
- $dW_t^1 \cdot dW_t^3 = \rho\, dt$;
- independence between W^1 and W^2, on the one hand, and between W^2 and W^3, on the other hand, may be assumed or not.

A positive drift μ in the second equation would translate to a rise, on average, of the value L_t toward which the commodity spot price S_t tends to revert, while this spot price itself may fluctuate significantly around L_t depending on the arrival of positive or negative news about the situation of world- and company-specific reserves. We should note in particular that the *stochastic volatility* $\sigma(t)$ may take large values on some days and be the mathematical explanation of major movements in spot price $S(t)$.

3.7 COMMODITY FORWARD CURVE DYNAMICS

We will start by reviewing some definitions and properties before analyzing the major challenges posed by the modeling of forward curve dynamics.

Definition The forward curve prevailing at date t for a given commodity is a graphical representation of the set $\{F^T(t), T > t\}$ of forward prices for different traded maturities T:

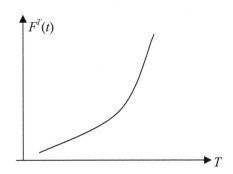

As mentioned before, this forward curve observed at date t is an important tool since:

- It depicts how the market prices the commodity for various future delivery dates T. If we believe in the rational expectations hypothesis, the forward curve tells us where the market sees the spot price in the future.
- It allows us to extract the convenience yield y and the spot price $S(t)$ from two liquid maturities.
  Recalling the spot–forward relationship:

$$F^T(t) = S(t) \, e^{(r-y)(T-t)}$$

we can derive y and $S(t)$ from two prices $F^{T_1}(t)$ and $F^{T_2}(t)$ since we have two equations and two unknowns. In the (unlikely) event of an arbitrage opportunity between several maturities, this one would be uncovered in the same way.

- It provides the *marking-to-market* to date of a portfolio of forward contracts.

This explains why utilities and trading desks invest time and effort in building a proper forward curve, in particular, through linear – or quadratic, or other spline – interpolation between liquid observed maturities.

Another crucial matter is the representation of forward curves that may prevail in the future (i.e., modeling of the dynamics of the set $\{F^T(t), T > t\}_{t \geq 0}$. Were all maturities observed, this would lead to a description of the random evolution of an infinite-dimensional system; for sure, the dimension of the problem is at least of the order of several units. Adding to the difficulty of this exercise, the model proposed should incorporate the no-arbitrage assumption since there will certainly be fewer and fewer arbitrage opportunities in markets with an increasing number of participants. Moreover, as argued before, one should never build a model where arbitrage opportunities are offered to the competitors.

The problem of a curve moving randomly over time was posed with its full complexity in the case of interest rates where the yields of zero-coupon bonds with maturities comprised between 1 day to 30 years constitute the yield curve. In the last 27 years *many* models have been proposed for the arbitrage-free dynamics of the term structure of interest rates. Even though there is no unanimity yet among financial institutions about the "best" model, a large number of important messages have been brought forward. Some authors have recently "imported" too abruptly results from the yield curve of interest rates to the forward curves of commodities. Our suggestion is to be more careful and analyze each property distinctly. Let us take a simple example: if we denote $\sigma(t, T)$ as the deterministic or stochastic volatility at date t of the price of a Treasury bond with maturity T, we clearly have:

$$\sigma(t, T) \rightarrow 0 \qquad \text{when } t \rightarrow T$$

since a default-free bond price must converge to its face value at maturity. The only source of risk, the *interest-rate risk*, vanishes and a close-to-maturity Treasury behaves like a riskless instrument.

Moving to commodities and denoting by $\sigma(t, T)$ the volatility at date t of a T-delivery forward price, we see that the above property no longer holds. When t goes to T, the T-forward price becomes a spot price and its volatility is higher in all commodity markets – extremely so in the case of electricity.

Returning to the forward curve dynamics, we are first going to recap a few properties that should be kept in mind at all times:

1. $F^T(T) = S(T)$ by no-arbitrage between spot and forward markets. In the case of electricity, the convergence:

$$F^T(t) \xrightarrow[t \to T]{} S(T)$$

   is not too clear because of non-storability, possible congestion transmission and a multi-form spot market: day-ahead, adjustment, within-day.
2. If we leave electricity aside, the spot–forward relationship:

$$F^T(t) = S(t)\, e^{(r-y)(T-t)}$$

   implies, under constant interest rates and convenience yield, that:

$$\frac{dF^T(t)}{F^T(t)} = \frac{dS(t)}{S(t)} - (r - y)t \tag{3.18}$$

   Hence:

   ○ there is a relationship between the dynamics of $(S(t))$ and $(F^T(t))$ under *any* probability measure;
   ○ if $(S(t))_{t \geq 0}$ is driven by a geometric Brownian measure, the same property will hold for $(F^T(t))_{t \geq 0}$, as long as we assume convenience yield and interest rates to be non-stochastic.

3. Forward price moves are always smoother than changes in the underlying spot price. One important explanation, among others, is that the time period prior to delivery allows the production process to adjust for shocks in supply and demand.
4. Anticipating Chapter 5, we know that under the risk-neutral probability measure Q, the Futures price $(F^T(t))_{t \geq 0}$ is a martingale, i.e., remains constant on average: there is no drift term representing the time value of money since there is no downpayment at inception of the contract (as is the case with an option) and the risk premium is embedded in Q. Keeping the representation of a geometric Brownian motion in mind as well as the martingale property and a volatility varying in t and T, a number of authors have proposed the following dynamics for forward prices $(F^T(t))$ under the risk-neutral measure Q:

$$\frac{dF^T(t)}{F^T(t)} = \sum_{i=1}^{n} \sigma_i(t, T)\, dW_t^i$$

   where:

   ○ n is the number of risk factors identified, say, through a Principal Component Analysis (PCA) of the forward curve;
   ○ Brownian motions $(W_t^1), (W_t^2), \ldots, (W_t^n)$ are possibly correlated.

In the case of an analogous representation of interest forward rates – which are embedded in the yield curve – many econometric studies have concurred about the choice of $n = 3$ risk factors to explain 97% of yield curve moves historically observed in various countries.

The first and most important one represents the parallel moves of the curve:

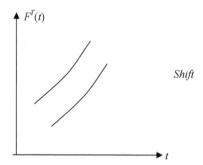

The second one in terms of explanatory power defines the changes in slope:

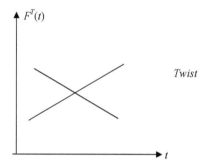

The third one is related to the curvature; so consistently with the Taylor expansion one may write for F^T:

$$F^T(t + \delta t, S_t + \delta S_t) = F^T(t, S_t) + \frac{\partial F^T}{\partial S_t} \delta S_t + \frac{1}{2}\frac{\partial^2 F}{\partial S_t^2}(\delta S_t)^2 + \text{term in } \delta t$$

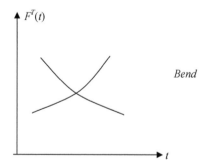

In the case of cvommodities, these three factors are certainly present. An interesting discussion may be found in Chapter 8 on metals which shows that $n = 4$ is more appropriate for metals. Koekbakker and Ollmar (2005) exhibit 10 factors to explain 95% of the changes of the forward curve dynamics in the Nordic electricity market, even though it has been and still is one of the best behaved among all the power markets in the world. Obviously, a model with 10 factors becomes cumbersome to implement and one needs to focus on the most significant ones to adopt a realistic approach.

4

Plain-vanilla Option Pricing and Hedging: From Stocks to Commodities

4.1 GENERAL DEFINITIONS

An option is a financial security granting its holder the right (but not the obligation) to buy (or sell) a given asset or commodity, called the underlying, at a predetermined price, called the "strike" of the option, at a given date, called the "maturity" of the option. This unique exercise date becomes a time interval in the case of American options or swing options (see Chapter 11).

Hence, the characteristics of the option may be summarized as follows:

- Underlying asset: stock, stock index, currency, bond, commodity, etc. (denoted as S).
- Option type: call C or put P.
- Position type: buyer (long) or seller (short).
- Strike price: purchase or selling price guaranteed by the ownership of the option (denoted as k).
- Inception date: day on which the option is "written" by the seller.
- Maturity date: or expiration date (denoted T in what follows); day on which the option may be exercised (European option) or upper bound of the exercise interval in the case of an American option.
- Option price: or premium, denoted $C(0)$ for the call and $P(0)$ for the put.

Indeed, two categories of options can be identified at the start: European options, which may only be exercised at maturity; and American options, which may be exercised on any business day during the lifetime of the option.

Another characteristic of an option, particularly important in the case of commodity markets, is the way the contract is settled: the buyer of the option may wish to take *physical delivery* of the underlying upon payment of the strike at maturity; in the case of commodities such as oil, where different grades exist, the exact type of commodity will be specified in the option contract as is done for Futures contracts. Or the option contract may be financially settled (e.g., using the last quoted price of the underlying asset at maturity). Index options – the index may be an equity index, a commodity index, an inflation index – are always financially settled and, according to our previous notation, the buyer of the call receives the cash flow $\max(0, S_T - k)$, where S_T is the value of the index at maturity. The notation "max" classically represents the larger of two quantities.

In what follows, the founding results will first be established for stocks as underlyings, then extended to commodities. The graphs and strategies displayed below hold, of course, for both. We can represent in simple graphs the pay-off C_T and P_T of a European call and a European put option at maturity as a function of the underlying asset price S_T:

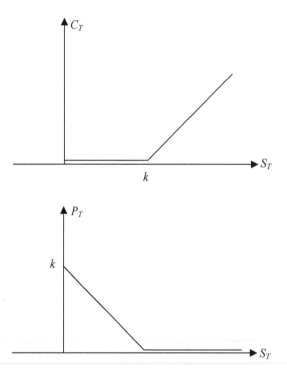

It is clear (and will be discussed in many ways further on) that the price at date 0 of the call (or put) is a positive number $C(0)$ (respectively, $P(0)$): by means of no-arbitrage, in order to get a payout which is zero or strictly positive, a positive premium has to be paid at date 0.

Hence, the algebraic gain profile or Profit and Loss (P&L) for the buyer of a call option between the dates 0 and T may be represented as follows:

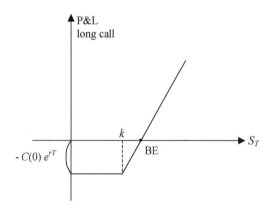

This graph is derived from the call pay-off diagram (above) by a downward translation of magnitude $C(0)\, e^{rT}$ since $C(0)$, the price paid by the buyer at date 0, must be augmented by accrued interest – represented by e^{rT} in continuous time – in order to be compared with the price S_T of the underlying asset at date T, expressed in dollars of day T. Note that BE is the breakeven point, i.e., the value of S_T making the P&L null. Since there is a zero-sum game between the buyer and the seller, the P&L of the call seller is obtained by symmetry with respect to the horizontal axis.

We show immediately below the P&L generated by a long position in a put bought at date 0:

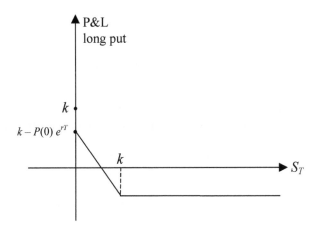

as well as the P&L of the short call and the short put:

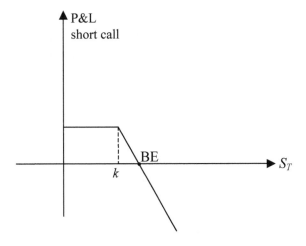

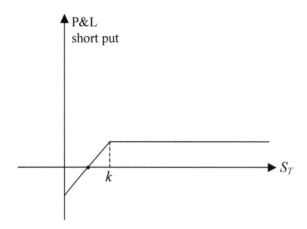

We can make at this point the following observations:

1. A market participant who anticipates an appreciation of the underlying asset will buy a call or sell a put; conversely, he shorts the call or buys the put if he foresees a decline of S.
2. Of the four P&L graphs, there is only one where the loss may be infinite: this is the short position in a call option. For practical purposes, this short position will always be hedged – using one of several possibilities that will be discussed in Section 4.4 – since no trader can leave open a position which may take the firm to bankruptcy.

4.2 CLASSICAL STRATEGIES INVOLVING EUROPEAN CALLS AND PUTS

Both because investors want to be able to bet on a more precise evolution of the underlying stock and because hedgers who need to buy options try to spend as little money as possible, strategies involving combinations of long and short positions in calls and puts have become quite familiar now and some of them, with no attempt at exhaustivity, are presented below.

1 Straddle

A long straddle consists in the simultaneous purchase of a call and put on the same underlying, with the same strike and maturity; the strike is most often chosen close to the current value of the underlying.

The investor has to pay both option premia but, in exchange, will benefit from the rise and the decline of the underlying:

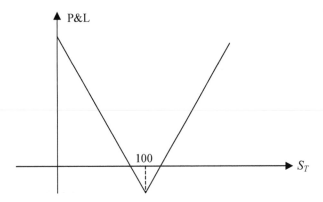

This strategy is appropriate if one anticipates a large move, upward or downward, of the underlying. It is a losing strategy in the case of "flat markets", the maximum loss being equal to the sum of the two option premia, with accrued interest. In the case of a short position in a straddle (i.e., anticipation of low volatility and small market moves), the loss may be massive in the case of major changes in the underlying price.

2 Strangle

A long strangle consists in the simultaneous purchase of a put with strike k_1 and a call with strike k_2, same maturity and $k_1 < k_2$:

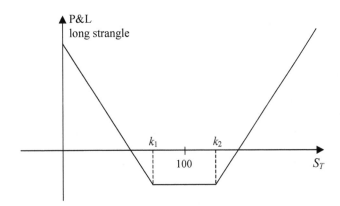

The investor buying a strangle anticipates a large move, upward or downward, of the underlying asset while one who shorts the strangle expects stable prices in the range $[k_1, k_2]$.

3 Call spread or vertical call spread

This consists in the purchase of a long call with strike k_1 and a short call with strike k_2, where $k_1 < k_2$, and the same maturity. Since a call with a lower strike has a higher price at time 0, a long call spread has a positive premium equal to the difference between the two call prices and the P&L profile at maturity is the following:

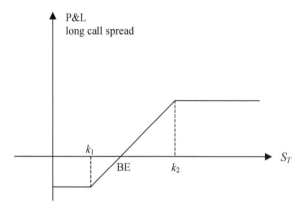

These instruments are very popular in the catastrophe options market and the weather market: the fact that the potential loss is bounded both for the buyer and the seller is a feature meant to generate liquidity, in particular in markets where the fair value of the option is not easy to determine (see Chapter 5 for more details on market "incompleteness"). It is easy to show that a vertical call spread is also a capped call (i.e., a call whose pay-off at maturity is bounded by a constant A specified at inception of the contract; in our example $A = k_2 - k_1$).

A *calendar spread* is the equivalent instrument, where the strike is replaced by maturity (i.e., the combination of a long call with maturity T_1 and a short call with maturity T_2, where $T_1 < T_2$). The buyer and seller of calendar spreads are taking views on a given *temporal* evolution of the underlying asset.

4 Butterfly spread

This is a very popular strategy, resulting from the combination of a long call spread and a short one, involving in total three strikes k_1, k_2, k_3 where $k_3 - k_2 = k_2 - k_1$. Equivalently, it consists in the purchase of two calls with strike k_2 and the sale of a call with strike k_1 and a call with strike k_2.

The P&L of a short butterfly spread at maturity has the following profile:

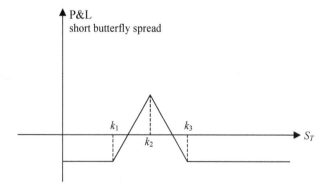

The seller of a butterfly anticipates no or small moves in the underlying asset price over the period $[0, T]$.

4.3 PUT–CALL PARITY

Before turning to the valuation at date 0 of the different European calls and puts involved in the above strategies, we are going to establish a result which requires *no assumption on the dynamics of the underlying asset price* and which will allow us to reduce the problem of pricing calls and puts to that of pricing calls. However, we do need a number of assumptions to establish put–call parity. One of them, central in this book and in the theory of option pricing, has already been discussed in the context of forwards and Futures: this is the no-arbitrage assumption. We recall that the first part of this chapter dealt with the context of a stock as an underlying. In order to prove put–call parity, we make the following assumptions (some of which will be relaxed later in the book):

A_1. No taxes, no transaction costs: "frictionless markets".
A_2. The underlying stock pays no dividend over the lifetime $[0, T]$ of the option.
A_3. Interest rates are constant; r denotes the continuously compounded rate.
A_4. There are no-arbitrage opportunities.

Then, at date t, the European put P, which has the same strike k, maturity T and underlying S as the European call C, has a price $P(t)$ related to $C(t)$ through the fundamental relationship:

$$P(t) + S(t) = C(t) + k\,e^{-r(T-t)} \qquad (4.1)$$

where t is any date prior or equal to maturity T.

Proof Let us build the following position P at date t: buy the stock S, buy the put P and sell the call C. The cash flows involved will be $-S(t), -P(t), +C(t)$. Since there are no dividend payments and the options are European, there is no *intermediate cash flow* until maturity T. At date T the options expire and the stock is sold in order to liquidate the whole position.

This position over the interval (t, T) can be represented by the following table:

	t	T	
		$S(T) < k$	$S(T) \geq k$
Buy the stock	$-S(t)$	$S(T)$	$S(T)$
Buy the put	$-P(t)$	$k - S(T)$	0
Sell the call	$+C(t)$	0	$-[S(T) - k]$
		k	k

At date T the final pay-offs of the call and the put depend on the stock being higher or lower than k. What is remarkable is that, in all states of the world, the total value $V(T)$ of the position at date T is equal to k. Since it has the merit of having a terminal value independent of $S(T)$ (i.e., *non-random* when viewed from date t), the portfolio P is *riskless*.[1]

Since P is riskless and a final value k at date T, building it at date t required an initial outflow of $k\,e^{-r(T-t)}$ dollars, which is also the sum of the numbers in the first column:

$$-S(t) - P(t) + C(t) = -k\,e^{-r(T-t)}$$

and the put–call parity relationship is established.

Note that the proof is exemplary in its simplicity and did not require at any point specification of the dynamics of S, such as continuous trajectories versus the possibility of jumps over the time interval $[t, T]$. Whenever it is feasible just to use such arguments in order to prove a result, it is clear that we should do so; unfortunately, this situation will be rare. Traders do try to identify such situations in practice; in their language, the put–call parity states that a portfolio consisting of a stock and a European put can be *statically* replicated by a call and a position in money market account M. This money market account is *the* riskless asset in the situation of constant interest rates and grows at the continuously compounded rate r.

Note also that at date T a portfolio P' comprising the stock – or commodity – and a put written on it has a final value equal to the sum of the components' market prices at date T:

$$S(T) + P(T) = S(T) + \max(0, k - S(T))$$

$$= \max(S(T), k) \tag{4.2}$$

If the stock or commodity market goes up between dates t and T, $S(T)$ is very high; the maximum of the two quantities will be $S(T)$ and the investor will have benefited from the rise in prices. Conversely, if markets crash, $S(T)$ is very low and the maximum is equal to k.

Hence, instead of collapsing to zero as it would have if the portfolio P' had contained only S, the investor's wealth is equal to k. This simple but fundamental use of put options is called *portfolio insurance*, the put providing protection against downward movements.

Formula (4.2) satisfies the first two fundamental motivations of any investor:

1. Benefiting from a market rise if it occurs, which may also be expressed by a wealth utility with a strictly positive derivative.
2. Limiting the investor's losses to a minimal wealth of k dollars in the case of market decline. This floor satisfies investor risk aversion, a feature that has been exhibited in experiments conducted for a long time by sociologists and economists; risk aversion is expressed by a concave utility function (i.e., a negative second derivative).

---

[1] We need to remember that *risk means randomness* or, equivalently, a strictly positive variance for the value of an instrument or a position at a future T. By definition, today is known since it is fully revealed, except in the case of opaque markets. Tomorrow is risky, except for a position carefully built today in order to eliminate all sources of randomness, in which case the position deserves the title of *riskless*; by means of no-arbitrage, the return on a riskless position cannot be lower or greater than the risk-free rate.

Many equity products are being proposed along these lines to investors wishing to be part of a rise in stock prices without losing everything in the case of a bear market; unsurprisingly, these products are very successful. It is clear that similar positions can be built with commodities and are being offered in commodity-linked notes or commodity-related funds (as discussed in Chapter 14). Note that for the desk which is selling product P', the difficulty and challenge will be to hedge over the interval (t, T) the put held in a short position, as well as the underlying commodity S; in the case of a producer or an originator, the latter part of the hedge poses no problem.

4.4 VALUATION OF EUROPEAN CALLS: THE BLACK–SCHOLES FORMULA AND THE GREEKS

This section could cover hundreds of pages if we wanted to account for all the valuable papers written on the subject since the early 1970s. We will limit ourselves first of all to the famous Black–Scholes model and will discuss a number of extensions later in this chapter and throughout the book.

The Black–Scholes–Merton model (1973)

The model presented below was developed in the papers of Black and Scholes (1973) and Merton (1973). The formidable development of option markets it permitted – because, somehow, market participants immediately believed in the model it became "a self-fulfilling prophecy", to quote the third author – gained for its authors the just dessert of the Nobel prize in 1997. The assumptions (among which we will recognize many of those used for put–call parity) are listed below and will be discussed to see to what extent they may apply to commodities:

A1. Trading in the underlying stock takes place continuously.
A2. There are no taxes nor transaction costs.
A3. The underlying stock pays no dividend over the lifetime $[0, T]$ of the option.
A4. Interest rates are constant over the lifetime $[0, T]$ of the option and will denote the continuously compounded rate.
A5. There are no-arbitrage opportunities in the markets.
A6. The dynamics of the underlying stock price S are driven by the stochastic differential equation:

$$\frac{dS_t}{S_t} = \mu \, dt + \sigma \, dW_t \tag{4.3}$$

where $\mu \in \mathbb{R}, \sigma \in \mathbb{R}^{+*}$.

We may also write:

$$dS_t = \mu S_t \, dt + \sigma S_t \, dW_t \tag{4.3'}$$

Since the geometric Brownian motion driving S_t in equation (4.3) was discussed at great length in Chapter 3, we will turn immediately to the problem of valuing a European call C written on S, with maturity T and strike k.

Obviously, the call price $C(t)$ will vary with time, will depend on the current value of the underlying stock price $S(t)$ and, because of the Markov property discussed in Chapter 3 and satisfied by $S(t)$, will not depend on any past value of the process S.

Hence, we can write:

$$C(t) = C(t, S(t))$$

C appears as a function of two variables: the first t varies in a deterministic manner; the second is driven by the stochastic differential equation (4.3). Using Itô's lemma, we can see that the change in the call price between dates t and $t + dt$ is given by:

$$dC(t) = \frac{\partial C}{\partial t} dt + \frac{\partial C}{\partial S} dS_t + \frac{1}{2} \frac{\partial^2 C}{\partial S^2} [dS_t]^2$$

Replacing dS_t by its expression from formula (4.3') and $(dS_t)^2$ by $S_t^2 \sigma^2 \, dt$, since all other terms in $(dS_t)^2$ are null, we obtain:[2]

$$dC(t) = dt \left[\frac{\partial C}{\partial t} + \mu S_t \frac{\partial C}{\partial S_t} + \frac{1}{2} \sigma^2 S_t^2 \frac{\partial^2 C}{\partial S^2} \right] + dW_t \left[\sigma S_t \frac{\partial C}{\partial S_t} \right] \qquad (4.4)$$

So far, our arguments have been primarily mathematical. Now, keeping in mind equations (4.3) and (4.4), we build at date t a portfolio $\mathcal{P}$ containing one call and n stocks, where n is a real number fixed over the interval $(t, t + dt)$:

$$V_p(t) = C(t) + nS(t)$$

$$dV_p(t) = dC(t) + n \, dS(t)$$

$$dV_p(t) = dt \left[\frac{\partial C}{\partial t} + \mu S_t \frac{\partial C}{\partial S_t} + \frac{1}{2} \sigma^2 S_t^2 \frac{\partial^2 C}{\partial S^2} + n\mu S_t \right] + dW_t \left[\sigma S_t \frac{\partial C}{\partial S_t} + n\sigma S_t \right] \qquad (4.5)$$

The change in value of the portfolio between dates t and $t + dt$ is random because of the second term involving dW_t. In the first term, all quantities have been observed at date t since, using more precise notation, we should write, say:

$$\frac{\partial C}{\partial t}(t, S_t)$$

In order to make $dV_p(t)$ non-random, we ask that:

$$\sigma S_t \frac{\partial C}{\partial S_t} + n\sigma S_t = 0$$

The parameter σ as well as the stock price S_t are non-null; otherwise, the option would not be traded. Hence, we need to choose:

$$n = -\frac{\partial C}{\partial S_t}(t, S_t) \qquad (4.6)$$

For this choice of the real number n not only does the term in dW_t disappear but also the two terms containing μ in the first bracket cancel out and the quantity $dV_p(t)$ is

---

[2] We recall the "fundamental rules" of Itô's calculus: assuming that any quantity in $(dt)^\alpha$ with $\alpha > 1$ is negligible, we have $(dW_t)^2 = dt$; $dt \cdot dW_t = 0$. Itô's lemma is nothing but a Taylor expansion of the function denoted in our problem $C(t, S_t)$; a contribution in dt comes from the second partial derivative in S_t because of the property $(dW_t)^2 = dt$.

reduced to:

$$dV_p(t) = dt\left[\frac{\partial C}{\partial t} + \frac{1}{2}\sigma^2 S_t^2 \frac{\partial^2 C}{\partial S_t^2}\right]\tag{4.7}$$

The portfolio P, whose value changes in a non-random manner during the time interval $(t, t + dt)$, is *riskless*; more precisely, it is *locally riskless* since this property is obviously not true over the whole interval $[0, T]$.

Using the no-arbitrage assumption for the first time, we state that the return of P over the interval $(t, t + dt)$ has to be equal to the risk-free rate r:

$$dV_p(t) = rV_p(t)\, dt$$

$$dV_p(t) = r\left[C(t) - S_t \frac{\partial C}{\partial S}\right] dt$$

Equating this expression of $dV_p(t)$ with the one obtained in (4.7) we obtain:

$$\frac{\partial C}{\partial t} + rS_t \frac{\partial C}{\partial S} + \frac{1}{2}\sigma^2 S^2 \frac{\partial^2 C}{\partial S^2} - rC = 0\tag{4.8}$$

This relationship is satisfied by $\dot{C}$ and its partial derivatives for any date t between 0 and T is called a Partial Differential Equation (PDE). Moreover, the terminal value of C is by definition:

$$C(T) = \max(0, S(T) - K)$$

The partial differential equation (4.8) is sufficiently "well-behaved" to provide, along with the boundary condition on $C(T)$, a unique solution $C(t)$ at all dates t in $(0, T)$. Discussion of unicity together with the expression of that solution goes back to the work of Einstein at the beginning of the 20th century when he studied the so-called *heat equation*:

$$\frac{\partial y}{\partial t} + a \frac{\partial^2 y}{\partial x^2} = 0$$

Classical results on PDEs (such as changes of variables and "variation of constants") show how the solution to equation (4.8) can be obtained through solution of the heat equation and lead to the price at the date of a European call option:

$$\boxed{C(t) = S(t)N(d_1) - k\, e^{-r(T-t)}N(d_2)}\tag{4.9}$$

where:

$$d_1 = \frac{\ln\left(\frac{S(t)}{k\, e^{-r(T-t)}}\right) + \frac{1}{2}\sigma^2(T - t)}{\sigma\sqrt{T - t}}$$

$$d_2 = \frac{\ln\left(\frac{S(t)}{k\, e^{-r(T-t)}}\right) - \frac{1}{2}\sigma^2(T - t)}{\sigma(T - t)}$$

$$N(x) = \int_{-\infty}^{x} \frac{1}{\sqrt{2\pi}} e^{-t^2/2}$$ is the cumulative function of a normal distribution $\mathcal{N}(0, 1)$

One of the remarkable features of the Black–Scholes model is that formula (4.9) provides an explicit value of the call price at date t, simply expressed in terms of the current price of the underlying stock $S(t)$, volatility σ, constant interest rate r and parameters k and T of the option. It is particularly worthy of note that μ, the second parameter defining the stock price dynamics in equation (4.3), is not present in the pricing formula. μ disappeared when we rendered the portfolio P riskless.

A second proof of the Black–Scholes formula (given in the following chapter and involving the so-called "risk-adjusted probability measure") demonstrates that the call price should *not depend on the drift* μ of the price process, a property which is not necessarily intuitive at first sight.

Consequences of the Black–Scholes formula

These are quite numerous and will be discussed in different parts of the book. For now, we will start with the most important ones:

1. Probably the most important consequence consists in observing that the price formula has been established *without any assumption on the preferences* and beliefs of market participants. The only economic assumption, A5, states that there are no ways of accumulating wealth if you start with no money and bear no risk.
2. We established put–call parity in Section 4.1. Now that the call price can be exhibited, we can derive:

$$P(t) = C(t) + k\,e^{-r(T-t)} - S(t)$$

$$P(t) = -S(t)[1 - N(d_1)] + k\,e^{-r(T-t)}[1 - N(d_2)]$$

which may also be written as:

$$P(t) = k\,e^{-r(T-t)}N(-d_2) - S(t)N(-d_1) \qquad (4.10)$$

3. Returning to the proof of the Black–Scholes formula, the portfolio P which is riskless over the interval $(t, t + dt)$ behaves like the money market account M:

$$V_p(t) = C_t + nS_t = -k\,e^{-r(T-t)}$$

and its evolution over the interval $(t, t + dt)$ can be written as:

$$dV(t) \approx (-k\,e^{-r(T-t)})r\,dt$$

Analogously, since:

$$C(t) = V_p(t) - nS_t = V_p(t) + S_t\frac{\partial C}{\partial S}$$

we obtain:

$$dC(t)_{(t,t+dt)} \approx \frac{\partial C}{\partial S}dS_t + (-k\,e^{-r(T-t)})r\,dt \qquad (4.11)$$

This formula exactly describes the replicating portfolio of call C (i.e., the hedging portfolio we should hold after having sold the call). It consists in a quantity $\partial C/\partial S_t$ of the underlying stock S and a (negative) quantity of the money market account M. The second term is less important since it is related to the *risk-free instrument* that banks or firms hold in all cases.

We will see below that the quantity $N(d_1)$ represents the partial derivative of the call price with respect to S_t (i.e., the quantity of the underlying stock we have to buy after selling the call).

Hence, the Black–Scholes model provides in the same formula the valuation of the call as well as the hedging strategy for the holder of a short position in the call.

Once a trader has sold a call, he receives the premium $C(t)$ and borrows the amount $k\,e^{-r(T-t)}N(d_2)$ (negative investment in the money market account), which added to the premium $C(t)$ allows him to buy $N(d_1)$ shares of stock S.

As time t goes by, $\partial C/\partial S_t(t, S_t)$ will change since both components are different. If this quantity increases at $t + dt$ (say, from 0.48 to 0.52), the hedge will be adjusted by buying an extra amount of the underlying S (namely, 0.04 shares). This adjustment over the lifetime of the call option is precisely the *dynamic hedging* of the short position.

In the case of a weather derivative, let us observe that the paradigm of hedging a short call by purchase of the underlying collapses because it is impossible to buy Celsius or Fahrenheit degrees. In the case of electricity, it is possible to buy at date t the appropriate amount of electricity to hedge a short position in a power derivative; however, it is not possible to carry the position to the following day $t + dt$ and, since the hedging portfolio has immediately vanished, there is no adjustment to make at date $t + dt$. Hence, the concept of dynamic hedging has to be reformulated appropriately in the case of electricity derivatives and replaced, for instance, by the *static hedge* provided by the physical asset.

The Greeks

The Greeks are partial derivatives of the call price with respect to the variables S and t and the different parameters involved in the option formula.

(a) Delta

This is the partial derivative of the call price C with respect to the price S of the underlying stock and, unsurprisingly, plays a key role in computing the exposures and Value at Risk of a position:

$$\Delta = \frac{\partial C}{\partial S}(t, S_t) = N(d_1) \tag{4.12}$$

Hence, the delta is positive and the call price, *at any date t*, is an increasing function of S_t. At maturity T, the simple graph of the call value C_T depicted at the beginning of the chapter clearly indicates that it is an increasing function of S_T. Formula (4.9) shows that this property holds at all times, in agreement with our intuition.

Let us note that for a small change δS in the stock price (e.g., positive), the corresponding change in C is given by:

$$\delta C \approx \frac{\partial C}{\partial S_t}\delta S = N(d_1)\,\delta S$$

Hence:

$$\frac{\delta C}{C} \approx N(d_1)\frac{S}{C}\frac{\delta S}{S}$$

Since $SN(d_1) > C$, we obtain:

$$\frac{\delta C}{C} > \frac{\delta S}{S} \tag{4.13}$$

If we anticipate a rise in the underlying S, the return generated by any amount of money invested in the call is strictly higher than the return on the stock during the same time period. This is called the *leverage effect* of derivatives and allows investors to increase their returns when betting on a given move of the underlying: inequality (4.8) holds in absolute values and provides the same result for returns on short positions in the case of an expected decline of the underlying stock.

(b) Gamma

Given the crucial importance of the delta, it is not surprising that the gamma (i.e., the derivative of the delta with respect to S) also deserves attention:

$$\Gamma = \frac{\partial \Delta}{\partial S} = \frac{\partial^2 C}{\partial S^2} = N'(d_1) \frac{1}{S\sigma\sqrt{T-t}}$$

$N'(d_1)$ represents the density of a normal variable $\mathcal{N}(0,1)$ at d_1. Since a density distribution is positive everywhere, the gamma of the call C_t is positive and the call is a *convex function* of the underlying stock S_t.

Again, this property can be seen to be obvious at maturity just from the profile of C_T as a function of S_T; what we have done here is to show that it is also true at all dates:

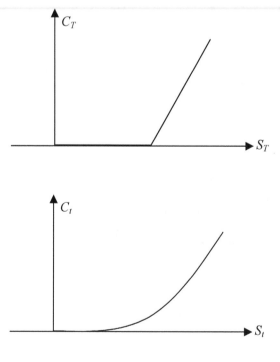

If we turn to the delta and gamma of the put, we know from put–call parity that:

$$S(t) + P(t) = C(t) + k\, e^{-r(T-t)}$$

Taking the partial derivative with respect to S on both sides, we obtain:

$$1 + \Delta_{\text{put}} = \Delta_{\text{call}}$$

$$\Delta_{\text{put}} = -(1 - N(d_1)) \tag{4.14}$$

Hence, the price of the put at date t is a decreasing function of S_t, as $P(T)$ is a decreasing function of $S(T)$.

Taking again the partial derivative in S in formula (4.14) we obtain:

$$\Gamma_{\text{put}} = \Gamma_{\text{call}}$$

The put price at date t is a convex function of S, as it is at date T; both put and call are convex functions of the underlying asset.

Let us consider a long position in a call option, denoted as C, and write a Taylor expansion of the option price between dates t and $t + \delta t$ when the underlying stock has moved from S_t to $S_t + \delta S_t$:

$$C(t + \delta t, S_t + \delta S_t) - C(t, S_t) = \frac{\partial C}{\partial t}\,\delta t + \frac{\partial C}{\partial S_t}\,\delta S_t + \frac{1}{2}\frac{\partial^2 C}{\partial S_t^2}(\delta S_t)^2$$

The left-hand side represents the P&L between dates t and $t + \delta t$. If we leave aside the term $\partial C/\partial t$ reflecting the passage of time, we see that, in order not to be exposed to a negative change in S_t which would damage the P&L, we need to add to the option a quantity $-(\partial C/\partial S_t) = -\Delta$ option of the underlying stock S.

Now the P&L of the *covered long position* (assuming no change in volatility) is:

$$C^{\text{cov}}(t + \delta t) - C^{\text{cov}}(t) = \frac{\partial C^{\text{cov}}}{\partial t}\,\delta t + \frac{1}{2!}\Gamma_{\text{option}}(\delta S_t)^2 \tag{4.15}$$

(note that $\Gamma_{\text{option}} = \Gamma_{\text{covered option}}$ since a linear quantity of S has a second derivative equal to zero).

Now, both for the call and put, Γ_{option} is positive and the covered position will benefit from large changes in S_t through the term $\frac{1}{2}\Gamma_{\text{option}}(\delta S_t)^2$.

More generally, for any position or portfolio, we will try to hold *positive convexity* in order to gain from major movements of the underlying; the same property has been exhibited many times in the context of bond portfolios where embedded options generate positive or negative convexity depending on whether the issuer or the investor owns the optionality. We will see that optionalities exist in standard electricity contracts which have been traded for a long time in the energy industry or in the nomination of cargoes in the oil industry.

(c) Theta

This is the partial derivative of the call price with respect to time:

$$\theta_{\text{call}} = \frac{\partial C}{\partial t} = -\frac{S\sigma N'(d_1)}{2\sqrt{T}} + rk\, e^{-r(T-t)}N(d_2)$$

In the case of a put:

$$\theta_{\text{put}} = -\frac{S\sigma N'(d_1)}{2\sqrt{T}} + rk\, e^{-r(T-t)}(1 - N(d_2))$$

Both quantities can be shown to be negative and represent the time decay of the option as it gets closer to maturity. One way of looking at it is to keep in mind that more time to maturity means more time for random moves of the underlying. These changes may be upwards or downwards but the option pay-off cannot be negative and the net result of more randomness will be positive.

In order to clearly identify the time value of the option, practitioners introduce for the holder of the option the notion of *intrinsic value*, which would be the pay-off of the option if it was exercised immediately – this value being zero if the current stock price is below the strike.

The remaining part is the *time value* and the option price can be decomposed as follows:

$$C(t) = \text{Intrinsic value} + \text{Time value}$$

When the option reaches maturity, the time value goes to zero and the intrinsic value is $S_T - k$ or zero.

(d) Vega

The option vega is the partial derivative of the option price with respect to the volatility parameter. In the context of the Black–Scholes model, the expression of the vega (which is not a Greek letter!) is:

$$\text{Vega}_{\text{call}} = \frac{\partial C}{\partial \sigma} = S\sqrt{T - t}\, N'(d_1)$$

and using put–call parity, we easily see that the put has the same vega as a call with the same strike and maturity:

$$\text{Vega}_{\text{put}} = \frac{\partial P}{\partial \sigma} = S\sqrt{T - t}\, N'(d_1)$$

Again, for these results it follows intuitively that the greater σ is, the higher the effect of the term σdW_t in equation (4.3) and the larger random moves become. The effect of downward moves (respectively, upward) is limited for the reasons mentioned above and the holder of the long position will benefit overall from higher volatility.

4.5 MERTON (1973) FORMULA AND ITS APPLICATION TO OPTIONS ON COMMODITY SPOT PRICES

As we will see, this formula plays an important role for options on commodities. For the time being, we keep the original Merton framework (namely, that the underlying asset is a stock) but, in contrast to the previous section, the stock pays dividends over the lifetime $[0, T]$ of the option. All the assumptions of the Black–Scholes model are kept except that the stock is supposed to make a continuous dividend payment at the rate g: the owner of a stock at date t receives at date $t + dt$ the dividend $gS(t)\, dt$.

The European call price is then given by the Merton formula:

$$C(t) = S(t) e^{-g(T-t)} N(d_1) - k e^{-r(T-t)} N(d_2)$$ (4.16)

where:

$$\begin{cases} d_1 = \dfrac{\ln\left(\dfrac{S(t) e^{-g(T-t)}}{k e^{-r(T-t)}}\right) + \frac{1}{2}\sigma^2(T-t)}{\sigma\sqrt{T-t}} \\ d_2 = d_1 - \sigma\sqrt{T-t} \end{cases}$$

Proof Let us first comment in this framework on the impact of a continuous dividend on the drift of geometric Brownian motion by describing in equation (A5) the dynamics of the stock price. Denoting this drift as μ', we can write:

$$\frac{dS(t)}{S(t)} = \mu' \, dt + \sigma \, dW_t$$

Note that in comparison with the case of no dividend payment, it must be that:

$$\mu' = \mu - g$$

For two firms with exactly the same activity and the same capital structure, the stock of the firm which distributes dividends will grow at a reduced rate, the difference account-ing exactly for the dividends received (continuously in our model).

Note also that the buyer of the option is not entitled to these dividends; he will have the right at date T to exercise and get for k dollars a stock less pricy than in the case of no dividends. Hence, we expect the call price to be lower than in the case of Black–Scholes and this is indeed translated by the factor $e^{-g(T-t)}$ which multiplies the positive term in the pricing formula.

We follow the same line of reasoning as in the previous section: the call price can again be written:

$$\begin{cases} C(t) \equiv C(t, S_t) \\ \text{where } dS(t) = \mu S(t) \, dt + \sigma S(t) \, dW_t \end{cases}$$

We write Itô's lemma:

$$dC(t) = dt \left[\frac{\partial C}{\partial t} + \frac{\partial C}{\partial S_t}\mu S_t + \frac{1}{2}\sigma^2 S_t^2 \frac{\partial^2 C}{\partial S_t^2}\right] + dW_t \left[\frac{\partial C}{\partial S_t}\sigma S_t\right]$$

and build the portfolio $\mathcal{P}$ at date t:

$$V_p(t) = C(t) + nS(t)$$

where again the choice $n = -\partial C/\partial S$ ensures that $dV_p(t)$ is reduced to:

$$dV_p(t) = dt \left[\frac{\partial C}{\partial S_t} + \frac{1}{2}\sigma^2 S_t^2 \frac{\partial^2 C}{\partial S_t^2}\right]$$

The fact that $\mathcal{P}$ is riskless implies that, by no-arbitrage, the return on $\mathcal{P}$ is equal to r, but in this new setting part of the return comes from the dividends received in cash for the ownership of n stocks which amount to $ngS_t\,dt$. Hence:

$$dV_p(t) = rV_p(t)\,dt - ngS(t)\,dt$$

$$= r\left[C(t) - S(t)\frac{\partial C}{\partial S}\right]dt + gS\frac{\partial C}{\partial S}\,dt$$

The PDE satisfied by the call price is now:

$$\frac{\partial C}{\partial t} + (r-g)S_t\frac{\partial C}{\partial S_t} + \tfrac{1}{2}\sigma^2 S_t^2\frac{\partial^2 C}{\partial S^2} - rC_t = 0$$

with the same terminal condition $C(T) = \max(0, S(T) - k)$. The solution is given by formula (4.13). Obviously, for $g = 0$, we recover the Black–Scholes formula.

Remarks
1. Since we assumed a *constant* dividend rate g, it is not surprising that the structure of the proof and the choice for n in the riskless portfolio are the same as in the Black–Scholes formula. The Greeks are derived using the same method as before (namely, computations of partial derivatives from the closed-form formula provide the option price).
2. Repeating the type of reasoning we used in Section 2.3, we can show that put–call parity in the case of a dividend paying stock becomes:

$$S(t)\,e^{-y(T-t)} + P(t) = C(t) + k\,e^{-r(T-t)}$$

4.6   OPTIONS ON COMMODITY SPOT PRICES

A fundamental and immediate consequence of the Merton formula is that it provides the valuation of European calls written on commodity spots. We saw in Chapter 2 that we may view commodity price behavior as that of a stock paying a continuous dividend equal to convenience yield. Hence, if we *assume that the geometric Brownian motion is an appropriate representation* of the commodity spot price, the price at date t of a European call written on the spot price S of a commodity with convenience yield y is obtained by replacing g by y in equation (4.16); that is:

$$C(t) = S(t)\,e^{-y(T-t)}N(d_1) - k\,e^{-r(T-t)}N(d_2) \tag{4.17}$$

where:

$$\begin{cases} d_1 = \dfrac{\ln\left(\dfrac{S(t)\,e^{-y(T-t)}}{k\,e^{-r(T-t)}}\right) + \tfrac{1}{2}\sigma^2(T-t)}{\sigma\sqrt{T-t}} \\[4mm] d_2 = d_1 - \sigma\sqrt{T-t} \end{cases}$$

and σ denotes the spot price of the commodity. Besides the condition of a geometric Brownian motion driving the spot price, this remarkable result holds as long as convenience yield y may be viewed as constant during the lifetime of the option (interest rates also need to be constant). If the option has a distant maturity, it becomes necessary to introduce a stochastic convenience yield in the dynamics of the underlying spot price S (see the model by Gibson and Schwartz, 1990 described in Chapter 3 and proposed for options on oil). If the stochastic process chosen for convenience yield is simple, such as an Ornstein–Uhlenbeck process:

$$dy(t) = a(b - y(t))\,dt + \sigma\,dW_t^1$$

where (W_t^1) is a Brownian motion possibly correlated with the Brownian motion (W_t) driving the spot price, and the option price is still not too difficult to obtain from a mathematical standpoint (e.g., using Monte Carlo methods). From a financial standpoint, however, we are facing a situation of *incomplete markets* since we have only the risky commodity to hedge two sources of risk, (W_t) and (W_t^1). Note that in this case the spot–forward relationship exhibited in Chapter 2 collapses since y is not constant and Futures contracts are no longer *redundant* for spot prices – except possibly for a nearby contract. Hence, if we can identify a *liquid* Futures contract, it may be the second instrument necessary to hedge both spot price risk and convenience yield risk.

Note that in the situation where σ is a random quantity, the relationship (4.12) which shows the change in the hedged long call becomes:

$$C^{\text{cov}}(t + \delta t, S_t + \delta S_t, \sigma + \delta\sigma) - C^{\text{cov}}(t, S_t, \sigma) = \frac{\partial C^{\text{cov}}}{\partial t}\delta t + \tfrac{1}{2}\Gamma_{\text{call}}(\delta S_t)^2 + \text{vega}_{\text{call}}\,\delta\sigma$$

Now, we have to manage optimally both the positive gamma and vega of the hedge call, using a term $\delta\sigma$ that may be positive or negative.

4.7 OPTIONS ON COMMODITY FUTURES AND THE BLACK (1976) FORMULA

These are traded much more than options written on the commodity spot price since, as we saw in previous chapters, most of the trading in commodities takes place in the form of Futures or forward contracts.

Fisher Black, in his 1976 paper, proposed the famous Black formula for options written on Futures. The Futures contract itself may be written on a stock or on a commodity; its maturity T_1 has obviously to be greater than the maturity T of the option:

Assuming once again no-arbitrage and a geometric Brownian motion for the dynamics of the Futures price process $(F^{T_1}(t))$ and noting that a Futures contract pays no dividend, it is easy to build again a riskless portfolio over the interval $(t, t + dt)$, comprising the call option and an appropriate number of Futures contracts and derive the PDE satisfied by the call price, leading to the Black formula:

$$C(t) = e^{-r(T-t)}[F^{T_1}(t)N(d_1) - kN(d_2)] \tag{4.18}$$

where:

$$
\begin{cases}
d_1 = \dfrac{\ln\left(\dfrac{F^{T_1}(t)}{k}\right) + \frac{1}{2}\sigma^2(T-t)}{\sigma\sqrt{T-t}} \\[2mm]
d_2 = d_1 - \sigma\sqrt{T-t}
\end{cases}
$$

and σ *now denotes the volatility of the Futures contract.* Note that in the particular case where $T_1 = T$, the option written on the Futures contract is equivalent to an option written on the spot price – if we assume no-arbitrage between the spot and Futures markets $S(T) = F^T(T)$. This is confirmed by writing the spot–forward relationship at date t:

$$F^T(t) = S(t)\,e^{(r-y)(T-t)}$$

Plugging this quantity into equation (4.18) gives:

$$C(t) = S(t)\,e^{-y(T-t)}N(d_1) - k\,e^{-r(T-t)}N(d_2)$$

which is exactly the Merton formula (4.16) for options written on the spot price of the commodity.

Finally, note that in the general case $T_1 < T$ the put–call parity for options written on Futures has the following form:

$$C(t) + k\,e^{-r(t-t)} = F^{T_1}(t)\,e^{-r(T-t)} + P(t)$$

and provides the price of the put written on the Futures contract.

This is consistent with the put obtained above and the fact that, as we will see in Chapter 5, the Futures price behaves like that of a stock paying a continuous dividend rate equal to r.

Comment

We observed that the volatility σ to be incorporated in formula (4.18) is the volatility of the Futures contract F^{T_1}. For practical purposes, it will depend on the maturity T_1 of this contract: for instance, in the gas or electricity market, σ_{T_1} will be much higher for $T_1 =$ January than April. If we want to be even more precise we can introduce a function $\sigma(t, T)$ that depends on both arguments t and T. If σ is deterministic, then it is easy to prove that formula (4.15) still holds as long as σ is replaced by Σ defined as:

$$(T - t)\Sigma^2 = \int_t^T \sigma^2(u, T_1)\,du$$

5

Risk-neutral Valuation of
Plain-vanilla Options

5.1 SECOND PROOF OF
THE BLACK–SCHOLES–MERTON FORMULA

When looking at the Black–Scholes formula written in equation (4.8), two remarkable properties appear immediately:

1. The parameter μ representing the drift term in the stochastic differential equation (4.3) which defines the dynamics of the underlying S is not present in the formula providing the European call price.
2. This price appears as the *difference* between two quantities: the current market price $S(t)$ of the underlying and the discounted strike price, both terms being multiplied by a coefficient smaller than one.

The first property is particularly intriguing since it is rarely the case that half of the parameters of a model disappear in the valuation of instruments derived from this model. A so-called "risk neutrality argument" was proposed in an intuitively correct way by Cox and Ross in 1976, but a thorough mathematical solution was provided by the seminal papers of Harrison and Kreps (1979) and Harrison and Pliska (1981). The reasoning involves the fundamental economic assumption of no-arbitrage together with a key result in probability theory and goes as follows.

Returning to equation (4.3) and taking the expectations of both sides, we obtain:

$$\mu = \frac{1}{dt} E_P \left[\frac{dS_t}{S_t} \, \middle/ \, F_t \right]$$

Hence, μ is the expected return per unit of time of a stock S in an economy where the only source of risk is the Brownian motion (W_t). From the no-arbitrage assumption and the Arbitrage Pricing Theory (Ross, 1976), we then know:

$$\mu = \underbrace{r}_{\text{risk-free rate}} + \underbrace{b}_{\text{risk premium}}$$

(*one* risk premium since *one* source of risk)

Since σ is non-null, we can write:

$$b = \sigma \frac{b}{\sigma}$$

and denote by λ the quantity b/σ. Since λ is defined as the risk premium expected by investors per unit of volatility, it will be called the *market price of equity risk* per unit of volatility.

Plugging the expression $\mu = r + \lambda\sigma$ into equation (4.3), we obtain:

$$\frac{dS_t}{S_t} = r\,dt + \sigma(dW_t + \lambda\,dt)$$

Now, from Girsanov's theorem, we know that there exists a probability measure Q such that the process $(\hat{W}_t)$ defined by:

$$\begin{cases} \hat{W}(0) = 0 \\ d\hat{W}(t) = dW_t + \lambda\,dt \end{cases}$$

is a Q-Brownian motion. We could say more about this measure Q from a mathematical standpoint. From a finance standpoint, we just need to know that under this probability measure, which is called risk-adjusted or *risk-neutral*, the dynamics of the non-dividend-paying stock have the following form:

$$\frac{dS_t}{S_t} = r\,dt + \sigma\,d\hat{W}_t \tag{5.1}$$

where $(\hat{W}_t)$ is a Q-Brownian motion.

At this point, the coefficient μ of the geometric Brownian motion, driving S under the real measure, disappears since it breaks into two pieces: the risk-free rate which remains in equation (5.1) and the risk premium that got incorporated in the probability Q. The weights this measure Q attributes to events will account for the risk aversion of investors.

Note that equation (5.1) first implies that the discounted stock price process $(S_t\,e^{-rt})_{t \geq 0}$ is a Q-martingale; that is:

$$S(t)\,e^{-rt} = E_Q[S(T)\,e^{-rT}/F_t]$$

We also observe that the same property holds for the money market account M since its discounted price is in fact constant over time and equal to $M(0)$. Since any option has a replicating portfolio in the Black–Scholes model, the martingale property is transmitted to the call price $C(t)$ and we can write:

$$C(t)\,e^{-rt} = E_Q[C(T)\,e^{-rT}/F_t]$$

or, since interest rates are supposed to be constant:

$$\boxed{C(t) = e^{-r(T-t)}E_Q[C(T)/F_t]} \tag{5.2}$$

This fundamental formula shows that the intuitive view of pricing the call as the discounted expected pay-off is correct as long the *risk premium is incorporated in the probability measure*.

We can now continue the computation all the way to the pricing formula by making explicit:

$$E_Q[C(T)/F_t] = E_Q[\max(0, S_T - k)/F_t]$$

where S_T is obtained at date t by integrating the stochastic differential equation (5.1) up to time T. We obtain:[1]

$$S(T) = S(t) \exp\left\{ \left(r - \frac{\sigma^2}{2} \right)(T - t) + \sigma \hat{W}(T - t) \right\} \qquad (5.3)$$

In order to compute its expectation, we write:

$$\max(0, S_T - k) = (S(T) - k)1_{\mathcal{E}}$$

where $1_{\mathcal{E}}$ denotes the indicator variable of the exercise set $\mathcal{E}$ and takes the value 1 if the final stock value $S(T)$ is greater than k and the value 0 otherwise.

We can then write:

$$C(t) = e^{-r(T-t)} E_Q[S(T)1_{\mathcal{E}} - k1_{\mathcal{E}}/F_t]$$

or:

$$C(t) = e^{-r(T-t)} E_Q[S(T)1_{\mathcal{E}}/F_t] - k e^{-r(T-t)} E_Q[1_{\mathcal{E}}/F_t]$$

The call price now appears as the *difference* between two quantities A and B. We will start with the computation of the simpler one:

$$B = k e^{-r(T-t)} E_Q[1_{\mathcal{E}}/F_t]$$

where:

$$E_Q[1_{\mathcal{E}}/F_t] = \text{Prob}_Q[\mathcal{E}/F_t]$$

$$= \text{Prob}_Q[S(T) > k/F_t]$$

$$= \text{Prob}_Q\left[S(t) \exp\left\{ \left(r - \frac{\sigma^2}{2} \right)(T - t) + \sigma \hat{W}(T - t) > k \right\} \right]$$

$$= \text{Prob}_Q\left[\left(r - \frac{\sigma^2}{2} \right)(T - t) + \sigma \hat{W}(T - t) < \ln\left(\frac{S(t)}{K} \right) \right]$$

After elementary rearrangements, we obtain:

$$\text{Prob}_Q[\mathcal{E}/F_t] = N(d_2)$$

where N is the cumulative function of a normal variable with mean 0 and standard deviation 1 and:

$$d_2 = \frac{\ln\left(\dfrac{S(t)}{k e^{-r(T-t)}} \right) - \frac{1}{2}\sigma^2(T - t)}{\sigma\sqrt{T - t}}$$

which is precisely the second term of the Black–Scholes formula.

The first term $A = e^{-r(T-t)} E_Q[S(T)1_{\mathcal{E}}/F_t]$ is more complicated since it involves the expectation of the product of two *dependent* random variables. However, we can recognize in $S(T)1_{\mathcal{E}}$ the random variable $S(T)$ *truncated* to those of its values greater than k. Hence, denoting g as its distribution under Q as defined in equation (4.18), we obtain:

$$E_Q[S(T)1_{\mathcal{E}}/F_t] = \int_k^{+\infty} xg(x)\, dx$$

---

[1] Since we will be essentially computing expectations, we identify $\hat{W}(T - t)$ and $\hat{W}(T) - \hat{W}(t)$ which are in fact only equal in law.

Well-known results on the distribution of the log-normal variable $S(T)$ lead to establishing that $A = S(t)N(d_1)$ and recovering from the difference $(A - B)$ the Black–Scholes formula.

5.2 RISK-NEUTRAL DYNAMICS OF COMMODITY PRICES

In Section 4.5, where we discussed the case of a stock paying a continuous dividend flow equal to g, we saw that this dividend implied a reduction of g in the drift of an analogous stock whose firm policy was not to distribute any dividend. Both mathematically and intuitively, it appears clear that the same drift reduction takes place under the real measure P and the risk-neutral measure Q since Girsanov's theorem only generates a drift translation in the geometric Brownian motion driving the stock price. Hence, the dynamics of a dividend-paying stock can be written as:

$$\frac{dS_t}{S_t} = (r - g)\, dt + \sigma\, d\hat{W}_t$$

where $(\hat{W}_t)_{t \geq 0}$ is a Q-Brownian motion.

For the purpose of this book, we observe that in the case of a *storable commodity* S with a constant convenience yield y over the lifetime of the option $[0, T]$, the risk-neutral dynamics have, under the assumption of a geometric Brownian motion for $(S(t))$, the expression:

$$\frac{dS_t}{S_t} = (r - y)\, dt + \sigma\, d\hat{W}_t \tag{5.4}$$

where r is supposed to be constant, as in the Black–Scholes–Merton model. Then there is one source of risk and one asset to trade and hedge it. The call price is unique and may be written as:

$$C(t) = e^{-r(T-t)} E_Q[\max(0, S(T) - k)/F_t]$$

We can rewrite the Merton formula for European calls written on *commodity spot prices*:

$$C(t) = S(t)\, e^{-y(T-t)} N(d_1) - k\, e^{-r(T-t)} N(d_2) \tag{5.5}$$

The computations are identical to those conducted in Section 5.1 except that the constant drift r is replaced by $r - y$.

It is useful to discuss equation (5.4) in greater depth. In the case of a non-dividend-paying stock, the drift under the pricing measure is r strictly positive. Hence, the holder of the call option sees the stock price grow at the risk-free rate and benefits from the volatility of the stock market, as shown in the Black–Scholes formula that was established for that specific situation. If the stock pays a continuous dividend at the rate g ($g > 0$), obviously the call option will still benefit from the volatility but the underlying stock price $S(t)$ will grow at a rate $(r - g)$ strictly smaller than the time value of money, and the call price is accordingly reduced by the factor $e^{-g(T-t)}$ in the first term of the Merton formula.

In the case of a commodity, the drift of the spot price dynamics is $r - y$, where the convenience yield y may be positive or negative; when y is positive, it may also be smaller or greater than r:

- If $y < 0$, $r - y$ is positive and greater than r – situation of sharp contango of the forward curve – the holder of the option will benefit from the expected rise in the underlying commodity spot price as well as its volatility. This is shown in the higher price he has to pay to purchase the option, as reflected by the term $e^{-y(T-t)}$, with $y < 0$, in the pricing formula (5.5).

- If $0 < y < r$, $r - y$ is still positive but obviously smaller than r – mild contango – and we are in the situation of having a dividend-paying stock.
- If $y > r$, the forward curve is in backwardation and the call price is lower since the market expects spot prices to go down, as reflected by $e^{-y(T-t)}$ which is much smaller than 1 in the call price given by formula (5.5).

Consequently, an important message to keep in mind is that the *option price is defined by the pair $(r - y, \sigma)$ of the drift and volatility* of the underlying dynamics under the pricing measure Q.

This message was not perfectly clear in the Black–Scholes partial differential equation-based proof of the famous formula;[2] it will become important when we discuss Asian or other exotic options.

5.3 COMMODITY FUTURES DYNAMICS UNDER THE PRICING MEASURE

We established in Chapter 2 the spot–forward relationship for storable commodities, namely the fact that the price $F^{T_1}(t)$ of a forward contract maturing at time T_1 is related to the spot price $S(t)$ by relationship (2.2):

$$F^{T_1}(t) = S(t) \, e^{(r-y)(T_1-t)}$$

where *r and y are assumed to be constant.*

This is an algebraic relationship involving quantities that are all constant except for $S(t)$ and $F^{T_1}(t)$. By differentiation, we obtain:

$$\frac{dF^{T_1}(t)}{F^{T_1}(t)} = \frac{dS(t)}{S(t)} - (r - y) \, dt$$

Note that this equation would have an extra term if r or y were a random quantity not independent of $S(t)$.

Using now the dynamics (5.2) of the spot price under Q, we obtain by subtraction:

$$\frac{dF^{T_1}(T)}{F^{T_1}(T)} = \sigma \, d\hat{W}_t \tag{5.6}$$

This fundamental equation holds whether y is zero or not and is *independent of y.*

Consequently, in the geometric Brownian motion setting, the *dynamics under the pricing measure Q of the Futures price are identical* whether the underlying be a non-dividend-paying stock, a dividend-paying stock or a commodity.

This explains the "universal" validity of the Black (1976) formula (which was even extended to interest rates by the so-called "market model for the pricing of caplets").

---

[2] In the Black–Scholes model, the underlying asset is a non-dividend-paying stock and it is true that the price of the option is the "price of volatility". In all other situations, the dividend yield or the convenience yield may "erode" over (t, T) the underlying delivered at date T.

Moreover, equation (5.6) may be integrated between dates t and t' ($t < t'$) to provide:

$$F^{T_1}(t') = F^{T_1}(t) \exp\left\{ -\frac{\sigma^2}{2}(t' - t) + \sigma \hat{W}(t' - t) \right\}$$

Hence, $F^{T_1}(t')$ is a log-normal variable, with mean $m = -F^{T_1}(\sigma^2/2)(t' - t)$ and standard deviation $\gamma = \sigma\sqrt{(t' - t)}$. It is well known that the expectation of a log-normal variable with mean m and standard deviation γ is $e^{m+\gamma/2}$, which gives here $F^{T_1}(t)\, e^{(-\sigma^2/2)(t'-t)}\, e^{(\sigma^2/2)(t'-t)}$. Hence, the future price process $(F^{T_1}(t))$ is a Q-martingale since:

$$F^{T_1}(t) = E_Q(F^{T_1}(t')/F_t) \qquad \text{for any date } t' > t \tag{5.7}$$

The Futures price remains constant on average under risk-neutral measures:

Hence, the no-arbitrage assumption implies that the rational expectations hypothesis holds for Futures prices, as long as expectations are computed under the risk-neutral probability measure Q.

This interpretation of the martingale property for the Futures price $(F^{T_1}(t))$ goes as follows: since there is no upfront payment to enter into a position (say, long) in a forward contract, there is no reward of this payment at the rate r. Moreover, according to Kaldor and Working, the dividend yield accrues to the holder of the physical commodity and not to the holder of the paper contract written on this commodity. Hence, y should not appear in the dynamics of $(F^{T_1}(t))$. The Futures contract, however, is a risky position and the *risk premium exists and is embedded in Q*. Lastly, the forward price moves randomly and its random fluctuations are translated by the term $\sigma\, d\hat{W}_t$.

This discussion shows that, as long as we accept the geometric Brownian representation, equation (5.4) will represent the risk-neutral dynamics of *any Futures price*, whatever the underlying. Moreover, choosing $t' = T_1$ in equation (5.7), we obtain:

$$F^{T_1}(t) = E_Q[F^{T_1}(T_1)/F_t]$$

or, if there is no arbitrage between the spot and forward markets and $F^{T_1}(T_1) = S(T_1)$:

$$\boxed{F^{T_1}(t) = E_Q[S(T_1)/F_t]} \tag{5.8}$$

Instead of the rational expectations *hypothesis* which was tested by famous economists and confirmed or infirmed according to the type of underlying and the period, we have *demonstrated* that the *Futures price is an unbiased predictor of the future spot price as long as the risk premium is embedded in the probability measure* under which the expectation is computed.

We can discuss this remarkable property in the context of many commodities. We will particularly document the case of electricity in Chapter 11: first, because of the unique properties of this commodity; and, second, because our claim is that equation (5.6) is still valid even though convenience yield does not exist in the case of electricity (see Eydeland and Geman, 1998).

5.4 IMPLIED VOLATILITY IN EQUITY OPTIONS AND LEVERAGE EFFECT

We have shown in Chapter 4 that, whatever the underlying, the option price is a strictly increasing function of the volatility parameter σ since:

$$\text{vega} = \frac{\partial C}{\partial \sigma}$$

is strictly positive for the call – and the put as well. When a function is strictly monotonous in a variable, it may be inverted in this variable and the *implied volatility* is precisely defined by solving in σ the equation obtained by making an option observed market price and the value given by the Black–Scholes formula equal:

$$C^{\text{mark}}(t) \xrightarrow[(\text{BS})^{-1}]{} \sigma_{\text{implied}}(t)$$

It is important to observe that, whatever models, with stochastic volatility or jumps, are today used in equity and commodity markets by various firms worldwide, the above definition of the implied volatility remains the same. Moreover, this one-to-one relationship explains why it makes no difference whether we quote the option by its price or by its volatility.

Volatility smile

If the assumptions of the Black–Scholes (or Black) formula were exactly satisfied in the markets, the volatility parameter σ should be constant over any time interval $[0, T]$ (and equal to the historical volatility – or *standard deviation* – computed at date T from the data series of spot prices $S(t)$ observed during the period $[0, T]$). Following the formidable success of the Black–Scholes–Merton (1973) model, participants in equity markets started in the early 1980s to compute the volatility implied in market option prices by the Black–Scholes formula.

If we place ourselves at date t and plot the volatility implied in a family of options written on the same underlying S, with the same maturity T and various strikes k:

$$C^{\text{mark}}(t, k) \mapsto \sigma_{\text{impl}}(t, k)$$

we obtain a graph which is *not* a flat line:

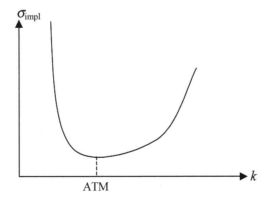

In the stock market prior to the 1987 crash, this graph used to have a symmetric shape – hence, its name *smile* – with a minimal point equal to the current value of the spot or forward price. This quantity is called "At The Money" (ATM). All call options with higher strikes have zero *intrinsic value*, where the intrinsic value of a European option is the pay-off of this option were it exercised immediately; in the same way put options with lower strikes than ATM have no intrinsic value. In classical practice, call options are used to build the right part of the smile (i.e., out-of-the-money calls), and out-of-the-money put options are used for the left part. The economic interpretation of this smile is that the writer of out-of-the money options takes higher risk since he provides a hedge against large fluctuations in the underlying price and, hence, should be adequately rewarded.

Interestingly, the shape of the smile has changed in the stock market after the crash of 1987 and now looks more like a *smirk*, with no symmetry between upward and downward movements:

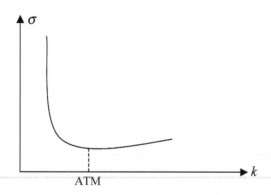

The classical explanation for this asymmetry is that the market as a whole is very averse to the occurrence of a new crash and prepared to pay a higher premium (i.e., a higher volatility) for low values of k. A discussion on the subject had started with historical volatilies, when Fisher Black (1976) observed that volatilities in the stock market go up when prices go down and termed this property the *leverage effect* (since indeed the debt-to-equity ratio increases). Even if they are not identical, it is not surprising that important properties are shared by the historical and implied volatility attached to the same underlying and time period.

Returning to the equity volatility smile, its shape and curvature are more than ever the subject of intense scrutiny in banks and financial institutions. Some practitioners represent the smile through a simple Taylor expansion around the ATM point of reference, namely:

$$\sigma^{\text{impl}}(k) = \sigma^{\text{impl}}(\text{ATM}) + a(k - \text{ATM}) + \text{Error}$$

where coefficient a has a different value for k smaller and greater than ATM.

Another way of explaining the *skew* characterizing the absence of symmetry of the volatility smile is to use a stochastic volatility model, as described at the end of this section.

Maturity effect

If we now freeze the strike k and consider at date t the volatility of options written on the same underlying S with different maturities, again the function:

$$C^{\text{mark}}(t, T) \mapsto \sigma_{\text{impl}}(t, T)$$

is not constant in T, a feature which is called the *maturity effect*. The volatility implied in short-dated options is usually higher, which is again the perception of the option's writer that a sharp move or crash may occur in any short period.

Time effect

Lastly, let us consider for a given underlying S, T and k fixed and extract every day t from the option price the implied volatility:

$$C_{\text{mark}}(t) \mapsto \sigma_{\text{impl}}(t)$$

again, this function is not constant as it should be if the Black–Scholes assumption of a constant volatility over the lifetime of the option prevailed in the markets.

Volatility not being constant over time is an observation consistent with the arrival of daily news and subsequent shocks on prices.

Volatility surface

If we take into account the combination of two effects, strike and maturity, on the implied volatility and fix the date of observation t, we obtain the volatility surface at date t:

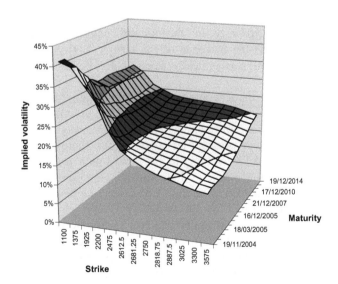

In the financial markets literature, this time-varying volatility has been addressed in several ways over the last 17 years:

1. Either, volatility is written as a deterministic function of time. For instance, in the case of a default-free yield curve, the volatility of a T-maturity bond has often been chosen in the form:

$$\sigma(t, T) = \sigma_0 \frac{1 - e^{-a(T-t)}}{a}$$

where a and σ_0 are two fixed parameters.

   It has, among other properties, the feature of going to 0 when the Treasury bond reaches maturity.

2. If we view volatility as non-deterministic but do not wish to bring in the complexity of an extra source of risk, a simple route consists in writing σ as a deterministic function $\sigma(S_t)$ of S_t, in which case the random changes in σ will occur through S_t. From a calibration perspective at a fixed date t, the problem can be solved in a fairly simple way (see Dupire, 1994; Derman and Kani, 1994)[3] as long as a large variety of strikes and maturities of traded options are available. Once the process (S_t) is calibrated on plain-vanilla options, it can be used as a better approach to the valuation of exotic options.

3. Thirdly, if we view volatility as being a stochastic quantity in its own right, a *stochastic volatility model* needs to be chosen. The most popular one in the financial markets today is the Heston (1993) model, where the dynamics of the spot price and volatility are described under the pricing measure Q by the equations:

$$\begin{cases} \dfrac{dS_t}{S_t} = r\, dt + \sigma(t)\, dW^1(t) \\[2mm] d\Sigma(t) = a(b - \Sigma(t))\, dt + \gamma\sqrt{\Sigma(t)}\, dW^2(t) \\[2mm] \text{and } \Sigma(t) = [\sigma(t)]^2; dW^1(t) \cdot dW^2(t) = \rho\, dt \end{cases}$$

The mean-reverting property in the second equation ensures that volatility remains bounded while the presence of the term $\sqrt{\Sigma(t)}$ precludes negative values for $\Sigma(t)$; the coefficient ρ is typically negative for equity options because of the leverage effect.

   Obviously, the mathematical complexity becomes higher but the greatest difficulty arises from the *incompleteness* of our model. We are now facing two sources of risk $S(t)$ and $\sigma(t)$ and we have only one asset, the commodity price, to hedge our position. Consequently, two possibilities arise: either there exists an option liquid enough (typically the ATM option) to be viewed as a *primitive* instrument whose price is provided by the market. Then, the hedging portfolio will consist of the underlying S and the option. If it does not exist, one has to decide either to give up on the sale or purchase of the option or to find another answer. Then, it becomes necessary to define a criterion under which a transaction becomes admissible (see Carr, Geman and Madan, 2001 for the notion of *acceptable risk* in a situation of non-perfect hedging). The recent literature has proposed a number of criteria to address the problem of market incompleteness since the no-arbitrage argument is insufficient to deliver a unique answer in terms of pricing and hedging. This explains

---

[3] These models are aimed at calibrating the volatility smile and are called "local volatility models".

why the Black–Scholes–Merton model, which leads to a unique price and hedging portfolio for all European calls and puts – and was designed to provide that remarkable property – remains the central reference.

4. Lastly, the introduction of a jump component in a diffusion process or of a pure jump process (see Geman, 2002) immediately creates stochastic volatility.

5.5   IMPLIED VOLATILITY IN ENERGY OPTION PRICES AND INVERSE LEVERAGE EFFECT

The volatility smile, in markets such as oil, heating oil or natural gas, where a fairly large number of strikes do trade, is today an important object of analysis for the trading desk of energy companies and commodity departments in banks. The shape of the smile and its curvature are again of particular interest.

Geman and Nguyen (2003) analyze a database of futures options traded on the New York Mercantile Exchange (NYMEX) and written on four important energy commodities: sweet crude oil, heating oil, unleaded gasoline and natural gas. In all cases, the volatility smile derived from option prices is *skewed to the right* showing that the market is more averse to a rise in commodity prices:

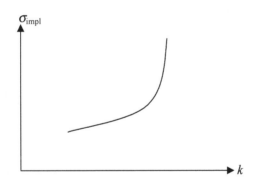

This *inverse leverage effect* is not surprising, given the negative effect on the world economy of higher energy prices. It is displayed in Figures 5.1–5.4. Figures 5.1 and 5.2 show that *historical volatility* increases sharply when oil and heating oil spot prices spike. Figures 5.3 and 5.4 show that energy volatility smiles are highly skewed to the right.

Moreover, the observed skew is more pronounced:

- For maturities corresponding to high values reached by the commodity price over its seasonal pattern.
- For options with short maturities. The high volatility implied in short-dated options is a feature we have already discussed (see p. 103): the market sees the possibility of *one* bad event in any time period, short or long.

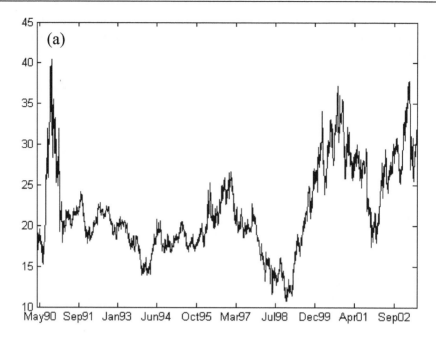

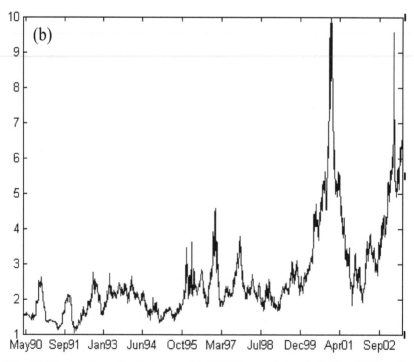

Figure 5.1 (a) Crude oil nearby Futures price (USD) over the period May 1990 to December 2002. (b) Natural gas nearby Futures price (USD) over the period May 1990 to December 2002.

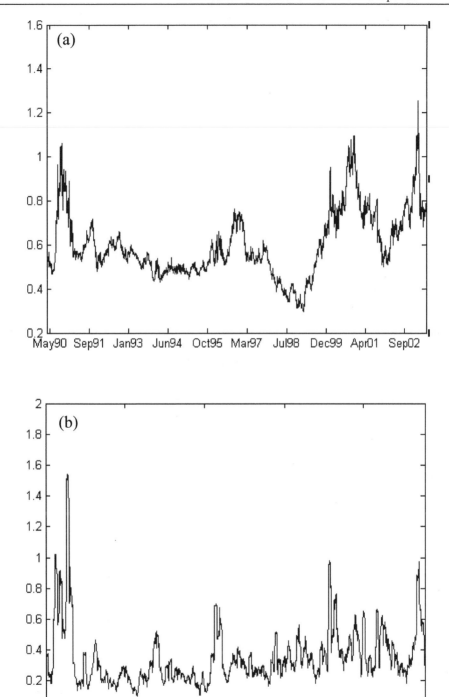

Figure 5.2   (a) Heating oil nearby Futures price (USD) over the period May 1990 to December 2002. (b) Heating oil nearby Futures volatility over the period May 1990 to December 2002.

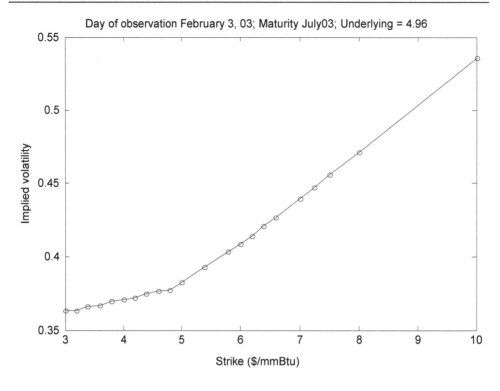

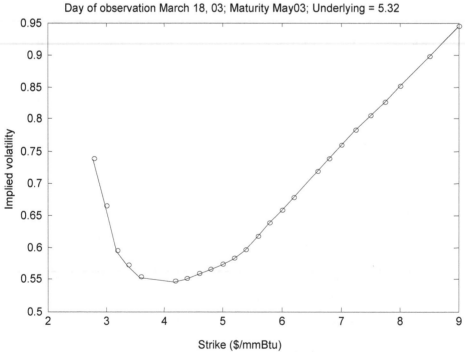

Figure 5.3   Maturity effect in NYMEX natural gas volatility smiles.

Day of observation April 30, 2003; Maturity July 03; Underlying = 0.78

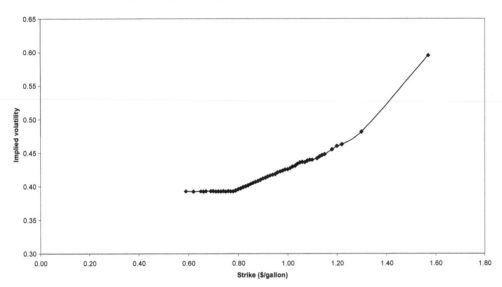

Figure 5.4   NYMEX unleaded gasoline volatility smile.

5.6   BINOMIAL TREES AND OPTION PRICING

In order to have a good comprehension of the key ideas, the underlying asset in what follows is supposed to be a non-dividend-paying stock S whose price at date 0 is denoted by S_0. We first consider the one-period case, where everything is settled at date 1.

(A) Market structure

Besides the stock S is traded at date 0 the money market account M that pays the risk-free rate r over the period. Hence, in all states of the world $M(1) = M(0)(1+r)$.

Now, we introduce the assumption that the number of states of the economy at date 1 is equal to 2; equivalently:

$$\text{card } \Omega = 2 \quad \text{and} \quad \Omega = \{\text{up}, \text{down}\}$$

where Ω denotes the probability space over which the random variable $\tilde{S}(1)$, market price of the risky stock at date 1, is defined.

Since card $\Omega = 2$, there are two possible values of $\tilde{S}(1)$: S^u and S^d where $S^d < S^u$.

Note that like M, S is a *primitive* asset since its value at all dates is *observed* in the market – and defined by the intersection of the *supply and demand order flows*.

(B) No-arbitrage assumption

In this simple setting, without any contingent claim in the picture, we introduce the no-arbitrage assumption already discussed in previous chapters. Interestingly, no-arbitrage implies a non-trivial constraint on S_0, S^u, S^d and r, namely:

$$S^d < S_0(1+r) < S^u \qquad (5.9)$$

Proof: Let us suppose, for instance, that the first inequality is not satisfied; that is:

$$S^d \geq S_0(1+r)$$

Now, we consider the position $\mathcal{P}$ built at date 0 in the following manner:

	date 0	date 1	
Buy the stock	$-S(0)$	S^u	S^d
Borrow to finance the purchase	$+S(0)$	$-S_0(1+r)$	$-S_0(1+r)$

At date 1, the position $\mathcal{P}$ is liquidated and its market value is:

$$S^d - S_0(1+r) \geq 0 \qquad \text{in the state of the world down}$$

$$S^u - S_0(1+r) > S^d - S_0(1+r) > 0 \qquad \text{in the state of the world up}$$

The portfolio $\mathcal{P}$, which required zero investment at date 0 and provides a strictly positive wealth at date 1 in some states of the world without any possible downside, is an arbitrage portfolio whose existence was precluded.
Hence:

$$S^d < S_0(1+r)$$

The other inequality is proved in an analogous manner.

(C) Pricing options on a tree

We now introduce a call option written on S at date 0, with strike $k \in]S^d, S^u[$ and maturity date 1. Hence:

$$\tilde{C}(1) = \max(0, \tilde{S}(1) - k)$$

In our simple economy, the call will pay $S^u - k$ in the state of the world *up* and 0 in the state of the world *down*.

The problem we wish to solve is to find the fair price $C(0)$ of the call at date 0, i.e., the price that both buyers and sellers would view as fair and admissible for a transaction. We see that despite the simplicity of the setting and the key addition of the no-arbitrage assumption – which already provided an interesting double inequality attached to S – the price $C(0)$ does not appear immediately, unless we think of introducing *replication* arguments: if we find a portfolio that only comprises primitive assets and has the same value as the call in all states of the world at date 1, then $C(0)$ has to be equal to the initial value of this portfolio (by no-arbitrage):

$$P = aS + bM \qquad \text{where } a \text{ and } b \in R$$

and we want to find a and b such that:

$$\begin{cases} aS^u + bM_0(1+r) = S^u - k \\ aS^d + bM_0(1+r) = 0 \end{cases} \qquad (5.10)$$

This is an elementary linear system of two equations with two unknowns, which will have a unique solution if (and only if):

$$S^u M_0(1+r) - S^d M_0(1+r) \neq 0$$

or, equivalently, $S^u \neq S^d$.

Hence, as long as the stock does indeed take two different values – hence, is non-colinear to the risk-free asset M or *non-redundant* with M – there exists a unique solution (a, b) where:

$$a = \frac{S^u - k}{S^u - S^d}, \qquad b = -\frac{S^u - k}{S^u - S^d} \times \frac{S^d}{M_0(1+r)}$$

We obtain the value $C(0) = V_p(0)$ of the call at date 0:

$$C(0) = \frac{S^u - k}{S^u - S^d} S_0 - \frac{S^u - k}{S^u - S^d} \frac{S^d}{1+r}$$

$$C(0) = \frac{S^u - k}{S^u - S^d} \frac{[S_0(1+r) - S^d]}{1+r} \qquad (5.11)$$

We observe that a, the number of shares of the stock replicating the call, is strictly positive, while b, the number of units of the money market account, is strictly negative. The quantity a is in fact the *delta* of the call in this simple setting since:

$$\frac{\partial C(0)}{\partial S} = \frac{\partial V_p(0)}{\partial S} = a$$

a is also smaller than 1, since $S^d < k < S^u$ and these results are in agreement with those of Chapter 4. Lastly, if an investor has sold the call at date 0, he is holding the position $(-P)$. In order not to be exposed to good or bad outcomes of S, he needs to add to his short position in the call a positive quantity of shares equal to a, the delta of the call. In this simple economy, his position is then *exactly* reduced to the money market account M and, hence, is riskless over the lifetime of the option $(0, 1)$. As we saw in Chapter 4, delta-hedging in a more complex continuous time setting allows us to nullify first-order exposure to underlying stock price moves, and leads to the second-order term in S, i.e., the gamma or second partial derivative, which is positive (hence, beneficiary) for a long position in a call. Here, there is no gamma term since the economy ends at date 1 and the delta is only defined at date 0; at date 1, the option expires. There is no exposure to volatility change either – as measured by the vega of the call – since the variance of $\tilde{S}(1)$ cannot change over time in our one-period model:

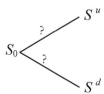

Another key observation is in order at this point: in the drawing representing the one-period tree, we *never specified* the probabilities p and $(1 - p)$ of occurrence of the states of the world up and down under the real probability measure P and these numbers do not appear in formula (5.11) providing the call price at date 0. Hence, they play no role and the input of the trader when pricing the option is totally contained in his choice of S^u and S^d.

(D) Risk-neutral probability measure

In principle, our analysis of the one-period binomial tree could stop here since we have obtained the option price as well as the hedging strategy. However, there is another remarkable result that we can derive from our discussion: let us introduce the quantity:

$$\pi = \frac{S_0(1 + r) - S_d}{S_u - S_d} \tag{5.12}$$

We know from Section 5.6(B) that π is positive and smaller than 1. Hence, we can *construct* a probability measure Q on Ω by specifying that:

$$\text{Prob}_Q(\{\text{up}\}) = p; \qquad \text{Prob}_Q(\{\text{down}\}) = 1 - p$$

We can observe that:

$$M_0 = \pi \frac{M_0(1 + r)}{1 + r} + (1 - \pi) \frac{M_0(1 + r)}{1 + r}$$

(in fact, this obviously holds for any π). Hence, we have:

$$M_0 = E_Q \left[\frac{M(1)}{1 + r} \right] \tag{5.13}$$

Now, *because of the choice of* π, an elementary rewriting of formula (5.12) shows that the same property holds for S:

$$S_0 = E_Q \left[\frac{\tilde{S}(1)}{1 + r} \right] \tag{5.14}$$

Note that (5.14) is equivalent to:

$$\frac{S_0}{(1 + r)^0} = E_Q \left[\frac{\tilde{S}(1)}{1 + r} \right]$$

hence, *the discounted price of S is a Q-martingale.*

It is important to observe that relationship (5.14) does not hold under the real probability measure P: no investor would buy a risky stock if its expected return were only the risk-free rate. He would be better off buying the risk-free money market account M, where for the same expected return he would not assume the risk represented by a strictly positive volatility. Recall from earlier that the Capital Asset Pricing Model (CAPM) provides at equilibrium the expected return on the stock S in terms of the expected market return:

$$E(\tilde{r}) = r_f + \beta(E(\tilde{r}_m) - r_f) \tag{5.15}$$

In formula (5.15), all the expectations are computed under the real probability measure P. Recalling the definition of the return over the period $(0, 1)$:

$$\tilde{r} = \frac{\tilde{S}(1) - S_0}{S_0}$$

relationship (5.15) leads to:

$$S_0 = \frac{E_p(\tilde{S}(1))}{1 + r_f + \beta[E(\tilde{r}_m) - r_f]}$$

If we consider the typical situation of a positive β, since stocks generally have positive covariance with the market, the price investors are willing to pay at date 0 to purchase the stock is *smaller* than the expected (discounted) selling price at date 1. The difference is the *risk premium* investors are entitled to receive for entering into a risky investment. In equation (5.14), the risk premium is embedded in the probability measure Q.

Retracing our steps, we constructed the probability measure Q through $\pi = \text{Prob}_Q(\{up\})$ defined in equation (5.12); π is comprised between 0 and 1 because of the double inequality derived in Section 5.6 (B) from the assumption of no-arbitrage in a simple economy where a riskless asset and a risky asset are traded.

Relations (5.13) and (5.14) constitute what is commonly referred today as the *First Fundamental Theorem of Asset Pricing*.

The no-arbitrage assumption implies there exists (at least) a probability measure Q called risk-neutral, or risk-adjusted (or equivalent martingale measure), under which the discounted prices of primitive securities are martingales. When a contingent claim H admits a replicating portfolio comprising only the primitive assets, no-arbitrage delivers a unique price for H at date 0 (namely, the price of this replicating portfolio). Moreover, the martingale property under Q extends by linearity to the contingent claim price. For instance, the call option price established in equation (5.11) exactly states that:

$$C(0) = \pi \frac{C^{up}}{1+r} + (1 - \pi)\frac{0}{1+r}$$

For operational purposes, the message is the same as before: it is by specifying *his* view of S^u and S^d that the trader will infer the option price. Moreover, if we view π (or Q) as given by the market through the market price of equity risk discussed in Section 5.1, these two numbers S^u and S^d would collapse to one since we can obtain S^d in terms of S^u and π from equation (5.12). The choice of S^u in that setting can be equivalently viewed as the choice of volatility parameter σ: indeed, the equation defining the variance σ^2 of the return:

$$\sigma^2 = \text{Var}\left[\frac{\tilde{S}(1) - S_0}{S_0}\right]$$

provides a unique positive solution in σ as a function of S^u. We recall that:

$$\sigma^2 = \text{Var}\frac{\tilde{S}(1)}{S(0)} = \frac{E([\tilde{S}(1)]^2) - (E[\tilde{S}(1)]^2)}{S_0^2} = \frac{\pi(1 - \pi)(S_u - S_d)^2}{S_0^2}$$

Hence, we obtain for this simple one-period binomial model the same conclusion as in the Section 5.1, namely, that *under no-arbitrage the price of a call option written on a non-dividend-paying asset is fully specified by knowledge of the volatility of the return on the underlying stock.*

(E) Extending the binomial tree to a trinomial tree

Let us suppose that we have the same number of primitive assets, M and S, in a one-period setting. But, we wish to introduce a more complex representation of the economy at date 1 and allow for three states in the probability space $\Omega = \{\text{up, level, down}\}$ where "level" represents the state of the world where the stock price remains roughly the same between dates 0 and 1 ("flat" markets). Now, our tree becomes a trinomial tree since it has three branches:

We consider again a call option written on S, with strike $k \in]S^d, S^u[$. We know from Section 5.6(C) that the existence of a replicating portfolio P for the option is the crucial piece leading to the price through the no-arbitrage assumption; moreover, the hedging portfolio will be the replicating portfolio itself.

We still have two primitive securities and need to find the pair (a, b) such that:

$$\begin{cases} aS^u + bM_0(1+r) = S^u - k \\ aS^l + bM_0(1+r) = \max(0, S^l - k) \\ aS^d + bM_0(1+c) = 0 \end{cases}$$

This linear system of three equations with two unknowns does not have a solution, in general; hence, there is no replicating portfolio for the call and the no-arbitrage argument cannot provide any message in terms of pricing and hedging. We are facing the situation of an *incomplete market*: there are *too few* primitive securities (two) compared with the number of states of the world at date 1 (three). Hence, either other types of considerations need to be introduced for pricing and hedging in incomplete markets, or we may decide there exists an option H with a particular strike (e.g., ATM) that is liquid enough to be viewed as a *primitive security*. Then, we can again find a replicating portfolio and get back on track. This option H may exist in such derivatives markets as the S&P 500 or the NYMEX oil market. It does not exist in agricultural and electricity markets, in which case it is wiser to use a binomial tree and keep the pricing and hedging under control. This observation will be mitigated in Chapter 12, however, since, although a binomial tree is a great tool for discretizing Brownian motion, it is not well suited to a mean-reverting process.

To conclude this section, we define a *complete market* as a market where any contingent claim admits at least a replicating portfolio and we can state the following theorem – which we proved in the simple case of two states of the world with two primitive securities.

Second Fundamental Theorem of Asset Pricing   *Assuming complete markets and no arbitrage, then:*

(i) *there exists a unique risk-adjusted probability measure Q.*
(ii) *any contingent claim has a unique price that is the discounted Q-expectation of its final pay-off.*

N-period binomial tree

If we are looking on date 0 at an option with maturity T, the fact of viewing the interval $(0, T)$ as a single period is simplistic since, for practical matters, traders rebalance their positions at least daily. Hence, we will divide the interval $(0, T)$ into N sub-periods supposed for simplicity to be of the same length T/N. Keeping the same structure of two primitive assets M and S traded in the markets and the assumption of two possible moves – up and down – for the risky stock at any date, we obtain the following tree:

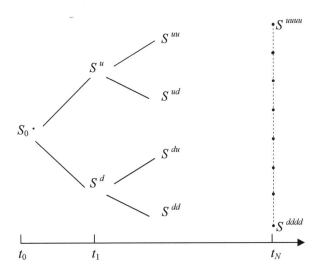

Note that we suppose the one-period rate r to be constant over the whole interval $[0, T]$, as in the Black–Scholes model.

The number of nodes at date $t_N = T$ is 2^N, which is a large number even for powerful computers. This brings about the idea of building a *recombining tree*, a property that is easily obtained by setting $S^u = aS_0$; $S^d = dS_0$ ($d < 1 < a$): more generally, any upward move is represented by multiplying the price at the previous node by a (respectively, d for downward movements). Obviously, adding a to S_0 would also provide a recombining tree but would not be consistent with the multiplicative dynamics of *geometric* Brownian motion that we wish to obtain at the limit. Cox, Ross and Rubinstein (1979), who were the first to introduce a binomial tree representation, proposed to choose $d = 1/a$. In this way, condition $d < 1 < a$ is obviously satisfied; moreover, in this discrete time setting a unique parameter a is defining the call price, as does the volatility σ in the continuous time limit case:

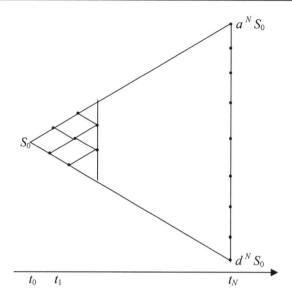

Each sub-tree:

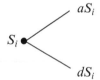

is attached to a complete market situation since there are two primitive securities and two states of the world. Hence, we can work recursively from the end nodes, which are now $(N+1)$ in number and derive the Cox–Ross–Rubinstein (1979) formula for the call price at date 0:

$$C(0) = \frac{1}{(1+r)^N} \sum_{j \in J} C_N^j \pi^j (1-\pi)^{N-j} (S_0 a^{N-j} d^j - k)$$

where:

- J denotes the set of integers between 0 and N such that $S_0 a^{N-j} d^j > k$ (nodes where the call ends in the money).

- $\pi = \dfrac{S_0(1+r) - dS_0}{(a-d)S_0}$ is the risk-neutral probability of an upward move at date t_{i+1} conditional on being at a given node at date t_i.

- C_N^j is the number of trajectories in the recombining tree leading from the initial state S_0 to one terminal node $S_0 a^{N-j} d^j$.

Comments
1. It can be shown that when N goes to infinity under the constraint $a = e^{\sigma \sqrt{T/N}}$ (and $d = e^{-\sigma \sqrt{T/N}}$), the Cox–Ross–Rubinstein price converges to the Black–Scholes

price. The objective of the authors, three years after the papers by Black–Scholes and Merton, was precisely to build a discrete time version of their continuous time model. In order to have convergence of the formula when the time step goes to zero, the tree had to be properly constructed. The *arithmetic* Brownian motion may be obtained as the limit of a random walk, where the random steps are *added* to the initial position. *Geometric* Brownian motion is obtained as the limit of the *multiplicative* version of the random walk.

2. The Black–Scholes–Merton (1973) formula was established in the spirit of continuous time finance models pioneered by Samuelson (1965) and Merton (1969). The idea of infinitesimal time periods may seem complex but the benefits are twofold:

   (i) The powerful Itô's calculus is fully available and allows us to obtain an explicit solution for $C(t, S_t)$, differentiable with respect to both arguments and leading to explicit expressions, for the Greeks as well.
   (ii) All the randomness of the problem is modeled under the real probability measure P, the only one used in finance in 1973 and the simplest to visualize.

3. A tree (the Cox–Ross–Rubinstein tree in particular) is a very attractive way of depicting the moves of a stock or commodity price. Moreover, discrete time is a more realistic representation of trading activities. The "cost", however, when using trees is the necessary introduction of the risk-adjusted probability measure Q under which expectations are computed. We will see in Chapter 6 that the same requirement will hold for Monte Carlo simulations.

4. We can summarize these important points in the following diagram:

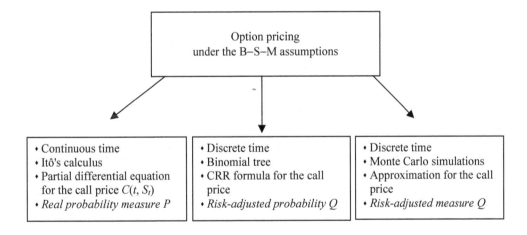

5.7 INTRODUCING STOCHASTIC INTEREST RATES IN THE VALUATION OF COMMODITY OPTIONS

In the previous sections of this chapter, as in Chapter 4, we supposed constant interest rates. This major assumption in the Black–Scholes model was meant to make the valuation problem simpler since only one source of risk – the stock price or the commodity price – needed to be faced. For a long-maturity option, however, it becomes highly questionable; this section provides the major results on this issue.

(A) General properties

From a hedging perspective, we can immediately state that the introduction of stochastic interest rates does not create "market incompleteness" since we have a whole variety of interest-related instruments (bonds in particular) to hedge this new source of risk. Hence, the "only" difficulty is mathematical.

Note first that, in this new setting, the short-term rate $r(s)$ evolves randomly over time and the money market account M is *no longer* riskless. If its face value at date 0 is $M(0) = 1$, its value at date t is:

$$M(t) = \exp\left(\int_0^t \tilde{r}(s)\, ds \right) \tag{5.16}$$

No-arbitrage arguments extended to stochastic interest rates imply that the price at date t of a random cash flow $\tilde{\phi}$ to be received at date T (e.g., the pay-off of an option) is:

$$V_t(\tilde{\phi}) = E_Q\left[\tilde{\phi} \exp\left(- \int_t^T \tilde{r}(s)\, ds \right) \bigg/ \mathcal{F}_t \right] \tag{5.17}$$

where:

- Q is the risk-neutral probability measure.
- $\mathcal{F}_t$ is the information available at date t.

The difficulty now resides in the fact that the quantity $\tilde{\phi} \exp(-\int_t^T \tilde{r}(s)\, ds)$ is the product of two random variables which are not independent (e.g., a credit crunch in the economy will impact both terms). As a general rule, one can safely state that two sources of risk in the economy are never independent.

(B) Change of numéraire, change of probability measure

Returning to the discussion of the riskless instrument, we see now that the only security whose value at date T is fully known at date t is the (default-free) zero-coupon bond B^T paying \$1 at date T. This instrument already appears in the part of Merton's (1973) seminal paper that discusses stochastic interest rates, as well as in Jarrow (1987) whose goal was precisely to address the valuation of options on commodities under stochastic interest rates.

Making no assumptions on the choice of a specific model of interest rates, Geman (1989) shows that:

- The "right" *numéraire* relative to which all security prices should be expressed is the zero-coupon bond B^T; its price at date t will be denoted $B^T(t)$ or $B(t, T)$.
- The "right" probability measure to introduce is the *T-forward neutral probability measure* denoted as Q_T and defined by its Radon–Nikodym derivative with respect to Q:

$$\frac{dQ_T}{dQ} = \frac{\exp(-\int_t^T \tilde{r}(s)\, ds)}{B(t, T)} \tag{5.18}$$

Formula (5.17) can now be rewritten as:

$$V_t(\tilde{\phi}) = E_Q\left[\tilde{\phi}B(t,T)\frac{dQ_T}{dQ}\bigg/\mathcal{F}_t\right]$$

The value $B(t,T)$ is the market price at date t of the zero-coupon bond (hence, fully observed at that date) and:

$$V_t(\tilde{\phi}) = B(t,T)E_Q\left[\tilde{\phi}\frac{dQ_T}{dQ}\bigg/\mathcal{F}_t\right]$$

A fundamental result from probability allows us to recognize $E_{Q_T}[\tilde{\phi}/\mathcal{F}_t]$ in the latter quantity and we can write:

$$V_t(\tilde{\phi}) = B(t,T)E_{Q_T}[\tilde{\phi}/\mathcal{F}_t] \tag{5.19}$$

If we choose $\tilde{\phi} = \tilde{S}(T) = $ selling price of a primitive security S at date T, $V_t(\tilde{\phi})$ represents the purchase price of this security today (assuming liquid markets). Hence:

$$S(t) = B(t,T)E_{Q_T}[\tilde{S}(T)/\mathcal{F}_t]$$

or:

$$\frac{S(t)}{B(t,T)} = E_{Q_T}\left[\frac{\tilde{S}(T)}{B(T,T)}\bigg/\mathcal{F}_t\right] \tag{5.20}$$

since $B(T,T) = 1 = $ face value of the zero-coupon bond.

We showed in Chapter 2 that, whether interest rates are stochastic or deterministic, $S(t)/B(t,T)$ represents the forward price of a non-dividend-paying stock or any primitive asset that does not pay any dividend or convenience yield. Equation (5.18) states that:

The T-forward price of a security that does not pay any dividend is a martingale under the T-forward neutral probability measure.

If we now replace $\tilde{\phi}$ by the selling price at date T of a commodity S, $V_t(\tilde{\phi})$ will represent its purchase price today and formula (5.20) holds identically.

However, we can no longer recognize in $S(t)/B(t,T)$ the T-forward price of the commodity. Formula (2.11) established the spot–forward relationship for a commodity under stochastic interest rates as:

$$f(t,T) = \frac{S(t)\,e^{-y(T-t)}}{B(t,T)}$$

We can at this point establish the following important relationship that links the forward price and the Futures price of the commodity under stochastic interest rates:

$$f(t,T) = F^T(t) + \frac{1}{B^T(t)}\mathrm{Cov}\left(\tilde{S}(T)\exp\left(\int_t^T \tilde{r}(s)\,ds\right)\bigg/\mathcal{F}_t\right) \tag{5.21}$$

Proof We have seen at various points in Chapter 2 and Chapter 5 that, because of convenience yield, it is not the discounted price of the commodity which is a martingale under the risk neutral measure Q, but the price augmented with the "lost" convenience yield. Put in other terms:

$$S(t)\, e^{yt} = E_Q\!\left[\tilde{S}(T)\, e^{yT} \exp\!\left(-\int_t^T \tilde{r}(s)\, ds\right)\bigg/ \mathcal{F}_t\right]$$

As y is assumed constant it can be pulled out of the expectation and we obtain:

$$S(t)\, e^{-y(T-t)} = E_Q\!\left[\tilde{S}(T) \exp\!\left(-\int_t^T \tilde{r}(s)\, ds\right)\bigg/ \mathcal{F}_t\right]$$

Let us, for simplicity, introduce the random variables:

$$X = \tilde{S}(T) \qquad \text{and} \qquad Y = \exp\!\left(-\int_t^T \tilde{r}(s)\, ds\right)$$

$$E_Q[XY/\mathcal{F}_t] = E_Q[X/\mathcal{F}_t] E_Q[Y/\mathcal{F}_t] + \mathrm{Cov}(X, Y/\mathcal{F}_t)$$

$$E_Q[X/\mathcal{F}_t] = E_Q[\tilde{S}(T)/\mathcal{F}_t] = E_Q[F^T(T)/\mathcal{F}_t] = F^T(t)$$

since the Futures price is a Q-martingale. Moreover:

$$E_Q\!\left[\exp\!\left(-\int_t^T \tilde{r}(s)\, ds\right)\bigg/ \mathcal{F}_t\right] = E_Q\!\left[1 \times \exp\!\left(-\int_t^T \tilde{r}(s)\, ds\right)\bigg/ \mathcal{F}_t\right]$$

$$= \text{Price at date } t \text{ of a dollar paid at date } T = B(t, T)$$

Hence:

$$S(t)\, e^{-y(T-t)} = F^T(t) B(t, T) + \mathrm{Cov}\!\left(\tilde{S}(T) \exp\!\left(-\int_t^T \tilde{r}(s)\, ds\right)\bigg/ \mathcal{F}_t\right)$$

Dividing both sides by $B(t, T)$, we recognize in the left-hand side the forward price of the commodity, hence formula (5.21).

This formula is very important in practice: it shows that, as long as we believe there is no significant correlation between interest rates and commodity prices – which has been so far a reasonable assumption – the *forward price and the Futures price of the commodity are equal*, even if interest rates are stochastic.

Whether one looks at long-term contracts or investments, long-maturity financial or real options, the forward price and the Futures price may be used indifferently; this holds in particular for the option formulas derived in Section 5.7(C). The market with the highest liquidity will provide the best representation of this forward/Futures price: in the oil market, it will be the Futures market, NYMEX or the International Petroleum Exchange (IPE). In electricity, it is for now the forward market in the specific region under analysis.

(C) Option pricing formulas under stochastic interest rates

(1) The Black–Scholes formula under stochastic interest rates

It is clear that a European option maturing at date T does not pay any dividend between t and T; it does have a unique price at date t when only the assumption of constant interest rates is relaxed in the Black–Scholes model. Formula (5.20) applied to the call price becomes:

$$\frac{C(t)}{B(t,T)} = E_{Q_T}\left[\frac{\tilde{C}(T)}{B(T,T)} \middle/ \mathcal{F}_t\right]$$

or:

$$C(t) = B(t,T)E_{Q_T}[\max(0, S_T - k)/\mathcal{F}_t]$$

Extending the computations conducted in the first section of this chapter to this setting, we obtain the remarkable result (see Geman, 1989; Geman, El Karoui and Rochet, 1995):

$$C(t) = S(t)N(d_1) - kB(t,T)N(d_2) \tag{5.22}$$

where:

$$\begin{cases} d_1 = \dfrac{\ln\left(\dfrac{S(t)}{kB(t,T)}\right) + \frac{1}{2}\sigma_f(T-t)}{\sigma_f\sqrt{T-t}} \\[3mm] d_2 = d_1 - \sigma_f\sqrt{T-t} \\[3mm] \sigma_f = \mathrm{Vol}\left(\dfrac{S(t)}{B(t,T)}\right) = \textit{Volatility of the forward price of } S \end{cases}$$

(2) Options on commodities under stochastic interest rates

Denoting the convenience yield by y and assuming y constant over the lifetime of the option, analogous arguments provide the price of a European call written on the spot price of a commodity S under stochastic interest rates:[4]

$$C(t) = S(t)\,e^{-y(T-t)}N(d_1) - kB(t,T)N(d_2) \tag{5.23}$$

where:

$$\begin{cases} d_1 = \dfrac{\ln\left(\dfrac{S(t)\,e^{-y(T-t)}}{kB(t,T)}\right) + \frac{1}{2}\sigma_f^2(T-t)}{\sigma_f\sqrt{T-t}} \\[3mm] d_2 = d_1 - \sigma_f\sqrt{T-t} \\[3mm] \sigma_f = \mathrm{Vol}\left(\dfrac{S(t)}{B(t,T)}\right) = \textit{Volatility of the commodity forward price} \end{cases}$$

Note that the introduction of a stochastic convenience yield would provide a model with both stochastic interest rates and stochastic convenience yield, which is obviously

---

[4] This formula was first written in Jarrow (1987) through a change of probability measure; the use of the zero-coupon bond B^T as part of the hedging portfolio for an option on a stock under stochastic interest rates was already in Merton (1973). Jamshidian (1988) redefines the probability Q^T introduced by Jarrow. Geman (1989) shows that this change of probability consists in fact in using the bond B^T as a new numéraire and that the approach can be extended to other changes of numéraire.

desirable for long-maturity options. Miltersen and Schwartz (1998) propose such a model, with a convenience yield driven by an Ornstein–Uhlenbeck process.

(3) Options on commodity Futures under stochastic interest rates

The Black (1976) formula for options on commodity Futures did not involve any convenience yield, nor does its extension to stochastic interest rates. If we denote by F^{T_1} the underlying Futures contract that has maturity $T_1 \geq T$, the call price has the following expression:

$$C(t) = B(t, T)[F^{T_1}(t)N(d_1) - kN(d_2)]$$

(5.24)

where:

$$\begin{cases} d_1 = \dfrac{\ln\left(\dfrac{F^{T_1}(t)}{k}\right) + \frac{1}{2}\sigma_{F_{T_1}}^2 (T - t)}{\sigma_{F_{T_1}} \sqrt{T - t}} \\[3ex] d_2 = d_1 - \sigma_{F_{T_1}} \sqrt{T - t} \\[1ex] \sigma_{F_{T_1}} = \text{Vol(Futures price)} \end{cases}$$

6

Monte Carlo Simulations and Analytical Formulae for Asian, Barrier and Quanto Options

---

We analyze in this chapter options whose pay-off is strictly more complex than the one involved in the Black–Scholes (1973) and Black (1976) models. This increased complexity typically arises in two forms, possibly combined:

1. The pay-off at maturity T is not only related to the sole value of the underlying asset S at date T. These options, often called "exotic", should be more precisely termed *path-dependent*. We will study those that are the most relevant for commodities (namely, Asian, barrier and digital) – American options will be studied in Chapter 12 on energy options where we will also introduce the take or pay and swing options, which are very important in the gas and electricity industry.
2. The pay-off at maturity T depends on the value on that date of several underlyings $S_1, S_2, \ldots, S_q$ in which case the option is a *multi-asset option*. The simplest, and probably the most important one in the specific terms and in the specific situation of commodities, is the *exchange option*. The holder of the option has the right at maturity to exchange a given amount of one commodity for another. This option will naturally appear when we use a real option approach (see Chapter 12) to the valuation of physical assets: a combined cycle gas turbine is a portfolio of options to exchange gas for electricity whenever it is profitable to do so – and do nothing otherwise.

   Extensions of this option include the spread option, the option "best of" and the options on the maximum or minimum of two commodity prices. In all cases, correlations between the various underlyings will play a key role.

   Since Monte Carlo methods happen to be an excellent tool for handling path-dependent options, whether they are written on a single or several underlyings, the first section of this chapter will be dedicated to their description.

6.1 MONTE CARLO METHODS FOR EUROPEAN OPTIONS

(1) The founding results

A central result in probability theory, not very difficult to prove but fundamental for its applications in different problems arising in insurance and finance, is the law of large numbers that we present below in its simple "weak" form.

Law of large numbers

Let $X_1, X_2, \ldots, X_n$ be a sequence of random variables with the same mean m and variance σ^2, where σ^2 is finite, and pairwise uncorrelated. Define:

$$U_n = \frac{X_1 + \cdots + X_n}{n} \qquad \text{for all } n > 0$$

Then, the sequence of random variables $(U_n)_{n \geq 1}$ *converges in probability* to the constant m; equivalently:

$$\text{for any } \varepsilon > 0, \qquad \text{Prob}(|U_n - m| > \varepsilon) \to 0 \qquad \text{for } n \to +\infty$$

Remarks

1. The proof is derived in a straightforward manner from the Bienaymé–Tchebitcheff inequality applied to U_n, and from the fact that, by absence of correlation between the X_i:

$$E(U_n) = m \qquad \text{Var}(U_n) = \frac{\sigma^2}{n}$$

2. If $X_1, X_2, \ldots, X_n$ have the same distribution, they will obviously have the same mean and variance (note that this variance has to be finite for the result to hold). In the same spirit, if $X_1, X_2, \ldots, X_n$ are independent random variables, they will be pairwise uncorrelated.

Fundamental consequence

If we consider a random variable X whose true distribution is unknown – which is in practice the case in finance, in insurance, or other applied sciences – we can still obtain an estimate of the first-order moment $m = E(X)$ as long as we are able to perform N *independent random draws*, called Monte Carlo draws, $X_1, X_2, \ldots, X_N$ of this variable X, by applying the law of large numbers:

$$\frac{X_{1+-} + X_N}{N} \approx E(X)$$

The true value of the expectation m of X may be approximated by the arithmetic average of the numbers obtained in a large sequence of independent draws of this random variable.

Generalization

In a famous paper, Metropolis et al. (1953) extended this result to the computation of $E[f(X)]$ where f is a fairly general real functional:

$$E[f(X)] \approx \frac{f(X_1) + \cdots + f(X_N)}{N} \tag{6.1}$$

This result was greatly applied in insurance and in industrial engineering in the 1950s and 1960s. It did not appear in finance before the end of the 1970s, precisely at the time when the option price started being written as the expectation of its (discounted) pay-off under an appropriate probability measure.

(2) Monte-Carlo methods for plain-vanilla options on non-dividend-paying stocks

We saw in Chapter 5 that in the Black–Scholes setting there exists a probability measure Q such that the dynamics of the non-dividend-paying stock are driven by the stochastic differential equation:

$$\frac{dS_t}{S_t} = r\,dt + \sigma\,d\hat{W}_t \quad \text{with } (\hat{W}_t)_{t\geq 0} = Q\text{-Brownian motion} \tag{6.2}$$

and the call price is then:

$$C(t) = E_Q[\max(0, S(T) - k)\,e^{-r(T-t)}/F_t]$$

Since interest rates are constant, the discount factor may be pulled out of the expectation and we recognize that the computation of $C(t)$ is equivalent to finding the expectation of a function of $S(T)$:

$$C(T) = e^{-r(T-t)}E_Q[f(S(T))/F_t]$$

where $f(S(T)) = \max(0, S(T) - k)$.

We know that if we can perform independent simulations of $S(T)$, the results of Section 6.1 will provide an approximate value for $E_Q[f(S(T))/F_t]$.

Hence, at date t, we need to simulate N times the quantity $S(T)$ in order to derive the corresponding values for the option pay-off $\max(S(T) - k, 0)$.

Let us integrate equation (6.2) between the dates t and T:

$$S(T) = S(t)\exp\left\{\left(r - \frac{\sigma^2}{2}\right)(T - t) + \sigma\hat{W}(T - t)\right\} \tag{6.3}$$

At date t, the current value of the stock or commodity $S(t)$ is fully observed, as well as the risk-free rate r. The key parameter σ is estimated by the trader, from historical values of $S(t)$ or as an implied volatility derived from liquid options.

Hence, simulating $S(T)$ is equivalent to simulating $\hat{W}(T - t)$, whose distribution under Q is normal $\mathcal{N}(0; \sqrt{T - t})$.

The cumulative function F of $\hat{W}(T - t)$ is easy to represent:

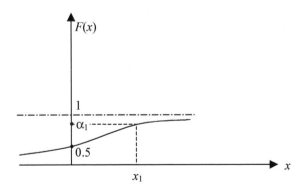

If we choose an arbitrary number α_1 between 0 and 1, it will define a unique x_1 which is a random simulation of $\hat{W}(T - t)$. In the above drawing, α_1 happened to be higher than 0.5, leading to a positive x_1. If we were to choose the second number α_2, we would tend to place it below 0.5, in order to reintroduce the symmetry exhibited by the density distribution of $\hat{W}(T - t)$. This would destroy the feature of independence required for the draws. Hence, it is a random number generator installed on our computer which is going to produce the numbers $\alpha_1, \alpha_2, \ldots, \alpha_N$ leading to N independent draws $x_1, x_2, \ldots, x_N$ of $\hat{W}(T - t)$. We plug each number x_i in (6.3) and obtain successively:

$$
\left.
\begin{aligned}
S^{(1)}(T) &= S(t) \exp\left\{ \left(r - \frac{\sigma^2}{2} \right)(T - t) + \sigma x_1 \right\} \\
S_T^{(2)} &= S(t) \exp\left\{ \left(r - \frac{\sigma^2}{2} \right)(T - t) + \sigma X_2 \right\} \\
&\cdots
\end{aligned}
\right\}
\qquad (6.4)
$$

leading in turn to the values $b_1, b_2, \ldots, b_N$ defined as:

$$
\begin{cases}
b_1 = \max(0, S^{(1)}(T) - k) \\
b_2 = \max(0, S^{(2)}(T) - k) \\
\cdots
\end{cases}
$$

positive or null depending on the position relative to k of the simulated values $S^{(1)}(T), \ldots, S^{(N)}(T)$. We then obtain as an approximation for the option price:

$$
C(t) \approx e^{-r(T-t)} \left[\frac{b_1 + b_2 + \cdots + b_N}{N} \right]
$$

We note that our approach has been parsimonious since we simulated the only quantity we need in the context of plain-vanilla options: namely, the price $S(T)$ of the stock at maturity as opposed to the whole trajectory. When the number of simulations gets very large, we can check numerically that, in agreement with the theory, the Monte Carlo price converges to the Black–Scholes price. It is important to observe that the Monte Carlo approach is a very simple and intuitive computation of the option price. The only difficulty resides in the introduction of probability measure Q; this step is necessary, however. It is only if we are prepared to believe that market participants are risk-neutral that we can assume $Q = P$ and apply the above results directly under the real probability measure P.

(3) Monte Carlo methods for plain-vanilla commodity options

We observed in Chapter 5 that, for storable commodities, the dynamics of the spot price under the pricing measure Q may be written, under the assumption of a geometric Brownian, as:

$$
\frac{dS_t}{S_t} = (r - y) \, dt + \sigma \, d\hat{W}_t
\qquad (6.5)
$$

Assuming the convenience yield y is constant over the lifetime of the option (as well as the continuously compounded interest rate r), we just need to change r to $(r - y)$ in equation (6.4) and nothing else is changed in the procedure which provides the Monte Carlo approximation of the option price.

Remark   As observed before, the numerical value of the convenience yield may be derived from knowledge of the spot price of the commodity together with the market price of a forward contract $F^T(t)$, thanks to the fundamental relationship:

$$F^T(t) = S(t) \, e^{(r-y)T - t}$$

If the spot price is not observed in a reliable manner, y may be obtained by using this relationship for the nearby Futures contract F^{T_1} and another liquid Futures contract F^{T_2}.

6.2   ASIAN (ARITHMETIC AVERAGE) OPTIONS AS KEY INSTRUMENTS IN COMMODITY MARKETS

These options appeared in the financial markets at the end of the 1980s and are particularly important today in currency and commodity markets:

1. In the case of Foreign Exchange (FX) markets, their validity can be explained in a simple example: consider a treasurer of a multinational company who knows that he will receive in a future period daily (or weekly) cash flows denominated in Japanese yen while he is based in Switzerland. In order to hedge his exposure to a collapse of the Japanese yen, he needs to buy *put* options on the underlying JPY/CHF value of the yen relative to the Swiss franc. If he is to receive 100 cash flows, he may protect each of them by a put option. This very exact hedge of 100 options is likely to be expensive. Hence, a less precise but adequate solution consists of buying a put option written on the arithmetic average of the 100 exchange rates (i.e., an Asian put option). This would typically be the example of the treasurer of an agrifood company hedging against currency risk revenues expected from exports to Japan. In a symmetric manner, this treasurer will need an Asian call option written on the value of the Brazilian real with respect to the Swiss franc to hedge against a rise in the cost of coffee imports from Brazil.
2. In the case of commodities, many indexes are given as arithmetic averages of the underlying spot price: this is to prevent momentarily wild fluctuations from impacting on transactions related to large exchanged quantities or volumes. In the case of oil, the quantity of time elapsed between the day a tanker leaves the production site and reaches its destination explains why oil indexes are arithmetic averages; accordingly, most options on oil are Asian.
3. Whenever the underlying spot price is not easily identifiable (and this is particularly true for many agricultural commodity markets) the party losing money on a position in plain-vanilla options may be tempted to sharply move the market on the date of maturity T in order to make the options expire worthless. A "large player" can fairly easily push the market up or down on a given day. This price manipulation becomes impossible in the case of an arithmetic average option since many numbers enter into

the computation of the average defining the pay-off and the exercise of market power becomes more problematic.

Because of points (1) and (2), Asian options are particularly appropriate for commodity markets and, unsurprisingly, represent a large fraction of the options traded in these markets.

Pricing issues

Placing ourselves in the Black–Scholes setting, the dynamics of the commodity price have the following expression under the pricing measure Q:

$$\frac{dS(t)}{S(t)} = (r - y)\, dt + \sigma\, d\hat{W}_t$$

where y is the convenience yield (positive or negative according to the period) and $(\hat{W}_t)$ is a Q-Brownian motion.

We know that, viewed from date 0, the values of S at future dates $t_1, t_2, \ldots, t_n$ may be obtained by integrating this equation:

$$S(t_i) = S(0)\exp\left\{\left(r - y - \frac{\sigma^2}{2}\right)t_i + \sigma\hat{W}(t_i)\right\}$$

Hence, the average $A(T)$ over the period, defined by:

$$A(T) = \frac{S(t_1) + S(t_2) + \cdots + S(t_n)}{n}$$

appears as a sum of exponentials, which is not a simple mathematical object.

It is important to remember that it is the simple distribution of $S(T)$ in the Black–Scholes setting (namely, a log-normal distribution) which is responsible for the simplicity of the valuation of European calls. The situation is quite different here, since a sum (or average) of log-normal variables is not log-normal.

The problem has represented a mathematical challenge since the beginning of the 1990s and still does to a certain extent. We are going to review the most tractable methods, and their limits as well.

(1) Approximation of the arithmetic average by a geometric average

Kemna and Vorst (1990) observed, when considering the geometric average, that:

$$A^{\text{geom}}(T) = [S(t_1), \ldots, S(t_n)]^{1/n}$$

log-normality is preserved, since the average appears as a product of exponentials.

They show that, in this case, the Asian option price at date 0 is obtained by a Black–Scholes-type formula:

$$C(0) = e^{-\alpha T}S(0)N(d_1) - k\,e^{-rT}N(d_2) \tag{6.6}$$

where

$$
\begin{cases}
\alpha = \dfrac{1}{2}\left(y - r + \dfrac{\sigma^2}{6}\right) \\[2mm]
d_1 = \ln\left(\dfrac{S(0)}{k}\right) + \dfrac{1}{2}\left(r - y + \dfrac{\sigma^2}{6}\right)T \Big/ \sigma\sqrt{\dfrac{T}{3}} \\[2mm]
d_2 = d_1 - \sigma\sqrt{\dfrac{T}{3}}
\end{cases}
$$

Consequently, the geometric average call option written on a commodity S can be priced by the standard Black–Scholes formula where the volatility σ is replaced by $\sigma/\sqrt{3}$ and the convenience yield y is replaced by α with $\alpha = \frac{1}{2}(y - r + (\sigma^2/6))$.

(2) Approximation of the distribution of the arithmetic average by a log-normal distribution

Levy (1991) and other practitioners proposed to approximate the true distribution of the arithmetic average by a log-normal distribution. In this case, it is important at least to incorporate in the representation of $A(T)$, by a log-normal distribution, the *true values* of the mean and the variance, in order to avoid the addition of errors. Geman and Yor (1992) provide an exact expression of the moments of all orders of the average $A(T)$. We are going to propose here an alternative route to the computation of the mean, one that has the merit of being simple and of illuminating some messages conveyed in Chapters 3 and 5. Recall that, for a large number of points in the average, we can write:

$$
A(T) = \frac{1}{T}\int_0^T S(u)
$$

and we are interested in the expectation (or mean) $E_Q[A(T)]$ under the *pricing measure*.

Remembering that the dynamics of S_t under Q are provided by equation (6.5), the process $(S(t)\, e^{-(r-y)t}, t \geq 0)$ is a Q-martingale; put in other terms:

$$
S(0)\, e^0 = S(0) = E_Q[S(u)\, e^{-(r-y)u}] \tag{6.7}
$$

expressing that the commodity price, discounted and compensated for the "loss" of convenience yield, remains constant on average under the Q measure.

Using now the *linearity* of the expectation operator, we can write:

$$
E_Q[A(T)] = E_Q\left[\frac{1}{T}\int_0^T S(u)\, du\right] = \frac{1}{T}\int_0^T E_Q[S(u)]\, du
$$

From equation (6.7), and because we *assumed r and y constant*, we can write:

$$
E_Q[S(u)] = S(0)\, e^{(r-y)u} \quad \text{for any } u > 0
$$

Hence:

$$
E_Q[A(T)] = \frac{1}{T}\int_0^T S(0)\, e^{(r-y)u}
$$

This integral is straightforward and provides the mean of the arithmetic average of $S(t)$ over the interval $[0, T]$:

$$E_Q[A(T)] = S(0) \frac{e^{(r-y)T} - 1}{(r - y)T} \tag{6.8}$$

This anticipated average value of the commodity price over the coming period $(0, T)$ relative to the current price $S(0)$ is defined by:

$$\frac{E_Q[A(T)]}{S(0)} = \frac{e^{(r-y)T} - 1}{T - t}$$

and an elementary expansion shows that it is: smaller than 1 if $r - y < 0$, the situation of *backwardation*; greater than 1 if $r - y > 0$, the situation of *contango*. Hence, the *shape of the forward curve* is reflected in the Q-expectation of the average of future spot prices expressed in the current value $S(0)$ as the numéraire. Lastly, it is interesting to observe that:

$$E_Q[A(T)/\mathcal{F}_0] = E_Q\left[\frac{S(t_1) + S(t_2) + \cdots + S(t_n)}{n} \middle/ \mathcal{F}_0\right]$$

$$= \frac{E_Q[S(t_1)/\mathcal{F}_0] + \cdots + E_Q[S(t_n)/\mathcal{F}_0]}{n}$$

$$= \frac{E_Q[F^{t_1}(t_1)/\mathcal{F}_0] + \cdots + E_Q[F^{t_n}(t_n)/\mathcal{F}_0]}{n}$$

$$= \frac{F^{t_1}(0) + \cdots + F^{t_n}(0)}{n}$$

which is the average of the current forward curve (here we have represented the average computed over a finite number of days, which is the case in practice).

(3) Monte Carlo simulations for Asian option valuation

One of the most popular methods used today by practitioners to price Asian options is the Monte Carlo approach described above for plain-vanilla options. A difference, however, from the previous situation is the fact that, in the case of European calls and puts, one needed only to produce N independent simulations of the terminal value $S(T)$. Now, we will need N *trajectories* of the commodity price over the period $[0, T]$; each of them will lead to one simulated average A and in turn to one simulated pay-off of the Asian option. The partition $t_1, t_2, \ldots, t_n$ of the period must be fine enough to incorporate all the dates included in the average and may be finer.

Let us return to the dynamic of the underlying commodity price $S(t)$ under the pricing measure Q:

$$\frac{dS(t)}{S(t)} = (r - y)\, dt + \sigma\, d\hat{W}_t$$

Integrating this equation between dates 0 and t_1 provides, as seen many times:

$$S(t_1) = S(0) \exp\left\{\left(r - y - \frac{\sigma^2}{2}\right)t_1 + \sigma\hat{W}(t_1)\right\}$$

A random draw of $\hat{W}(t_1)$ will lead to one simulated value $\hat{S}(t_1)$.

Starting from this point – since we need to have "consistency" in the construction of the trajectory according to our chosen model, we have:

$$S(t_2) = \hat{S}(t_1) \exp\left\{ \left(r - y - \frac{\sigma^2}{2} \right)(t_2 - t_1) + \sigma \hat{W}(t_2 - t_1) \right\}$$

Now, a random draw of $\hat{W}(t_2 - t_1)$ (whose distribution is the same as the one $\hat{W}(t_1)$ for equally spaced points t_1, t_2, t_n over the period $[0, T]$) leads to a simulated value $\hat{S}(t_2)$. Proceeding piecewise, we simulate a first trajectory $\mathcal{T}_1$ of the underlying commodity S over which we can compute a simulated average a_1:

$$a_1 = \frac{\hat{S}(t_1) + \cdots + \hat{S}(t_n)}{n}$$

and a simulated pay-off $b_1 = \max(0, a_1 - k)$.

We repeat this procedure N times and obtain an approximate value for the Asian option at time 0:

$$C(0) \approx e^{-rT} \frac{b_1 + \cdots + b_n}{N}$$

This Monte Carlo approach gives a very good approximation of the exact Asian option price because of the smooth nature of the pay-off. However, since we have no explicit formula[1] for the price $C(0)$, we cannot take its partial derivative with respect to $S(0)$ to obtain the delta of the Asian option. A classical answer adopted by practitioners is to use a "finite difference method" and approximate the *delta* (i.e., slope of the tangent) by the slope of a segment centered in $S(0)$, the current price of the underlying commodity:

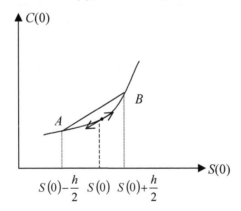

Using the same random draws as before for $\hat{W}(t_1), \hat{W}(t_2 - t_1), \ldots, \hat{W}(t_n - t_{n-1})$, we now compute the Asian call price, but for a starting value $S(0) + h/2$; lastly, we use as a starting value $S(0) - h/2$, where h is a small number (e.g., of the order of $S(0)/100$). We then write an approximate value for the delta:

$$\Delta^{As} \approx \frac{C^{As}\left(S_0 + \dfrac{h}{2}\right) - C^{As}\left(S_0 - \dfrac{h}{2}\right)}{h} \tag{6.9}$$

---

[1] One of the beauties of the BSM formula is the existence of a closed-form expression of the call price, hence of all its partial derivatives.

Note that by doing so we accumulate three errors:

1. The first two come from the Monte Carlo approximations used in computing $C^{As}(S_0 + h/2)$ and $C^{As}(S_0 - h/2)$.
2. The third one is generated by the replacement of the tangent at the point $S(0)$ by the slope of the segment AB.

Obviously, when going to the gamma, i.e., the second derivative of the call price with respect to the underlying commodity, the approximation error will become even larger; this explains why exact methods are desirable, even though they are mathematically complex.

(4) Exact results (Geman and Yor, 1993)

Geman and Yor (1993) wish to address the exact issue, namely an arithmetic average for the underlying, in an exact manner (i.e., with no approximation for the distribution of this arithmetic average $A(T)$ nor for the computation of the option price):

1. Using several probabilistic tools, including a stochastic time change, they are able to provide an exact formula for the Laplace transform with respect to maturity of the Asian option price. Because of the *linearity* of the Laplace transform, the same approach applies to the delta and other Greeks. Eydeland and Geman (1995) show how to invert this Laplace transform and also exhibit the loss of accuracy occurring in computation of the different Greeks (as defined in Chapter 3) with approximate methods. The fast inversion procedures existing today for the Laplace transform (and the Fourier transform) provide the option and the Greeks within a very short time.
2. In the same paper, Geman and Yor underline that the valuation of the Asian option does depend on the date at which the pricing takes place relative to the averaging period. Supposing for simplicity that the averaging period coincides with the lifetime of the option:

At date 0, none of the values $S(t_1), S(t_2), \ldots$ is known and the price $C^{As}(0)$ is related to the *expectation* of the average of all quantities. Now, suppose that the date t of analysis lies between the date t_j and t_{j+1}:

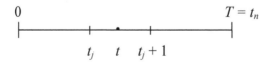

The values $S(t_1), \ldots, S(t_j)$ are then *fully observed* at that point and the average may be written as:

$$A(T) = \frac{S(t_1) + \cdots + S(t_j) + \tilde{S}(t_{j+1}) + \cdots + \tilde{S}(t_n)}{n}$$

where randomness resides only in the last terms, hence diminishes to zero as one gets closer to the maturity date. We observe that if the values $S(t_1), \ldots, S(t_j)$ registered prior to date t are large, it may happen that the quantity $[S(t_1) + \cdots + S(t_j)]/n$ is larger than k. Since the unknown quantities $S(t_{j+1}), \ldots, S(t_n)$ are positive, it is already certain at date t that:

- The Asian call option will finish in the money.
- $\max(0, A(T) - k) = A(T) - k$.

Hence, it becomes legitimate to write:

$$\left.\begin{aligned} C(t) &= e^{r-(T-t)} E_Q[\max(0, A(T) - k)/F_t] \\ \text{as } C(t) &= e^{r-(T-t)} E_Q[(A(T) - k)/F_t] \end{aligned}\right\} \tag{6.10}$$

The linearity of the expectation operator allows us to obtain an explicit formula for the Asian call in this particular case, namely:

$$\boxed{C^{\mathrm{As}}(t) = S(t)\frac{1 - e^{-r(T-t)}}{rT} - e^{-r(T-t)}\left[k - \frac{S(t_1) + \cdots + S(t_j)}{n}\right]} \tag{6.11}$$

Geman and Yor observe that this formula has interesting resemblances to the Black–Scholes formula, where the strike k is adjusted for already-observed values and the coefficient of $S(t)$ can easily be shown to be positive and smaller than 1. However, the quantity in brackets is in fact negative since we are in the particular case where $[S(t_1) + \cdots + S(t_j)]/n > k$, exhibiting the high value of the Asian call in the particular case under analysis.

Lastly, in this situation the delta of the option does not depend on $S(t)$ and depends only the date of analysis; its computation is derived in a straightforward manner from equation (6.11):

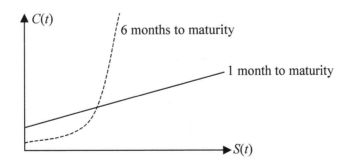

We are in the unusual situation where the price of the call at date t is a linear (still increasing) function of the underlying commodity price $S(t)$.

(5) Comparison of the Asian call and plain-vanilla call with the same strike and maturity

It is clear that the arithmetic average of n quantities $S(t_i)$ has a smaller volatility than a single quantity $S(t_i)$. Consequently, the common view is that an Asian call option should *always* be cheaper than a plain-vanilla one with the same strike and maturity, and this was stated in some papers written in the early 1990s. Geman and Yor (1993) show that this statement is not true: even though volatility is a key component of an option price, it is not the only one.

To take an elementary example, let us consider an Asian option based on an average over three points $t_1, t_2, t_3 = T$ of a dividend-paying stock whose values are $S(t_1) = 80; S(t_2) = 60; S(t_3) = 40$. The average $A(T)$ is equal to 60 while $S(T)$ is equal to 40. Hence, for all strikes between 40 and 60, the Asian option has a positive pay-off and the European one a zero pay-off. Consequently, the price at date 0 of the Asian call option should be higher than the European one, even though the volatility of the average is lower.

This observation is particularly important in our situation, namely commodities: as seen many times in this book, the convenience yield plays the role of a dividend payment. If the convenience yield y is positive and very high or, more precisely, if the *forward curve is backwardated, $r - y$* is negative and an Asian call option *may be more expensive* than a European call with the same characteristics.

Geman and Yor (1993) show the following:

- If $r - y$ is positive, the Asian call option is indeed cheaper than the European one; this is true in particular in the classical Black–Scholes setting of a non-dividend-paying stock since $y = 0$.
- If $r - y$ is negative, the answer is not clear and depends on the relative impact of volatility reduction in the average versus the declining value, in expectation, of the underlying commodity spot price. Detailed results may be found in their (1993) paper.

An important conclusion of this discussion, beyond the specific case of Asian options, is to remember that the price of any option depends not only on the volatility parameter σ but also of the drift term $(r - y)$ of the price dynamics *under the pricing measure Q*, as exhibited in Chapter 5. For options written on commodities, this message is indispensable since $r - y$ may be positive or negative. It is interesting to observe that many practitioners, even if they are unfamiliar with the pricing measure Q, have instinctive knowledge of these properties as the sign of $(r - y)$ has a direct impact on the *shape* of the forward curve as well as on the price of the Asian call option relative to the standard European call.

6.3 TRADING THE SHAPE OF THE FORWARD CURVE THROUGH FLOATING STRIKE ASIAN OPTIONS

As indicated by the name, floating-strike Asian options do not have a fixed strike, but instead the value of the underlying commodity at maturity, $S(T)$.

Since a call option has the property of giving a positive pay-off when the underlying price goes up, a floating strike Asian call option is *defined* by the following pay-off at maturity:

$$C_{fl}^{As}(T) = \max(0, S(T) - A(T))$$

Symmetrically, the floating strike Asian put option pays at maturity:

$$P_{fl}^{As}(T) = \max(0, A(T) - S(T))$$

In the first case, one may exchange the average over the period $[0, T]$, *represented approximately by the forward curve* (as seen above), for the final value $S(T)$ if it is beneficial to do so or, otherwise, do nothing. Unsurprisingly, these options are extremely popular in commodity markets (in particular, in the oil market since the owner of a tanker cargo usually has a time window flexibility in the nomination, hence cost, of the corresponding oil). These options may easily be priced by the Monte Carlo simulations described in Section 6.2(3) since each simulation of a trajectory provides $A(T)$, on the one hand, and $S(T)$, on the other hand. Analytical formulas can be worked out, observing, for instance in the case of a floating Asian call, that:

$$C_{fl}^{As} = S(T) \max\left(0, 1 - \frac{A(T)}{S(T)}\right)$$

hence, the right numéraire in the problem is the underlying commodity price (see Geman, El Karoui and Rochet, 1995). The benefit of the call option is to be able to exchange the forward curve for its end point, the value of the optionality being magnified by the current price of the commodity – which factors out in the above formula. In the expensive oil markets of today, these "operational" options represent a significant component of oil companies' expertise and revenues.

6.4 BARRIER OPTIONS

In all markets, barrier options have been very popular from the very start, barrier options were first discussed by Merton (1973), because they are less expensive than the standard European option while allowing for a hedge against a catastrophic (or viewed as such) state of nature. The commodity market is not an exception, quite the opposite: an agrifood company, or a coffee shop chain, wants to protect the cost of purchasing the raw commodity. It may buy a call option with a strike k equal to the price in dollars above which the cost of coffee may damage the profitability of the company. However, to make the hedge cheaper, the company may prefer to introduce in the call option an *up-and-in* feature at a level U (U being higher than k), which represents a price which may threaten the feasibility of other payments and really endanger the viability of the firm. A similar example is provided by an airline company buying a barrier call option written on the price of jet fuel and activated only if this price goes over a level U during the period $[0, T]$.

Definition

A barrier call option is a standard European call paying the Black–Scholes pay-off only if (unless) a given barrier is touched by the underlying asset at any time during the life $[0, T]$ of the option. The way to represent the different cases is to specify the (de)activation procedure as:

- Up-and-in, down-and-in for the "knock-in" options.
- Up-and-out, down-and-out for the "knock-out" options.

To avoid any dispute between the buyer and the seller, the price that triggers (de)activation has to be specified: it is usually the closing price for equity barrier options. In the case of FX markets, it may be a price observed at any time of the day, i.e., continuous (de)activation of the option. In the case of commodities, this number is in general the index provided by a respected publication viewed as a reliable source of information.

From a mathematical standpoint, the valuation of barrier options is not too difficult since it may be expressed, in the spirit of the computations in Chapter 5, as:

$$C(t) = e^{-r(T-t)} E_Q[\max(0, S_T - k) \mathbf{1}_B / F_t] \tag{6.12}$$

where

- $\mathbf{1}$ is the indicator variable.
- B is the event activating the barrier; for instance, in the case of an up-and-in barrier option:

$$B = \{\text{states of nature such that } S(t) \geq U \text{ for some } t \text{ in } [0, T]\}$$

The price of the option involves the expectation of the product of two *dependent* random variables and, hence, is not totally straightforward. However, the fact that the distribution of the bi-dimensional process $(S_t, M_t)_{t \geq 0}$, where by definition $M(t) = \max S(u)$ for $0 \leq u \leq t$ is totally known for simple functionals of Brownian motion (see Geman, 2000), implies that an explicit solution can be obtained for the barrier option. For instance, the price at date t of a down-and-out call is:

$$C_{DO}(t) = S(t) e^{-y(T-t)} N(x_1) - k e^{-r(T-t)} N(x_2)$$

$$- \left[S(t) e^{-y(T-t)} \left(\frac{U}{S(t)} \right)^{2\frac{(r-y)}{\sigma^2}+1} + N(y_1) - k e^{-r(T-t)} \left(\frac{U}{S(t)} \right)^{2\frac{(r-y)}{\sigma^2}+1} - N(y_2) \right] \tag{6.13}$$

where:

$$\begin{cases} x_2 = x_1 - \sigma\sqrt{T - t} \\[2mm] y_2 = y_1 - \sigma\sqrt{T - t} \\[2mm] x_1 = \dfrac{\ln\left(\dfrac{S(t) e^{-y(T-t)}}{\max(U, k) e^{-r(T-t)}} \right) + \frac{1}{2}\sigma^2(T - t)}{\sigma\sqrt{T - t}} \\[6mm] y_1 = \dfrac{\ln\left(\dfrac{U^2 e^{-y(T-t)}}{S(t) \max(U, k) e^{-r(T-t)}} \right) + \frac{1}{2}\sigma^2(T - t)}{\sigma\sqrt{T - t}} \end{cases}$$

Note that $C_{DO}(t) + C_{DI}(t) = C(t)$ since one of the two calls, down-and-out or down-and-in, will be equivalent to the plain-vanilla call at maturity and the other will be worthless:

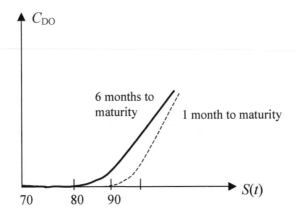

In the example above, $U = 80; k = 100$.

It is important to observe that the barrier effect has a high impact on the delta and the gamma of the option: the delta has a discontinuity point at the barrier while the gamma may become negative for an up-and-out call in a region where the underlying $S(t)$ is close to the barrier U:

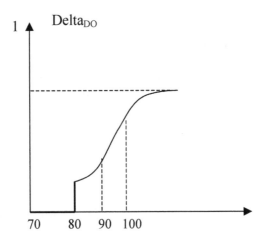

Unsurprisingly, the discontinuity of the delta around the barrier $U = 80$ translates for practitioners into a delicate readjustment of the hedging strategy.

Monte Carlo methods for barrier options

Given the Monte Carlo procedure, which consists in building a piecewise simulated approximation of the real trajectory, it is clear that Monte Carlo methods are not very appropriate for barrier options: the real trajectory may hit the barrier while the approximate one does not, and conversely. Hence, corrections and adjustments must be made in order to reduce the extra error due to the Monte Carlo approach to barrier options. Note, however that, in contrast to Asian options, exact solutions do exist (as seen above) under a closed-form expression for barrier option prices in the Black–Scholes setting; Monte-Carlo methods become particularly worthy of consideration for barrier options if one moves away from the Black–Scholes setting. A number of papers have recently proposed "improved" Monte Carlo methods for barrier options (see, for instance, Glasserman, 2000).

6.5   COMMODITY QUANTO OPTIONS

The terminology of quanto options has been introduced in the context of equity markets for multi-asset options where one of the risk factors is currency risk. These quanto options are obviously particularly relevant in commodity markets since producing regions export to various countries in the world. Energy commodities provide numerous examples of the validity of such instruments: if we consider an Italian municipality buying gas on the basis of a formula indexed to oil prices, it will need to take a position on the International Petroleum Exchange (IPE) in London to hedge its exposure to a rise of oil prices, since the IPE index is liquid and reliable. Typically, the municipality will buy European calls paying at maturity T:

$$C(T) = \max(0, S(T) - k)$$

where S denotes the spot price of the IPE index. If oil prices and, in turn, gas prices in continental Western Europe do rise, the positive pay-off of the options will offset the increase in the cost of operating schools and other public equipment. However, in this process, currency risk appears since the possible decline of pounds sterling against the euro will impact the option pay-off which is, like S, denominated in sterling. The benefit of the hedge would be destroyed while the option premium would be paid upfront. Hence, a proper solution for the municipality is to buy from a bank, located in Italy, the UK or anywhere else, a *commodity quanto option*. The most appropriate one in the example under analysis would pay at maturity:

$$C(T) = \max(0, S(T)X(T) - k_d) \tag{6.14}$$

where $X(T)$ is the exchange rate prevailing at date T (number of euros per pound sterling), and k_d is the strike of the call option expressed in the domestic numéraire of the municipality and represents the level above which the cost of oil translated into gas prices and euros would damage the finances of the municipality.

Assuming that S, the spot price of oil in sterling, and X, the exchange rate GBP/EUR, both follow a geometric Brownian motion, the product $(S(t)X(t))_{t\geq 0}$ is also a geometric Brownian motion. Unsurprisingly, the price of the commodity quanto call at date t is given by a Black–Scholes-type formula, namely:

$$C(t) = S(t)X(t)\,e^{-y(T-t)}N(d_1) - k_d\,e^{-r_d(T-t)}N(d_2) \tag{6.15}$$

where:

- y is the convenience yield of the commodity.
- r_d denotes the interest rate in the domestic economy.
- $d_1 = \dfrac{\ln\left(\dfrac{S(t)X(t)\,e^{-y(T-t)}}{k_d\,e^{-r_d(T-t)}}\right) + \frac{1}{2}\Sigma^2(T-t)}{\Sigma\sqrt{T-t}}.$
- $d_2 = d_1 - \Sigma\sqrt{T-t}.$
- $\Sigma = \mathrm{Vol}(SX) = \sqrt{\sigma_S^2 + \sigma_X^2 + 2\rho\sigma_X\sigma_y}.$
- σ_S and σ_X denote, respectively, the volatilities of S and X.
- ρ is the correlation coefficient between S and X.

Note that, except in the totally unlikely situation of a perfect correlation between the oil price in sterling and the exchange rate GBP/EUR, ρ is strictly smaller than 1 and the volatility Σ strictly smaller than $\sigma_S + \sigma_X$. Hence, the price of the quanto option – and the cost of the hedge for the municipality – is strictly lower than the added premia of an option written on the oil price and an option written on the FX rate.

Proof   When one moves to a multi-economy problem, the no-arbitrage assumption needs to be extended to this new setting. It can be shown that the non-existence of arbitrage opportunities between two economies implies, as long as geometric Brownian motion is viewed as acceptable, that the dynamics of the exchange rate X under the world-adjusted risk-neutral measure Q have the following remarkable expression:

$$\frac{dX(t)}{X(t)} = (r_d - r_f)\,dt + \sigma_x\,dW_t^X \tag{6.16}$$

where:

- r_d (respectively, r_f) denotes the domestic (respectively, foreign) interest rate.
- σ_X denotes the volatility of the exchange rate.

Assuming now that the IPE oil index *denominated in sterling* also follows a geometric Brownian motion, the dynamics of S under the Q measure have the same expression as discussed before, namely:

$$\frac{dS(t)}{S(t)} = (r_f - y)\,dt + \sigma_s\,dW_t^S \tag{6.17}$$

where y denotes the convenience yield of the commodity S.

Introducing ρ, the correlation coefficient between Brownian motions W^X and W^S, it is easy to see from equations (6.16) and (6.17) that the terminal value $S(T)X(T)$ is a log-normal variable with volatility Σ. The drift of the process $(S(t)X(t))_{t\geq 0}$ under Q is equal to $(r_f - y) + (r_d - r_f) = r_d - y$, hence leading to the pricing formula (6.15) through the developments proposed in Chapters 4 and 5. Note that the expression of volatility Σ translates the "vector additivity" of the volatilities σ_S and σ_X:

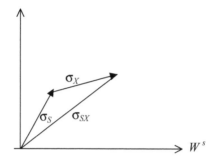

Many other types of commodity quanto options can be formulated. We will only describe one more, the popular "foreign commodity quanto struck in the foreign currency", to paraphrase the terminology used in equity markets.

The call pay-off at maturity T is:

$$C(T) = X(T) \max(0, S(T) - k_f) \qquad (6.18)$$

where the strike is now expressed in the foreign currency and the difference $S(T) - k_f$, if positive, is multiplied by the final value of the exchange rate to define the terminal value of the commodity quanto.

Note that since $X(T)$ is a random quantity at the date t when the call is purchased, the right-hand sides of formulas (6.14) and (6.18) cannot be reduced to the same quantity. Hence, we have indeed another form of commodity quanto and the buyer of the option will decide which one better suits his needs. The valuation problem in the case of the pay-off expressed in (6.18) is even simpler than in the example studied before. Using arbitrage arguments, one can show that:

$$C(t) = X(t) \text{ [price at date } t \text{ of a foreign call written on the commodity } S]$$

hence:

$$\boxed{C(t) = X(t)[S(t)\, e^{-y(T-t)} N(d_1) - k_f\, e^{-r_f(T-t)} N(d_2)]}$$

where:

- $d_1 = \dfrac{\ln\left(\dfrac{S(t)\, e^{-y(T-t)}}{k_f\, e^{-r_f(T-t)}}\right) + \frac{1}{2}\sigma_S^2(T-t)}{\sigma\sqrt{T-t}}.$

- $d_2 = d_1 - \sigma_s\sqrt{T-t}.$

Accordingly, the hedging strategies will be different for the seller of these options: the hedging portfolio will involve positions in the commodity and in the foreign currency but the corresponding quantities will differ according to the option. In both cases, however, the weights in S and the foreign currency are given by the pricing formula, which illustrates once more the remarkable virtues of the geometric Brownian motion setting. Lastly, note that the above results can be extended to stochastic interest rates in both economies, a generalization that becomes necessary for long-dated commodity quantos.

To conclude this chapter, note that the different categories of path-dependent and multi-asset options that experienced exponential development in the stock market over the last 15 years are equally relevant for commodity markets. In Chapter 12 we will describe other types of "exotic" options, such as swing or take-or-pay, that are specific to energy commodities as they involve volume flexibility as well. We will see that the pricing approach will become more involved and the existence of closed-form solutions very rare, even in the simple setting of a geometric Brownian motion for the underlying commodity price dynamics.

7

Agricultural Commodity Markets

7.1 INTRODUCTION

The building blocks used in the analysis of agricultural commodities consist, as for other commodities, of supply, demand and inventory, with the additional considerations of perishability and quality (e.g., arabica versus robusta coffee). Some elements of vocabulary specific to agricultural commodities are recalled below.

Supply

For agricultural commodities, supply comprises three components:

1. Surplus stocks left from the previous year also known as "carry-in" in the jargon of practitioners and as "inventory" in the economic literature.
2. Current year production.
3. Imports from other countries.

Demand

It essentially covers two categories:

1. Domestic use.
2. Exports.

For these two categories, further subdivisions can be considered, such as animal feed versus human food. In the first category, products are generally used as such while, in the second, food that needs to be processed will have different costs and lead to various quantities of the raw product.

Carry-over

This is defined as the remaining supply from the previous year plus current year production and any imports minus demand. It is this carry-over that links Futures prices in different crop years. In particular, when there is a decrease in demand in one crop year, carry-over to the next crop year will increase and prices will generally drop that year.

Stocks-to-use ratio

This important indicator for trading activities is defined as current year ending stocks divided by current year use. For instance, if the year's ending stocks in wheat are 540 million bushels and the year's usage totals 2.7 billion bushels, the stock-to-use ratio is 20%. This number expresses how short supplies may be: typically, it should lie between 20% and 40%. It will obviously have an impact on price volatility: in a tight market, any shock in supply while demand is steady is likely to send prices very high. This explains why the stock-to-use ratio is a key number in technical analysis rules of trading in commodity markets and option pricing as well.

7.2 THE GRAIN MARKETS

The US Department of Agriculture (USDA) publishes every month an updated balance sheet containing the current year exports, domestic use, carry-out from last year and expected carry-over for next year. It also contains the USDA's estimates for production in the major foreign nations that either compete with US producers, such as Brazil and Argentina which have become major competitors for soybeans, or are traditional importers, such as India, Russia, Pakistan and Egypt.

A monthly report on all grains comes out during the second week of the month. If the USDA's numbers differ greatly from private reports, a price shock may occur in the market.

In addition to the monthly reports, the USDA issues two planting reports: (1) the Planting Intentions report, which comes out at the end of March, and (2) the Final Acreage report, which comes out at the end of June and shows what farmers actually planted. For instance, a decline in acreage translates into an expected decline in production; or, if the Planting Intentions report shows that farmers intend to plant less corn in the coming season, corn prices will rise relative to soybean prices. Together with USDA's reports, events that can impact prices may be the announcement of a large purchase by an export customer, a weather-related event such as a frost on the winter wheat crop just before harvest or the decision of a country to develop extensively the planting of a new commodity (such as coffee in Vietnam in recent years).

Soybeans

Soybeans were used in China more than 4,500 years ago, and first appeared in France in the middle of the 18th century. In the US, they were first used in the east and southeast of the country, with culture appearing around the end of the 19th century. At the time soybeans were mostly used as animal feed, with plants originating from eastern Asia.

Soybean culture increased strongly throughout the 20th century in the US, one reason for this expansion being its similarity to corn culture. Beans are planted in the spring, generally April and May, but they can be planted as late as early July. A late-planted crop runs the risk of being caught by an early frost in the fall and may have difficulties flowering and setting pods in August. For these reasons, a late-planted crop will generally lead to a higher premium. Through the summer prices gyrate with the weather, especially at the time when pods are set. Soybeans are known as "miracle plants" because of their remarkable resilience.

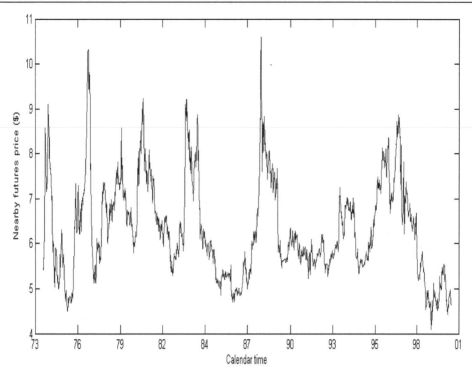

Figure 7.1   Soybean nearby Futures price over the period July 1974 to October 2000.

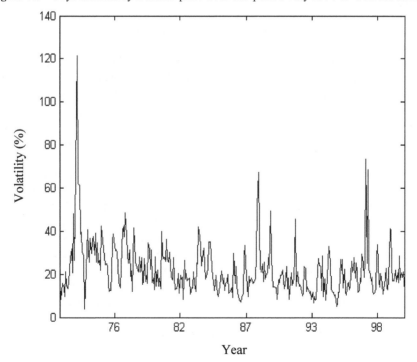

Figure 7.2   Soybean price volatility over the period July 1974 to October 2000

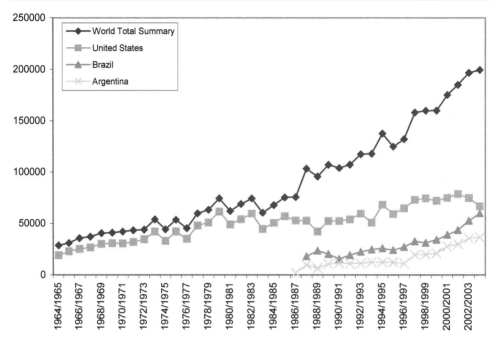

Figure 7.3   World soybean production.

South American soybeans

Prior to the 1970s, the US was the only place to buy soybeans and soybean products, and was responsible for more than three-quarters of world production. In the 1960s, because of a feed shortage in proteins, soybean-growing skills were passed on to Brazil and Argentina, through firms like Archer Daniels Midland. Today, these two countries combine to produce almost as many soybeans as the US, with 36% of world production against 45% for the US. Their combined production 5 years ago represented only about one-half of US production. Total South America soybean production from 1985 to 2003 underwent a four-fold increase, with Paraguay entering the market in the mid-1990s.

Moreover, Brazil has more than 100 million acres of uncultivated grasslands in the center and north of the country that are ideal for bean crops. Plantations there are producing as much as 50 bushels an acre, these yields being on a par with US yields. In the near future, the Brazilian government envisions this area being fully cultivated. At present, what these regions mostly lack for mass-production is an adequate transportation system. These 100 million acres exceed the size of the US Corn Belt. If Brazil is successful in developing its agricultural land for soybeans, then the growth of expected world demand for beans will be met easily. Imports of soybeans to the European Community mostly arrive in the ports of Rotterdam and Saint-Nazaire (France),[1] as the EU is the world's largest soybean importer. Figures 7.3, 7.4 and 7.5 illustrate the Brazilian boom in soybean production and exports.

---

[1] Saint-Nazaire is home to a major soybean-processing center operated by the US commodity company Cargill.

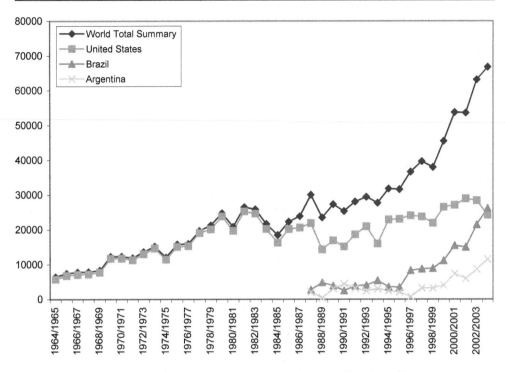

Figure 7.4   Soybean world exports – the "Brazilian boom".

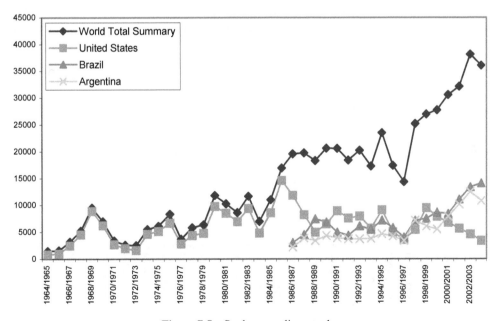

Figure 7.5   Soybean ending stocks.

As a percentage of total supply, the US exports more than the other two producers (30% versus 20%), but consumption represents roughly the same proportion in all three countries (around 60%). Thus, exports alone explain the fact that the ending stock percentage in the US accounts for a smaller part of total supply: 10% compared with 20% in the other two countries.

Note that, over the last 5 years, Brazil has exported much more and consumed less in percentage terms with no significant change in ending stock percentage.

Soybean acreage in the US increased from 1.8 million in 1924 to 72.7 million in 2000. Cultivation takes place in most central and eastern states, from Wisconsin to Alabama, with Iowa and Illinois predominating, each having more than 10 million acres under culture. Today, soybean represents the number one US export crop. An extensive study of soybean inventory and its relation to price volatility over the last 15 years can be found in the articles by Geman and Nguyen (2002) and Richter and Sorensen (2002).

Historically, soybeans were mainly prized for their seeds, which were processed into different types of food products. Today, soybeans account for more than one-half of the total fats consumed in the US. Indonesian consumers are turning to that source of proteins and fats, with a sharp increase in their imports over the past decade. Soybeans are also traded under the form of soybean meal and soybean oil; the three forms constitute what is called the "soybean complex".

Soybean meal and oil

Soybeans are crushed to produce meal and oil. The crush spread is the expected gross margin of soybean processing. It is a very popular agricultural spread and traded by the simultaneous purchase (sale) of soybean Futures and the sale (purchase) of soybean oil and soybean meal Futures. Meal makes up 75–80% of the content of a bean and is used for animal feed as a direct competitor with corn. It is a higher quality protein than corn and, as such, exhibits a premium over corn. Factors affecting meal prices include: the

Figure 7.6 Soybean nearby Futures price.

availability of meal from crushing operations; the price of fish meal, produced from anchovy fished off the Pacific coast of South America; the price of corn and the size of livestock herds. Soybean oil is mostly used for cooking. Its competitors range from India's groundnut oil to Canada's canola oil, as well as sunflower oil and palm oil, mostly produced in Indonesia and Malaysia. An important product extracted from soybean oil is lecithin, used in many food preparations as an emulsifier.

If meal demand is high and oil demand is not, processors promptly turn to crushing and allow oil stocks to build up in anticipation of future demand. This explains why trading the spread between meal and oil is very popular in this industry.

As will be seen in Chapter 12, options on this spread are highly traded between participants in this market. Each month the US Census Bureau and the National Oil Processor Association (NOPA) release estimates of the crush rate and the stock of meal and oil.

Corn

Corn was first cultivated in Central America about 5000 B.C., when it was mainly used for human food. The cereal was brought to Europe and North America, but remained poorly grown until the 19th century. As strains of the plant were further developed, it led to a high-yield plant that could grow under different conditions and in different climates. Plants were also modified to increase their content of proteins, above all in the amino acid tryptophan, a lack of which in populations that mainly depended on corn led to skin disease.

Corn must be planted no later than mid-June and, even then, it may be too late as late-planted corn will need to flower and be pollinated in the high heat of the summer in late July to mid-August. Late-planted corn is also vulnerable to early frosts in the fall. If corn is to be planted late, farmers have the option to switch to a variety that has a shorter growing season. Today, corn represents about 70% of the world coarse grain markets. The five leading producers in 2003 were the US (38%), China (20%), Brazil (7%), EU (7%) and Mexico (3%). The main consumers in 2003 were the US (32% of world consumption, equivalent to about 88% of production), China (20%) and the EU (7%). Yields in the US or EU countries are about three times those of Brazil and Mexico. In recent years, China has aggressively increased its corn production so that from a net importer it became a net exporter of corn. Production in the Ukraine has increased markedly in the past years, with a 16.7% increase from 2001/2002 to 2002/2003, and a 50% increase in 2003/2004 relative to the previous year (source: USDA).

The main competitors of corn as animal feed are wheat, sorghum and soybean meal. One of the drawbacks of corn is its low content of essential amino acids, which is much higher in soybean. Corn production has been subject to scientific controversy in recent years. Use of Genetically Modified (GM) seeds that bear insecticide-producing genes or other modified features has prompted an ethical debate; some GM corns have for instance been qualified as improper for human food by the US Environmental Protection Agency (e.g., Aventis's StarLink product).

As was the case for the first known Central American populations, some in South America still use corn for human consumption. In Europe and the US, it is mainly used for forage. In Northern America, 75% of the corn produced is on average used for animal feed; this variety is called "dent corn". About 8% is transformed into vegetable oil or wheat for incorporation in food preparations, and 6% is used for food (in particular, sweet corn which possesses a higher quantity of sugar). Moreover, corn is used in alcohol distilleries, and in the production of alcohol for engines. Due to the major increase in crude oil prices in 2000, the use of corn for ethanol production is expected to increase considerably. Over 5% of US corn is currently used for the production of ethanol and other alternative fuels, and about 95% of North America's ethanol is made from corn. Programs on ethanol production from corn will therefore have a constant influence over corn prices, such as the $300m program announced at the end of 2000 by the US to expand ethanol production.

The corn that is traded on the Chicago Board Of Trade (CBOT) is animal feed, not the sweet corn bought in the supermarket. The competitors of feed corn are wheat, sorghum and soybean meal. Foreign competition in production are primarily China, South Africa and Argentina.

Electronic trading and new Futures on grains

In February 2002 the Minneapolis Grain Exchange (MGEX), which was established in 1881, launched corn and soybean derivatives: Futures and options contracts, respectively written on the National Corn Index (NCI) and National Soybean Index (NSI), started trading while the MGEX launched at the same time its new electronic trading platform MGEXpress.[2] NCI and NSI Futures and options trade exclusively on the MGEXpress. They were the first cash-settled grain and oil seed Futures and options and represent the industry's first exclusively electronically traded contracts as well.

The NCI and NSI are indexes composed of country elevator bids. As such, they tend to track prices where grain is originated – the cash market – more closely than corn and soybean contracts traded at the CBOT, which are based on delivery to a few major elevators.

The indexes are calculated by Data Transmission Network (DTN), an electronic commerce and information services company which collects bids from roughly 1,500 elevators and, in turn, calculates the indexes. These indexes are based on bids in the country and, hence, tend to correlate closely with cash prices, making the Futures contracts an effective tool for risk management. The indexes also reflect a broad spectrum of cash market participants, which precludes the possibility of index manipulations; for instance, the single largest bidders for corn and soybeans represent respectively 3.3% and 3.6% of the index and more than 90% of US elevators are represented. The contract size is 5,000 bushels for both NCI and NSI Futures.

Wheat

A grass similar to wheat was cultivated in the Middle East earlier than 8000 B.C. Its culture, in the area called the "Fertile Crescent", at that time most probably constituted the birthplace of agriculture. Wheat is the oldest commodity contract and started trading around 1850 on the CBOT. It is used as food for both humans and animals. For many nations, wheat is the staple diet and is certainly a major part of the US diet.

World wheat production reached a maximum in 1998 with 609 million tonnes (note

---

[2] OM Technology, a company based in Stockholm, provides the technological expertise behind MGEXpress.

Table 7.1 Different kinds of wheat in the US

Wheat	Ratio of total production (%)*	Farmer price (crop 2003, $)	Domestic use/export (million bushels)*
Hard red winter	45.5	3.2–4.4	520.4/510
Hard red spring	21.4	3.5–4.5	246.5/260
Soft red winter	16.2	3.0–3.8	250.6/135
Soft white	12.8	3.2–4.0	116.5/180
Durum	4.1	3.6–4.5	85/40

* Projected for 2003/2004.

that a tonne is the metric unit equivalent of 1.1 US tons), which was mainly due to large crops in the major producing countries: the US, former Soviet Union and China. US production has been unstable, with small crops in 2000 and 2001. Total trade projected for 2003/2004 is up 2% since 2000 to 99.5 million tonnes.

Kinds of wheat

Wheat is traded on three US exchanges: the CBOT, the Kansas City Board of Trade (KCBOT) and the MGEX. *Chicago wheat* is a soft winter wheat. It is planted in the fall and harvested in the late spring and early summer. It is grown primarily in Tennessee, Arkansas, Missouri, southern Illinois, Indiana and Ohio. It is a low-grade wheat used as animal feed and as flour for cheap bread and pizza dough. It is often exported to Third World countries because of its low price.

Kansas City wheat is the largest crop. It is a hard, red, winter wheat and is grown in Texas, Oklahoma, Kansas, eastern Colorado and southern Nebraska. It represents prime bread and pizza dough wheat. About one-half of this crop is exported. Like Chicago wheat, it is planted in the fall and harvested in the spring and summer. Chicago wheat and Kansas City wheat account for 60–75% of the wheat grown in the US. *Minneapolis wheat* is grown in the northern states of Montana, the Dakotas, northern Nebraska and Minnesota. It is the highest grade of wheat, planted in the spring and harvested in the fall. It is used for pastry and is not exported.

In the US, the harvest generally begins in June in Texas and continues north through the summer until it is completed in September in Minnesota. Storage facilities exist to store approximately one-half of it; the rest gets sold immediately. This produces a temporary oversupply, depressing the market until all the wheat can be used or sold abroad. So, every year, wheat gets depressed during the summer harvest. When the harvest is complete, the selling pressure comes off the market and the price gradually rises each fall until supplies become available from the southern hemisphere around December.

Hence, we obtain a regular seasonal pattern in prices that are exhibited by observed price trajectories. The fundamentals that produce this pattern are clear: if the price approaches the bottom third of the historical trading range for wheat during the months of May, June or July, it is likely that this will be the low for the year. The combination of approaching historical low prices in the right seasonal time frame can be a buying signal for technical analysis speculators. These observations are part of the

Figure 7.7   Wheat nearby Futures price.

elements that constitute the technical analysis rules often used in the trading of agricultural commodity Futures, by Commodity Trading Advisors (CTAs) in particular.

Note that 75% of the wheat grown in the US is winter wheat that is planted in the
fall. It germinates, sprouts, is then covered with snow and lies dormant for the rest of
winter. In late winter or early spring, it begins to grow once more and is ready to
harvest by early summer.

Global wheat

World wheat production reached a maximum in 1998 at 609 million tonnes, which was
mainly due to bumper crops in the major producing countries: the US, Russia and
China. The forecast for global production in 2004 is 548 million tonnes; this low value
comes from a number of factors, not least of which has been variable US production
over the past few years.

The competitors of the US in wheat production are most EU countries, along with
Argentina, Canada and Australia. The main customers are Egypt, Morocco, Pakistan,
India, Russia and China. Wheat is grown in almost every part of the globe, including
Saudi Arabia.

Global wheat stocks have been decreasing since 2002. Ending stock forecast for 2004
and the stock-to-use ratio have reached their lowest values in a long time, stocks being
depleted by 128 million tonnes. At the same time global consumption has slightly
increased. Such conditions will make 2004 the sixth consecutive year that global consumption has exceeded production. Ending stocks in the US were at their peak in 1999
and 2000, reaching close to 40%, but have been decreasing ever since, and should end
the year 2004 around 23%. China has seen its production fall in the past 3 years and has
been using its own stocks to meet demand. India also had to face a small decrease in its
stocks, due to rising consumption.

Wheat is a hard-to-kill grass and the only danger to the wheat crop is the loss of yield and quality in the case of too much rain at the end of the crop cycle when it is time to harvest (see Grandmill, 1991).

7.3   SOFT COMMODITIES: COFFEE, COTTON AND SUGAR

The soft group is an odd mix. It is often referred to as "tropics" because these commodities are grown primarily in tropical or subtropical regions. In most cases, they are grown in developing countries where information is often harder to get.

Cocoa

Cocoa beans grow on trees and, hence, changes in production occur over very long cycles. New trees take approximately 7 years to mature and fruit, which makes grain production easy to forecast.

If prices get too low, cocoa farmers abandon marginal growth. This is what happened in the early 1990s when prices reached $795 a tonne, down from $4,500 in 1976; the seventh consecutive year of overproduction was 1991. After the lows of 1992, the market rallied between then and 1998 with prices reaching $1,787.

Since early 2000, cocoa production has been expanding as a result of the additional trees that were planted as prices began to rise in the early 1990s. The Ivory Coast, by far the biggest cocoa-growing nation, has achieved record high production levels recently. Cocoa statistics are released every year by the International Cocoa Organization (ICCO) at its annual conference in London, where the headquarters of ICCO are located.

Measuring demand is difficult. Cocoa grind statistics are released country by country, but more cocoa is being ground in the production countries and shipped afterwards. As with other commodities, the stock-to-use figure is the most important one.

Because of the key role of London in cocoa trading, cocoa is also priced in sterling on the world market, in contrast to most other commodities.

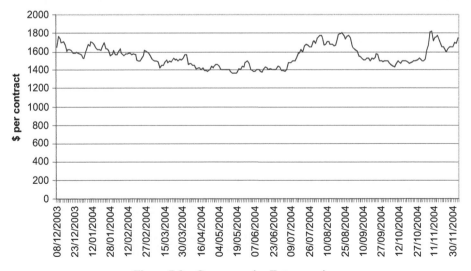

Figure 7.8   Cocoa nearby Futures price.

Coffee

This tropical crop is grown in so many different varieties that the Coffee, Sugar and Cocoa Division of the New York Board of Trade (NYBOT) has established a scale that determines the ratio at which the different types of coffee can be delivered against the contract traded on that exchange. The main difference, however, is between African coffee, which is arabica coffee, and Latin America, which is robusta. The London coffee contract is arabica and the New York contract is robusta. The US almost exclusively imports robusta coffee, probably because US consumers have gotten used to its taste. Coffee is the second largest US import (it was the largest until the 1960s) – one of the reasons the coffee market has become subject to dramatic price volatility. It is interesting to note, for instance, that the development of the Starbucks coffee chain, which is now present in most towns of the US and will be in 65 countries by the end of 2005, has given rise to an estimated increase of 10% in world coffee consumption.

Coffee grows as bushes. It takes 3–5 years for new bushes to mature sufficiently to produce fruit. Brazil is by far the largest robusta producer, followed by Colombia, Ecuador, Costa Rica and other Latin American countries.

The International Coffee Organization (ICO) is a consortium of producing and consuming nations. For years, the US, as the largest consuming nation, blocked a program meant to buy surplus production from farmers. Now some countries, most notably Brazil, have established their own price support programs independently; but these programs may collapse if they prove difficult or unpopular.

Overproduction of coffee (mediocre coffee in particular) in the world explains the consistent decline of coffee prices since 1998, as depicted in Figure 7.9. This phenomenon is occurring despite the sharp increase in US coffee drinking.

The Coffee Quality Program (CQP), promoted by the ICO with the aim of checking that coffee meets minimal standards before being sold on the markets, is not really effective. African producers, however, are trying to bridge the gap between robusta and arabica prices, the former having recently reached an all time low. African producing countries, regrouped in the African Coffee Organization, are determined to improve the quality of the robusta coffee they produce and promote a "robusta gourmet"-type coffee.

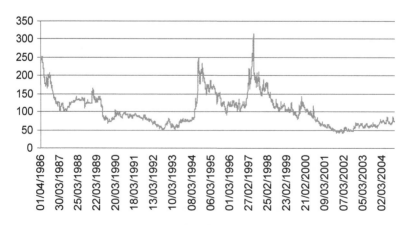

Figure 7.9 Arabica nearby price

Sugar

The year 2003 was disastrous for sugar, with spot prices of 6 cents per pound at the beginning of 2004, a number which is barely the production cost of the most efficient producers in the state of Sao Paulo (Brazil) and way below the cost of 40 cents per pound characterizing some old sugar-producing entities. The explanation for this drop is essentially oversupply. During 2002/03, the world production had generated large stocks, totaling between 3 and 6 million tonnes according to estimates. The season 2003–04 followed the same pattern, with an excess supply totaling between 2 and 3 million tons. Brazil again had a remarkable harvest, with the production of cane sugar increasing by 6% over the previous year. With potential exports of 13.5 million tonnes (out of its production of 24 million tonnes), Brazil dominates all its world competitors. India has become a structural exporter, while Australia and Thailand are following the same path. Only if consumption of sugar in China approaches Western levels would a number of the order of 20 million tonnes (see Chalmin, 2004) be reached and push prices up, but this is not the case yet.

In June 2003 a meeting took place in Bangkok between Brazil, Australia, South Africa, Guatemala and Thailand – countries representing 25 million tonnes of exports. Not much was decided, except for a complaint directed to the World Trade Organization (WTO) against the sugar export policy of the EU. The complaint which Brazil filed, along with Australia and Thailand, argued that the close-on $2bn in annual export subsidies the EU pays to sugar beet and sugar cane farmers encourages over-production, which floods the world, drives down market prices and hurts the economies of poor nations that depend on the crop. According to the international relief agency

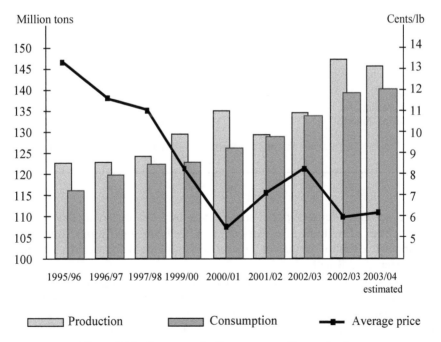

Figure 7.10   Sugar production, consumption and price.
Source: USDA.

Table 7.2 Sugar production. consumption, exports and imports (in million tonnes)

	1998/99	1999/00	2000/01	2001/02	2002/03	2003/04
World production	**130.9**	**136.5**	**130.5**	**134.9**	**147.3**	**144.6**
Brazil	18.3	20.1	17.1	20.4	23.8	24.8
India	17.4	20.2	20.5	20.5	22.1	19.9
European Union	17.8	19.5	18.5	16.2	18.7	17.1
China	9.0	7.5	6.8	8.3	10.6	10.1
United States of America	7.6	8.2	8.0	7.2	7.6	8.1
Thailand	5.4	5.7	5.1	6.4	7.3	7.7
Mexico	5.0	5.0	5.2	5.2	5.2	5.5
Australia	5.0	5.4	4.2	4.7	5.4	5.1
Cuba	3.8	4.1	3.5	3.7	2.0	2.0
Russian Federation	1.3	1.5	1.6	1.6	1.6	1.8
Ukraine	2.0	1.7	1.7	1.8	1.6	1.4
World consumption	**124.2**	**127.4**	**130.2**	**134.8**	**137.7**	**139.3**
India	17.0	17.3	17.8	19.8	20.8	21.5
European Union	14.3	14.5	14.1	14.1	14.4	14.4
China	8.9	8.5	8.7	9.4	9.9	10.3
Brazil	9.1	9.1	9.3	9.5	9.8	10.1
United States of America	9.1	9.0	9.3	9.1	9.1	8.8
Russian Federation	5.0	6.1	6.8	7.0	6.3	6.0
Mexico	4.5	4.6	4.6	5.2	5.2	5.3
Ukraine	2.0	1.9	2.1	2.0	2.4	2.2
World exports	**37.4**	**41.4**	**37.7**	**41.2**	**45.7**	**45.1**
Brazil	8.8	11.3	7.7	11.6	14.0	14.3
Thailand	3.4	4.1	3.4	4.2	5.1	5.8
European Union	5.3	6.1	6.6	4.8	5.6	4.9
Australia	4.1	4.1	3.1	3.6	4.2	3.9
Cuba	3.1	3.4	3.0	3.1	1.4	1.3
World imports	**36.0**	**36.1**	**38.6**	**37.7**	**39.2**	**37.2**
Russian Federation	5.4	5.2	5.7	4.9	3.9	3.8
United States of America	1.7	1.5	1.4	1.4	1.6	1.4
Japan	1.5	1.7	1.5	1.4	1.5	1.4
China	0.5	0.7	1.1	1.4	0.6	0.6
Indonesia		1.7	1.8	1.7	1.8	1.9

Source: USDA.

Oxfam, EU subsidies depress global sugar prices by 23%, depriving developing countries of hundreds of millions of dollars in revenues from sugar crops. Indeed, the EU exports about five million tonnes of sugar a year, making it the world's second-largest sugar exporter after Brazil.

In August 2004 the WTO declared the EU sugar subsidy program to be in violation of international trade agreements. In July 2004 the EU agriculture commissioner proposed extensive changes to EU sugar subsidies, including cutting support prices and exports. The WTO decision could hasten planned reductions in sugar subsidies in the EU and, more generally, help developing nations by reducing farm subsidies in the rich nations by 20%.

Cotton

This is another hot-weather crop. In the US, cotton is grown from Georgia through Arizona and California. California cotton is among the best quality cotton in the world. Cotton is also grown in Latin America and Asia. Cotton exporters include such nations as Kazakhstan, Pakistan and Australia. China also produces a large quantity of cotton and alternates from being an importer to an exporter depending on its crop size and domestic usage.

Cotton prices in the US are mostly affected by world prices, but they are also subject to such government programs as the "Step I: Export Subsidy Program". This program is variously applied as it must be voted on each year by Congress.

Because cotton is such an important US crop, the USDA produces a very complete report that includes supply and demand figures for the US and for the world. Cotton is used primarily for clothing fiber and is increasingly being consumed in developing countries as their economies improve.

The Cotlook A Index – the major cotton index – averaged 68 cents per pound in 2003/04, a 6-year high. Higher prices are boosting the world cotton area by an estimated 8% in 2004/05. The harvest has begun in the northern hemisphere without incident, and the world yield is forecast to climb to a record 663 kg per hectare in 2003/04, up 26 kg from the previous season. As a result, world production is forecast to go up 13%, from 20.5 million tonnes in 2003/04 to a record 23.1 million tonnes. This would be the largest year-to-year increase in absolute terms since 1984/85.

Expectations of rising stocks and lower imports by China in 2004/05 caused the Cotlook A Index to fall from 75 cents per pound in January 2004 to 52 cents per pound in August 2004. World cotton consumption in 2004 will be stimulated by lower prices, as cotton is currently price-competitive with polyester. Mill use is forecast to go up 400,000 tonnes, nearly 2%, to a record of 21.6 million tonnes in 2004/05.

The shortfall between production and consumption in China is expected to shrink by 1 million tonnes from more than 2.2 million tonnes in 2003/04. However, depleted

Figure 7.11   Cotton nearby Futures price.

Table 7.3 World cotton supply and distribution

	2003/04	**2004/05**	**2005/06***
Production	20.485	23.08	22.04
	94.09	106.0	101.2
Consumption	21.256	21.63	21.98
	97.63	99.4	101.0
Exports	7.280	3.56	6.95
	33.44	30.1	31.9
Ending stocks	7.761	9.21	9.26
	36.65	42.3	42.5

* Projected; the first number is in million tonnes, the second in million bales.

stocks, including government reserves, need to be replenished. Chinese imports are expected to decline from more than 1.9 million/tons in 2003/04 to 1.5 million tonnes in 2004/05.

Despite record consumption, world ending stocks are projected to increase from 7.8 million tonnes last season to 9.2 million tonnes in 2004/05. Market fundamentals suggest that the season average Cotlook A Index will decline to 52 cents per pound in 2004/05, 16 cents (24%) below the average in 2003/04.

7.4 CITRUS AND ORANGE JUICE

Citrus represents a very important group in world fruit production. It constitutes roughly one-quarter of total fruit volume, but there is a high variability in production. All the main producing countries have reduced their output: Brazil by 9%, the US by 7%, China by 13% and Spain by 3%. These four countries account for 53% of world production, and the first ten countries account for 71%.

The international citrus market is divided into two types of products: fresh fruit and juices. One-third of world citrus production is transformed into juices. Brazil (the state of Sao Paulo) and the United States (state of Florida) are the principal regions in the world for citrus juices (in particular, orange juice) and account for 75% of transformed citrus volume. Italy and Mexico for orange juice, Argentina for lemon juice and Cuba for grapefruit juice complete the world offer. The EU has slightly reduced its imports in the recent past, while the US has increased its imported volumes and no significant change has happened in Asia. The price of frozen concentrate orange juice (i.e., the reference product) remains stable between $1,000 and $1,200 per tonne (free on board) in Europe, despite a sharp decline in the Brazilian crop for the season 2003/04, the worst since 1989. This is due to the high level of inventory and the expectation of a record harvest in Florida.

Table 7.4   Concentrate orange juice in Brazil (in thousands of tonnes)

	2000	2001	2002	2003	2004 (estimated)
Beginning inventory	346	263	151	240	92
Production	1,197	978	1,354	1,005	1,260
Exports	1,265	1,078	1,250	1,135	1,195
Consumption	15	15	15	18	18
Ending inventory	263	141	240	92	139

Source: USDA.

A recent and fundamental evolution in juice consumption is the shift in interest to "not-from-concentrate" orange juice. The market share of such juice in the US is today at 52% and should increase at a rate of 3–5% per year. Accordingly, many plants in Florida are transforming their capacity to production of not-from-concentrate orange juice.

Frozen Concentrate Orange Juice (FCOJ) was first traded in an organized way around 1947. Innovations in packaging and transportation permitted the emergence of an international market. In 1966 the NYBOT launched FCOJ Futures contracts, and options on Futures appeared in 1985. Both instruments translated the impact of the weather on the commodity price and, in turn, its risk: production in Florida is very sensitive to frost while orange trees in Brazil languish in a dry climate.

The quality of orange juice is measured by two criteria: "brix" and the acidity (brix represents the fraction of sugar in the juice). The taste of the fruit is determined by the sugar-to-acid ratio.

Table 7.5   Orange juice (in thousands of tonnes) and the main exporting countries

	1998/99	1999/00	2000/01	2001/02	2002/03	2003/04
World production	2,416.9	2,489.3	2,199.9	2,604.2	2,142.7	2,602.3
Brazil	1,360.0	1,197.0	978.0	1,354.0	1,005.0	1,260.0
United States of America	879.0	1,071.7	966.7	992.8	898.3	1,108.9
Spain	45.3	52.0	58.0	58.0	56.0	58.0
Israel	14.5	74.0	52.0	40.0	44.0	35.0
Italy	25.0	40.0	38.0	38.4	45.3	37.0
South Africa	15.8	23.5	20.8	27.4	23.7	23.1
Australia	17.6	23.1	13.0	26.1	13.5	18.1
Mexico	45.3	41.0	40.5	34.0	13.0	20.0
Main exporting countries						
Brazil	1,295.0	1,265.0	1,075.0	1,250.0	1,135.0	1,195.0
United States of America	106.8	103.5	87.2	128.89	73.3	125.0
Spain	56.6	73.7	59.0	55.0	56.0	57.0
Italy	28.0	38.0	43.0	16.1	18.0	20.0
Mexico	45.0	37.8	37.9	0.7	9.9	16.9

Source: USDA.

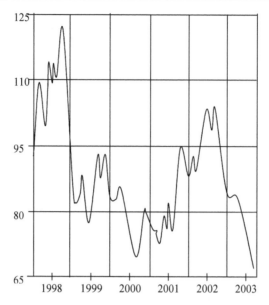

Figure 7.12   Price of orange juice in New York (in cents per pound).

Table 7.6   FCOJ Futures contract specification

Trading unit	15.00 pounds (±3%)
Trading hours	12:30 p.m. to 2:45 p.m.
Traded months	January, March, May, July, September, November
Symbol	OJ
Tick	0.05 cent per pound or $7.5 per trading unit
Last trading day	The 14th business day prior to the month's last business day
Quality	Grade A, with a minimal brix degree of 62.5
Delivery location	Defined locations in Florida, New Jersey, Delaware and California

7.5   LIVESTOCK MARKETS

Unlike grain markets, where almost one-half of the use is exports, livestock markets are much more domestic. Although exports have become more important they only represent 10–15% of total use. The advance of agribusiness is noticeable in the livestock markets. Producers now sell their production directly to packers and this may lead to the demise of livestock Futures markets. For the time being, cattle and hogs are still auctioned on the open market.

Cattle

The USDA releases its "cattle-on-feed" report every month; this shows the supply and demand numbers of cattle on feed, their placement and marketing. Cattle on feed means the total number of cattle in feedlots, placements mean the number of cattle placed in feedlots and marketing is the number of cattle marketed by these feedlots.

Each month, the USDA also releases a "cold storage" report that includes pork, beef and orange juice in cold storage throughout the country. At the end of January, the USDA releases its annual cattle inventory report, which is not only the best indicator of supply in the coming year, but also of increasing or decreasing production in the long term. However, the total number of calves (and their ages) is not enough to describe supply: the price of feed (corn) makes a big difference since animals are fed longer if corn is cheap. In contrast, when the price of corn approaches $4, the market is flooded with large numbers of animals. Over the last 14 years, the cattle price has plunged whenever corn prices reached $3.25 or higher.

The demand for cattle is more elastic than the supply (e.g., when the public at large experiences the feel-good factor a preference for beef is observed).

Studies show that when the number of available cattle is tight, producers tend to try to hold their cattle in order to get a higher price. Likewise, when supply looks like becoming plentiful, they will try to sell their cattle while prices are still good.

To trade feeder cattle, one has to watch the feeder cattle market, the cattle market and the corn market at the same time. As a result of such an amount of necessary information, there is a lack of liquidity in the cattle market.

Hogs

The cycle for hogs is significantly shorter than the cycle for cattle. Hogs are taken to the market when they weight around 230 lb, i.e., at the age of 6 months. The USDA's quarterly *Hogs and Pigs Report* is filled with important details regarding the nation's hog supply. As mentioned earlier, another important report is the monthly "cold storage" report.

Pork bellies

Pork bellies are the flanks and ribs of hogs and are largely used to make bacon. They may be stored up to 1 year when frozen and represent the underlying of the CME contract. The hog Futures contract represents 40,000 lb of carcass and (unsurprisingly) is cash-settled based on an index of prices collected by the USDA. The belly Futures contract represents 50,000 lb of frozen bellies; each point move (one-hundredth of a cent) represents $5 per contract. There is a 300-point limit in the belly market which is known for numerous limit moves. The reason usually given for that high volatility is the high percentage of speculators – as opposed to hedgers – in this market.

7.6   TECHNICAL ANALYSIS IN AGRICULTURAL COMMODITY MARKETS

(A) Some reminders of fundamental analysis

We recap here the main components of the fundamental analysis already mentioned in previous sections of the chapter.

(1)   Supply and demand characteristics

Total supply is defined by the beginning stocks carried over from the previous year's production plus imports:

- Beginning stocks are in general published by the USDA and analogous publications.
- Production is the crop estimate for the current year and is a key number to figure out. Sources of information on this key number, production, are the USDA weekly *Crop Progress* report as well as news collected from information providers worldwide. For instance, those who closely followed the political upheaval which has been brewing in the Ivory Coast for more than a year and which culminated in November 2004 with the massive departure of French producers were certainly able to benefit from the sharp rise in cocoa prices at the end of November 2004. Last but not least, major agrifood and agribusiness companies such as Nestlé, Cargill or Louis Dreyfus Corporation locate their own staff in major producing countries in order to have real-time information on what the fields, trees and future crops look like.
- Imports are relevant at the level of a country or a region. From a worldwide perspective of prices in a given commodity market, they play no role.

(2)   Ending stocks (or carry-over stocks)

These are defined by total supply, i.e., production plus beginning stocks (plus imports) minus demand, including the raw commodity used in the crush process. Obviously, in the case of agricultural commodities, there are no underground reserves as in the case of oil and natural gas. An interesting piece of information, however, is represented by commodities "in transit". There is a weekly report produced in the US by the Commodity Futures Trading Commission (CFTC) which publishes the changes in terms of volume of corn, wheat, soybeans and oats which are in the elevators licensed to deliver on the CBOT. This information is particularly relevant for those willing to trade the first nearby Futures contract.

(3)   Weather

As will be discussed again in Chapter 13, weather is a key component of fundamental analysis of agricultural commodity markets. Given the location in both hemispheres of major producing countries of soybean, corn, coffee, etc., each calendar quarter represents either a planting season (winter in the US), a crop development season (summer in the southern hemisphere for Brazilian coffee) or a harvest season. Besides the major TV and radio channels, other sources of information are available such as the weekly USDA *Weather Bulletin* or private companies' publications.

  To conclude this section, we observe that, just like in equity markets, large volumes in commodity markets will move prices and volatility (see Geman and Ané, 1996). In practice, these large volumes go together with news arrival on one of the quantities discussed above and constitute an important signal both for fundamental and technical analysts.

(B) Technical analysis

In agricultural commodity markets, the "locals" in the pits together with the major agrifood companies and crush spread traders represent the major players; banks and other financial institutions are essentially not present, while they do intervene in metals and energy markets. Moreover, the trading sessions are short, lasting for a few hours (from 10 : 30 a.m. to 2 : 10 p.m. New York time) and it is quite risky to keep open positions from one day to another. These open positions are mostly held by hedgers. For the other market participants, technical analysis is a particularly popular tool. Without trying to be exhaustive on this subject to which dozens of books are dedicated, we provide below some minimal elements of this approach. The technical approach to investment in commodity markets relies on the premise that prices move in trends which are determined by the changing attitudes of investors toward a number of factors, including the ones defining a fundamental approach to the markets as listed above. According to Perfetti (1992), "technical analysis is the ability to identify trend changes at an early stage and to maintain an investment position until the weight of the evidence indicates that the trend has reversed." It is important to observe that technical analysis does not try to forecast trends in the economy nor to assess the attitudes of investors toward those changes. It aims to identify turning points in the market's assessment.

Charts

The bar chart is the first basic tool of the technical analyst. It consists in representing every day with a bar (vertical line) where the top represents the day's high and the base the day's low. Most professionals subscribe to a service which updates the charts in real time. In any given price chart, analysts will try to identify patterns. The first goal is to determine the trend of the market, uptrend or downtrend, as well as changes in the trend.

Trend-determining techniques

The trendline is the most basic and the most popular of all chart tools. It can be either an uptrendline or a downtrendline. In an uptrend (respectively, downtrend) the market tends to show higher lows and higher highs. In a rising (or bull) market, the trendline is obtained by drawing a straight line between higher lows; the more points connected, the more conclusive the trend is. When an uptrendline is broken, this is viewed as a negative signal and long positions should be liquidated. But it may be that the market returns to the preceding trend, and a new trendline should be drawn using the new significant high.

Channels

In the "best" trends, prices trade within a channel. A channel is identified by constructing a parallel line to the major trendline:

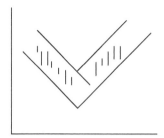

A classical view in technical analysis is that when a market trades above the upper channel line in an uptrend, there are good chances that the market is entering an accelerated phase – usually because of some news arrival about supply or demand.

Support and resistance

"Support" and "resistance" represent two of the most important words in technical trading. Support is an area where buying interest was observed in the past, hence is expected to develop again. Resistance is the symmetric notion: it represents a level market prices have difficulties to go beyond, hence the name. Support and resistance levels can be drawn graphically by using a horizontal line on the bar chart connecting the low points in the case of support and the top points in the case of resistance.

Figure 7.13 shows the evolution of wheat prices during the period 29 November to 6 December 2004. Looking at the price chart on 6 December, the technical analyst will draw a support line at 300 and a resistance line at 304. He recognizes a buying signal when the market breaks the 304 resistance level.

Flags

As indicated by the name, a flag indicates a market trend where the price trajectory is included in a slanted rectangle, upward or downward sloping, and signals a pause after a significant move. When the flag is passed, prices return (in principle) to the same drift as the one prevailing before the flag, and in bigger volumes – since market participants do not in general like trendless markets:

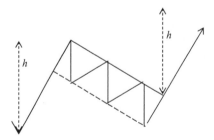

Figure 7.14 exhibits a bearish flag because of its inverted shape. The market entered the flag in a downward trend; the lower side of the flag represents a support line. When it is

Figure 7.13   Intraday wheat prices from 29 November to 6 December 2004.

Figure 7.14   Corn prices over the period October 2003 to December 2004.

Figure 7.15 Intraday soybean prices from 30 November to 3 December 2004.

broken in September 2004, the technical analyst recognizes a selling signal. Everyone, including non-technical analysts, can visualize on this graph the extreme volatility of agricultural commodity markets!

Elliott waves and Fibonacci series

Ralph Elliott published the results related to his famous waves in 1939. His "theory" relies on the observation that natural cycles have been observed since the beginning of the universe, in the planets' trajectories, in the immutable alternation of nights and days. These cyclical evolutions have to be transmitted to financial markets since prices have to reflect the current psychology of market players.

Fibonacci sequence

This is named after the mathematician Leonardo Fibonacci, who lived in the 13th century and introduced the sequence:

$$1, 2, 3(1+2), 5(2+3), 8(3+5), 13, 21, 34, 55, \ldots$$

The ratio between two consecutive numbers is equal to 0.618 and 1.618, depending on which order it is computed; moreover $1.618 = \dfrac{1+\sqrt{5}}{2}$ is called the gold number.

The relation between Elliott's considerations on the repetition of natural cycles and Fibonacci's sequence is based on the "observation" that many natural phenomena occur according to this proportion: for instance, out of the 89 petals in a sunflower, 55 are oriented in the direction of the wind, 34 in the opposite direction; both 34 and 55 belong to Fibonacci's sequence! Assuming that the same rules apply to financial markets, the same ratios are used to build the *retracements* lines.

Figure 7.15 depicts the intraday evolution of soybean prices over the period 30 November to 3 December 2004. On 3 December at $12:00$ a.m., the technical analyst draws the extreme lines of support and resistance at 520 and 538.5, as well as the middle line 529.3. Moreover, he draws two other lines related to the Fibonacci ratios: the Fibonacci ratio 0.618 multiplied by 18.5 and leading to the horizontal line at the level $520 + 11.3 = 531.4$; and $(1 - 0.618) \times 18.5$ leading to the level $520 + 7 = 527$. When this 527 line is reached, the technical analyst may decide to get out and take his profits or wait until the market reaches the middle line 529.2. In all cases, consolidation will occur at one of the three levels 527, 529.2 or 531.4 (according to Fibonacci ...).

8

The Structure of Metal Markets and Metal Prices

by Chris Harris

8.1 INTRODUCTION

In this chapter we characterize the movement of metal prices using the language and techniques of the fixed income and equity markets. We will do this by viewing the relevant physical characteristics of metals, their production and consumption, and the mechanics of the traded metal markets. We will then view some generic forward price structures that are characteristic of metals.

Traded markets can be characterized by the nearby price, the forward price and the slope of the price curve, and, generally, characterization of two of these allows us to construct the third. In this chapter we will see that for metals each of these elements has a distinct economic life, and that "whole curve" price movements are strongly influenced by the tension between them. We will also see that the changes in relative forces across time leads to a heterogeneity in the dynamics of metal price movements.

8.2 ABOUT METALS

Relevant physical characteristics

Metals have been used and exchanged for thousands of years. The physical characteristics of primary[1] elemental[2] metals make them uniquely suitable as candidates for currency.

Metal production

The metal prices that we will be considering are the prices of the standard ingots[3] of nearly pure metal that are traded in the markets. These are approximately halfway through the life cycle. Metal also exists as a semi-liquid commodity at other parts of the cycle, including underground, as concentrate, in non-reduced form such as oxide, in semi-fabricated form and as alloy. In addition, some *processes* have become

---

[1] "Primary" means produced directly from natural resources, rather than recycled.
[2] "Elemental" means composed of a single element from the periodic table, rather than being an alloy of elements.
[3] "Commodity metal" is cast or grown electrolytically as cathode, and occasionally forged. There are several forms and the term "ingot" is generally used here.

Table 8.1   Relevant characteristics of primary elemental metals and their importance in relation to market structures and prices

Characteristic	Importance
Divisible	Tradable in price per mass unit at all scales and, thereby, communicable as a measure of exchange.
Extracted	Stable forward price driven by the economics of production from an underground natural resource base.
Consumed	Stable fundamental economics and with potential to be a stable "numéraire" asset.
Dense	Leading to cheap storage, which limits the "contango" slope of forward price curve, and to cheap movement which reduces the geographical differentials of prices.
Durable	Stock degrades only little, thereby enabling the "cheapest to deliver" mechanism that promotes price uniformity and depth at the exchanges.
Elemental	Standardized for trading. Suitable for composition basis reference in the physical market. Reduced cost for assay/audit.
Historic	Fundamental use and exchange values are relatively slow-moving, thereby enabling equilibrium economics to be applied.

commoditized, such as smelting (reduction), rolling (semi-fabrication), scrap collection, segregation, mixing and remelting.

Figure 8.1 is a generalization of the metal life cycle, focusing on the degree to which the physical forms of metal, and the processes themselves, are commoditized.

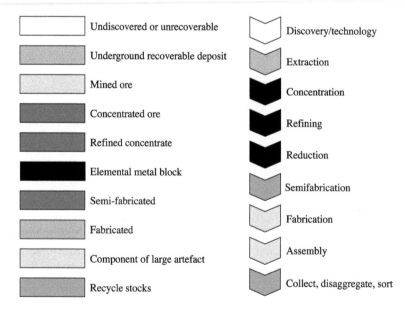

Undiscovered or unrecoverable   Discovery/technology

Underground recoverable deposit   Extraction

Mined ore   Concentration

Concentrated ore   Refining

Refined concentrate   Reduction

Elemental metal block   Semifabrication

Semi-fabricated   Fabrication

Fabricated   Assembly

Component of large artefact   Collect, disaggregate, sort

Recycle stocks

Figure 8.1   Generalization of the metal life cycle. The shading of the box/arrow represents a generalization of the degree to which the form/process is commoditized.

The movement of metal prices is greatly dependent on the balance of power between the production tiers, and the degree of integration between them. There are many contributing factors, but the key ones are:

- *Access to downstream customers*, thereby securing a route to a non-commoditized higher margin market.
- *Ability to store product*. Withheld stock, if durable, can eventually be sold or used, whereas unused capacity and non-durable stock is wasted for ever.
- *Inherent retention of terminal market price risk*. A sector with low risks has low entry barriers and will eventually become a sector with low margins, as new entrants arrive.
- *Negotiating strength*. This can maintain higher profits in one part of the life cycle for long periods – it depends on financial strength and the ability to replace inputs and outputs and counterparties with alternatives.

Metal consumption

Commodities such as gas and coffee trade in a very similar physical form downstream at retail level and upstream at wholesale level. The same is essentially true of financial assets such as cash, bonds and equities. Industrial metals are however generally *assembled* when finally sold in the retail market so that they are only a part of a complex commodity such as a car, white good or house. The raw material metal cost has a relatively minor influence on the short-term product price and the result is that short-term metal demand is highly inelastic. In the medium term, *product* demand is still fairly inelastic, and *metal* demand elasticity arises only where metal and other materials are substitutable in the short term for making particular products, or where metal-based products are substitutable in the short term for products made from other materials.

Metal production rates are relatively inflexible, since reduction in production rate wastes invested capacity and committed non-storable resources such as labour. Hence, stored metal plays an active role in swing supply and demand – surplus metal arriving on the market is stored, and extra demand leaving the market to be consumed is withdrawn from stock.

8.3 OVERVIEW OF METAL MARKETS AND THEIR OPERATION

Most industrial metals and major alloys have some form of reference price and a price basis, but for an understanding of metal prices, in terms of the stochastic processes that are used for financial assets, we look to the actively traded industrial and precious metals. These are gold, silver, platinum, palladium, copper, tin, lead, zinc, nickel, and aluminum.

Metal exchanges

Exchanges act to concentrate liquidity. Most exchanges work on a number of principles the most important of which for our purposes here are summarized below:

1. *Storage* allows delivery to and from the exchange and, thereby, connects the exchange index price to the price of physical metal.
2. *Standardization* defines the range of allowable delivery specifications and makes "good delivery"-grade relevant to physical participants.
3. *Seller's choice* (akin to "cheapest to deliver") allows sellers to deliver anything to the exchange within specification when the prompt[4] period arrives. This attracts stock to the exchange, adds to liquidity and creates a definable price relationship for the range of specifications of stocked material, which are all classed as good delivery.
4. The *clearing system* matches bilateral purchases and sales so that all transactions are cleared through the clearing house, and all forward purchases that run to delivery are allocated bearer warrants through a process such as randomization of warrants delivered to the exchange on the previous day. The clearing system facilitates the concentration of liquidity in the market and uses credit in a very efficient manner.
5. "Integrity" is maintained by having a licensing system for registered warehouses/ vaults, conforming brands and trading counterparties. This greatly reduces performance risk on traded contracts.

In general, the four key delivery specifications for metals are date, location, composition and shape. Since sellers of "good delivery"[5] material can always realize the clearing price by delivery to the exchange, then buyers of specific material must commonly pay a physical premium that reflects the difference in value relative to the "average" material that is delivered to buyers through the clearing system. This premium is generally less than 1% of the commodity price, but occasionally trades as high as 10% of it.

The delivery and storage system supports the functioning of the exchanges. The amount, location and specification of metal at exchange-listed locations are a key source of information for market participants, and storage provides the buffer for the mismatch between production and consumption volumes. In our examination of forward curve mechanics and dynamics in Section 8.5 we will see the role of storage, and in doing so we must recognize that storage exists not only at exchange-listed warehouses, but at other points in the supply chain. There are five principal inventory categories:

1. Good delivery material in listed warehouses.
2. Good delivery material in producer location, consumer location, in transit, in non-listed warehouses, in listed warehouses but not "on warrant" (delivered through a sale on the exchange).
3. Material in the same life cycle position as good delivery but not good delivery (off-grade material, premium material, good delivery specification but not listed, or of similar value to good delivery but not conforming to good delivery specification).

---

[4] The prompt date is the contract date on which purchased and sold material must be delivered. On the Futures exchanges the seller has the choice of delivery date within the contract period.
[5] Material that has its brand registered on the exchange and which conforms to the exchange specification.

4. Material upstream in the life cycle (most of which can become good delivery).
5. Material downstream in the life cycle (the destination of most good delivery material).

We will see later that the physical and geographical closeness of physical material to commodity (i.e., good delivery in a listed warehouse) has an important effect on metal pricing.

Industrial metals on the London Metal Exchange

The London Metal Exchange (LME) has a series of open outcry sessions called "rings" for each metal one by one, and all-metal sessions called "kerbs". Each individual delivery day is discretely tradable, and liquidity concentrates around the cash, 3-month and third-Wednesday-of-the-month contracts. Brands, warehouses and counterparties are licensed by the exchange and/or associated clearing house.

The industrial metals traded are aluminum, copper, zinc, lead, nickel and tin. While the six main contracts are for primary metal, the exchange listed an aluminum alloy contract in 1992. This contract later divided into two different specifications and the exchange has several times considered listing a stainless steel contract. There is in addition an index "LMEX", and a current intention to launch contracts in polypropylene and linear low-density polyethylene.

The non-elemental[6] contracts are important in the study of metal prices because they are harder to standardize. Aluminum alloy is expensive to store due to slight surface deterioration,[7] which leads to relative strong gradation in warrant prices (see Figure 8.9). Steel adds the additional specification of thermomechanical treatment which affects mechanical properties and corrosion resistance, and this adds further interest to basis trading.

In both industrial and precious metals, spreads[8] are actively traded, particularly between the most active dates such as the cash, 3-month and third-Wednesday-of-the-month contracts. European and average rate options are also actively traded.

The denominating currency is US dollars, as it is for the London bullion market.

Precious metals on the London bullion market

Gold has been held historically as an international currency, independent of individual countries and their fiscal and monetary policies. At various times in history, domestic currencies have been backed by gold (e.g., in the gold standard) or pegged to gold (e.g., in Special Drawing Rights).[9] Countries have held gold so that they can engage in international exchange, to pay for goods or currency. To a large extent, countries hold gold now because the gold is already there and, indeed, there has been some

---

[6] Note that the less reactive metals such as copper and the industrial metals are relatively easy to purify and, hence, there is little distinction between primary and secondary sourcing. Aluminum is a reactive metal that is hard to purify and, hence, aluminum alloy is made mainly from secondary sources, rather than "waste" pure metal on alloying.

[7] While the deterioration is superficial, it adds cost to the industrial consumer in the form of surface cleaning or heating to remove trapped moisture.

[8] "Spreads" are contracts involving simultaneous purchase for one delivery date and sale for a different delivery date.

[9] The unit of account of the International Monetary Fund used to be denominated in gold, but now a currency basket is used for indexation.

reduction of gold holdings. History suggests that, in all nations and all events, gold will always be valid as a specie[10] currency of intrinsic value, which can operate effectively at all levels from individuals to nations. This is supported by the features of metals, in general (which gold exemplifies), that were illustrated in Table 8.1.

The holdings of gold ingot have a high influence on market behavior. On the one hand, gold holders wish to defray the opportunity cost of carry by lending the gold in a manner that does not excessively compromise the reason for holding gold in the first place. On the other hand, gold is a convenient currency to borrow in for those who have the ability to repay in gold.

"Good delivery loco London gold" in the London bullion market means cast bars of 400 Troy[11] ounces, at 99.5% purity from listed refineries and stored in listed vaults. The London Bullion Market Association (LBMA) oversees the market.

Gold is generally traded in "unallocated" form in which a buyer of gold only has an account balance rather than a bearer warrant for a numbered bar.

The key markets in the London bullion market are:

1. *Spot market* This also has a daily clearing or "fix" price found by balancing purchases and sales ordered through the fixing members.
2. *Forward "gofo" rate market.* The gofo transaction is a simultaneous spot[12] sale/ purchase and forward purchase/sale. The "gold forward" or "gofo" rate is expressed as an annualized percentage. For example, if the spot price is \$400/oz and the 3-month gofo rate is 4%, then the implied 3-month forward price is \$404/oz.
3. *Lease rate.* A lease is a short-term loan denominated in gold. The rate is expressed as an annualized interest rate for gold. For example, if the 3-month lease rate is 2%, then 1 oz of gold could be exchanged for 1.005 oz of gold for delivery in 3 months' time. The lease rate can be calculated approximately using the gold forward market and the dollar interest-rate market, but, since leasing involves borrowing, the lease rate is sensitive to bilateral credit.

The option markets are active for gold and silver, and structured and complex derivatives continue to increase in activity. Gold, in particular, is eminently suitable for option transactions because mines have natural long "real option" positions, and the low borrowing cost of gold means that production delays do not incur great risk to the gold option seller.

The rules for silver are essentially the same as for gold. Speculative and investment interest in silver tends to be much more sporadic than in gold.

Other markets

There are many other metal markets for industrial and precious metals, such as the New York Mercantile Exchange (NYMEX), and many local gold markets. They differ

---

[10] "Specie" means money with some physical value, as opposed to notes, which are money of account.
[11] There are 32.15 Troy ounces in 1 kg. Gold is traded in fine Troy ounces (ounces of actual gold in the ingot), whereas in silver the weight of the ingot at designated purity is used as contract weight.
[12] Forward/forward rates also trade, which are settled financially against the Dollar LIBOR and GOFO indexes.

in "good delivery" specification, geographical reach, denominating currency and delivery rules. There is some arbitrage activity between markets (particularly, NYMEX, LME and LBMA).

There are some important rule differences:

- Settlement. Futures contracts create a cash settlement if the purchases and sales match, whereas forward contracts, such as those on the LME, will settle on the delivery date.
- Settlement date. Futures contracts have monthly settlement, and the delivery date within the month is "seller's choice".
- Credit. Futures contracts are with the exchange. LME contracts are initially bilateral until they "match' with the clearing house, almost always on the same day.
- Price basis. Not all contracts can be settled by physical delivery and must be financially settled against an index, which is determined by polling participants.

Platinum and palladium commonly trade in association with gold and silver. Platinum is an "inherently" more valuable metal than gold both in jewellery and industrial use, but does not have the "specie" status that gold does, and hence would be less valuable at the very times when the use of gold as principal/sole currency would be invoked. The dynamics of platinum prices are therefore quite different to those of gold.

8.4 CHARACTERIZING GENERAL PRICE MOVEMENTS

It is our aim in this chapter both to capture the modeling tools from other markets to help us better model metal prices and, by interpreting metal prices in a standard framework, to see what light metal prices can shed on other markets. For our present purposes there are three categories of instrument: namely, assets with no yield (convenience or other) across a holding period, assets with a yield and non-assets. So, for example, between coupon payments a bond is an asset with no yield, across the coupon payments a bond is an asset with a yield and the price drivers of bonds such as prior probabilities of default and interest rates are non-assets.

We wish to model the "whole curve" movement of metal prices, and will find it useful to regard the curve in terms of three factors, the prompt/nearby price, the forward price and the price slope. Clearly, they are related, and it is the priority of construction that will guide us. There are three mechanisms by which the curves can be constructed:

1. Spot price plus forward slope implies forward price.
2. Forward price minus spot price implies forward slope.
3. Forward price minus forward slope implies spot price.

We will see that metal prices can follow any of the three mechanisms in different circumstances and also at the same time in different parts of the forward curve. If we can understand when to use which mechanism we will be able to use the stochastic process tools that we use in other markets such as the fixed income markets.

Table 8.2   Initial assumptions for commodity assets

	Assumption
Credit	Zero credit risk for all participants
Physical storage	Direct and associated costs zero
Deliveries	All good delivery identical with no location differential
Uncertainties	Everything certain (prices, supply breaks, demand, etc.)
Freight and other transport	Free and immediate
Use value convenience	Zero
Inflation rates	Zero
Cost of risk	Zero
Interest rates	Flat and constant

To place metals in context we will briefly characterize the other key markets. To do this, we must first establish the arbitrage relationships for price slopes, where relevant.

Let us first make a set of assumptions that we will refer to throughout this chapter. While these assumptions are more true for metals than other commodities, deviations from the assumptions have important effects on metal forward price slopes.

The forward slope–arbitrage relationship for assets during periods in which they deliver no yield was described in detail in Chapter 2. The same relationship must hold for metals if they deliver no yield (convenience or other), and in addition the assumptions listed in Table 8.2 hold good. We can construct the relationship simply by considering the choices of metal consumers, producers and arbitragers, and the choices that they have with respect to holding physically and trading forward. Hotelling's rule for the equilibrium price growth rate of physical holdings in natural resources essentially takes this approach, makes the same assumptions and arrives at the same curve. One of the key challenges for metals is identifying the various forms of yield so that the pricing of the yield-free metal and of the yield can be separated.

8.5   CHARACTERIZING METAL PRICE MOVEMENTS

We will examine metal prices in terms of the interplay of the nearby price, long-term price and forward slope. First, we examine metals in the same manner as for the other asset classes and then consider some specific behavioral characteristics.

Spot prices

Prompt commodity prices are generally amenable to supply/demand analysis. However, there are two reasons that, on any given day, it is hard to get a quantitative answer using this method.

First, only a small percentage of physical throughput remains uncontracted when the prompt date arrives. While this does represent the most elastic (and hence marginal) production and demand, the volume of material that is traded as a conduit of physical supply to physical demand is small compared with the volume traded as redistribution of market positions. The market positions act as supply and demand with prices that

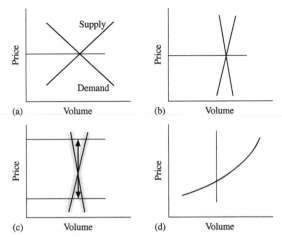

Figure 8.2 Supply and demand relationships: (a) normal linear elastic supply and demand; (b) short-term inelastic; (c) the potential effect of stocking actions; (d) short-term equilibrium with inelastic demand, use of stock to lend and borrow against future production and convex short-term production curve.

are determined more by behaviour[13] than by fundamentals. Therefore while average spot prices are generally representative of economic fundamentals, on any one day, they can differ substantially from the fundamental price.

Second, while stock can act as either a buffer for receiving or releasing material, market behaviors such as withholding stock can lead to "technical tightness". For example, a producer may increase supply by selling material that it holds in stock or reduce supply by stock building instead of selling. Similarly, a consumer can increase demand by stock building or reduce it by drawing from owned stock. The net result is that voluntary stock actions can cause strong movements in supply and demand curves. The effect of stock action on a short-term (and therefore inelastic) market is shown in Figures 8.2b and c. The shaded areas in Figure 8.2c show how stocking actions by producers and consumers can increase or decrease effective supply and demand, and result in a wide potential range of clearing prices. In Figure 8.2d, market behavior with inventory is treated as a production activity.

Long-term price

At any one time there is, for any metal with stable production economics, a forward price that is, broadly[14] speaking, equal to the fully loaded cost of production for the marginal producer, including the cost of risk premiums at which capital[15] is attracted to new production. The fully loaded cost of production includes the capital cost of the land, technology and equipment. Even in the long term, price elasticity of demand is

---

[13] For example, for three participants with long positions, one may sell at the market close whatever its level, another may sell only into a price fall on a "stop loss" basis and another may buy more material after price falls.
[14] The precise definition of each term is important in practice. For example, the marginal producer could be a producer who is already producing, one who has a business plan, one who is considering the asset or one yet to arrive.
[15] This includes market cost of commodity price risk if unhedged, or if hedged the market price includes the market cost of commodity price risk. The risk cost should not be double-counted.

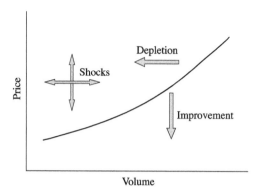

Figure 8.3   Effects on the long-term supply stack.

assumed to be low. The stability of long-term economics means that instantaneous volatility of long-term contracts is usually low. This is the Samuelson effect mentioned in Chapter 2.

The changes in long-term prices arise from visible factors such as:

1. Currency effects. This is the main source of the long-term volatility of metal prices. Since metal prices are denominated in currency, then the volatility of the currency value will drive metal price volatility even if the cost and "value" of the metal is constant when expressed in a fundamental numéraire asset.
2. Variation in supply and demand for risk capital. Risk capital is largely provided from established routes such as debt and equity, and is highly dependent on the cash earnings of the borrower. This causes a relationship[16] between long- and short-term prices.
3. Gradual changes in long-term economics. These are brought about by the gradual decrease in production costs, due mainly to technology enhancements, the gradual finding of new exploitable resources, due to more searching and improved exploration techniques, and the gradual exhaustion of known resources.
4. Shocks. Unexpected changes in production technique (such as electrochemical methods for aluminum and titanium, and bacterial heap leach for gold), massive finds, changes in exploration techniques, changing access and supply arising from geopolitics, cartel instability, environmental regulation with respect to the production process, the product itself or the consumer.
5. Gradual changes in consumption trends, due in part to price elasticity of demand.

Denomination of the price has a significant effect on volatility, since the denominating currency has volatility in its own right when expressed in terms of some other numéraire asset, and the relationship between numerator asset and denominator asset takes the form of correlation which then affects the volatility of the price.

For example, medium-term copper prices denominated in US dollars have low volatility, due to the high proportion of dollar-denominated factor costs, and the volatility of copper denominated in euros is driven by the volatility of the dollar/euro rate.

---

[16] High spot prices cause high cash earnings, which reduce risk capital costs, which increases investment in production, which causes long-term prices to fall.

Aluminum itself acts as a currency for the purchase of alumina, and power for the smelters. Long-term aluminium/alumina is non-volatile due to the commonality of factor costs, and dependence on demand for aluminium. Long-term aluminum/power is more volatile if the power producer is not dependent on the smelter to consume the power production. These relationships do not affect short-term prices. In fact, aluminium/alumina can have high volatility as smelter stoppages cause a glut of (poorly storable) alumina and a shortage of aluminum and, hence, negative correlation of prices.

In the long term, the dollar itself is a source of volatility, as fiscal and monetary policy can cause its absolute value in terms of fundamental numéraire assets (such as goods baskets, or units of labour) to change by inflation. Aluminum is in fact a good candidate for a numéraire asset.

Conventions for pricing commodities in particular currencies tend to make prices more sticky in those currencies, because the supply chain underneath the cost structure also tends towards the same currency. However, we should be careful to remember that stickiness is quite distinct from low long-term volatility. Stickiness is associated with a lag on movement towards fundamentals and discrete rather than continuous movements. Low long-term volatility is associated with slow-moving fundamentals. Stickiness affects short-term prices, and commonality of factor costs and of demand dependence affect long-term prices.

Controlled prices tend to have higher long-term volatilities, since fundamental equilibrium is never really established, and short-term decisions can have instant effects on long-term prices. Short-term prices are sticky, but collapse of cartels, "squeezes" and other controlled prices tends to be rapid and, hence, the most extreme movements are caused by these collapses. Well-known price control examples from the past include the gold standard, the tin buffer stock, and the "corner" of the silver market by Bunker Hunt. Price control, whether officially or unofficially, is becoming rarer and smaller in scale. However, while price control and the use of market power tends not greatly to affect annual average prices, it remains an important force in the dynamics of forward price curves.

Forward slope

We saw in Section 8.2 that, in the absence of convenience yield, the slope of asset price curves is equal to the FRA slope and, therefore, that other slopes may be partly explained in terms of convenience yield. It was noted in Section 2.2 that convenience yield arises for a variety of reasons, and it is the purpose of this section to examine these in more detail for metals, in order to understand the idiosyncrasies of metal price movement. We will also see that different segments of the metal forward curve can have distinct economics, and that the transition can be sharp.

Convenience yield and repo rate

For consistency of terminology, we will use the term "repo"[17] for the actual forward curve slope differential relative to the FRA or term interest rate, and the

---

[17] "Repo", short for "repossession" is a common transaction in the bond market, in which a prompt position in a bond is rolled forward by a simultaneous prompt purchase/sale and a forward sale/purchase. The transaction is effectively a securitized loan and the repo rate is the difference between the transaction rate and that dictated by forward arbitrage.

term "convenience yield" for the elements that contribute to the repo rate. In using this term, we should be mindful that neither repo nor convenience yield are terms in common use in the metal markets.

In order to quantify convenience yield and understand how it changes, we will divide metal into two roles, use value and exchange value. Use value is the value derived by the holder of metal in his private or industrial activities, Exchange value is the value derived by the holder of metal in gaining cash from market actions.[18]

Use value convenience yield – equilibrium

RECYCLE PERCENTAGE AND LIFE CYCLE

Suppose that the good that we make from the metal has a recycle rate of $R\%$ and a lifetime of L. When purchasing the good, we may consider that we are borrowing $R\%$ of the metal for period L and consuming $(1 - R\%)$ of the metal over period L. The disposal cost of the metal should also be relevant, and acts as an effective uplift to the prompt price of consumed metal. In practice, the practical option of domestic users to dump illegally, and the response of local councils in providing recycling facilities means that there is commonly a zero floor price for disposal of the assembled good.

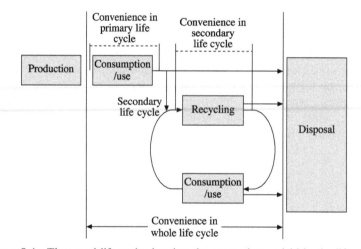

Figure 8.4   The metal life cycle showing the convenience yield in the life cycle.

CONSUMER USE VALUE

Consumption value is defined here as the value derived by the individual consumer from an activity that is facilitated by the metal. In the case of precious metals this also includes the value derived to the holder that is specifically associated with the metal itself[19] rather than the function that it performs. Jewelry is an example of this. The consumer use value of the fully commoditized form is zero in almost all instances and,

---

[18] The recognition of, and action responding to, exchange value as distinct from the use value of commodity contracts leads to the "ruthless" execution of terms specified in such contracts.
[19] This is closely associated with existence value – the value derived by "knowing that it is there".

hence, we must consider the fabricated form. To then consider the impact of convenience yield on commoditized form we need to consider the friction cost to convert
from one form to another. Since metals are not consumed instantaneously, we are
concerned with the net cost paid over the consumption period.

PRODUCER USE VALUE

Producer use value is defined here as the value derived by the participant who uses the
metal to gain revenue. The economics are essentially similar to the economics of
consumption, except that we are able to deal not with subjective evaluation of utility
but with hard facts, such as supply break probabilities, cost of production capacity and
acceleration, and the price curves of metal and metal-containing products in different
stages of the production cycle.

DELAYED CONSUMPTION AND PRODUCTION

Delayed consumption is equivalent to borrowing from the consumer. It is in fact very
difficult to construct an economic argument to value this. This problem can be illustrated by the use of utility curves to value the delay. A delay means less consumption
and less utility now, and more consumption and more utility later. The loss of utility
from a delay in consumption is shown in Figure 8.5, and we note that the same cost is
incurred by the "round trip" regardless of duration and, hence, we cannot construct an
interest rate. In practice, the utility curve in one period is affected by the history of
consumption and this path-dependence has a temporal structure. To use a simple
example, a missed lunch can be compensated by a large dinner, but not by an extra
lunch the next day. However, a delay in a visit to the cinema may incur little loss in
utility as the timing of the consumption experience may be less critical.

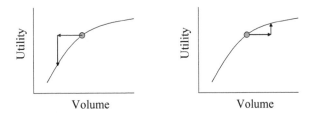

Figure 8.5 Net utility loss from delaying consumption by reducing in one period and increasing
by the same amount in the next period, assuming no dependence of utility on consumption
history.

So, in metal terms, while we could consider a steep backwardation as a good time to
delay consumption, we must instead regard backwardation as an expression of the
unwillingness to delay. The option to adjust throughput is important to producers.
In a backwardated market, the producer can destock at different parts of the production cycle (with corresponding lead times to delivery) and lend into the backwardation.
This requires an increase in throughput rate and incurs an increased risk in the financial
cost of supply breaks (risk can be reduced, at a cost, by operational measures). Unlike

the cost of delay to end-consumers, which is subjective, the expected net cost of accelerating production and destocking can be calculated and, therefore, the supply cost can be quantified.

FRICTION AND TRANSFORMATION

If commodity can be transformed into usable metal instantly, costlessly and in one place, then this is not an issue. In practice, the fact that use value is derived from metal in non-ingot form and exchange value is derived from metal in ingot form means that friction between the two is important.

Let us now suppose that we can store the metal in a form in which it can have use value without consumption. For example, silver in the form of electrical wire.[20] Suppose that we borrow silver ingots and promise to return the same atoms of silver as ingots at some defined date in the future. We pay a tolling fee to a wire-drawing firm now to make the wire, and to a refining firm later to convert the wire back to ingots.

We truly have borrowed the silver, as we have returned the same atoms, and if our drawing and refining fees are zero, then our use value convenience yield paid by the wire user and exchange value convenience yield received by the ingot holder will be easy to define. The need to return the same atoms of silver is not critical to the holder. Hence, a commodity loan is directly equivalent to a spot purchase, a forward sale and a loan of cash.

We physically transform the silver twice and, hence, the use value of silver wire at equilibrium is higher than silver ingot to a wire buyer (mn), but lower than silver ingot to an ingot investor (op). So, wire and other physically useful forms of pure metal have different values relative to ingots to different people. The "basis" differential is bounded by the conversion price from one to another. If silver wire were a deliverable form of the commodity, as copper wire rod used to be, then it would not have a discounted exchange value.

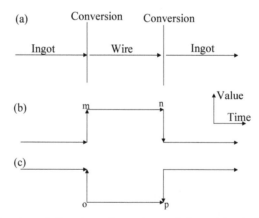

Figure 8.6 (a) The drawing of silver ingot into wire, and the melting/refining to ingot after use; (b) the value of the silver to the wire user; (c) the value of the silver to the refinery.

---

[20] A good example of the dichotomy between use value and exchange value is found in silver. During the Second World War, an aide of Brigadier General Groves approached the US Treasury to borrow thousands of ton of silver for wiring in nuclear power stations. The rejoinder was "In the Treasury, we do not speak of tons of silver. Our unit is the Troy ounce."

The lower the friction cost from ingot to artefact and back, the closer the relationship between the convenience yield on the artefact and the price curve for the commodity.

UNCERTAINTY

Commodity metal, as shown in Figure 8.1 is approximately halfway through the metal life cycle. There is serial dependence on all activities along the critical path of the flow of metal. If the life cycle runs with no stock, then a disruption in any part of the life cycle causes both wasted capacity for each and every part of the life cycle to the consumer and beyond (to recycling), and consumer costs in the form of the cost of delayed consumption. This is very expensive. However, it can be alleviated by holding stock between each and every stage of the life cycle by providing a buffer for supply breaks.

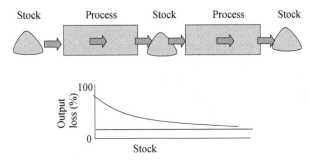

Figure 8.7   The use of stock to reduce the impact of production breaks.

Stock levels can be managed on a probabilistic basis. Apart from the opportunist value of exchange value variation, then optimum levels can be calculated by the cost of holding the stock, on the one side, and the probability-weighted cost of supply breaks, on the other. The cost of a supply break is calculated in the form of liquidated damages. In practice, in many industries, such as copper cathode[21] production, the optimum stock levels between each production level are carefully managed.

PRICING

Equation (2.4) and Hotelling's rule tell us that, in the absence of convenience yield and storage costs, the forward price of metal rises at the same rate as the money market account and that, if there is a convenience yield, this causes the forward prices to rise at a lower rate. However, zero general inflation and inflating[22] commodity prices are economically not compatible from a use value perspective. The consumer[23] pays an ever higher amount for loan and consumption of material. The situation is partly

---

[21] Cathode is the "good delivery" form that is produced as the last stage of copper refining from concentrate and/or scrap.
[22] There is in fact little evidence for commodity inflation, let alone at the growth rate of a money market account as indicated by Hotelling's rule (Halvorse and Smith, 1991; Slade, 1982).
[23] The general incompatibility results from implicit simultaneous use of two numéraire assets, one being the goods basket for use value and one being the rolled-up money market account for exchange value. This in turn makes implicit assumptions about intertemporal relationships for price elasticity of demand and the conversion cost and time from one form of metal to another.

resolved by decreasing the price of money, which causes us to lower the commodity price curve. At a particular inflation rate, the "own rate" of return, in which the repo rate is paid in commodity rather than currency, is constant.

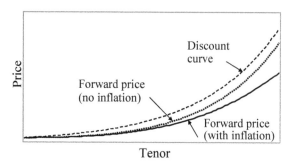

Figure 8.8   Consumer equilibrium price term structure for metals with 100% recycling.

The gold forward price structure commonly rises above the general inflation curve for short and medium tenors, but for long tenors the market is structurally long due to greater hedge requirements for mines than for consumers, and the absolute cost of risk for holding a long forward position or a short forward position increases with holding period. Hence, forward prices do not follow an upward curvature.

The forward price curve with inflation shown in Figure 8.8 is a sustainable equilibrium curve. Curves with steeper upward (contango) slopes, or with downward (backwardation) slopes, are non-equilibrium slopes and, thereby, indicative of volatility. Indeed, the slope, curvature and change of curvature of the curve give us strong clues about volatility and volatility term structure. For modeling here, we will assume that the metal is continuing "trying" to revert to an equilibrium curve such as that shown above, but that it is continually assaulted by exogenous forces. The curve dynamics in contango are different from those for backwardation, because the arbitrage limit acts as a boundary condition.

EXCHANGE VALUE CONVENIENCE YIELD

If there is no physical differentiation between metal contracts, there is no reason to hold physical metal in preference to a paper contract that will deliver physical metal when required. In practice, there is physical differentiation, which causes there to be an exchange value convenience yield for commodity metal. In addition, there are other sources of convenience yield for metal in different stages of the production cycle that can be identified by assessing a quasi-market value for the commodity (e.g., holding to reduce the cost of supply breaks). These are described here.

EXCHANGE VALUE CONVENIENCE YIELD – EFFECT OF PHYSICAL DIFFERENTIALS

For a monolithic metal such as gold, one good delivery ingot is very much like another, but industrial metals differ by composition, shape, and location.[24] We can form a value

---
[24] Stainless steel, which is planned to be traded on the LME, is in addition specified by thermomechanical treatment.

"stack" of all material stored in listed warehouses. Traders receiving material will sift the stock each day. The material "better" than the "best" cleared on Figure 8.9 may not be returned as deliveries against sales contracts, and the holders may pay the repo rate rather than give up the physical position. Material "worse" than the "average", if not withdrawn for use, will be returned to the exchange. We can also see in this figure that the volume of warrants delivered to prompt buyers is equal to the aggregate of net purchases, and that if the physical stock does not change by deliveries and withdrawals, and all participants take an interest in physical premium and have equal access to credit, and warrants are allocated randomly, then buyers will receive average value over the lowest value stock that is dependent on the volume cleared.

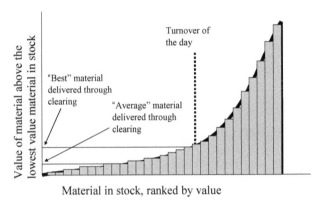

Figure 8.9 Representation of the value of physical premium for material in stock.[25]

The decision on whether to hold on to physical stock and pay the repo rate depends on the prospective use and exchange value of the physical premium as well as the use and exchange value of convenience yield at market prices.

The respective factors change in influence. For example, a participant could endeavor to borrow a volume equivalent to the total stockholding from some future date to another, and then wait for the position to become prompt. If this action could be undertaken for a low repo rate, then the participant may either gain hold of the whole physical stock, including high-value warrants, or make a backwardation profit as the stockholders elect to borrow back their positions rather than release the stock.

It is clear that the seller of high-premium material would prefer to gain the premium by selling direct to customers of the illiquid market in physical premiums, thereby gaining the premium, rather than delivering to the exchange and losing it. However, the exchange is the "buyer of last resort", and almost by definition a delivery of material to the exchange signifies a downturn in general demand. In such times, the buyers are building a long position not for immediate use but for later use or exchange. The only way to keep the premium is to keep the stock and to finance it.

The arbitrage relationship discussed in Chapter 2 involved physical storage at zero cost. In reality there are three costs for storage: (i) warehousing/handling costs;

---

[25] Note that while the cheapest delivery mechanism exposes the "worst" stock to stay until the stocks are run to zero, they could degrade so much that they become worthless. The high durability of metals avoids this.

(ii) insurance; and (iii) material degradation. In addition to this, there is the cost of diverting[26] material to a storage location away from the supply chain.

While balance sheet treatment, liquidity and general convenience encourage stocked material toward the listed warehouses, stocks can be held in any of the five ways described earlier. Just as with production costs, we can build a stocking cost stack. In Figure 8.10 we have included the cost of deviating material from the most efficient supply chain in order to stock.

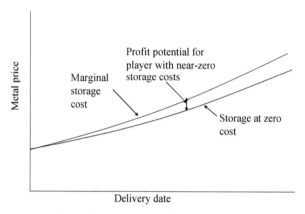

Figure 8.10   Convenience yield available to a participant with low storage costs if the contango slope is set by a participant with high storage costs.

It is quite possible to store a large amount of material at very low cost by keeping it in the producer location. This maintains flexibility for saving transport and handling costs by driving stock upstream and avoiding delivery to exchange-listed warehouses, but does not make use of the liquidity that the exchanges provide, and denies the holder of the potential to make gains by lending material when the prevailing convenience yield (backwardation) is high. Material held upstream "on consignment" by financiers at the producer location must be financed "on balance sheet",[27] thereby connecting the storage to interest-rate differentials, and will also commonly involve a profit-sharing agreement with the producer.

EXCHANGE VALUE CONVENIENCE YIELD – CREDIT EFFECTS

Suppose that all the other assumptions in Table 8.2 are correct but that the participants have different credit standings.

All stock is owned and must therefore be financed or lose opportunity cost. Let us assume that the borrowing rate for a particular participant is $(r + s)$ where r corresponds to the FRA rate and s is the credit premium that the participant must pay to borrow for the transaction. If the participant needs material after date T, then they will

---

[26] Additional transport costs, plus additional handling. Warehouse charges for "in and out" and bilateral arrangement incentives for delivery to particular warehouses also affect this.
[27] Depending on capital adequacy rules and capital calculations, the balance sheet impact can be zero, as a forward hedge with an AAA-rated exchange can be considered to reduce the risk to zero.

buy forward rather than spot if:

$$P(T, t) < P(t, t) * \exp(r * (T - t)) * \exp(s * (T - t))$$

The slope is the same if they are an arbitrager with no use for the material or a stockholder wishing to sell.

As a result, the forward slope for metal is determined by the marginal borrower, and the more creditworthy borrowers make a profit equal to the marginal value of creditworthiness. Since this profit has very low risk,[28] we would expect the cash available to be high and, therefore, the forward slope margin to be small.

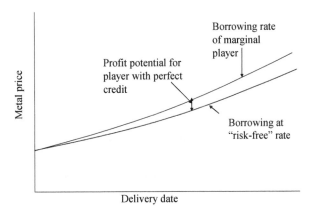

Figure 8.11 Convenience yield for low-cost borrowers if the forward slope is set by high-cost borrowers.

This effect is of relatively minor significance for nearby prices (less than 6 months, say), since many players can borrow to finance metal spread positions from prompt and even more can take on forward spread positions without the immediate need for cash. In addition, even an interest-rate differential that has a 1% effect over a year has only a 0.002% effect per day.

Now consider the inventory stack and the interest stack together. In the example shown in Table 8.3, there are four participants with the cost structure.

Table 8.3 Interest rate and stock costs for four participants

Participant	Inventory cost for the period	Interest cost for the period
A	1	1
B	1	4
C	4	2
D	2	2

Supposing that there are 2 units in stock, it is clear that we cannot separately build the inventory cost and interest-rate stacks, but that we must combine them. In the above case, separate stacking would give us a marginal inventory cost of 1 and a

---

[28] Risks include operational, tax, legal, regulatory and credit.

marginal interest cost of 2 and, hence, a total of 3, whereas building the stack in one go gives us a marginal cost of 4.

The presence of different elements of value for physical premium, and the difficulty of "shuffling" them between participants, increases the spread of values between the "best" and "worst" ingots in the exchange warehouses, thereby increasing the repo rate for physical stock.

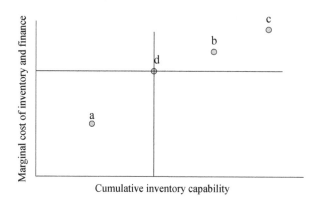

Figure 8.12 The inventory stack when stockers have both borrowing and physical stocking costs (as shown in Table 8.3).

There are several features of note here:

- Market sectors with low borrowing costs are not closely associated with those with low physical stocking costs.
- Low stock cost locations are specific and not accessible in the multilateral market. Similarly, cheap credit is not readily transferable. Therefore, the cheapest physical and credit costs cannot be shuffled to create a low-cost stack.
- Partly because of the low liquidity of stock/credit pairings, the stock stack is opaque and transitory.
- The storage stack is upward-curving in the short term due to limitation of warehouse space, and downward-curving in the long term due to the accessibility of a wide array of storage options for durable metal, when there is time to make the arrangements. The credit stack is downward-curving in the long term due to the size of the banking market, and upward- or downward-curving in the short term in different circumstances.

EXCHANGE VALUE CONVENIENCE YIELD – UNCERTAINTY EFFECTS

This is very closely associated with the instant access value described in Section 8.5, except that now we assume that the market price for prompt material is affected by forces shared by all participants.

The maximum loss on a short spread position is theoretically infinite even for a spread as short as 1 day. Therefore, traders are particularly wary of them. Indeed, they have a morbid fear of the slightest "hole" in their forward positions, since they assume a systematic attack[29] on the position with a plan that has not yet been revealed. In addition, there tends to be concentration of activity around short spread positions.

A long contango position then, even if conferring no convenience in its own right, provides the ability to trade without getting "caught short". This component of convenience yield is variously regarded as a cost of doing business, an option premium for a possible pay-off in backwardation or a cost of risk[30] premium.

CONVENIENCE YIELD – LIQUIDITY OF EXCHANGE – METAL AS CURRENCY

We hold paper currency in our pockets because it provides us instantaneous access to purchasing power, without the need for associated transactions such as withdrawing money from the bank. In holding the paper currency we are forgoing the interest that we would have received in our current account. Similarly, a current account with instantaneous withdrawal access pays less interest than an account with required notice. The convenience that we are paying for is liquidity of exchange and this liquidity is a form of American[31] option with a value that is dependent both on the variation in our private needs and in the velocity of money.

The liquidity provided by a long position in physical metal is similar in nature. In industrial metals, this liquidity is primarily related to a metal warrant granting immediate access to specific metal and a metal contract which may require further conversion for specific material in a specific location. The value of liquidity is intimately related to uncertainty.

When considering commodity metal with no discernible physical differentials, then the liquidity value refers only to the exchange value of metal, and since commodity metal is always instantly accessible on the exchanges there is no obvious liquidity benefit in having a long physical position, particularly since it ties up cash and reduces liquidity in that way. Metal in this form only has exchange value liquidity if this liquidity has a greater value than cash, and such circumstances are very special ones. In practice, this can only really happen for gold; so, we will only illustrate the situation for gold.[32] Other metals can be considered in relation to gold.

To understand the dynamics of gold lease rates, we must also understand the dynamics of borrowing.

It is more effective to borrow gold than to borrow money, when the ability to repay is naturally denominated in gold. This would be either (i) because gold is being produced, or (ii) gold is already held physically, and the holding could be reduced if necessary.

To illustrate the movement of gold and the behavior of the various participants let us consider the transaction tranches by which gold production is financed and gold reaches the consumer. The roles are stylized and in practice are overlapping.

---

[29] "Squeeze" positions were commonly built up with three or four discrete market plays that, when finally netted off, revealed a long position on particular spreads. Regulation has substantially reduced the incidence of overt squeeze positions over short periods.

[30] Cost of risk is normally applied to the first moment of price movements (movement in mean). The cost of risk here refers to the cost of volatility risk (i.e., higher moments).

[31] An American option is a traded option in which the delivery date can be chosen by the option buyer.

[32] Note that when we considered long-term prices, we noted that a metal basket was a more effective numéraire asset than a unit of currency. However, this use of metal-as-currency does not translate into the short term.

The mechanism of tranche 1 is as follows:

- The Central Bank lends 100,000 ounces of gold short term to the Bank on a leasing arrangement (Transaction 1).
- The Bank lends 200,000 ounces of gold long term to the Mine using the gold forward rate with a credit cost adjustment (Transaction 2).
- The Mine sells 200,000 ounces of gold to the Spot Trader (Transaction 3).
- The Spot Trader sells 150,000 ounces of gold to the Investor (Transaction 4) and 50,000 ounces to the Jeweler (Transaction 5).
- The Investor lends 100,000 ounces of short-term gold to the Forward Curve Trader (Transaction 6) using the gold forward rate and retains 50,000 physical.
- The Forward Curve Trader lends on a swap basis 100,000 ounces of gold medium term to the Bank using the gold forward rate (Transaction 7).

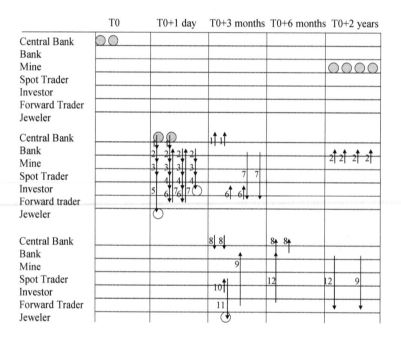

Figure 8.13 Opening position, transaction tranche 1 and transaction tranche 2 for gold (see text).

In the second tranche of trades:

- The Central Bank rolls 100,000 ounces of lease (Transaction 8).
- The Bank rolls the lease (Transaction 8) and borrows 100,000 ounces forward on a swap basis (Transactions 9 and 12).
- The Investor sells 50,000 ounces (Transaction 10) and retains 100,000 ounces on account.
- The Forward Curve Trader lends "forward forward" on a swap basis (Transaction 9).
- The Spot Trader has intermediated.
- The Jeweler buys 50,000 ounces for consumption (Transaction 11).

So after all this:

- The Mine has raised cash and committed production to repayment.
- The Investor has bought most of the Mine's production, and has deferred delivery of most of it for a short period.
- The Spot Trader has intermediated with no final position.
- The Central Bank has leased gold for a short period with the intention to roll the lease.
- The Forward Curve Trader has a short forward swap position.
- The Bank has a short forward swap position and primary[33] credit exposure to the Mine.
- The Jeweler has removed some metal from the total stock of ingots.

We learn from this that the lease market is effectively structurally short in the medium to long term (as demonstrated by the fact that the Bank cannot lay off all long-term swap risk to the Forward Curve Trader) and is structurally long in the short term (as demonstrated by the long account[34] position of the Investor). Hence, long-term forward lease rates are generally higher than short-term ones. If this equilibrium is stationary, then it should be possible to gain a risky arbitrage profit by taking short forward lease positions and borrowing back as the prompt date arrives. Indeed, this is generally the case, and the lease rate drift is reconciled by the cost of risk. The risk on a short-term lease position offers unlimited loss for limited profit, and the wait for profit on a long-term lease position is a long one and ties up risk capital for a correspondingly long period.

We simplistically viewed the sequence of transactions as early consumption of mined gold, facilitated by a loan of stock. The "convenience" here is the liquidity that the Central Bank provides. The gold itself does not actually get used or even moved. In fact, it does not even get seen! There is clearly some resonance of existence value here. A depiction of how the participants in the gold market act to "bring forward" physical gold for consumption from the mined product is shown in Figure 8.14.

The resulting contango structure for gold looks something like that shown in Figure 8.15. While there is no hard and fast long-term forward rate, the currency interest rate represents a sensible upper bound because miners, while they wish to borrow, do not wish to sell into a backwardation and, hence, the dollar interest rate represents an effective upper bound lease rate that corresponds to a flat forward price in dollars.

Whole curve behavior

In this section, we look to model some common characteristic metal price movements in terms of the standard building blocks of stochastic process analysis. To do so, we need to establish different behaviours and limits in different time periods.

---

[33] Primary credit exposure arises from an explicit debt obligation. Secondary credit exposure arises from variations (e.g., forward price movement on a forward sale contract).
[34] The investor would like to lend, but the velocity of gold is finite.

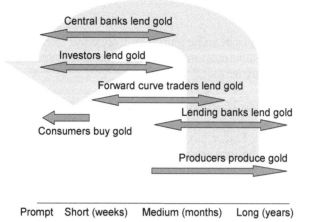

Prompt   Short (weeks)   Medium (months)   Long (years)

Figure 8.14   Depiction of the position of different actors in gold trading.

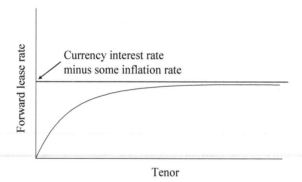

Tenor

Figure 8.15   Repo-rate term structure for gold.

Let us initially ignore the arbitrage relationships in contango, and characterize the metal price curve by:

$$P(T,0) = P(\infty,0) + (P(0,0) - P(\infty,0)) \exp(-k_1(T,0)T)$$

where:

- $P(\infty,0)$ is the long-term equilibrium price.
- $P(0,0)$ is the spot price.
- $k_1(T,0)$ is the mean-reversion rate of the price (observation date is now $t=0$).

We can depict the simple shocks to spot price, long-term price and decay rate as shown in Figure 8.16.

When modeling forward curves in the financial markets, we are accustomed to using principal components. These are formalized breakdowns of price movement into a series of independent movements of decreasing size. Anecdotal experience is that, out of 100% total movement in a forward curve, movements of 70%, 20%, 5% and 2% of the first four principal components would be considered normal. Hence, 97% of price

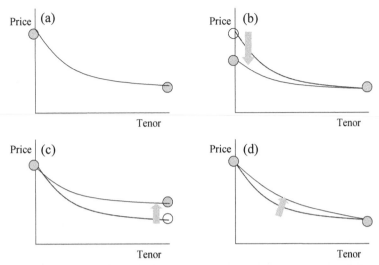

Figure 8.16 (a) Initial curve; (b) shocked cash price; (c) shocked equilibrium price; and (d) shocked mean-reversion rate.

Figure 8.17 Generalized depiction of the first four principal components of movement of the forward price.

movement is commonly explained by the first four principal components and the shape of these can be characterized,[35] in order of size, by "shift", "tilt", "bow" and "flex" (as shown in Figure 8.17).

Simplistically, the first principal component generally represents a shock to the spot price, or a shock to the spot price and a corresponding shock to the long-term price in the same direction and at a particular ratio. The second principal component generally represents a shock to the spot price and a shock to the forward price that is opposite in direction and at a particular ratio. Hence the first two principal components can represent most structured shocks to spot and long-term price. The third principal component represents a shock to the decay factor (responsivity of market to shocks on the spot price), and the fourth principal component generally represents a simple term structure to responsivity. The fourth principal component (flex) is important for metals, at least conceptually, since, as we will see, the effect of near-term contango, the effect of stock and the strength of short-term movements in metals means that the flexing of the curvature of the metal price curve can be strong. This can be interpreted physically as a change in the term structure of the responsivity of metal production and consumption.

---

[35] This is a slight oversimplification. For example, "shift" does not actually mean parallel shift, but a one-factor movement that could, through volatility attenuation with tenor, actually look like tilt.

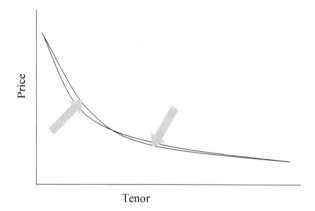

Figure 8.18   Manifestation of the fourth principal component in metal prices.

Characterization of generic structures of metal forward curve and curve movements

In looking at the fundamentals of using and trading metals, we have seen two particular features: (i) the sporadic influence of the full contango limit, and (ii) backwardation that can be very steep. We will now review some characteristic price structures for metals that show these features, and review the resulting term structures of volatility.

Contango limit

We saw in Chapter 2 how arbitrage limits the upward slope of the forward curve (the maximum contango limit). Now consider what happens during a collapse in cash price. If there were no contango limit, then in the one-factor case we would see an exponential price curve. However, as the price falls and the FRA slope is approached, contango borrowers buy cash metal and sell forward metal. This has the effect of a tilting force that is strongest in the near term (i.e., with flex).

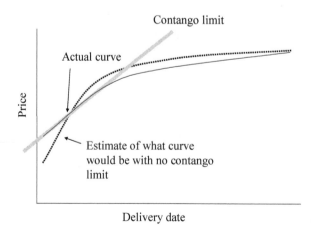

Figure 8.19   Maximum contango forward curve structure.

Now all prices within the maximum contango area move in lock step (not just tenor-attenuated movements with 100% correlation but actually in parallel). Our volatility term structure[36] now looks unusual.

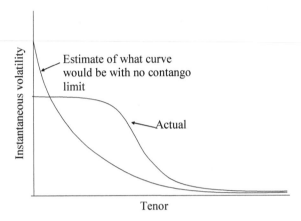

Figure 8.20   Volatility term structure for a market with maximum contango.

Note again that we substantially affect mid-tenor behavior. We have in effect pushed spot price behavior (albeit at a lower volatility) to that of mid-tenor.

We depict the evolution of volatility term structure in Figure 8.21.

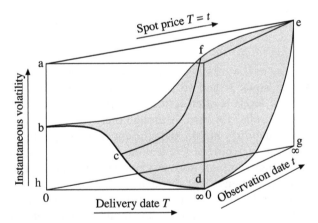

Figure 8.21   Volatility evolution for full contango market.

Plane afdh is the standard graph for instantaneous volatility with respect to the delivery date that was depicted in Figure 8.21.

The surface dcbfe is the volatility surface for evolving contracts.

The projection onto plane dgef of the respective volatility paths, such as cf, is the

---

[36] In practice, instantaneous volatility falls with tenor in the near term because a "lock step" movement is a lesser proportion of the forward price that is higher than the spot price. This effect is not shown, for ease of illustration.

volatility evolution of individual contracts, with de – the volatility evolution of a long-term contract bfe on the plane ghae – being the evolution of the spot contract.

Average, or option, volatility is found by integrating variance across line integrals, such as cf.

The equivalent curve for gold is slightly different because, while it has a low repo rate that is treated as sporadic in base metals, it is the common condition for gold. Therefore, the "S" shape (bcd in Figure 8.21) can be stable for long periods.

Structural backwardation with rolling contango

Another characteristic structure is shown in Figure 8.22.

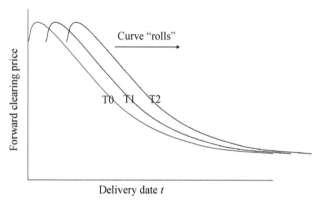

Figure 8.22 Short-term contango–long-term "rolling" backwardation for observation dates $T_2 > T_1 > T_0$.

In this structure, the backwardation structure prevails but, as metal comes close to prompt, the metal on stock is lent to form a nearby contango. A backwardated[37] market with high stock levels is often termed "technically tight". The curve seems to move to the right, as it "rolls" forward. Although there is a common belief in the metal markets that this is structurally stable, the efficient market hypothesis seems to make such a structure subject to arbitrage (by lending medium-term metal and borrowing back when it is in contango) and this must be explained. The explanation is that, once in a while, backwardation tightens right through to the cash market, and to very high levels. The cost of risk related to this event also maintains backwardation as traders maintain long spread positions (to retain trading liquidity) and then lend them to defray backwardation, financing and stockholding costs.

Our volatility evolution is shown in Figure 8.23. The three key characteristic features are (i) that the short term displays the contango behavior shown earlier, (ii) back-wardation is an indication of spot volatility higher than equilibrium and (iii) high skewness of volatility with respect to strike (which could be depicted with a series of surfaces for options with different deltas). Note that point j is at the same volatility as point e in Figure 8.22.

---

[37] Note, however, that, when expressed in terms of a zero interest-rate currency, backwardation is the norm, even for gold.

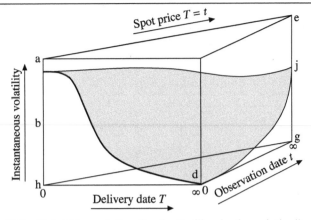

Figure 8.23 Volatility evolution for the "rolling backwardation" market.

This behavior has much in common with jump processes and the "smile" structure of volatility is consistent with this, as call options trade at much higher volatility than put options. This is described in the section on strike price structures (see p. 191).

DISLOCATED CONTANGO

The final important generic structure is forward backwardation. It is shown in its most extreme form in Figure 8.24.

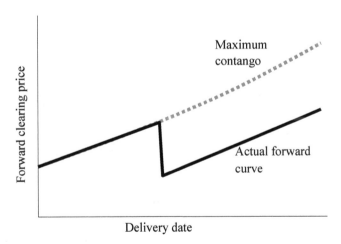

Figure 8.24 Forward backwardation in most extreme form.

In this structure a specific period is "squeezed". It can be the result of speculative activity to force participants to buy back short spread positions at high prices, a stock exercise to gain physical premium or simply a consequence of the concentration of activity (e.g., in European options or other specific derivative products).

Here, movement in the spread dominates the curve. In extreme instances the left and right side completely disconnect. A trade with a shorter tenor than the backwardation date causes a parallel shift of the left-hand side. A trade with a longer tenor causes a smaller parallel shift on the right, at least as far as the full contango period.

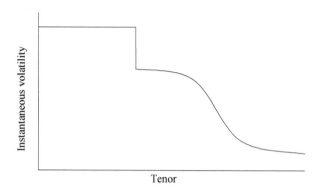

Figure 8.25   Instantaneous volatility in a "forward backwardation" market.

In summary, both backwardation and full contango markets are regarded as non-equilibrium conditions, and the market will "try" to revert to a curve in which the metal price inflates gently over time.

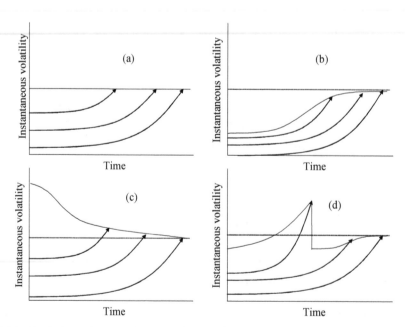

Figure 8.26   Evolution of spot price volatility and the volatility of short-, medium- and long-tenor contracts for four market structures: (a) normal inflation; (b) full contango; (c) rolling backwardation; and (d) forward backwardation.

Strike structures

Metal options are actively traded. The strike structure of volatility, commonly called "smile" and "skew", is a large subject that is not covered in detail here. Metals display the same effects as other traded entities, including: (i) "kappa convexity" arising from stochastic volatility; (ii) the market cost of volatility risk; (iii) the path-dependence of volatility; and (iv) the price dependence of volatility. There are in addition two features of metals that give them the distinctive strike structures of volatility: the effect of full contango and the effect of sharp backwardation.

Effect of full contango

We have seen how full contango locks contracts together. For medium-tenor options, this has the effect of flattening volatility term structure for lower strike options, thereby lowering the nearer tenors (within the medium-tenor range) and raising further tenors. This effect is additive to other strike structure effects.

Effect of sharp backwardation

The effect is opposite to the effect of full contango. At high prices, the correlation between adjacent contracts falls, with the effect that high strike options have very high "smiles", as longer tenor options are an ineffective hedge for shorter tenor options. In the same vein, rising prices cause the increasing independence of contracts and, hence, a long position on a forward contract gives less protection for a short position in a short-term contract. Therefore, the volatility smile is pronounced for short-term high-strike contracts. This is partly a fair value effect and partly a cost of risk effect.

A generic depiction of the overall strike structure of traded metal options, relative to at-the-money options, is shown in Figure 8.27.

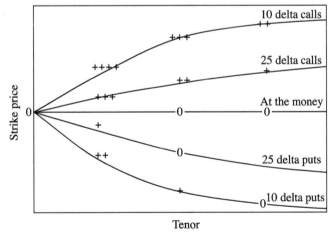

Figure 8.27 Generic strike structure of volatility relative to "at the money".[38]

---

[38] In "at the money" options, the strike price equals the prevailing forward price.

8.6 CONCLUSION

The analytic disciplines that apply to financial markets, such as principal components analysis, stochastic process characterization, equilibrium term structures and arbitrage relationships, can all be applied to metal prices, and, in addition, the fundamentals of metals and metal economics gives us strong indications for quantitative characterization. However, analytic disciplines are more useful for characterization of specific instances and specific parts of the curve than they are for general application. Despite the difficulty in modeling, the quantitative characterization of both term structures and strike structures of volatility is considerably enhanced by the use of formal techniques.

Metal prices are strongly influenced by the (separate) economics of spot price movements, long-term equilibrium price movements and by the arbitrage relationships for forward curve slope movements. These are in constant tension, and relative strengths change both over time and simultaneously across different tenors of the metal price curve.

The Oil Market as a World Market

By Etienne Amic

9.1 WHY OIL IS TRADED AND ITS RELATIONSHIP WITH WORLDWIDE ENERGY PRICES

Over the past 20 years oil has become the biggest commodity market in the world and it has evolved from a primarily physical activity into a sophisticated financial market with trading horizons now extending to over 10 years forward. In the process, it has attracted a wide range of participants which now include investment banks (Goldman Sachs, Morgan Stanley), asset managers for mutual funds, pension funds or endowments (Pimco, Fidelity), insurance companies (AIG), hedge funds (Citadel, Tudor Jones) as well as the traditional oil majors (BP, Total), the independents (Apache, Oxy Petroleum) and the physical oil traders (Vitol, Glencore).

The initial momentum for the expansion of the oil market came from the changing structure of the industry in the 1970s. The nationalization of the upstream interests of the major oil companies by their host countries caused a decoupling of their Exploration and Production (E&P)[1] and refining operations. Having lost access to large volumes of equity oil, the majors were forced to buy at arm's length from their former associates (i.e., the national oil companies), and the physical base of the international oil market expanded rapidly as a result. With more oil being traded, external markets began setting the price for internal transfers as well as third-party sales; companies started to buy and sell oil outside their own supply network if better opportunities existed, fueling the growth of the physical market. After more than 30 years of this regime, only a small percentage of the volume of oil produced by each of the majors is now refined in their own system.

In parallel, the volatility of the oil price (see Figure 9.1) and the hedging needs this created for industry participants triggered the development of a financial sphere of derivative contracts (Futures, forwards, swaps and options) which now dominate the process of worldwide oil price formation. However, since oil is an inherently non-standard commodity, the industry has had to choose a small number of "reference" or "marker" grades of crude oil and refined products that provide the physical basis for a much larger derivatives market and attract most of the liquidity. The most prominent oil-related derivative is without doubt the Futures contract on light sweet crude that is quoted on the New York Mercantile Exchange (NYMEX); it is usually known as "WTI" since the West Texas Intermediate grade of crude oil for delivery at Cushing, Oklahoma still underpins the market (despite the introduction of fungible delivery grades for physical settlement of the contract in recent years).

---

[1] E&P is commonly called "upstream".

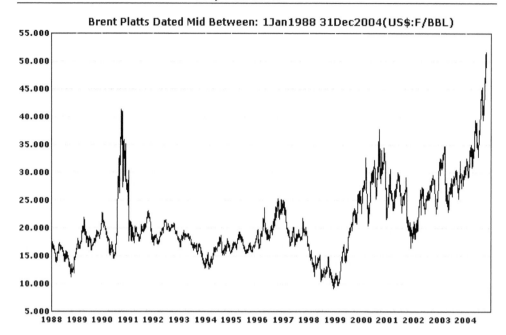

Figure 9.1   Evolution of the price of crude oil 1988–2004.
Maximum: 51.585, minimum: 9.130; last: 49.035; mean: 20.992. *Source: Platt's.*

It is important to understand that oil is physically traded twice: first, as a refinery feedstock, and, second, as a finished product. Even if crude and refined products have rather different characteristics, they are inextricably linked by the technology and economics of refining. Although product prices may, and do, fluctuate widely relative to each other, they must together be related to crude oil price because refineries will not continue to operate long on negative margins and competition will set a ceiling to high margins in return. This is true for both physical and derivatives transactions, although some temporary discrepancies might emerge in the latter.

In the 1980s and 1990s, the oil markets extended their influence to the prices of virtually all primary fuels. For instance, long-term contracts for delivery of natural gas in Europe have their price directly tied to reported prices for fuel oil and gasoil in the Amsterdam–Rotterdam–Antwerp (ARA) refining hub. The price of Liquefied Natural Gas (LNG) produced in Asia, Africa, the Middle East and Central America is more often than not indexed on baskets of crude oil. Even when there is no explicit price relationship, as is the case for US natural gas, the value of the latter closely follows that of oil because of physical arbitrage by industry participants: when gas becomes more expensive than distillates, it is substituted with heating oil in dual-fired power plants and the resulting increment in oil demand contributes to reducing the price gap between both commodities. International coal prices are also affected by the price of oil, although more loosely. In the UK, for instance, where coal and natural gas compete at the margin of the power stack, any significant increase in the price of natural gas triggers more imports of coal from South Africa as a substitute feedstock. In Europe at least, this is likely to cause higher electricity prices in return, driven by the dominant markets in Germany and the UK,[2] as utilities attempt to pass through their higher costs to consumers.

In more ways than not, the outright price of oil has thus acquired a deep influence on the whole energy complex (refined products, coal, natural gas, electricity), transforming oil into a major financial indicator of the global economy, far beyond its relevance of 40% of worldwide primary energy consumption. The Asian financial crisis of 1997, the 9/11 attacks in the US or the recession of 2001 can all be read directly in the historical price of oil.

But, because there are many different types of crude oil and refined products, the majority of oil trading is actually concerned with price differentials between grades, locations, markets and delivery periods. As a result, it has evolved into one of the most complex commodity markets in existence today, with an interlocking set of physical and financial instruments that interact 24 hours a day, 7 days a week, all year long.

9.2   CRUDE OIL MARKETS

Physical crude oil markets are highly fluid, global and volatile. For instance, the international trade flows on which they are based are radically different from those of precious metals (gold, silver, platinum) since oil is an asset destined to be consumed, not a store of value. In 2004, annual oil sales are still significant at the macroeconomic scale: around 2% of world GDP, compared with 7% in 1980. World demand was 79.4 million barrels per day (Mb/d) on average in 2003, or close to $1 trillion of nominal. The resulting transfer of wealth from industrialized nations to less developed, oil-producing countries has a measurable effect on the financial system: from 2002 to 2003, the revenues accrued to the OPEC 10 members from hydrocarbons sales jumped from $180bn to $240bn, as the price of WTI averaged $31.10/b (an increase of 30% on the previous year). These revenues are easily expected to reach $400bn in 2004, a figure comparable with the much-talked-about $500bn US current account deficit. As a result, it matters to know where this money (the so-called petrodollars) will be invested or spent because it has the potential to move currencies, stocks and interest rates.[3] As an illustration, Figure 9.2 plots the returns of major equity indexes in the Persian Gulf, with the base set on 1 January 2003, and their correlation to the oil price, defined as the rolling first nearby futures on NYMEX.

The global crude oil supply, at 79.5 Mb/d in 2003 – of which 27.0 Mb/d is produced by OPEC[4] – follows demand very closely, the adjustment being made through inventories. Because a surprisingly large amount of oil is required just to fill the supply chain from well-head to consumer (the average delivery time of crude to market is 30 days, with 85 days from long-haul crude transported from the Middle East to the Gulf of Mexico), the oil industry has long adopted "just-in-time"' inventory management methods and the level of stocks held by market participants has fallen steadily since

---

[2] The German and British power markets are particularly relevant in Europe, not only because of their size, but also because they act as price makers. France, the second largest consumer of electricity in Europe, exports about 75.0 TWh to its neighbors (the equivalent of nine nuclear reactors running at baseload) and does not set the wholesale price as a result.
[3] For instance, the market capitalizations of most Persian Gulf stock exchanges doubled between January 2003 and September 2004, following the oil price.
[4] OPEC, Organization of Petroleum Exporting Countries, comprises Saudi Arabia, Kuwait, the United Arab Emirates (UAE), Iran, Qatar, Algeria, Libya, Nigeria, Venezuela and Indonesia.

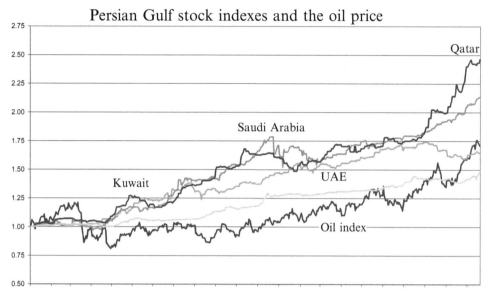

Figure 9.2   The macroeconomic effect of petrodollars.
Source: Bloomberg.

the early 1980s.In 2004, the forward cover[5] provided by OECD[6] companies stands at 53 days (21 days for crude and 32 days for refined products), an absolute record low,[7] while demand growth is expected to reach more than 2.7 Mb/d (or 3.1%), on the back of synchronized global economic expansion (5.0% GDP growth in 2004, compared with 4.7% in 2000) and of ever-increasing demand from China (+0.8 Mb/d in 2004 alone, or a 15% increase year-on-year). Spare production capacity, essentially located in the politically unstable Middle East, only amounts to 1.6 Mb/d in 2004, slightly below 2% of the expected total demand of 82.2 Mb/d.

The main producers of crude oil are North America (11.9 Mb/d in 2004), Saudi Arabia (8.8 Mb/d), Russia (8.4 Mb/d) and Iran (3.9 Mb/d), while the major consumers are the US (22.7 Mb/d), Western Europe (14.8 Mb/d), China (6.4 Mb/d)[8] and Japan (5.5 Mb/d). These geographical imbalances create the need for massive exports from the Middle East (19.2 Mb/d), the Former Soviet Union (7.4 Mb/d) and West Africa (6.5 Mb/d) to the Far East (15.6 Mb/d), North America (10.8 Mb/d) and Western Europe (8.4 Mb/d). All in all, the flows between the main producing and consuming regions accounted for an average 35 Mb/d in 2003, excluding barrels moving from the North Sea to Europe, which themselves totaled about 8 Mb/d (see Figure 9.3)

---

[5] Forward cover is calculated by dividing stocks at the end of a given period by consumption in the following period (the result is expressed in days).

[6] OECD: Organization for Economic Cooperation and Development.

[7] As a comparison, a detailed study of the US oil industry published by Exxon in 1981 showed that the US held a total of 89 days of oil stocks at the start of 1981, measured in terms of forward consumption: 7 days' worth was held by the government in the Strategic Petroleum Reserve (SPR), and 82 days' worth was held by companies (a figure comparable with the 53 days mentioned in the text).

[8] China had the same oil consumption as Japan in 2003 (5.6 Mb/d) but has clearly overtaken the latter in 2004: 6.4 Mb/d compared with 5.5 Mb/d.

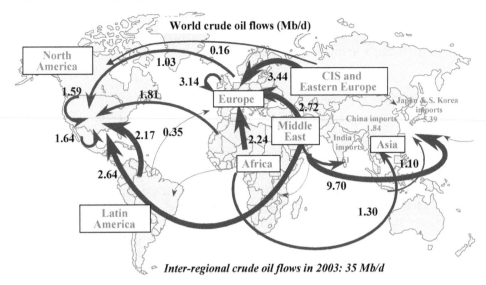

Figure 9.3 The global crude oil market.
Source: Total, *Platt's*.

Oil is transported either in ships or in pipelines. In the international market, oil moves almost exclusively in ships, and it is therefore the size of the cargo that forms the basic unit for physical trading. In the North Sea, the most active waterborne crude market in the world, 500,000-barrel cargoes are the norm, but, for longer haul crudes from West Africa and the Middle East, oil often moves in Very Large Crude Carriers (VLCCs) which can take up to 2 Mb at a time. The scale of financial exposure associated with crude oil trading can thus be very large, often exceeding a nominal $50m in a single transaction.[9] Crude oil is usually sold close to the point of production and title is transferred as the oil flows from the loading terminal to the ship (FOB: Free On Board). Once loaded, however, oil can be traded at sea or at the point of discharge, so that the same cargo may be priced differently according to its destination. Since a ship on her way to a refinery can be bought and sold more than once, the actual volumes of physical crude oil handled by traders across international borders are actually greater than the mere physical flows; they are estimated to have reached 55 Mb/d in 2003, or 157% of actual exports.

Oil is also traded in pipelines, essentially in the US, where third-party access to the transportation infrastructure is guaranteed in law and supervised by the FERC;[10] in this type of trading, crude is usually sold Free In Pipeline (FIP) at designated locations, as a flow rate (i.e., a specified number of barrels per day over an agreed delivery period).

In the following we describe in detail how different grades of crude oil are valued by the market, as well as the pricing arrangements that dominate international trade of the

[9] One of the most important services provided by international banks in the oil market is the financing of imports and exports among countries. This is done through *Letters of Credit* (L/Cs). An L/C is a financial instrument issued by an importer's bank that obligates the bank to pay the exporter (or its designated beneficiary) a specified amount of money once certain conditions are met, including receipt of a Bill of Lading (BL) acknowledging possession of the oil with the right specifications by a common carrier. With an L/C, the bank substitutes its good faith and credit for that of the importer.

[10] FERC: Federal Energy Regulatory Commission.

commodity today. The interplay between the physical and financial spheres of the market will appear more clearly in a thorough examination of one of its major compartments: the market for Brent blend (now Brent BFO[11]).

(1) Physical markets for crude oil. Quality and crude streams

The market value of a specific grade of crude oil (Arabian Light, Bonny Light, Forcados, Urals or Brent) depends essentially on two factors:

1. The relative yields of products (butane, propane, gasoline, jet/kerosene, heating oil, fuel oil) that can be extracted in the refining process; these yields are related to the density of the grade of crude oil under consideration.[12]
2. The energy that must be spent in refinery treating units to remove the sulfur contained in the crude in order to meet the stringent quality specifications for refined products imposed by customs authorities in most consuming nations.

These two features – density and sulfur content – ultimately define the desirability for refiners of a grade of crude and, therefore, the price they are ready to pay for it.

Density and sulfur content

Crude oil being a mixture of molecules formed by carbon and hydrogen atoms, there are as many different types of crude oils as there are oilfields (around 400 so-called "grades" are traded worldwide), some more valuable than others. Heavy crude oils are very thick and viscous and are difficult or impossible to produce, whereas light crude oils are very fluid and much easier to exploit. Crude oils are therefore compared and described by density, the most commonly used scale being the °API, which is inversely linked to specific gravity.[13]

As a benchmark, freshwater has a °API of 10, whereas the degree of crude oils varies from 5 to 55, average weight grades being in the range 25 to 55. Light oils have low viscosity, are often transparent, rich in gasoline and are the most valuable; they are rated between 35 and 45. In contrast, heavy oils, such as those produced in the Orinoco Basin of Venezuela, are below 25. They are viscous, dark-colored and contain considerable asphalt: they have to be "refined" and blended to become marketable.

Crude oils are also classified as *sweet* and *sour* on the basis of their sulfur content. By definition, *sweet crudes* have less than 1% sulfur by weight and the refiner usually pays a premium of $1 to $3 per barrel for them (although this premium is highly variable – more of it later); the adjective *sour* refers to other, less desirable grades. Sulfur in hydrocarbons is a burden: when it is burnt, it forms sulfur dioxide, a gas that pollutes

---

[11] BFO stands for Brent, Forties, Oseberg, which are three oil/natural gas fields located in the North Sea (the first two on the UK continental shelf, the last on the Norwegian shelf).
[12] For instance, Brass River, a Nigerian crude (41°API, 0.1% S) typically yields 26.4% gasoline/naphtha, 15.5% kerosene, 29.3% gasoil/diesel and 27.0% atmospheric residues (allowing for losses of 0.5% in the refining process). The Arab Light, a Saudi crude (34°API, 1.8% S), gives less light products in a simple refinery: 18.0% gasoline/naphtha, 12.3% kerosene, 23.6% gasoil/diesel and 45.0% atmospheric residue.
[13] API stands for American Petroleum Institute, the association based in Washington, DC that standardizes the industry's equipment and procedures.

the air and contributes to acid rain. Sulfur must also be removed if end-users' facilities and motor engines are not to be damaged.

In general, heavy oils tend to be sour, whereas light oils tend to be sweet.

Crude streams and benchmarks

Most of the crude oil from exporting countries is sold packaged as a *crude stream*. A crude stream can either be extracted from a single field, if its output is more than a few hundred barrels per day, or it can be a blend of oils from several fields which are close together and for which it is economic to share facilities such as pipelines, storage tanks or shipping terminals. Most of the North Sea streams are such blends (e.g., Brent and Flotta). The physical characteristics of oil from constituent fields are usually different and, as respective production rates are not constant, variations in the quality of the stream tend to vary slightly, although for obvious commercial reasons it is in the best interest of operators to smooth out such fluctuations (see Table 9.1).

Table 9.1 Some well-known crude streams, their country of origin, °API and sulfur content

Crude stream	Country	°API	%S	Pour point (°F)
Arabian Light	Saudi Arabia	33.4	1.80	−30
Bachequero	Venezuela	16.8	2.40	−10
Bonny Light	Nigeria	37.6	0.13	+36
Brass River	Nigeria	43.0	0.08	−5
Dubai	Dubai	32.5	1.68	−5
Ekofisk	Norway	35.8	0.18	+15
Iranian Light	Iran	33.5	1.40	−20
Kuwait	Kuwait	31.2	2.50	0
North Slope	Alaska	26.8	1.04	−5

With such a diversity of crude oils, one might wonder how a unified market has been able to develop. The solution lies in a simple, stylized fact: the outright price of oil is usually much more volatile than the differentials in value caused by their qualities. As a result, the industry has been able to concentrate on a limited number of reference qualities, or *benchmarks*, that form the backbone of the international oil market, both for physical and derivatives trading.

By definition, a benchmark is a standard crude oil against which other grades are compared *and prices are set*. There are three major benchmarks in the world of international trading today:

1. West Texas Intermediate, or WTI, in the US (38–40°API and 0.3% S) and, to a lesser extent, West Texas Sour (33°API and 1.6% S).
2. Brent blend, the reference crude oil for the North Sea, which is very similar to WTI in quality: 38°API and 0.3% S.
3. Dubai, the benchmark crude oil for the Middle East and Far East (32°API and 2% S), which comes from four offshore local fields: Fateh, SW Fateh, Falah and Rashid.

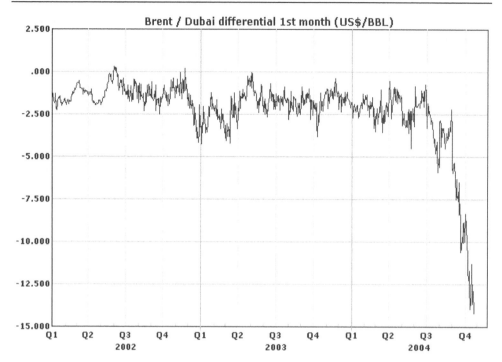

Figure 9.4 The spot differential between Brent and Dubai.
Maximum: 0.280; minimum:−14.180; last: −14.180; mean: −2.259. *Source: Platt's.*

These three markers are used as references in their respective areas: even if all crude oils traded FOB on the international markets are paid for in US$ per barrel by refiners and traders, their pricing formulas (floating prices) are explicitly indexed on the price of Brent blend if they are bound to Europe, WTI for the US or Dubai/Oman for Asia.

It should be noted that the relative value of the three markers changes all the time, sometimes spectacularly (Figure 9.4). When global crude oil supplies are tight or when there are uncertainties over the supply from the Persian Gulf (as was certainly the case in 1991, 2000 and 2004), swing producers such as Saudi Arabia must tap more deeply into their spare capacity, which consists mainly of medium sour grades, in order to satisfy demand. Since the refining system's ability to transform heavy, high-sulfur crudes into the lighter, most desirable products (gasoline, distillates) is constrained globally, these grades attract relatively little buying interest unless they are granted larger-than-usual discounts compared with low-sulfur crudes. The market value of Dubai versus Brent will then drop (from an average of just under −$2.0/barrel in 2003 down to −$11.0/barrel in the fall of 2004). Similarly, since WTI is an onshore crude oil whose price movements essentially reflect expectations of extra imports into the US, barring exceptional squeezes its relative value versus Brent behaves as an indicator of the shipping costs necessary to move supplies across the Atlantic. In February 2003, when strikes at Venezuela's national company, PDVSA, stopped the production of close to 2.0 Mb/d of crude mostly sold to US and Caribbean refineries (on a national production of 2.5 Mb/d), the Brent–WTI spot differential adjusted

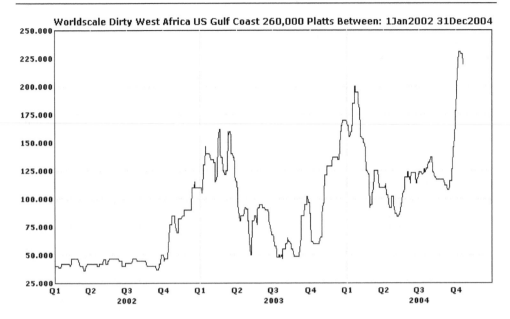

Figure 9.5 The explosion of freight rates 2002/2004.
Maximum: 231,000; minimum: 36,000; last: 230,000; mean: 91,455.

immediately to factor in the fact that supplies had to come from farther away to meet US needs. In 2004, freight rates have skyrocketed to reflect the increasing appetite of Asia for Atlantic Basin crudes and new restrictions on old vessels. While in 2002 it cost $1.0m to charter a 2-million-barrel VLCC from West Africa to the Gulf of Mexico, this rate had jumped more than seven-fold at the end of 2004 to reach $7.4m (Figure 9.5). As a result, the Brent–WTI spread widened significantly over the same period.

How is the price of a crude oil cargo set?

Historically, the first publication to quote international crude oil prices regularly was *Platt's*, an agency of financial reporters which has been tracking transactions since the 1930s. It has been a central piece in the oil market jigsaw since then and, despite some competition from *Petroleum Argus*, it still retains the ability to set oil market prices rather than just report them (more on that later). Practically, most spot transactions for cargoes are priced at a differential to one of the qualities whose price is reported in the daily *Platt's* report.

For instance, Urals is a local reference stream in the Mediterranean; it is exported through Novorossiysk, a major Russian terminal on the Black Sea, and then through the Bosporus to the major refining centers in France, Italy or Spain (3.0 Mb/d of oil flow through the strait). A cargo of Urals FOB with a loading window of 3 days centered on 15 December may be traded at "dated Brent – $1.50/barrel", where the benchmark is the mean of the means of *Platt's* and *Petroleum Argus* high and low quotations for "dated Brent" on the Bill of Lading (B/L) date.[14] Most often, crude oil is priced on an average of 11 published quotes (i.e., the price on the B/L date plus and minus 5 working days around this date).

Some flexibility may also be offered by sellers as an incentive to lift their particular crude oils. Nigeria, for example, is known to have offered flexible date ranges during which buyers could price their purchases. Instead of pricing a cargo 5 days after the date of B/L, the buyer could either price it over a 5-day period starting 14 days after B/L or the 5 days preceding B/L.[15]

Rather than using published prices on which to base a formula, some transactions are now made at a fixed differential to International Petroleum Exchange (IPE) Futures prices. For example, the price of a cargo of Bonny Light – a high-quality crude oil – transacted in the first days of December may be the settlement price of the January Brent Futures contract at the close of business on the date of B/L, plus a fixed differential of $0.50/barrel. Or it may be the settlement of the January Brent Futures, plus a floating differential, defined as the spread between the prices for Bonny Light and dated Brent on a future date, as published by *Platt's*.

Over one-half of internationally traded crude oils is quoted at a fixed differential to Brent in either of these ways, since this stream is felt to be sufficiently transparent to be a valid benchmark. Another underlying factor, especially important in the early days of volatility, is that Brent, coming from a politically stable democracy, has been a reliable source of crude oil supply over the past 30 years. Brent is also considered to be of a consistent quality and volume, and not to vary over time. Any change in the differential to Brent BFO for a given crude oil (the discount of $1.50/barrel for Urals or the premium of $0.50/barrel for Bonny Light) will reflect relative market interest in that crude compared with Brent and will vary much more slowly than the price of Brent itself. In this sense the market is able to distinguish between the outright price movements of a very limited number of "markers" ("the price of oil") and the relative fluctuations of all other grades around these benchmarks.

(2) Market(s) for Brent blend

Brent is one of the older fields of the UK Continental Shelf (UKCS). Originally, its crude stream was sufficient to sustain a very active spot market and its fragmented ownership made it a suitable physical basis for a forward paper market (at one point, 30 companies had an equity share in the stream). The field has naturally declined over time and it was decided in July 1990 to combine the output from the Brent and Ninian systems[16] in order to preserve the physical depth of the market. Recently, an index has been created which includes two additional streams, Forties (770,000 b/d) and Oseberg (430,000 b/d): the Brent BFO. Since there are no longer enough spot (cargo) transactions to allow the determination of a daily price for Brent on its own, this new index is widely used as the preferred benchmark for crude oil transactions. On average, there are

---

[14] The B/L is a receipt issued to the exporter by a common carrier (shipping company) which acknowledges possession of the oil described on the face of the bill. It serves as a contract between the exporter and the shipping company, specifying the services to be performed, the charges for those services and the disposition of the goods if they cannot be delivered as instructed. The B/L is also a document of title that follows the merchandise throughout the transport process; it can be used by the exporter as collateral for loans prior to payment by the importer.

[15] This is clearly an option given to the buyer on the front end of the forward curve for Brent.

[16] The blend represented a flow of about 670,000 b/d in 1997, which has declined to 470,000 b/d in 2004.

between 80 and 100 cargoes of BFO available each month, which could be nominated against forward contracts for physical delivery, although half that number is destined to the spot market.

One of the reasons for the continued success of the Brent waterborne market has been the historical tax regime operating in Great Britain. A Petroleum Revenue Tax (PRT) of close to 80% is levied on E&P companies by the British Oil Taxation Office (OTO) on the basis of "the market price". In the case of transactions with a third party, the reference is the price of the actual deal; but when the transaction is an internal transfer between the E&P and the refining subsidiaries of an integrated oil company, the reference for a given month used to be arbitrarily taken as an average of reported prices over a 45-day window, using information supplied by companies. In a falling market, there was thus a strong incentive for integrated companies to release cargoes out to third parties, to get more favorable tax treatment.

Practically, the outright price for Brent blend is determined in five market compartments that are deeply intertwined:

1. The spot market, or dated Brent, that trades cargoes about to be loaded in the next 2 to 10 days, FOB Sullom Voe (Shetland Islands, UK).
2. The forward market, or "15-day Brent", that trades physical cargoes whose loading window is not known at the time of the transaction and will only become known 15 days prior to the first day of the loading window. The forward curve formed on this segment can extend up to 12 months; it is less active now than it used to be in the 1990s, due to the emergence of Futures contracts.
3. The market for CFDs (Contracts For Differences), which are purely financial swaps allowing companies to hedge the basis risk between the first nearby 15-day forward month and the average of dated Brent quotations over a given loading week; typically, the nearby 8 weeks are quoted.
4. The Brent Futures contract(s),[17] that is settled financially against the assessments of the 15-day forward market on the final day of trading of the contract;[18] the maturities of IPE Futures extend 36 months forward.
5. The market for Brent fixed-for-floating swaps, which are Over The Counter (OTC) instruments, and whose underlying is the first nearby IPE Futures contracts.[19] The maturities traded extend 10 years forward in the swaps market.

(A) THE DATED AND 15-DAY BRENT MARKETS

The 15-day Brent market trades forward cargoes of Brent blend for delivery FOB at Sullom Voe, during any future calendar month, with most of the liquidity concentrated

---

[17] The main Brent Futures contract is traded on the IPE in London. But, during 2001, NYMEX also introduced a Brent contract that put itself in direct competition with the IPE; activity on NYMEX Brent Futures has been lacklustre though.
[18] The IPE contract also allows physical delivery through an EFP (Exchange For Physical), but that procedure is not common nowadays.
[19] Technically, swaps are quoted for calendar months, whereas trading on the IPE expires on the last business day before the 15th day of the month preceding delivery. As a result, the Futures contract that is used as underlying for the floating part of the swap will change during the month. For instance, Brent January swaps will be calculated as an average of February Brent Futures during the first 15 days of January and of March Brent Futures during the last 15 days. Another peculiarity of the Brent swaps market is that on the day of expiry of the February contract, whereas the latter is still the first nearby, its close will be replaced by the settlement of the March contract. This trick was originally intended to exclude from swaps' calculation the last day of trading of Futures, which was deemed too volatile to reflect true fundamentals; it has remained to this day.

in the shortest maturities (between 1 and 5 months ahead). The standard cargo size is 500,000 barrels, which is subject to an operational tolerance of ±5%. The market is known as the "15-day" because the standard contract specifies that each seller must give his buyer at least 15 days' notice of the first day of the 3-day loading date range for the physical cargo that is to be nominated against the paper contract.

Cargoes loading with less than 15 days' notice cannot be nominated against a paper contract. They are traded as spot or *dated* cargoes because a specified loading window has already been attached to them. The loading program for Brent is published on the 15th day of the month preceding delivery (i.e., 1 day before expiry of the associated Futures), which means that cargoes can be nominated against forward contracts during the last half of the month preceding the delivery month, or the first half of the delivery month. To cope with this schedule, the 15-day forward of a given month (e.g., Brent January) ceases to be quoted between the 10th and 12th day of the month preceding delivery (i.e., December).

Interestingly enough, 15-day forward contracts need not be settled through the delivery of a dated cargo for all parties involved in the market. A procedure called a *bookout* allows participants who have purchased and sold a nominal cargo in the future to net out their position with other counterparties, thereby exiting the "daisy chain" between the equity producer and ultimate refiner of the crude.

How are the values of dated Brent calculated by *Platt's*? On day D, the agency will record the transactions for the time window $(D + 10, D + 21)$. If, on 1 December, only one spot cargo has been traded at a formula of "January Brent Futures − \$0.20/barrel", for instance, and if the closing price for that particular contract turns out to be \$49.80/barrel on the IPE, *Platt's* will publish an assessment for dated Brent of \$49.60/barrel.

To determine the price of various maturities in the 15-day forward market, *Platt's* and competing agencies just record the transactions that have been completed OTC for a given maturity (e.g., Brent March) on day D, at a fixed price. They publish the corresponding assessments (where the agency infers the market has closed) on day $D + 1$.

(B) THE MARKET FOR BRENT CFDS

What springs to mind immediately from articulation of the dated and 15-day markets is that traders are left with a potentially devastating basis risk between the spot and the first month of the 15-day (devastating because this is the part of the forward curve where volatility is highest).

Let us assume, for instance, that in late April a Belgian refiner has bought a cargo of Forties, loading in 2 weeks' time, at a price of "dated Brent + \$0.15/barrel"; the pricing period for the benchmark is defined as the average of the week 16–20 May. Clearly, at the end of April, the May 15-day is no longer quoted by traders, and the first maturity of the forward market is Brent June (implied: 15-day). If the refiner wishes to convert the purchase from floating to fixed price, he will have either to buy a June Brent cargo on the 15-day, or to go long 500 lots of IPE June Brent Futures (each lot has a nominal rate of 1,000 barrels). Both hedges leave him with some risk, however, since during the pricing period for the dated Brent index (16–20 May), the June forward and Futures contracts will in all likelihood show only moderate correlation with the dated Brent spot index. Let us assume further that the Belgian refiner opts to buy a June Brent cargo at \$45.50/barrel.

To deal with the risks associated with the very short maturities of the Brent forward curve, the need has arisen to introduce financial swaps, or CFDs, that allow the exchange of payments based on the difference between the average of the dated Brent index for a given week (16–20 May in our example) and the average of the 15-day first nearby (Brent June here), as reported by *Platt's*. In a market in backwardation, at the end of April, traders could find quotes for the week 2–6 May at "Brent June + \$0.14/barrel", 9–13 May at "Brent June + \$0.11/barrel" and 16–20 May at "Brent June + \$0.06/barrel", for instance.

Our Belgian refiner could thus enter into a CFD whereby he would pay the average of Brent June over the period 16–20 May and simultaneously receive the average of dated Brent. He would then be left with the following purchase cost, with no residual risk (provided he sold 20% of his Brent June position each working day of 16–20 May):

- Buy a cargo of Forties at: dated Brent + \$0.15/barrel.
- Buy June Brent 15-day at: \$45.50/barrel.
- Buy 16–20 May CFD at: Brent June + 0.06/barrel.
- Net purchase cost for the cargo of Forties: \$45.71/barrel.

Although a NYMEX Futures contract is more active than its IPE counterpart (the open interest for the first nearby of the former is close to 200,000 lots when the latter only records 90,000 lots), Brent is a more common pricing reference for waterborne crude than WTI, and there are two main reasons for this:

1. WTI is ultimately a domestic crude oil that cannot be exported and that is traded in pipelines.
2. With the high volatility in the short-term end of the forward curve, companies need hedging instruments for the next few weeks' pricing exposures. And while the current combination of 15-day Brent and Brent CFDs fulfill this function very efficiently, US pipeline operators expect traders to nominate their delivery programs before the delivery month. As a result, the "spot" in the US crude oil market is usually equivalent to the first forward month in the Brent market.

(C) THE MARKET FOR FUTURES AND BRENT SWAPS

The physical Brent market described above is completed by a set of purely financial instruments, essentially Futures and swaps (and options on Futures and swaps). IPE Brent futures contract trades in lots of 1,000 barrels and expires around the 15th day of the month, just before the first nearby 15-day forward ceases to be quoted by market participants because of the nomination mechanism described above. Futures are cash-settled against the 15-day index on the day of expiry; alternatively, they can lead to delivery through an Exchange for Physical (EFP) agreement. The EFP is a transaction whereby two parties, one long Futures and short a physical cargo and the other short Futures and long a physical cargo, agree to offset their respective positions; the EFP has to be declared to the clearing house of the exchange (in this case the LCH: London Clearing House) by both parties.

The market for Brent swaps has been by far the fastest growing segment of the past ten years. It has become a little more transparent since 2001, with the introduction of a popular electronic platform, ICE,[20] which now owns the IPE. One of the peculiarities of the oil market is that the underlying prices used for Brent and WTI swaps, its most liquid trading instruments, are usually monthly averages of Futures prices, not spot indexes (although some swaps are based on dated Brent, for instance). This obviously creates direct arbitrage between the OTC Brent swap market and IPE Futures, whose prices are in turn settled on the 15-day forward market. Physical arbitrage between the 15-day and dated Brent closes the loop of interactions between all instruments. These relationships, and the potential for profits they generate should the segments fall temporarily out of sync, tie closely together the five compartments of the Brent market.

(3) Other crude oil markets

Over the past few years, many physical forward markets for crude oil have been supplanted by financial swaps, so that only a small number of them have survived to this day:

- The forward WTI, which is a blend of crude oils collected by pipeline from New Mexico and West Texas, is based on deliveries into the BP/ChevronTexaco pipeline at Cushing, Oklahoma, for typical quantities of 50,000–75,000 barrels. Only the first 3 months see some decent activity.
- The forward Dubai trades 500,000-barrel cargoes FOB the Fateh terminal, with a tolerance of ±5%. Physical production has diminished over the last few years to 12–15 cargoes per month, calling into question its validity as a major price determinant for Persian Gulf crudes going to the Far East. Paper trades are now a mere 5–10 per day and they are mainly carried out as spreads to the 15-day Brent.
- The forward Tapis is based on 600,000-barrel cargoes FOB the Kerteh (Oman) terminal, with 14–16 cargoes per month and about 5 paper trades per day. The forward market has now been almost completely replaced with swaps on the so-called Asian Petroleum Price Index (APPI) which trades in typical quantities of 100,000 barrels.

A double trend has thus emerged in the crude oil markets over the past few years:

1. Liquidity has concentrated into a very limited number of grades against which all others are priced.
2. Trading has become a primarily financial activity. Indeed, most of outright price trading is now concentrated in the huge derivatives markets for Brent and WTI. WTI trades further forward than any of the existing Futures contracts (7 years ahead) and its daily volume easily reaches 250,000 contracts, with an open interest in 2004 of close to 700 Mb, or the equivalent of 8 days of worldwide production. The spread between these two grades is also very actively monitored because it reflects shipping conditions across the Atlantic (delivery commitments on NYMEX can be honored with North Sea and African crudes that are needed to satisfy the US demand in light

---

[20] ICE: Intercontinental Exchange.

crudes).[21] In practice though, the derivatives market often adjusts to new conditions before oil tankers actually take the sea across the Atlantic.

(4) The changing landscape of oil trading

With hindsight, the introduction of Futures and, subsequently, of swaps, options and other derivative instruments has completely changed the way in which crude oil is priced and, most importantly, valued by the market. The physical commodity is now priced at a differential to Futures prices, which are themselves linked by arbitrage to the value of long-dated swaps. If investors (funds) decide that they want to own long-term claims on crude oil in an attempt to anticipate an expected tightening of the so-called "fundamentals", they will typically buy swaps from their brokers/dealers for long-dated maturities (5 to 10 years forward). The selling banks will carry the positions on their books by determining a "reasonable" value for spreads between the most actively traded maturities (e.g., the years 2005 and 2006 in 2004) and they will hedge themselves by buying relatively short Futures maturities. This will cause an increase in the price of the latter and, subsequently, in the price of all physical crude oils traded as spot cargoes. The financial sphere has thus a direct impact on the price paid for oil in the physical world. Trees cannot grow to the sky, though: if there is more physical material than demand from refiners, commercial inventories are going to increase to the point when the latter will not feel comfortable buying any extra oil, physical cargoes are going to be sold at a discount to the first nearby futures (the curve will move in "contango") and market participants will push the whole forward curve down to take into account their revised supply/demand expectations. In practice, the forward curve of Brent and WTI moves from contango to backwardation on a regular basis: when spot prices are "high", forward curves are generally in backwardation, and the reverse when spot prices are "low" (Figure 9.6).

Let us take a few recent examples: in September 2001, oil Futures dropped sharply immediately after the re-opening of NYMEX, as the market factored in the potentially recessionary effects of the 9/11 attacks on the World Trade Center. Similarly, at the beginning of 2003, as the second Gulf War was about to be launched, a "global insecurity trade" had become fashionable among "global macro" investors, consisting in going long oil and gold derivatives, which would be positively affected by turmoil in the Middle East and the likely flight to non-monetary, inflation-hedged assets, while simultaneously shorting equivalent amounts of copper futures on the LME or COMEX,[22] in anticipation of a worldwide decline in industrial production.

In the fall of 2004, as WTI oil futures were reaching 21-year highs of more than $55.0/barrel, most analysts were disconcerted by the apparent breakdown of the well-tested relationship between the level of OECD inventories and the differential between short- and long-dated oil prices: put simply, prices were too high on the short end of the curve, despite the considerable increase in 5- to 10-year swap prices (see Figure 9.6 once more). Again, this could be explained, at least in part, by the effect of commodity funds

---

[21] At present, the list of alternative grades for delivery on NYMEX is confined to three North Sea crudes (Brent blend, Oseberg and Forties), two Nigerian crudes (Bonny Light and Qua Iboe) and a Colombian crude (Cusiana). Brent, Forties and Oseberg are currently priced at a discount of $0.30/barrel to WTI, Bonny Light and Cusiana at a premium of $0.15 and Qua Iboe at a premium of $0.05/barrel.

[22] LME: London Metal Exchange. COMEX: New York Commodity Exchange.

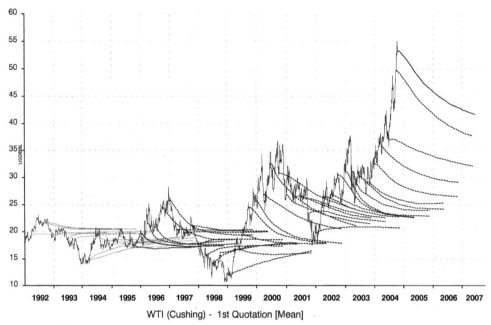

Figure 9.6 From contango to backwardation ... and the end of cheap oil.

attracting more and more investment dollars. The amount of savings passively invested in commodities (i.e., indexed on the GSCI, AIG-Dow Jones or CRB series[23]) has increased sharply in 2003–2004 (some estimates now put the tally at close to $30bn, which implies about $15bn indexed on crude prices alone), as investors have come to realize that, over the long run, commodities as an asset class have performed at least as well as stocks, and far better than bonds, when corrected for inflation.[24] A simple calculation allows quantifying the magnified effect that a global reallocation of investments towards commodities could have on oil prices. The value of NYMEX oil options/Futures open interest is close to $50bn, or 0.3% of US equity market capitalization (about $17 trillion in 2004). Practically, this means that if only 1% of funds invested in US stocks were to be re-assigned to commodities investments an additional demand for oil derivatives of close to $140bn[25] (roughly three times the open interest on NYMEX) would materialize. Needless to say, one can expect some effect on the price of oil.

Financial institutions and investment funds have thus become major players in the oil derivatives markets over the past 10 years; in this sense, it is the investors who now decide the level of oil prices, not the industry. Speculation should not be blamed too quickly though; as the saying goes: "in the short term, the market is a voting machine

---

[23] GSCI: Goldman Sachs Commodity Index; CRB: Commodity Research Bureau.
[24] See, for example: "Facts and fantasies about commodity futures", G. Gorton and K.G. Rouwenhorst, Yale ICF working paper, June 2004, *www.ssrn.com/abstract=560042*.
[25] $140bn = 80% × 1% × $17 trillion. For example, the GSCI Total Return Index represents the compounded return of a fully collateralized position in a number of first nearby Futures contracts, which are rolled forward every month, invested according to each commodity's share in worldwide production. Roughly 75% of the index is made up of energy Futures (WTI, Henry Hub natural gas, heating oil, gasoline), the rest coming from precious and base metals (gold, silver, palladium, copper), as well as soft commodities (wheat, soybeans, livestock).

but, in the long term, it is a weighing machine." By contrast, producing countries and international oil companies increasingly behave as *price-takers*, even if their trading departments are among the major derivatives players when optimizing their own systems or serving customers. From time to time, the majors re-align the reference price of oil used in budgeting investments, but, more often than not, they do not sell their output forward and, therefore, almost never express an opinion about the price of oil.

9.3 REFINED PRODUCTS MARKETS

Because of its chemical nature and liquid state, crude oil is a very compact source of energy. This said, it is not normally used in its raw state[26] and must be processed through a refinery in order to be turned into marketable products such as gasoline, heating oil or fuel oil. There are over a hundred refineries in Europe and many hundreds worldwide, with a global capacity of about 84.0 Mb/d at the end of 2003. This capacity is now growing at a moderate pace – 1.7–1.8 Mb/d each year – with most of the investments in Asia. This is not much, given that refinery utilization rates are between 85% and 90% in the US and Western Europe.

Refining is a complex, large-scale business: most facilities have crude intake capacities in the range 50,000 to 150,000 b/d and cost a few billion dollars to build as "greenfield" projects. In a refinery, crude is basically heated in a furnace and goes through a fractional distillation process in which its various components are separated by their volatility and molecular size into so-called *refinery cuts*. The longer the hydrocarbon molecules, the higher their boiling temperature; heavy fractions thus come out at the bottom of the distillation column, whilst light ones come out at the top of the column. Schematically, the main groups of refined products are, in order of ascending cooling temperatures:

1. Liquefied Petroleum Gases (LPGs), such as propane, butane or a mixture of the two.
2. Gasoline and naphtha, which include motor gasoline as well as petrochemical feedstocks.
3. Jet/kerosene, including most aviation fuel.
4. Gasoil and diesel, used mainly for home heating and for small- and medium-sized engines, mostly in Europe and the US.
5. Fuel oil used in furnaces, boilers and in large engines (factories and ships).

Gasoline is the refining product in highest relative demand, especially in the US. Oil has indeed virtually no substitute as a transportation fuel, and there is no immediate prospect for that to happen at current prices. A process called *cracking* (thermal and catalytic) is therefore implemented in refineries in order to extract more gasoline from the other cuts (in particular, residues from the fractional distillation process), by breaking their longer, less valuable molecules.

Generally speaking, the lighter products are priced higher than their heavier counterparts (Figure 9.7). Substitution of other energies is also a consideration: fuel oil and

---

[26] The only exception is low-sulfur crude oil which is sometimes burnt directly in power stations, in Japan in particular.

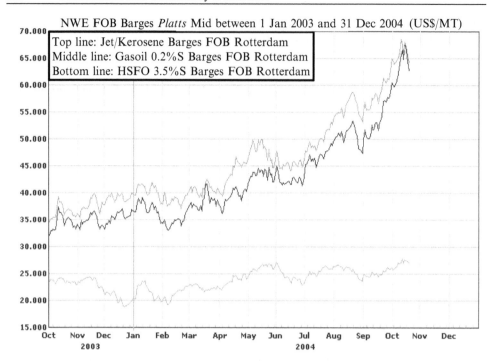

Figure 9.7   Light products are more expensive than heavy cuts.
Source: Platt's.

LPGs face competition from coal and natural gas and this certainly limits their prices; therefore, LPGs do not always enjoy the premium associated with being the lightest product. Motor gasoline usually costs more to produce than diesel and, therefore, is priced higher, except during short episodes. Jet fuel is also more expensive than diesel because special care must be taken in its transportation and storage and part of the kerosene fraction can be made into gasoline, whereas diesel cannot. Because they are co-produced in the refining process, there are strong relationships between the various cuts: the price of kerosene is well correlated to gasoil, for instance; an airline that is willing to hedge its forward purchases of aviation fuel for pre-sold tickets will typically use some Brent swaps 2 to 3 years forward, will roll them over into gasoil swaps (by buying the "crack spread"), eventually converting them into swaps on kerosene cargoes CIF when the delivery period gets closer (by buying the "jet differential"). Although this spread is fairly stable compared with the outright price of products *most of the time*, hovering between $20.0 and $50.0/MT (Metric Ton), it can diverge dramatically on some occasions. It spiked to $200/MT just before the First Gulf War in 1991 when military requirements for fighter jets and bombers caused a sharp increase in the demand for aviation fuel compared with heating oil. On the contrary, the crisis of air travel in 2001–2002 led to a narrowing of the spread to unheard-of levels (Figure 9.8) while the 2003 recovery caused its widening.

Refined products markets differ from crude in several respects. First, the scale of operations is usually much smaller: a typical product deal might only involve 5,000 or 10,000 barrels; as a result, the money at stake is also much lower. Second, quality

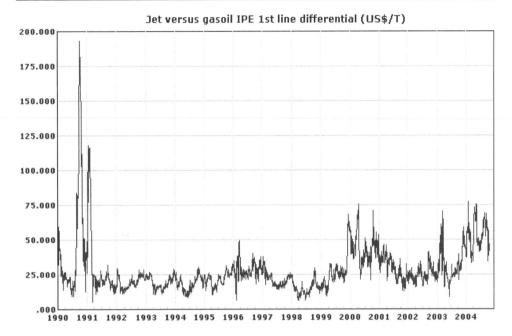

Figure 9.8   The jet/kerosene versus IPE gasoil differential.

Maximum: 193,000; minimum: 5,500; last: 42,000; mean: 28,177. *Source*: *Platt's*, Argus Petroleum Products.

considerations are paramount: refined products must meet very stringent quality specifications if they are to be sold to final consumers and the delivery of an off-spec cargo would be regarded as a breach of contract by the buyer. Rigorous quality tests therefore form an important aspect of any deal, through the appointment of independent inspectors. Finally, price differentials between the various grades of refined products are constantly shifting and the complexity of the physical market open opportunities for traders, either in blending or in moving cargoes around the world.

The size of the market is smaller, though. Because refineries have historically been built close to consuming centers, the markets for products are more regional than for crude oil. Indeed, no refiner or marketer is able to operate a completely balanced system and the primary function of the physical market is to redistribute the individual surpluses and deficits that inevitably arise at each location. In 2003, inter-regional flows are estimated to have totaled 500 million MT, or the equivalent of 10.0 Mb/d (i.e., less than one-third of international crude oil exports).

Although these patterns change over time, there are regular flows of products from one region to another and relative price levels are set accordingly (Figure 9.9). Europe, for instance, not only exports gasoline to the US and fuel oil to the Far East, but also imports naphtha and fuel oil for use as refinery feedstock[27] from Russia and the Middle East. With a large number of sophisticated refineries, it is able to purchase profitably

---

[27] Indeed, Europe has a well-developed petrochemical industry and a large number of sophisticated refineries specializing in the production of gasoline. As a result, there is a ready market for both naphtha with a high paraffin content, which is preferred as a feedstock for ethylene crackers, and naphtha with a high naphthenic and aromatic content, which is preferred as a feedstock to refiners to make gasoline.

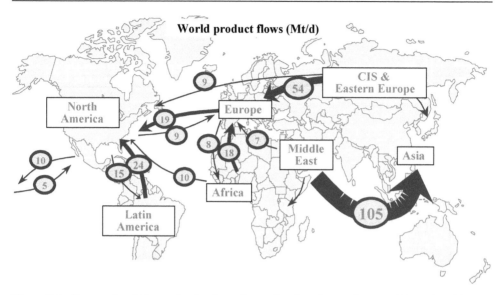

Figure 9.9 International flows of refined products. *Product flows* reflect specific regional imbalances between refining and demand. The market must be balanced. Inter-regional flows total 500 MT, or 30% of crude flows.
Source: Total, PIRA.

low-quality feedstocks and turn them into high-quality products, such as gasoline and jet fuel, for re-sale. The US exports distillates to South America and the Far East (there are also some occasional flows of diesel to Europe), while the Middle East is a net exporter of naphtha and fuel oil to both the Far East and Europe. In aggregate, the breakdown by product of international physical flows in 2003 was the following: residual fuel oil 24%, gasoil 25%, gasoline 15%, LPGs 8%, naphtha 11% and jet fuel and kerosene 8%. Other, more exotic products, such as coke, bitumen, asphalt and lubricants, accounted for the remainder.

Because they require specialized knowledge, an exhaustive description of all the markets for refined products in Europe, the US and Asia is clearly beyond the scope of this chapter. It is best to concentrate on two particular markets: gasoil and diesel in Europe, on the one hand, and gasoline in the US, on the other hand.

(1) Gasoil and diesel in Europe

The European products market is the second largest in the world. The greatest concentration of refining capacity is to be found in the ARA region of the Netherlands and Belgium where crude intake is nearly 2.0 Mb/d and which is strategically placed at the mouth of the Rhine River. The four major consuming countries are, unsurprisingly, Germany, France, Italy and the UK, with significant cross-border flows of products between them.

Gasoil is used extensively throughout Europe both as a fuel for domestic central heating systems, especially in Germany, and as an automotive fuel (diesel); over the past decade, it has become the largest European product market by far. Quality standards for heating oil and automotive diesel have become more stringent and the market appears to be increasingly fragmented as blending opportunities are constrained. At the end of 2003, the sulfur content in German gasoil could not exceed 0.10% in weight and its winter CFPP had to be below $-7°C$,[28] whilst its French counterpart's acceptable levels were defined as 0.35% S and $-5°C$ CFPP, respectively, a difference explained by colder weather in Germany. By contrast, there is now an EU-wide diesel grade (EN590), whose sulfur content will have to be below 0.005% starting in January 2005 (it will then be renamed ULSD, for Ultra Low Sulfur Diesel) but whose cold properties will still vary from country to country.

The market for European gasoil divides into the northwest (ARA) and the Mediterranean (Genoa). Northwestern European gasoil is traded in cargoes of 20,000 to 25,000 MT, on both a CIF (imports) and an FOB (exports) basis. Prices are typically negotiated at a fixed differential to the IPE gasoil Futures contract, which is closely related to the spot ARA barges market (see p. 214). Barges correspond to unit lots of 1,000 to 5,000 MT after the product has been discharged from the incoming cargoes (the price of 1 MT is usually higher in a barge than in a cargo to reflect handling costs); most of the time, the barges move inland, into the Benelux countries and Germany.

Because of tax incentives at the pump and a continued improvement of motor engines, diesel has been a high-growth story over the past decade in Europe: its French consumption is now twice as high as that of gasoline or gasoil, for instance. Despite this success in the retail market, diesel cargoes are mostly sold at a fixed differential to the first nearby IPE gasoil Futures on the wholesale market.

How is the spot price of EN590 formed in practice? The methodology of the assessment is defined very precisely by *Platt's*: on any day D, the agency will record all transactions involving cargoes of 20,000 MT (with a tolerance of $\pm 10\%$) which are able to discharge at Bordeaux and whose price is set on the basis of deliveries at Le Havre between $D + 10$ and $D + 25$. This is the so-called "EN590 flexi-market". If a trader bids a 20,000-MT cargo CIF Le Havre, with delivery between 12–18 March, at a formula price of "April IPE gasoil + $20.0/MT", *Platt's* will record a low quotation for EN590 of $420.0/MT, if the April futures closes at $400.0/MT.

This series of daily assessments is used as a basis for floating price transactions and diesel swaps. Let us take a practical situation: a Parisian transportation company has agreed to buy 10,000 MT of diesel directly from a refiner, at a price defined as the monthly average of *Platt's* EN590 CIF NWE (North West Europe), and it now wishes to convert its physical diesel purchase into a fixed price transaction. Let us assume further that the forward value of diesel is at a premium of $22.0/MT over IPE gasoil for the period under consideration (e.g., March 2005). The transportation company will need to make two simultaneous transactions:

1. Buy a 10,000-MT fixed-for-floating swap for March 2005 on IPE gasoil.
2. Buy a floating-for-floating swap whereby it commits to pay the average of "IPE gasoil + $22.0/MT" and to receive in exchange the average of *Platt's* quotations of EN590 CIF NWE in March 2005 (see Figure 9.10 for the historical series of 1-month forward differentials).

---

[28] The stability of gasoil in cold weather is important in its two main uses. At low temperatures, the heavier components of a gasoil tend to crystallize and cause filters to plug. There are several tests of quality, all of which are designed to detect the formation of crystals (the Cold Filter Plugging Point, or CFPP, is the most common test).

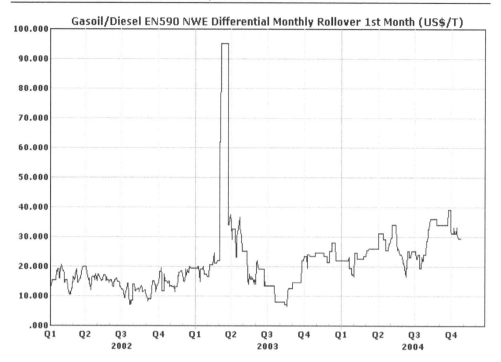

Figure 9.10 Differential between EN5920 and IPE gas oil.
Maximum: 95,000; minimum: 6,500; last: 29,500; mean: 21,669. *Source*: Argus Petroleum Products.

It can be seen from this example that European heating oil and diesel markets closely follow the model prevailing for crude oil: in essence, the outright price of middle distillates is formed on the IPE through financial trading of their main benchmark[29] – gasoil 0.2% S barges FOB Rotterdam – and all the other grades or shipping terms are priced at a differential to the benchmark; this is true for both spot cargoes and swaps based on *Platt's* indexes for forward delivery periods. Such an organization allows liquidity to concentrate on a very limited number of Futures contracts, canceling out the actual complexity of different quality specifications between countries.

(2) The US gasoline market

The US is the single largest user of oil products in the world, consuming 20.5 Mb/d of refined products in 2004. Its demand barrel is exceptionally light compared with most other countries: gasoline, heating oil, diesel and jet fuel account for 70% of US product demand, whilst gasoline alone constitutes about 45% of the total (i.e., 9.0 Mb/d, or roughly 40% of a worldwide demand of 21.75 Mb/d), which explains why the "driving season" of the US is monitored so closely by oil traders.

Despite having the world's largest and most sophisticated refining system, the US

---

[29] In 2004 the typical daily volume of gasoil Futures traded on the IPE was 40,000 lots, with an open interest of 170,000 lots; its US counterpart, the NYMEX heating oil contract, had volumes of 65,000 lots per day, with an open interest of 200,000 lots.

remains, more than ever, dependent on imports of refined products from Venezuela, Canada, Algeria, Europe, the Caribbean and Asia. Net imports averaged 2.0 Mb/d in 2003 – 10% of total US product demand – and the key consuming markets in the northeast rely on imports to meet about one-fifth of their gasoline demand. Waterborne imports, especially for gasoline and gasoline-blending components, play an important role in the overall supply/demand balance of the country since the forward cover for this product is fairly low in the US: 25 days of consumption on average in 2004.

Because settlement of NYMEX Futures contracts – the industry benchmark – is done through an FOB delivery in barges in New York Harbor, the US gasoline market is centered on the northeast. The 1.9-Mb/d Colonial Pipeline takes products from refineries in Texas, Louisiana and Mississippi and serves the Atlantic coast markets with the exception of Florida. Most finished gasoline is imported by US distributors on an FOB basis from Europe. In contrast, blendstocks are sold CIF into New York and some of the finished gasoline is shipped through the Buckeye Pipeline to the Midwest. There are spot markets at different exit points along the Colonial Pipeline (e.g., 25,000-barrel batches sold FIP in Pasadena, Texas), in New York (25,000-barrel barges sold FOB from anywhere in the harbor) and in Boston (max. 225,000-barrel cargoes sold CIF).

Gasoline is a blended product that is characterized by its octane number[30] and vapor pressure as well as its benzene, lead and oxygenate content. In 1990 the US Clean Air Act (CAA) was amended to limit sulfur, carbon monoxide and ozone-forming emissions in transportation, the law being interpreted and enforced by the powerful Environmental Protection Agency (EPA). CAA rules have significantly altered the physical characteristics of gasoline in the past ten years. The first concrete measure was the lead phasedown program, which has resulted in only unleaded gasoline being permitted for sale in the US today. The second phase placed limits on the volatility of gasoline throughout the year and was introduced to reduce vapor emissions resulting from the extensive use of butane as a blending component. The introduction of Re-Formulated Gasoline (RFG) in 1995 was intended to reduce the build-up of ozone in the atmosphere in the nine urban areas most severely affected in summertime and led to further tightening regulations regarding olefin and sulfur contents. In addition, some states had allowed MTBE[31] as a blending component to compensate the mandatory removal of lead in gasoline; but this additive has subsequently been declared toxic and is now forbidden in California, New York and Connecticut (it must be replaced with methanol). These layers of complexity, coupled with further planned reductions in sulfur content from 0.030% to 0.003% in 2006, have had the effect of fragmenting the US gasoline market in a high number of grades that all trade at a differential to NYMEX. The most common qualities are, in order of increasing price, unleaded 87 octane 0.3 S (*regular*), 89 octane 0.3 S (*midgrade*) and 93 octane 0.3 S (*premium*).

Outright price formation for US gasoline is done on NYMEX, through the regular unleaded gasoline Futures contract, where trading is brisk: average daily volumes easily reach 60,000 lots and the open interest stood at a comfortable 160,000 contracts at the

---

[30] The octane number measures the tendency of motor gasoline to "knock" in engines; the higher the octane number, the lower the knocking tendency. There are two octane number tests for motor gasoline: the F1 or "research method" and the F2 or "motor method". For instance, premium unleaded, or *Eurograde*, has a minimum F1 specification of 95 and a minimum F2 of 85.

[31] MTBE: Methyl Tertiary Butyl Ether = an additive for gasoline.

end of September 2004. The contract requires delivery to be made FOB seller's facility in New York Harbor, ex-shore (i.e., into barges) with all duties, taxes and other charges paid and the specifications must conform to Phase II complex model reformulated gasoline.[32] In a similar fashion to crude oil and heating oil, all grades, shipping terms and delivery points are traded at a differential to the first quoted month of NYMEX gasoline Futures. For instance, on 3 October, Premium 93 Gulf Coast could trade at a premium of 6.0 cents/gal over NYMEX November while RFG unleaded 87 barges NYH and Conventional 87 FIP into Buckeye would sell at discounts of 50.0 cents/gal[33] and 25.0 cents/gal under NYMEX, respectively.

The US also retains two forward gasoline markets that operate in parallel with much more liquid futures: the Colonial Pipeline and the so-called "Boston Bingo" cargo markets. These segments allow companies to take positions against the basis between the highly standardized quality and delivery terms of the Futures contract and the slightly different terms associated with physical delivery in the most active spot markets. But, although the delivery terms are different, the pricing mechanism remains the same and all forward clean product contracts are negotiated at a differential to gasoline Futures.

9.4 CONCLUSION

The main lesson that can be drawn from the evolution of crude and refined products markets over the past 20 years is the trend to go beyond the physical details of the commodity. A limited number of "markers" have managed to capture most of the trading volumes of industry participants, financial institutions and investors in the form of highly standardized contracts that are exchanged in small-size lots. While some may argue that this trend has created noise in prices and has therefore been detrimental to the expression of the so-called "fundamentals" of the oil industry, this clearly misses the point. The spectacular development of the market has only been allowed because of the ample supply of high-quality downstream infrastructure that had been accumulated after the oil shocks: refining capacity, ships and storage. If a refiner has purchased 12 Dubai cargoes over 1 year but finds it more desirable to replace one of them with Bonny Light, he can easily charter a ship and buy the alternative crude FOB off Nigeria. The spot market will easily accept the unused Dubai cargo, at a price, because there is always enough slack capacity in the system to absorb it. This very simple fact creates a lot of re-combinations that greatly enhance physical trading and allow price changes to propagate across the spectrum of qualities and locations.

Comparisons with the US natural gas market will help us to understand the phenomenon. As explained in Chapter 10, Henry Hub in Louisiana is a spot market renowned for its efficiency. Trading of energy is done at a pipeline node, which is located at the heart of the main producing region within the US, namely the Gulf of Mexico. Numer-

---

[32] The first step of the RFG program required refiners to produce gasoline with a lower content of ozone-forming and other specified toxic air pollutants than the actual supplies they produced in 1990. Each refiner established its own "baseline" gasoline quality and used a "simple model" to certify its RFG output based on the reduction in oxygen, benzene and aromatics content. The second step, which began in 1998, required refiners to achieve additional reductions in olefins, sulfur and the percentage of fuel evaporated at 200 and 300°F. This is known as the "complex model" and imposes a new statutory baseline for sulfur and olefins which all refiners must meet.

[33] gal = gallon; 1 barrel = 42 gallons.

ous pipelines originating from the Permian Basin (Texas), San Juan and New Mexico, as well as the Lake Charles LNG terminal, extend towards the large urban centers of Chicago and New York/New England. Thousands of producers, transporters, traders and storage companies carry out their physical transactions here for the day ahead, the month ahead or several years in advance. Since the price of Henry Hub has long been reliable, NYMEX launched a Futures contract in 1991 for natural gas delivered at the hub. Traded volumes have experienced exponential growth and Futures are now a reference for long-term contracts in the US natural gas industry. They have even acquired global status. If natural gas prices increase suddenly in the Gulf of Mexico (e.g., due to a hurricane), the industrial regions of Chicago and New York will switch to supplies from the basins of Alberta (British Columbia) or Anadarko (Oklahoma). Almost instantly, the price of natural gas will increase throughout the US and even in Europe and Japan, under the effect of diverted LNG cargoes. This shows that the transportation infrastructure is clearly an essential factor to the quality of the US market, measured by its depth, its reactivity and the relevance of the prices it generates.

It can be said today that the oil market has reached a similar degree of seamlessness, but on a worldwide scale. If consumption of light products increases strongly in Asia, the traditional export flows of distillates to the US and Europe will diminish as less material crosses the Suez Canal northbound. This will trigger in turn a price rise of heating oil in the West, which will itself pull natural gas higher as a substitute fuel for power generation. Similarly, if freight rates jump upward, since fuel oil has to be sold from Europe to the Far East to clear physical inventories, the spread between both locations has to widen almost mechanically. It can be seen from the above examples that physical oil is almost as liquid as money itself: at any time, it is possible to collect any grade of oil from any shipping terminal and find a buyer for it. As a result, performance risks are limited, market prices have acquired worldwide relevance and industry participants have come to trust these prices,[34] even if they are still heavily influenced by political intervention, particularly with the decisions of OPEC on output and spare capacity. In this respect, the oil market is a model that remains to be challenged.

---

[34] In contrast, US and European electricity markets are too fragmented. They do not have trading hubs of global relevance and, to this day, there are some countries, such as France, where 95% of customers pay their electricity on a regulated tariff, not a retail price deducted from wholesale prices.

10

The Gas Market as the Energy Market of the Next Decades

10.1 THE WORLD GAS OUTLOOK

Once the neglected child of the global energy industry, natural gas is increasingly the "belle of the ball". Gas is indeed the fastest growing energy commodity today: first, because of the virtues of gas in its own right; second, because of the increasing use of gas in power generation worldwide; and, third, while the exact amount of reserves of major oil companies such as Shell Royal Dutch has been recently readjusted to lower numbers, the state of gas reserves remains remarkably promising. Because of reduced emissions, the share of gas in power generation will increase from 100 billion m^3 in 1995 to more than 200 billion m^3 projected in 2010, an increase of 4.8% a year (compared with an increase of 1.4% a year in gas consumption for other uses). As oil supplies tighten and prices march every day to new highs, major oil companies have recently unveiled a flurry of multi-billion dollar deals for new projects whose target is not oil, but natural gas.

Worldwide, prices of gas have risen: for instance, at Henry Hub, a major trading point located in the south of the US on the Gulf of Mexico (the most active hub in the world), prices went from $2.76 per million British thermal units in the third quarter of 2001 to $3.20 in mid-2002 and above $8 in October 2004. Price volatility is higher in gas markets than in oil markets – gas is more similar to electricity in this respect. Trading of Liquefied Natural Gas (LNG) is starting, with gasification plants being built along various shores: for the major players, the possibility of rerouting methane tankers is certainly a way of taking immediate advantage of gas shortage in a given region and exploiting arbitrage opportunities between continents. Large differences remain between such countries as the US and the UK, where gas is a commodity in its own right and price is set by supply and demand, and Western Europe, where, in contrast, deregulation of gas markets is far from complete while gas prices continue to be defined as linear functions of oil prices. The supply of gas in such countries as France and Italy takes place through *long-term contracts* with Take Or Pay (TOP) clauses (i.e., penalties if a minimum volume is not purchased at any time over the contract period).

Reserves of natural gas around the world are abundant. They have more than doubled in 20 years and amounted to more than 176 million m^3 at the end of 2003. The largest reserves are in Russia, followed by Iran and Qatar. The next largest can be found in the US, Abu Dhabi, Norway, Venezuela and Algeria. Existing resources, including reserves still to be discovered, should cover world needs for more than 150 years. Figures 10.1 and 10.2 show the proven reserves of gas (at the time of writing),

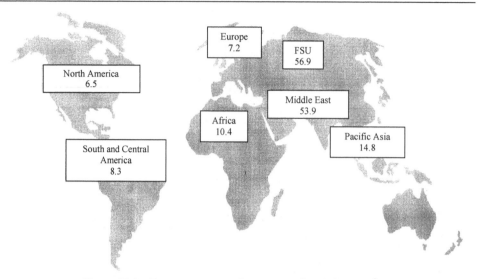

Figure 10.1 Proven reserves of gas per region (trillion m^3).

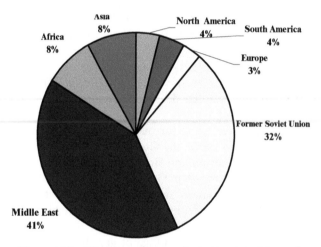

Figure 10.2 World gas reserves in 2003: 176 trillion m^3.
Source: BP Statistical Review World Energy 2004

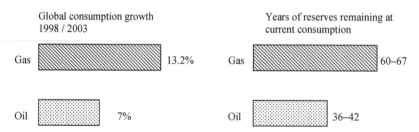

Figure 10.3 Global consumption and years of reserves remaining at current consumption.

expressed in trillion m^3. Figure 10.3 shows consumptions and years remaining at the present level of consumption.

Note that natural gas mainly consists of methane and ethane which occurs naturally in the earth's crust; it is often found in association with crude oil.

Principal gas markets

Until recently, three regional markets could be identified in the world, with limited trade between them because of the cost of gas transportation over large distances:

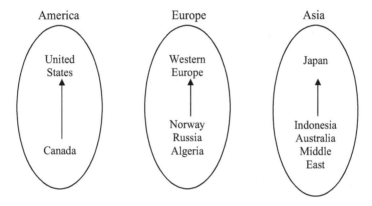

Numbers on the transportation of LNG will be given in Section 10.4. But, for the moment we need to keep in mind that it only costs $2 to transport a barrel of oil across the world, i.e., a small percentage of the price of a barrel. This explains why oil is a global market while gas is not (electricity is restricted to local markets because of its unique non-storability). Increased LNG transport should help to break down the current world segmentation.

Note that gas fields are unevenly spread: 37% lie in the Former Soviet Union, about the same in the Middle East, 7.2% in Africa and 3.2% in Europe, Norway included. American reserves represent 3% of the world total, enough for just 9 years of consumption; Europe has reserves for 24 years.

Today, gas represents 25% of the total energy balance and will amount to 30% in 2020, by which time it should represent one-half of all new electricity production, reducing the contribution of coal, although coal will remain the most common energy source.

Europe needs gas in high amounts and is trying to diversify its supply. The rate of increase in gas consumption varies from one year to the next, and depends on the evolution of other energy prices. However, the trend is clearly positive for domestic use and for electricity production, largely because of increasing limits on nuclear energy production. In 2001 the consumption of gas in the EU amounted to 423 million m^3, 2.7% higher than in 2000, and the increase has been sharper in 2002 and 2003.

Local production in Europe represents 241 billion m^3 (up by 0.9%), but it imports 173 billion m^3 (down by 4%). The main exporters to Europe are Russia (70 billion m^3), then Algeria (50 billion m^3, the same amount as exported by Norway). Regarding the eight gas pipelines which connect Norway to Germany, Belgium, France and the UK, their capacity amounts to 88 billion m^3. Those coming from Algeria have a combined capacity of 35 billion m^3. LNG covers only about 10% of EU consumption, but its importance should rapidly increase and imports are expected to amount to 60 billion m^3 within a few years. Deregulation of most European gas markets should be completed by then, but it is not clear whether the opening of competitive markets will be sufficient to avoid any disruption risk. The three companies importing the highest volume of gas – roughly 40 billion m^3 each, representing more that 50% of the imports between the three of them – are ENI (Italy), Ruhrgas (Germany), which was recently acquired by the German electricity giant E.ON, and Gaz de France.

Turkey is expected shortly to become one of the world's main gas importers, with contracts already signed for 68 billion m^3 over the period 2010–2015. In 2002 Russia was the first to start delivery of gas through the Blue Stream Pipeline under the Black Sea and the capacity of the pipeline (16 billion m^3) should double by 2015. Russian gas also reaches Turkey through above-ground pipelines via the Ukraine, Romania and Bulgaria. The other providers are Iran, Algeria (as LNG) and Nigeria (as LNG). Gas imports are expected to total 40 billion m^3 as of 2005. The volume of gas coming from Iran has been reduced by Turkey because of its poor quality.

The US faces serious difficulties in meeting demand for gas as domestic production is decreasing. Solutions are provided partly by gas imports from Canada and partly by LNG; Canadian production, however, is also declining and some promising gas fields have proved disappointing. Natural gas accounts to date (2004) for almost a quarter of US energy consumption, since nearly all new power plants are Combined Cycle Gas Turbines (CCGTs), two peaks can be observed in prices: in winter because of the cold and in summer because of air conditioning. In Asia, energy needs are severe in eastern Asia, particularly Korea and Japan, while they are also a primary concern in China. Abundant and cheap coal remains a central source of energy, but increasing use of gas would allow China to curb emissions and satisfy the rapidly growing demand for electricity. Korea does not have any energy sources of its own and increasingly uses gas (in particular, for electricity production), the imports of which doubled between 1995 and 2001. China has undertaken major gas pipeline projects in central Asia but is also considering the importation of LNG. Japan is the third largest world importer of natural gas after the US and Germany and the largest importer of LNG. In fact, all Japanese gas imports (more than 75 billion m^3 in 2002) are LNG.

Gas production and quality

Gas in its natural state is a mixture of hydrocarbon gases, carbon dioxide and nitrogen. Among hydrocarbon gases, methane (CH_4) is the major constituent, with a proportion in volume comprised between 82% and 95%, then ethane (C_2H_6) between 2.5 and 7.5%; propane and butane are present in smaller fractions. The component of carbon dioxide (CO_2) varies between 0.2 and 1% of the volume, and nitrogen (N_2) between 1.5% and 15%.

The quality of gas is measured by its calorific value and can fluctuate between 33 and

40 megajoules per cubic meter (MJ/m^3). The higher hydrocarbons release more energy when burned. Other gas characteristics include:

- Hydrocarbon dewpoint (the temperature at which there will be condensation of gas in a pipeline).
- Wobbe index (which measures the compatibility of gas and a burner).
- Odorization (which permits detection of gas leaks by adding a distinctive odor to gas, which is odorless in its natural state).

Natural gas is produced from hydrocarbon deposit reservoirs located in porous rock. The production side of the natural gas industry involves the exploration, development, extraction and processing of gas. The transportation of gas between production areas to onshore terminals and processing facilities is considered as part of the "upstream" process. Note also that natural gas is often found in conjunction with crude oil.

10.2   THE GAS-PRODUCING COUNTRIES

(1) Russia

Gazprom, the Russian company that is also the world's largest producer, accounts for nearly all Russian production. The current government has been trying to encourage competition from Russian oil companies; however, the recent events related to the oil company Yukos have muddied the picture. Domestic gas prices increased in 2002 but still represent only 20% of the export price. Gazprom increased its investments by 50% in 2002 and got together with Shell in the project "Sakhalin 2", which involves oil production and the construction of an LNG terminal in the south of Sakhalin Island for exportation of gas to Japan and South Korea.

However, Gazprom production has been decreasing in the last few years. The main problems it had to face were aging infrastructure and difficulties accessing the country's enormous reserves (26,000 billion m^3 in distant Siberia and under the Arctic Ocean). Huge investment is necessary to exploit them. For instance, the development of the vast Yamal fields (with an estimated potential of 6,000 billion m^3) may require an investment of $70bn between now and 2030. This explains why Gazprom is looking for joint projects with international companies; these, however, have to include participations in gas pipelines. The goal of Gazprom is to stabilize its production around 530 billion m^3 per year. Its exports amounted to $14.5bn in 2002. Long-term contracts involve 2,400 billion m^3 for a total amount of $250bn and are expected to fulfill the needs of one-quarter of the European market for the next 10 years.

Gazprom intends to develop its exports to Asian markets, which may surpass European ones by 2020. In November 2002, Gazprom signed an agreement to reactivate the project to finish the Iran–Pakistan–India (IPI) Pipeline which will pass through Pakistan to India. This project is supported by the World Bank, which views it as a possible way of improving the Afghan economy. Nevertheless, political obstacles are prohibitive at this point.

At the same time, Russia wants to maximize its exports to Europe. Exports to the EU amounted to 88 billion m^3 in 2002. Total exports to Europe amounted to 130 billion m^3

and should rise to 200 billion m^3 by 2008. This agrees with the opinion of strategists who believe that, in the mid to long term, Russia will try to balance its exports between Europe and Asia.

Gazprom wants to build a gas pipeline under the Baltic Sea to directly serve Europe (the "Northern European Pipeline" will be 2,000 miles long and is expected to cost $5.7bn and transport 20–30 billion m^3). The plan is for it to reach Bacton, already a major hub in England.

Gazprom has also signed a project with Petrochina to participate in the construction of a gigantic pipeline linking the northwest part of China and Shanghai. It will be 2,500 miles long and will cost $18bn, with a possible extension to Japan and Korea. Gazprom would own 45%, and the other 55% would belong to the Chinese.

Lastly, Russia is re-establishing its position in the Former Soviet Union by allowing the transfer of gas to Europe through its pipeline network from Kazakhstan, Turkmenistan and Uzbekistan. This strategy also allows it to control potential competitors and, eventually, prevent them from selling their gas at a very low price.

In September 2004, the oil company Total SA bought a 25% stake in the Russian natural gas company Novatek for $1bn. In December 2004, Gazprom was in the process of taking over a major subsidiary of the former oil giant in Russia, Yukos.

(2) Algeria and Libya

Algeria currently exports 65 billion m^3 of natural gas per year; one-half is transported through pipelines, the other half in the form of LNG. Not only does Algeria want to increase its share of the European market but it is also aiming at the US market which has a big need for LNG. America's internal consumption should double in 2010 and reach 22 billion m^3 by 2020. A new decree reduced from 51% to 30% the required participation of Sonatrach, Algeria's national company, in new exploitation/production projects that would be conducted in Algeria by foreign companies and, at the same time, allowed these companies to build their own gas pipelines and terminals. The capacity of the Algeria–Tunisia–Italy Pipeline is expected to increase from 24 to 27.5 billion m^3 per year and a new link to Italy with a capacity of 10 billion m^3 is expected to be built. Financing for a gas pipeline going directly to Spain, with a capacity of 8 billion m^3, has been secured. This would allow Algeria to avoid using the Algeria–Morocco–Spain Pipeline during periods of tension with Morocco. Algeria has ordered two butane tankers from Japan, facilitating the transportation of its Liquid Petroleum Gas (LPG).

In October 2004 Libya began pumping natural gas to Europe through a recently completed undersea pipeline. The Greenstream Pipeline is part of a €7bn gas project by Italy's ENI and Lybia's National Oil Co. Libya is involved in a major tender process to attract Western investment to develop 15 new energy exploration areas.

The Greenstream Pipeline has an undersea length of 520 km and a total capacity of 8 billion m^3 per annum; the pipeline links Libya to Sicily. The deepest part of the pipeline is 1,127 m below sea level. By the end of 2005, 8 billion m^3 of gas will be pumped to Sicily, roughly 10% of Italy's annual consumption. As far as Libya is concerned, its goal is to attract billions of dollars in new investment for its oil and gas infrastructure over the next decade. When the country's exports were subject to sanctions imposed by the UN as a result of its weapons program, Libya had only one customer for exported gas, Enagas SA of Spain, which has been importing about 1.5 billion m^3 a year of gas in liquefied form.

(3) Other producers

In the Middle East, Qatar owns the largest gas field in the world. Qatar's LNG equipment has been providing the Asian market with gas since 2000. The capacity of this equipment surpasses 14 billion m^3 per year and should reach 35 billion by 2010. A gas pipeline is soon expected to send gas from Qatar ito those Gulf countries that need it and, in the longer term, there is the possibility of an intercontinental gas pipeline to Europe. Moreover, Qatar is in the forefront of Gas To Liquid (GTL) projects, where natural gas is transformed into liquid oil (using sulfur) for the transportation industry; projects are run in conjunction with the South African company Sasol which has a lot of expertise in this area. In July 2004, Exxon Mobil signed an agreement with the Qatar Government to develop a $7bn natural gas-to-liquid project.

Iran has enormous reserves of natural gas (13% of the world total), in particular in the gigantic field of South Pars which is a remarkable continuation of the Qatar field. The French company Total is already involved, while the Norwegian company Statoil aims at developing another end of the field. In February 2004, Total signed an agreement with the state-owned National Iranian Oil Co. and Malaysia's Petronas to build an LNG plant and export facility in Iran.

In Egypt, a gas project conducted by British Gas, which brings together a consortium of companies including Gaz de France, is very advanced (Gaz de France is expected to receive 3.5 billion m^3 per year). Meanwhile, Electricité de France is building two gas turbines near the Suez Canal. Another LNG project is currently under study.

The San Diego-based energy company Sempra disclosed in August 2004 details of its LNG projects in Mexico. Construction should start at the end of 2004 on a jointly owned LNG receiving terminal at Costa Azul in North Baja. Bids for construction were due at the start of the fourth quarter of 2004.

In January 2004, Saudi Arabia awarded to the Russian company Lukoil rights to explore and produce natural gas near Ghawar, the world's largest oilfield.

10.3   GAS SPOT MARKETS

Natural gas is traded in contracts for physical delivery in the spot market or through long-term contracts. As the world market for natural gas is fragmented into different regional markets, it is not possible to talk about a world price for natural gas – in sharp contrast to oil. In North America, for example, where the market is highly liberalized, prices are very competitive and respond to demand and supply forces. By contrast, in the Russian Federation, where there is a clear monopoly, domestic prices are kept artificially low while gas is sold in foreign markets at higher prices in order to recover losses. In western Continental Europe, the sales price for natural gas is based on competition with alternative fuels and mostly indexed on oil product prices (as in France and Italy). The same holds in Japan. In the UK the gas market is liberalized and prices in principle are defined by a competitive mechanism. The existence of the interconnector between Bacton (UK) and Zeebrugge (Belgium), however, brings to the UK market the European price of gas, closely related to the formula used for calculation of the oil price. The interconnector started functioning in 1998. It is about 140 miles long and has a capacity of 20 billion m^3 when used from the UK to the Continent, or 8 billion m^3 in the other direction.

Natural gas prices may be measured at different stages of the supply chain, starting with the wellhead price. Natural gas prices in the market will reflect a number of components:

- Wellhead price (the cost of natural gas itself).
- Long-distance transportation cost.
- Local distribution cost.

Note that as of today the cost of transportation within western Europe does not increase with distance but with the number of zones crossed between the two end points.

This is not the case when long distances are covered because gas needs to be regularly repressurized in dedicated and costly stations.

In the US, wellhead prices were the first to be deregulated while transportation costs are still regulated by national energy boards.

The major demand factors are weather and economic activity. Due to the importance of the weather factor, natural gas demand is highly *seasonal*. Other factors affecting demand are population and trend changes. New legislation concerning air pollution control may lead to increased demand for this clean fuel.

In most regions of the world, gas prices reflect competition with alternative sources of energy:

- *At the level of a country* – competition between gas and imported oil, such as in Japan, implies that gas prices are defined in terms of crude oil prices and inflation.
- *In a given market segment*, such as the European gas companies – competition takes place between gas and oil products used in the manufacturing industry. Hence, gasoil and crude oil become the indexing parameters for gas prices.
- *For a given project*, such as gas used in European gas turbines – here, gas competes with coal and the indexing parameters become coal, inflation, consumer price index.

In all these cases, the pricing formula will be:

$$P = P_0 + a(X - X_0) + b(Y - Y_0)$$

where the values X and Y are computed as averages over the last 3- to 9-month period. The new value P will prevail during a time period varying from 1 to 9 months before being readjusted.

Two major examples

(1) JAPAN

All gas demand is covered by LNG imports undertaken by a small number of LNG importers. The principal use of gas is electricity production; this is because gas is a clean source of energy and because of nation's commitment to reduce pollution. Since crude oil is the principal competitor of natural gas as an energy commodity, a typical formula for the LNG price (at the point of disembarkment) is:

$$P(\text{ex-ship}) = P_0 + a_1(\text{JCC} - \text{JCC}_0) + a_2(\text{Inflation} - \text{Inflation}_0)$$

where:

- JCC = Japanese Crude Cost, the average cost of imported crude oil.
- P_0 is the price at time 0.
- a_1 and a_2 are constants.

(2) IN EUROPE

1. Gas used by manufacturing companies and services competes with oil products, and typical pricing formulas are of the type:

$$P = P_0 + 60\%[0.8(\text{GO} - \text{GO}_0)] + 40\%[0.9(\text{FO} - \text{FO}_0)]$$

where:

- GO is the price of gasoil.
- FO is the price of fuel oil.

Sometimes inflation is also taken into account:

$$P = P_0 + 30\%[\text{GO} - \text{GO}_0] + 30\%[\text{FO} - \text{FO}_0] + 40\%(I - I_0)$$

where:

- I denotes the inflation rate.

2. For electricity generation in Europe, natural gas is competing with coal, and a typical pricing formula for gas is of the form:

$$P = P_0[(35\%(C - C_0) + 20\%(E - E_0) + 20\%(I - I_0)$$
$$+ 20\%(S - S_0) + 5\%(T - T_0)]$$

where:

- C is the coal price.
- E is electricity.
- I is inflation.
- S denotes salaries.
- T denotes equipment.

Risk-sharing in long-term gas contracts

Since its emergence in the 1960s, gas in western Europe has been founded on the use of long-term contracts between integrated natural gas companies, such as British Gas, Ruhrgas or Gaz de France, and major producing countries, such as Russia or Algeria, represented by Gazprom and Sonatrach. In the process of restructuring of the energy industry, some of these companies have disappeared: Ruhrgas has been absorbed by the German electricity giant E.ON; British Gas demerged in 1997 into two groups, BG and Centrica. BG got the ownership and operation of the British pipeline system and Centrica the British Gas supply business. Despite the growth of spot markets allowing for greater flexibility, most of the gas that is internationally traded is still today in the form of *long-term supply contracts*. The producing countries are thus ensured a steady flow of revenues securing the high capital investment necessary to develop, produce, transport and supply gas. Optimization of a short-term/long-term supply and service contracts portfolio is conducted at the level of the major gas or energy companies.

Some key considerations must be kept in mind:

- The risks and opportunities arise from the number of actors in the market under analysis: producers, transporters, distributors, industrial consumers.
- *Long-term contracts* with TOP provisions have so far permitted the financing of very costly infrastructures. They involve long durations and large volumes, made necessary by the cost of the transmission infrastructure (the cost of gas transportation is five times higher than oil).
- In these long-term contracts both parties have obligations concerning the duration of the contract, price, reliability of supply and volume taken.
- The producer makes sure his production is sold by signing long-term contracts. The TOP clause protects him against volume risk. TOP describes a buyer's obligation to pay for a certain percentage of the annual contracted volume whether or not he takes delivery of this gas. Typical TOP levels would be 90% of contracted volume. To take the British example, in 1997 Centrica started reducing the TOP exposure it inherited from British Gas long-term contracts. By 2000, Centrica had spent £1bn to reduce its TOP liabilities, which resulted in a sharp increase in the market value of the company. Regarding the buyer, he holds volumetric flexibility in the form of a so-called *swing* optionality attached to his contract. A typical contract will allow a buyer to receive 1 million m^3 of gas per day for a year, with a volume flexibility of $\pm 10\%$ every day and a constraint of total delivery of 365 million m^3 over the year.
- The distributor, on the other hand, faces volume risk since he has purchased long-term TOP contracts and demand will fluctuate with weather conditions and cycles in economic growth. But he is protected against price risk since the selling price to customers is also indexed to oil products.
- Deregulation of the gas industry is becoming effective in many European countries, together with concentration and restructuring (e.g., Ruhrgas and E.ON in Germany; ENI and Lasmo in Italy).
- The European gas industry is experiencing fundamental changes with the emergence of short-term contracts, while the Zeebrugge–Bacton Interconnector tends to bring about convergence between competitive gas prices in the British market and oil-related gas prices in western Continental Europe.
- The increasing share of power generation in the gas balance could cause a break between the gas price and the crude oil price in favor of the gas industry.
- New gas projects (particularly in Russia) consume such vast amounts of capital that long-term contracts are no longer sufficient and *production-sharing agreements* are signed to bring some security to investors (such as those signed between Gazprom and international oil companies).

Gas spot markets are at this point most active in countries where the gas industry has been deregulated for a number of years: typically, the US, the UK and some other

European countries such as the Netherlands or Norway. These countries also share the common feature of having vast amounts of indigenous supply. For instance, the UK is still mostly independent of imported supply and produces 40% of the gas in Europe. In these countries, gas markets are located in areas where there is a concentration of buyers and sellers and where there are arrival points of of major pipelines or interconnectors.

DEVELOPMENT OF PHYSICAL FLEXIBILITY TOOLS

As physical markets mature, the value of market flexibility gets higher, as well as the number of available instruments. Typical developments include the following tools:

- *Storage–* all downstream gas supply systems are designed with some storage capacity to meet the structural fluctuations in gas demand. Moreover, as short-term trading expands, the flexibility offered by gas storage becomes more valuable. This leads to the development of new storage facilities by independent storage providers, and the sale of *virtual storage* services.
- *Swing –* the value of swing optionality in daily supply increases with the liquidity of spot markets, leading to a pronounced request for swing in contract negotiations.
- *Basis trades –* these allow prices at one location to be based on prices at another location where there is a more liquid market, with a premium or discount determined by the price differential between the two markets.
- *Physical swaps –* these allow both parties to reduce transportation costs by swapping gas deliveries with another party. A famous example of a physical swap involved Gaz de France which took delivery in Britanny of Nigerian LNG contracted to Italy while Gazprom sent to ENI in Italy an equivalent volume of gas that was contracted to Gaz de France.

THE US AND THE UK AS EXAMPLES OF ACTIVE GAS SPOT MARKETS

The US is a very competitive market, with a large number of actors and direct contact between producers and consumers. In contrast to the situation in southern Europe and many countries in western Europe, most supply contracts are short term while spot and forward markets are quite liquid. The main references for gas spot prices in North America are:

- The Henry Hub Index in the Gulf of Mexico, by far the most liquid because of the network of pipelines intersecting at that point.
- The New York City Gate.
- The Chicago City Gate.
- The Texas Pipeline Pricing Index.
- The Katy Hub Index, Texas.
- The South California Border Index.
- AECO (Alberta Gas Price Index) in Canada.

The UK is another liquid gas market. Natural gas is the dominant fuel in the UK, both for domestic heating and power generation. In 2002, gas accounted for about 37% of primary energy use. In the same year, gas-fired stations produced 33% of UK electricity output and there is a prospect of at least 60% of electricity being produced from gas by 2020. The UK has substantial gas reserves but the North Sea is now a mature field. It must compete with newer areas where production may be either less costly or less technically difficult. The Department of Trade and Industry has forecast that the UK will import by 2020 as much as 80% of its total consumption. The predicted shortfall in indigenous supply will be, at least initially, made up of imports of gas from Norway and from the European market via the Bacton–Zeebrugge Interconnector. However, in many projections, the EU as a whole will become increasingly dependent on gas supplies from foreign countries, notably from Russia, Algeria, Iran, Egypt and Libya.

The UK gas market was the first to be liberalized in Europe in 1996. Gas in the UK today is primarily traded in the Over The Counter (OTC) market. Trades are bilateral deals that are physically or financially settled. Gas can be bought within day, day ahead or for any maturity up to several years. Trades are in general in multiples of 25,000 therms. Although the great majority of OTC trading occurs at the National Balancing Point (NBP), some trading occurs at the beach terminals (particularly, Bacton). The On-the-day Commodity Market (OCM) was introduced in October 1999. Its aim is to provide a liquid, within-day market that combines Transco's requirements to buy or sell gas for balancing purposes with shippers' trading requirements. The OCM is provided by an independent market operator, Enmo, and is accessed either through dedicated communication links or via the Internet.

THE MAIN GAS TRADING HUBS IN EUROPE

As in the US, most hubs develop at intersections of pipelines. Access to storage facilities and the ability to acquire capacity to transport gas to and from hubs is another important factor. Most hubs are physical locations with infrastructure capabilities, but *notional* points may also become virtual hubs. A major example is the NBP (National Balancing Point) in the UK, which, interestingly, is also a notional hub. Hub operators in general offer hub services such as:

- *Parking* – temporary storage of gas at the hub.
- *Flexibility* – shippers and users of the hub can use the balancing services to reduce imbalance liabilities.
- *Nomination-matching*.
- *Capacity-trading* – in which systems for acquiring and selling transportation capacity on connected pipelines are made available to hub users.
- *Wheeling* – transferring gas from one pipeline to another.

THE NBP

Because of its virtual nature, all UK gas flows through this hub, insuring liquidity and making the NBP price the reference for many forward transactions and for the International Petroleum Exchange (IPE) Futures contracts:

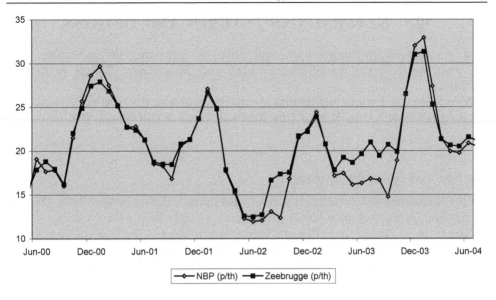

ZEEBRUGGE

This is the arrival point in Belgium of the interconnector departing from Bacton in the UK, and the major hub in continental Europe. In order to facilitate trading at the hub, the Belgian gas transmission company Distrigas has set up Huberator, a fully independent company, to operate the hub.

Because of the interconnector, prices at Zeebrugge reflect arbitrage between UK gas prices which are based on UK supply and demand fundamentals and European gas prices which are typically indexed to oil prices. When gas prices on the continent are higher than in the UK, the flow goes from Bacton to Zeebrugge and gas at Zeebrugge trades at a small premium to NBP gas. If UK prices are higher than continental prices, the Interconnector is likely to flow in reverse, leading to gas sales at the NBP at a premium to Zeebrugge. Some restrictions need to be introduced into this picture because of limited capacity and technical difficulties associated with reversing the flow quickly.

EMDEN

This is a rising hub in Europe, close to the main German production region and the Groningen Field and part of the well-developed onshore and offshore pipeline system of northwest Germany.

HUB HOLLAND

Hub Holland's existence is related to the highly flexible Groningen Field. Through Groningen, the Dutch company Gasunie has the possibility of offering seasonal storage and swing services to long-distance, long-term suppliers such as Gazprom or Norwegian producers.

10.4   NATURAL GAS FUTURES AND OPTIONS

Risk management instruments are well suited to managing the increasing price risk resulting from gas market liberalization and other major changes in the gas industry.

Worldwide, gas Futures and options are mainly traded on the New York Mercantile Exchange (NYMEX), the Kansas City Board of Trade (KCBOT) and IPE.

The New York Mercantile Exchange

NYMEX launched the world's first natural gas Futures contract in April 1990. Options on natural gas Futures were launched in October 1992. Open outcry trading is conducted from 9:30 a.m. to 3:10 p.m. After-hours trading in Futures and options is conducted via NYMEX's Access electronic trading system from 7 p.m. to 9 a.m. on Sundays and 4 p.m. to 9 a.m. on Mondays to Thursdays. NYMEX has also introduced an electronic platform (Enymexsm) for forward trading and clearing contracts in a wide variety of energy and metal products.

Kansas City Board of Trade

The natural gas Futures contract offered by NYMEX was mostly oriented to the eastern US market. Western natural gas marketers who face supply and demand situations different from those in the east needed a risk management tool. This was provided by the western natural gas contract launched by KCBOT.

Intercontinental Exchange (*www.ngx.com*)

The Intercontinental Exchange is an Internet-based marketplace for the trading of OTC energy. It represents a partnership between world leading financial institutions and some of the world's largest energy companies and natural resource firms.

Natural Gas Exchange (*www.ngx.com*)

NGX, located in Calgary, Canada, has provided since 1995 electronic trading and clearing services to natural gas buyers and sellers, one of the largest and most significant production areas of natural gas in North America. Among the customers at NGX are most of the major North American players in the energy market. NGX has quadrupled its turnover since 1997 and is expected to grow in the future on the basis of a new clearing structure and a wider range of products. In September 2003 NGX acquired from Canadian Enerdata the daily spot, one-month spot and midweek spot gas price indexes (Alberta gas price indexes). NGX is a wholly owned subsidiary of the Swedish company OM.

NYMEX Henry Hub Natural Gas Futures and Options

- Trading unit

  Futures: 10,000 MBtu.
  Options: one natural gas Futures contract as the underlying.

- Price quotation

  Futures and options: dollars and cents per MBtu.

- Trading hours

  Open outcry trading from 10:00 a.m. until 2:30 p.m. After-hours Futures trading via the NYMEX ACCESS Internet-based trading platform beginning at 3:15 p.m. on Monday through Thursday and concluding at 9:30 a.m. the following day. On Sundays, the session begins at 7:00 p.m.

- Trading months

  Futures: 72 consecutive months commencing with the next calendar month.
  Options: 12 consecutive months plus contracts extending up to 72 months and traded in a quarterly manner.

- Minimum price fluctuation

  Futures and options: $0.001 per MBtu (or $10 per contract).

- Maximum daily price fluctuation

  Futures: $3.00 per MBtu for all months.

- Options

  No price limits.

- Last trading day

  Futures: trading terminates 3 business days prior to the first calendar day of the delivery month.

- Options

  Trading terminates at the close of business on the business day preceding the expiration of the underlying Futures contract.

- Options strikes prices

  20 strike prices in increments of $0.05 per MBtu above and below the at-the-money strike price in all months. The at-the-money strike price is nearest to the previous day's close of the underlying Futures contract.

- Delivery location

  Sabine Pipe Line Co. Henry Hub in Louisiana. Seller is responsible for the movement of the gas through the hub; the buyer from the hub. The hub fee is paid by the seller.

- Delivery period

  Delivery takes place across calendar days of the delivery month. They are supposed to be made at a uniform hourly and daily rate of flow over the course of the delivery month.

● Alternative Delivery Procedure (ADP)	An alternative delivery procedure is available to buyers and sellers who have been matched by the exchange after the termination of trading in the spot month contract. If buyer and seller agree to finalize delivery under terms different from those prescribed in the contract specifications, they may proceed accordingly after submitting a notice of their intention to the exchange.
● Positions limits	Any month/all months: 12,000 net Futures, but not to exceed 1,000 in the last 3 days of trading in the spot month or 5,000 in any 1 month.
● Trading symbols	Futures NG; options ON.

NYMEX also makes available for trading a series of basis swap Futures contracts that are quoted as price differentials between 30 natural gas pricing points in the US and Henry Hub. The basis contracts trade in units of 2,500 MBtu on NYMEX's Clear Port[sm] trading platform. Transactions can also take place off the exchange and submitted to the exchange for clearing via NYMEX's Clear Port[sm] clearing website: they include exchanges of Futures for physicals or exchanges of Futures for swaps.

International Petroleum Exchange

In 1997 the IPE (Europe's leading energy Futures and options exchange) began trading its first non-oil contract with the launch of natural gas Futures. These contracts were launched on the bespoke electronic platform which has since been enhanced and is now allowed to trade oil Futures as well.

The natural gas Futures contract traded on the ETSII (IPE automated trading system) has the following characteristics:

● Unit of trading	Therms of gas per day.
● Trading period	– Monthly – 9 to 11 consecutive months, 6–7 quarters, 2 seasons; – balance of month (BOM) – 1 month – the remainder of the current month; – daily close of business on the last business day immediately prior to the contract date.
● Last trading day	– For monthly contracts, close of trading on the business day that is two business days prior to the first calendar day of the delivery month; – balance of month: close of business on the business day which is two business days prior to the penultimate calendar day of the delivery month; – daily: close of business on the last business day immediately prior to the contract date.

- Quotation   Sterling pence per therm.

- Minimum price movement   0.01 pence per therm.

- Maximum price movement   No limits.

- Tick value   − Monthly: 1,500 pence (considering 30 days per month);
                                  − balance of month: 1,500 pence (considering 30 days per month);
                                  − daily: 50 pence (1 day).

The IPE natural gas Futures price is expected to become an international benchmark as Europe develops competitive markets. The underlying index is the Heren Index published by *Petroleum Argus*, *Platt's* and *British Spot Gas Markets*. We already mentioned that the NBP is also a *notional* point in the UK National Transmission system (NTS), i.e., already in the NTS rather than "at the beach" or, in other words, at one of the major British harbors. For accounting and balancing purposes, all gas in the UK is deemed to flow through this point and be in the system until it is removed via customer offtakes. There is no need to acquire entry capacity for trades at the NBP since gas is already in the system. Allocation and title-tracking issues are also avoided: after each deal, only the parties' balance positions on the Transco system are adjusted. Here is an illustration of the NBP:

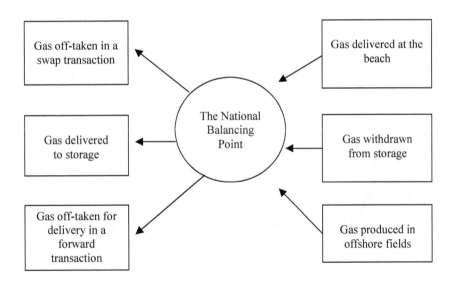

Figures 10.4–10.6 show that both in the US and in the UK natural gas spot and nearby Futures prices exhibit seasonality. Price spikes essentially take place in winter. Analyzing the NBP price in the UK, we see that the level around which prices tend to mean-revert was about 20 pence per therm[1] in 2004 while it was about 12 in 2002. In the

---

[1] A therm is the caloric equivalent of 23.30 kilowatt-hours.

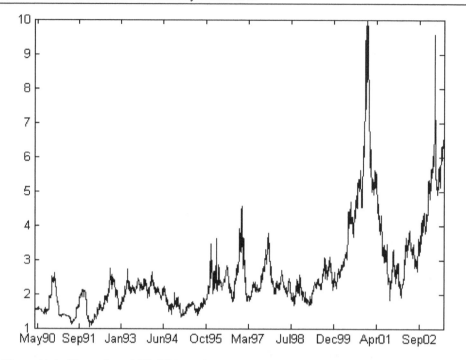

Figure 10.4   Natural gas NYMEX nearby Futures price (in USD) between 1990 and 2003.

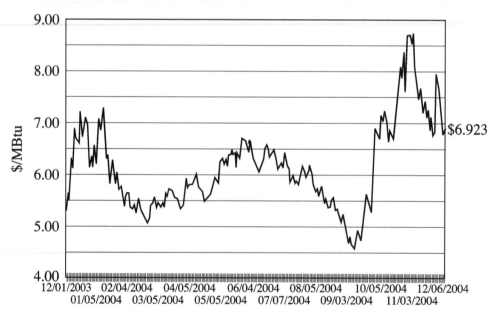

Figure 10.5   NYMEX natural gas Futures close (front month): 1 December 2003–6 December 2004.

Source: WTRG Economics © **2004** *www.wtrg.com* (479) 293-4081.

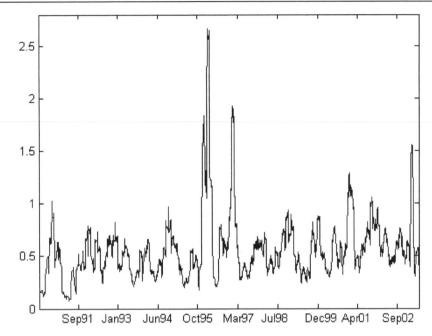

Figure 10.6   Natural gas NYMEX nearby Futures volatility between 1990 and 2003.

US, a sharp rise took place at the end of 2000, after development of the California crisis and the increasing use of natural gas in US power generation. In November 2004, despite the beginning of the winter season, the spot price at Henry Hub was at the relatively low level of $5.5 per MBtu because of the amount of natural gas in storage of 3.299 billion cubic feet reported in November, 11.2% above the 5-year average (Table 10.1).

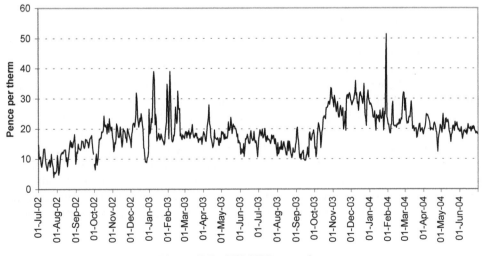

Figure 10.7   UK NBP gas price.

Table 10.1 Examples of the price differentials between Henry Hub and some other major locations in the US

Spot prices ($ per MBtu)	Thursday 18 Nov. 2004	Friday 19 Nov. 2004	Monday 22 Nov. 2004	Tuesday 23 Nov. 2004	Wednesday 24 Nov. 2004
Henry Hub	5.58	4.79	5.25	5.23	4.95
New York	6.03	5.11	5.67	5.64	5.62
Chicago	5.56	4.80	5.51	5.50	5.24
California Com. Avg²	5.53	4.65	5.89	5.88	5.37
Futures ($ per MBtu)					
December delivery	6.873	7.115	6.762	6.793	7.976
January delivery	7.652	7.791	7.540	7.621	8.639

Source: NGI's Daily Gas Price Index (*http://intelligencepress.com*).

10.5 THE GROWING INTEREST IN LNG

Cooling natural gas to about −260°F (−162°C) at normal pressure results in its liquid form, LNG. Besides the gain in transportability, liquefaction has the merit of removing oxygen, carbon dioxide and sulfur, resulting in a type of gas whose emissions are much lower if fired later in a power plant. Note that LNG can make economically profitable some stranded natural gas deposits for which the construction of pipelines is not an option.

LNG spot markets are developing and bringing flexibility to world gas supply. They increased by 42% in 2001, representing 182 cargoes (10.8 billion m³). The main exporters in spot trading are Trinidad, Algeria, Indonesia, Nigeria and, of course, Qatar. Spot trading went from 1.3% of LNG trading in 1992 to more than 8.5% in 2002. Swap contracts allow arbitrage positions to be built between different geographical zones according to price differentials.

If all discussed projects are undertaken, the capacity of liquefaction and transportation of LNG should increase by the energy equivalent of 79 million tons of oil per year until 2007, reaching a volume of 214 million tons per year. LNG offers an alternative to long-distance transmission pipelines and brings more options to supply since cargoes may come from different sources. The flexibility provided by LNG explains its increasing role in international trade. The orders for methane tankers are sky-high; the total fleet will increase by 56% in the next 5 years and is expected to increase by 7.5% a year until 2015. The size of tankers is growing, as is the distance they can cover; today they are capable of traveling more than 7,000 miles without refueling. Innovations have also been found for the financing of infrastructure, that bring together producing countries, oil and gas companies, transporters and distributors:

---

² This number is an average of prices at Malin, PC&E citygate and Southern California Border Average.

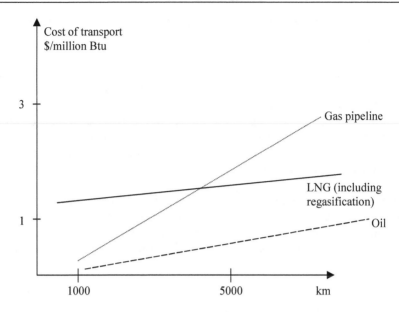

Globalization of the LNG market is on the way. With the multiplication of projects, there is strong competition between countries owning reserves that can be exported as LNG. Australia has reduced the price of its deliveries to China, in order to compete with offers from Qatar. Qatar is trying to become the provider of choice for the Asian market, but this has so far not happened. The extra cost of transporting LNG from the Gulf to eastern Asia is significant, compared with the cost of shipping LNG from Australia or Indonesia. Should they turn to Europe for customers, the Gulf producers of LNG would face the competition of natural gas from Nigeria and Trinidad.

Algeria wants to diversify its customers by selling LNG to the US, which similarly wants to diversify its supply. The very fact of the US opening up to imports highlights the concerns about the capacity of the North American continent (especially Canada) of being self-sufficient. The construction of new terminals is necessary, but, as usual, their location is problematic because of the pollution and risks brought by the necessary infrastructure ("not in my backyard"!).

The extension of LNG production in Oman has taken place; an offshore LNG project is being studied in Equatorial Guinea. In Venezuela an agreement between Shell and Mitsubishi is expected to lead to new infrastructures in 2007. The joint venture "Med LNG" between Gaz de France and Sonatrach established in 2001 has already sold three cargoes of LNG to Korea. China is starting to import large amounts of LNG since its total gas consumption is expected to rise to at least 66 billion m^3 in 2010.

Transportation of natural gas and LNG

Some numbers to keep in mind at the start:

- Natural gas fills a volume that is 1,000 times greater than oil for the same energy content. Liquid gas occupies a volume 600 times lower than gas itself.

- The cost of transportation of gas over long distances is 5 to 10 times higher than in the case of oil.

For instance, a methane tanker transporting 135,000 m³ costs $180m; equivalently, a tanker transporting 70,000 tons of oil costs $60m. A gas pipeline that permits 100-terawatt-hour energy equivalent of gas to flow per year costs $1.5m per kilometer, whereas an oil pipeline permitting 500-terawatt-hour energy equivalent of oil to flow costs $0.7m per kilometer. Moreover, LNG-receiving terminals have the inherent capacity of operating as a form of gas storage while they take delivery of large quantities of liquid gas from LNG tankers and then release it slowly into the gas supply system. Unlike other forms of storage that depend on geological formations, above-ground LNG tanks can be constructed anywhere. For example, in the UK, five LNG facilities are located at the extremities of the pipeline system to maintain transmission at peak demand. LNG storage sites allow high deliverability and occupy comparatively little space. However, the process of liquefaction is expensive and limits the use of LNG storage that is typically dedicated to *peak storage*.

Cost of the LNG chain

Let us take as an example an LNG chain corresponding to a volume of roughly 9 billion m³ per year and linking two points that are distant by 6,000 miles:

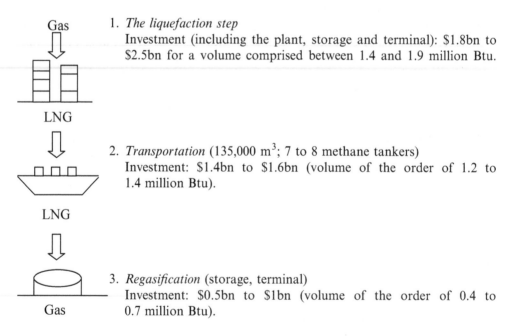

1. *The liquefaction step*
   Investment (including the plant, storage and terminal): $1.8bn to $2.5bn for a volume comprised between 1.4 and 1.9 million Btu.

2. *Transportation* (135,000 m³; 7 to 8 methane tankers)
   Investment: $1.4bn to $1.6bn (volume of the order of 1.2 to 1.4 million Btu).

3. *Regasification* (storage, terminal)
   Investment: $0.5bn to $1bn (volume of the order of 0.4 to 0.7 million Btu).

Let us conclude by observing that it costs only $2 to transport a barrel of oil across the world (i.e., a small percentage of the price of a barrel). This shows that only a drastic reduction in transportation cost will permit gas to reach the same global market as oil at the present time.

The future of LNG

A major meeting about LNG took place in Washington in December 2003, showing the massive interest of the US Administration and energy industry for this new form of gas. LNG imports to the US represented 0.17 trillion cubic feet of natural gas in 2002 and are expected to increase at an average annual rate of 15.8% to reach 4.80 trillion cubic feet by 2025. Hence, LNG will become a growing part of the supply picture in the US, with shipments coming from Trinidad, Qatar, Algeria and even Indonesia and the UAE. According to the Chairman of Exxon, the Atlantic market will replace the Pacific region as the biggest world gas market by 2015 or 2020 and the liquidity of the American market may attract suppliers at the expense of Europe. The world demand for LNG should increase by 7% per year between now and the year 2020, compared with 1.7% for all energies, 1.6% for oil and 2.4% for all types of natural gas. LNG trading should reach 546,000 million m^3 in 2020 and the oil majors such as Exxon, Chevron, Texaco and Total are investing large sums in this new energy. Moreover, new technologies are emerging: GTL allows the transformation of natural gas into fuel and will enlarge the offer of oil products. Industrial production is expected to start in Qatar in 2005 and a project is on the way in Nigeria. In the case of smaller and distant natural gas fields, new techniques are being conceived: floating barges to carry the liquefaction equipment for gas to be then transferred into methane tankers. Among the methane tankers that are being built, some are reserved for long-term contracts but a number will be available for short-term trading, increasing gas-to-gas competition.

11

Spot and Forward Electricity Markets

11.1 INTRODUCTION

The recent introduction of competition in the electricity industry worldwide followed in a natural manner the process that had already taken place in the gas industry, on the one hand, and in the telecom industry, on the other hand. In all three, deregulation was justified by the perceived benefits of introducing market forces in an industry previously viewed as a monopoly. However, the design of efficiently functioning electricity markets has proven to be a difficult exercise.

Electricity among all commodities is characterized by some unique features:

- It is an essential commodity, some would say vital.
- It is mostly non-storable (except for hydro, which represents a small fraction of the electricity produced worldwide), entailing the necessary real-time balancing of supply and demand.
- It has to be transported in a transmission network, with no alternative existing today to physical high-voltage lines, in contrast to the telecom industry where satellites may replace underground cables.

Electricity, which can act as a substitute for oil and gas and can be generated by either fuel, shares with these two commodities the need to invest high amounts of capital; consequently, the electricity industry used to be organized in many cases as a state-owned monopoly.

When we combine all these elements it is easy to understand why deregulation of the electricity industry was no easy matter in any part of the world. The 1990s started with great enthusiasm for such a change. It ended with the demise of Enron and the rattling bankruptcy of US energy merchants such as Dynegy, Mirant and El Paso. These companies had to close the offices they had opened in Europe, with the object of benefiting in that continent from the trading expertise they had acquired in the US market. They are today subject to Chapter 11 legislation, and the poor image built up as a consequence of their activities has led the US public to question the viability of deregulated electricity markets and the validity of deregulation itself. Regarding Europe, the consequences of deregulation are puzzling at the present time: the two countries with the lowest cost of producing electricity in April 2004 were:

- The most deregulated one, the UK, with a cost of production of €0.048 per kilowatt-hour.
- The most centralized one, France, with a cost of production of €0.051 per kilowatt-hour.

These numbers are enough on their own to express the complexity of the issue of deregulation and the impossibility, at this date, to draw clear conclusions on its virtues for consumers and for economic growth as a whole in countries where deregulation has been introduced.

Today, the new entrants in the electricity industry are the bankers: those who have been trading commodities for a long time such as Morgan Stanley and Goldman Sachs, as well as Deutsche Bank, Bank of America or Barclays. Given the unique features of electricity, which will be repeated throughout the chapter, the new players are acquiring physical assets in order to back their financial positions. They do so at a relatively low cost at this time, since a number of generation units have been put on the market by the energy companies mentioned earlier which are facing a need for cash.

Another fundamental feature of electricity, related to the properties described before and explaining the risks and rewards in the deregulated electricity industry, is the presence of spikes in price trajectories (i.e., very sharp movements upwards shortly followed by drops of the same amplitude). The order of magnitude of these jumps which have been known to take prices from normal levels of $30 per megawatt-hour to $1,000 or more is totally absent from other commodity markets, even the more volatile ones like oil and gas. This is totally consistent with the *theory of storage* that was analyzed earlier in this book and explains why price volatility is an inverse function of inventory level. Here, we face the property in its extreme form: in total absence of inventory, price volatility may be unbounded. From an economic standpoint, this is explained by the following facts:

- An equilibrium between supply and demand needs to be secured at any time.
- Demand is a fairly inelastic function of price. Residential customers must be serviced at all times. Interruption rights may be exercised by the utility in the direction of some industrial customers but not all of them. High-tech companies, for instance, are adversely affected by power blackouts.
- Supply may abruptly change in the case of a plant outage or a failure in the transmission network. The non-existence of the buffering effect of inventory as in the case of oil and gas explains the price spikes regularly observed in power markets worldwide.

11.2 STRUCTURE OF THE ELECTRICITY INDUSTRY: FROM VERTICALLY INTEGRATED UTILITIES TO UNBUNDLING AND RESTRUCTURED OLIGOPOLIES

The electricity sector is a transformation industry which seems fairly simple at first sight:

- Generators burn fuels such as coal, natural gas or enriched uranium in power plants, or use the gravitational energy liberated by water from rivers of mountain lakes, or capture the wind force to activate alternators that inject electricity into a high-voltage network (typically 380 kilovolts or more).
- Marketing companies and distributors get the electricity from the high-voltage

network, cascade it down to network distributions with lower voltage and sell it to industrial or residential consumers and handle the metering and billing.
- The network operator (an Independent System Operator, or ISO) is responsible for global balance – as much electricity must come into the system as the quantity that exits – and makes sure there is no local congestion. He maintains the system software that allows merchants to exchange electricity on the high-voltage network, which is the natural place for wholesale trading.

In the former organization of electricity markets, utilities typically undertook at the same time the generation, transmission and distribution of electricity over a wide geographical area. Each utility included a center for the monitoring of equipment and dispatching of electricity, with a power management system executing such functions as automatic generation control, reactive power control and preventive and emergency security control – one important regulation activity being that of *system frequency*. For many years, the generation part of the electricity industry was organized as a natural monopoly because of the economies of scale that could be obtained by using large power plants, and, until the early 1980s, the optimal size of generating units increased continuously. Examples are provided in particular by the construction of a number of nuclear plants in the US and of a vast nuclear park in France, which today allows Electricité de France to be a major exporter to many countries in Europe.

Recently, under the combined effect of ecologists who question the nuclear solution, and other "green" groups represented in international organizations and pushing for treaties such as the Kyoto Protocol which demand the limitation of emissions (carbon dioxide, sulfur-derived gases), Combined Cycle Gas Turbines (CCGTs) are becoming increasingly popular and in many countries are the only type of plants that are currently built. These generating units are smaller and cheaper; hence, they reduce the difficulties of finding large amounts of long-term investment capital and diminish the barriers to entry in this industry. Moreover, their remarkable flexibility allows plants to be switched on when power market prices are high, thus explaining their name of "peakers".

Unbundling vertically integrated utilities means identifying and separating the different tasks attached to a single entity in the traditional organization, so that these tasks could be open to competition whenever feasible and profitable. Previously, when these tasks were coordinated by a unique operational center, cost minimization under the constraint of reliability was the sole optimization criterion. The vertically integrated utility was able to change the rates it could charge after negotiations with an independent regulatory body, comprising representatives of consumers, local municipalities and government agencies. As already mentioned, the transport of electricity takes place through the grid. High-voltage network operation is usually in the hands of a single entity, the Transmission System Operator (TSO or ISO), for the obvious purpose of unicity of management. Flows of electricity present some important features that must be kept in mind:

- They have to follow the laws of physics called "Kirchoff laws".
- Particular flows from hub A to hub B cannot be identified.
- When generators change their production schedule or experience plant failure, the entire high-voltage system is affected and action needs to be taken immediately to

avoid a general collapse, such as the major blackout that took place in August 2003 in those regions of the US and Canada located between Nigeria Falls and New York.

Managing the grid system means ensuring that:

- Generation and load are balanced at any time under whatever transmission constraints.
- The electrical flow over the system is controlled in such a way that the system is continuously in equilibrium in each part of the network.

11.3 SPOT POWER MARKETS AND ISSUES IN MARKET DESIGN

Given the unique characteristics of electricity as a commodity, regulators and governments must reflect on a number of issues when they introduce deregulation in electricity markets. A non-trivial difficulty arises from the existence of a (few) large player(s) in most countries or regions.

(1) California as an example of poor market design

A lack of investment in power plants at the end of the 1990s certainly represents the deep roots of the problem. While demand grew by about 5,500 MW between 1996 and 1999, in particular because of the steady growth of the economy, the explosion of high-tech industry and other start-ups in this attractive state, generation capacity increased by only 672 MW over the same period. A drought in 1999 created poor hydro conditions and reduced the generation capacity of hydroelectric dams. The neighboring states (Oregon, Washington) which used to traditionally export to California were themselves facing rising demand and cut down their exports. Lastly, this period witnessed a large increase in the price of natural gas which was the main fuel for *power plants at the margin*, i.e., providing the most expensive electricity necessary to satisfy demand (see Figures 11.2 and 11.3 on p. 257).

The market design

In terms of market structure, the situation can be summarized as:

- Distribution companies were forbidden by regulation to sign *long-term forward* contracts to hedge their exposure to *price risk*.
- All buyers had to buy from the three local utilities (among them was PG&E – Pacific Gas and Electricity).
- Retail markets were not deregulated and were subject to fixed prices that were set for 4 years. Because of this it was not possible to pass on higher wholesale prices to consumers, and these had no motivation to reduce their demand.
- There were two uncoordinated wholesale markets: one operated by the ISO, the other by the California Power Exchange (CPX). Different caps on the price of

electricity created incentives for suppliers to use the ISO real-time market during peak hours rather than the CPX.

- California had more than a dozen regulatory authorities with overlapping responsibilities while the state Public Utility Commission (PUC) had no authority over municipal utilities within California nor over interstate transmission companies. The PUC was responsible for approving the retail prices that private utilities could charge for electricity while the Federal Energy Regulatory Commission (FERC) was responsible for approving wholesale prices that producers could charge for power and use of transmission lines. This division among regulatory bodies made the identification of "round-tripping" electricity between two merchants with no physical exchange difficult, while this practice was artificially inflating electricity prices.

Note that the problem is currently present in Europe where regulatory responsibility is divided between the EC, national regulators, authorities ruling over competition in all sectors of the economies in general and even regional authorities.

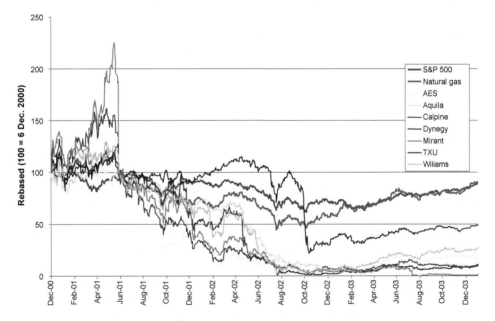

Figure 11.1   Energy merchants and Independent Power Producer (IPP) share prices.

Development of the California crisis

After the drought of 1999, prices started climbing and during peak hours repeatedly reached the price of $1,000/MWh. Interestingly, this number was the *price cap* imposed by the regulatory authority and incorporated in the software of the CPX which defined the *clearing price* resulting from bids and offers. In October 2000, PG&E had already lost several billion dollars from buying at these price caps while the California System Operator had to buy electricity in the *adjustment market* at the price of $10,000 for a few hours. The CPX closed in February 2001; FERC imposed a cap of $250 in the day-ahead market. In the within-day market operated by Cal ISO (the California Independent System Operator), a cap of $150 was established for the first 5% traded and a cap of $250 for the rest. Producers saw their selling price collapse from $1,000 to $250 and announced they would rather export their electricity to Oregon, a region with no price cap. The state of California decided at that point to buy electricity in the forward market for 25 years at the price of $150/MWh.

Today prices are capped at the level of $250 over the three western states of Oregon, Washington and California. California has renegotiated the forward contracts it had bought too late at too high a price and rolling blackouts have been essentially eliminated.

(2) Spot power markets

These refer to the wholesale trading of electricity. Even in a competitive environment, the first role of a spot market is to ensure that total generation meets demand (and, obviously, the regulatory authority has to oversee its well-functioning). Second, the transmission system operator will arrange the physical aspects of delivery.

So far, deregulated spot power markets have been mainly organized in two forms that are suitably illustrated by the UK example prior to 2001 and after 2001 (and discussed on p. 259).

(a) Pool and single buyer

The pool is organized as a system, mandatory or not, where generators place their bids in terms of prices and quantities for each hour (or half-hour) of the following day. The System Operator acting as the *Single Buyer* collects these bids, ranks them by merit order from the least expensive to the next least expensive and so forth, building the *supply function* (also called the "power stack function" in electricity markets; see Eydeland and Geman, 1998). This supply function is a key piece of the economic fundamentals of a given market, and all market participants invest heavily in its construction. Figures 11.2 and 11.3 depict the shapes of the supply function in two regions, one covered by the East Center Area Reliability Coordination Agreement (ECAR) and the other by the Energy Regulatory Council of Texas (ERCOT), of the US. These shapes are typical of any electricity market, since in all cases prices at some point start rising exponentially when increasingly inefficient power plants come into play in order to meet demand. The left parts of the curve correspond to the baseload that is met by hydropower plants, nuclear plants and other low-cost units. As we move to the right, less efficient plants, on the one hand, and peakers, on the other hand, come into play. It is interesting to observe that both in ECAR and ERCOT, additional capacity at a reasonable price was introduced between 1999 and 2002.

Returning to the system operator, we see that he manages two possible pool designs:

- Either it is only suppliers who make bids to the pool and the system operator is responsible for computing the *expected demand* for each hour of the following day; intersecting this demand with the supply function provides the *System Marginal Price*, or SMP.

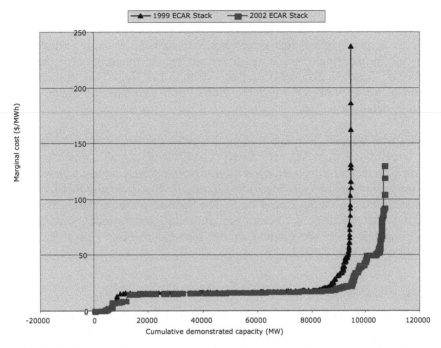

Figure 11.2   ECAR generation curve: marginal cost versus cumulative demonstrated capacity.

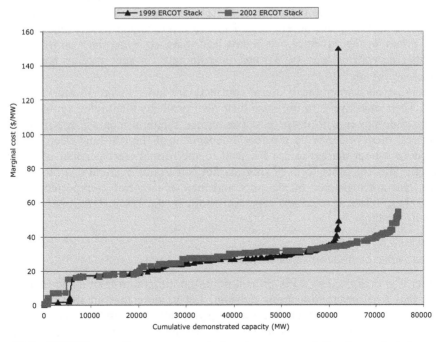

Figure 11.3   ERCOT generation curve: marginal cost versus cumulative demonstrated capacity.

- Or it is both buyers and sellers who make bids to the pool and then the system operator has to build a demand function analogous to the supply function except that it is a quasi-vertical line since electricity demand is fairly inelastic to price changes. The marginal price is again defined by the intersection of the curves of supply and demand. Examples of pools include the New York Intrastate Access Settlement Pool (NYPOOL) and the Nord Pool (Scandinavia) which will be discussed in detail on p. 260.

In 2004 Italy introduced electricity trading through a day-ahead market organized by a system operator (Gestore Mercato Elettrico, or GME). Spain, which was the first country in Continental Europe to open its electricity market, created a power exchange called Compañía Operador del Mercado Español de Electricidad (OMEL) where electricity is also traded on a day-ahead basis. The Spanish power exchange is a voluntary market, but bilateral trade is discouraged since capacity payments (i.e., rewards for providing capacity) are not granted to the bilateral market. Hence, most Spanish consumption trades on OMEL.

(b) Power exchange

A power exchange (PX) is a competitive wholesale trading facility for electricity; it is usually a private entity owned by market participants. These participants include generators, distribution companies, traders and large consumers.

Spot trade on the exchange is not mandatory and is conducted through bilateral contracts. Bilateral bids will specify quantities and prices; trades have to be completed the day before delivery in order to give both market participants and the TSO the necessary time to arrange the physical aspects of delivery. Matching the supply and demand of electricity on the exchange leads to a public market-clearing price. These hourly prices, or their average over a day, lead to an *exchange index* on which Futures and other derivatives may be written once liquidity in spot trading has reached a satisfactory volume.

Generally, participants in bilateral contracts are not required to make their offers public. Their objective is to optimize their own profit by identifying counterparties to directly trade power with in the best conditions. Bilateral bids will specify quantities and prices, these prices being possibly independent of the real-time electricity market price. Both a pool market and a PX lead to the formal establishment of the system clearing price. The other form of spot market consists of bilateral contracts which, in general, are not registered by the pool and may or may not be reported to the PX. Today, these bilateral contracts represent, both in the US and Europe, the bulk of electricity trading.

THE BASIC ROLE OF A SHORT-TERM SPOT MARKET

Whether it is organized as a **PX** or as a **pool**, the ultimate role of a spot market is to ensure that total generation meets demand. Let us note that an ISO does not own generation and is only responsible for supplying total demand efficiently. However, there is no guarantee that demand will be completely met at any point in time. Hence, a mechanism which is termed *reserves capacity* (discussed in Section 11.4) is necessary to provide additional generation and bring about a balance between supply and demand.

Taking the example of Europe, where more than 60% of the power supply was opened to competition at the end of 2002, the structure of electricity markets is given in Table 11.1.

Table 11.1 Structure of the electricity markets

Country	Date	Name
England and Wales	1990–1999 2001	Electricity pool UK Power Exchange (UKPX) *www.ukpx.co.uk*
Norway	1993 1996	Nord Pool Scandinavia Nord Pool – *www.nordpool.no*
Spain	1998	OMEL
Netherlands	1999	Amsterdam Power Exchange (APX) *www.apx.nl*
Germany	2000 2001	Leipzig Power Exchange (LPX) European Power Exchange (EEX) *www.lpx.de*
Poland	2000	Polish Power Exchange (PPX)
France	2001	Powernext *www.powernext.fr*
Italy	2004	Gestore Mercato Elettrico (GME)

The UK pre and post the New Electricity Trading Arrangements (NETA)

Deregulation started in the UK in 1990 with the establishment of the England and Wales Electricity Pool:

- Trading in the pool was mandatory and organized as a *day-ahead* market for each half-hour of the following day.
- Only sellers made bids to the pool by quoting prices and quantities for each time period.
- The *system operator*, acting as a "Single Buyer", received all the offers.
- In the England and Wales Pool, buyers did not make any bid. The system operator had to estimate the demand relative to each half-hour of the following day as the intersection of that demand with the supply function and defining the SMP.
- The price paid to generators, called the Pool Purchase Price (PPP), was the marginal price plus a *capacity payment* (meant to reward their reserves).
- In addition to pool activity, generators and suppliers were trading short-term financial contracts called *Contracts For Differences* (CFDs). Typically, a supplier wishing to find a hedge against excessive volatility of the pool price would trade an Over The Counter (OTC) contract with another player in the pool where he would pay a fixed

price and receive the pool price. CFDs are in fact swaps where fixed and floating payments are exchanged.

The pool faced many criticisms, due in particular to the fact that bids made by generators in the pool were allowed to be *non-firm* – meaning they could be placed and not executed if accepted. This flexibility implied that the supply function was not a solid line but a dotted line, increasing price volatility and making strategic behavior on the part of the major players possible, which probably did occur.

In March 2001, the England and Wales Pool was abolished and replaced by the New Electricity Trading Arrangements (NETA). The United Kingdom Power Exchange (UKPX) was established; it has the following features:

- It is a private structure.
- Participation is voluntary.
- Trading takes place through bilateral transactions.
- The electricity price at any moment is, as in any market, the price of the latest transaction.

Nord Pool as an exemplary PX

Nord Pool was the very first power exchange. It began operating in Norway, then was extended to Sweden, Finland and Denmark. Participation in Nord Pool is voluntary; still, by 2001 some 300 market participants were already trading and the number of bilateral transactions fairly limited. Nord Pool covers several markets:

- Elspot, the spot market organized as a day-ahead market. Prices are determined by looking at the supply and demand curves for each hour of the following day. This price is the Nord Pool Index, which is used as the reference for the settlement of financial power contracts as well as a *benchmark* for bilateral transactions.
- Elbas is an adjustment market for short-term physical delivery. It allows market participants who had previously taken positions on Elspot to adjust these positions up to 2 hours before delivery.
- Eltermin is a purely financial market, involving no physical delivery. Forward and Futures contracts are traded for hedging or speculating purposes, over periods which are days, weeks, blocks of weeks and years. As usual, forward contracts settle at maturity while daily margins are called on Futures positions. Liquidity remains fairly good for maturities going beyond 3 years.
- Eloption is a financial market, dedicated to options as indicated by its name. It offers options written on the various Futures contracts mentioned above as well as arithmetic average options.

The success of Nord Pool is attributable to a number of reasons, in particular:

- There are a great number of participants and the largest player in the market owns less than 25% of production assets. This facilitates both the accession of new entrants and the confidence of financial traders in a market where price manipulation is not easy.

- A large fraction of electricity traded on the Nord Pool is hydroelectricity, which is storable; water can be stored in reservoirs and lakes and its optimal use is defined over a year time frame starting at the end of March. This storability makes hydro-electricity more similar to other commodities, lowers the height of spikes and reduces price volatility.
- The northern countries of Europe have low populations, a wide transmission network and a tradition of dialog between governments, system operators, munici-palities and associations of end-users.

The United States

In 1992 the Energy Policy Act opened up competition in electricity production by introducing a new category of independent producers, "Exempt Wholesale Genera-tors", who were allowed to sell electricity outside their home state. At the same time, traditional utilities were permitted to own plants located in competitors' zones. The high-voltage network became open under the supervision of the FERC and everyone could "wheel" its wholesale electricity after paying the access fee.

Geographically, the US comprises two large regions for electricity separated by the Rocky Mountains:

- In the east, a set of zones between Quebec and Florida which consume 2,800 TWh (terawatt-hours) of electricity.
- In the west, regions extending from British Columbia to California which consume 660 TWh of electricity.

Texas, with its 285-TWh consumption, is unconnected to its neighbors and represents the Electric Reliability Council of Texas (ERCOT) market. Some other states, such as

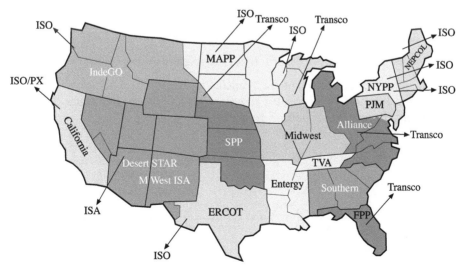

Figure 11.4 The different electricity markets in the US.

Arizona, Nevada, Wyoming, Colorado and Minnesota, have done little to restructure their electricity markets, possibly because of the low density of population and, in turn, potential gains from competitive markets.

Some elements about the US network transmission

Network operation through the US is managed either by private companies (called "transcos") or non-profit entities managed by utilities (called "ISOs").

It is in the highly populated regions of the northeast (New York state, Pennsylvania, New Jersey) that deregulation was the most successful, mainly because of the quality of the network – which was in no way responsible for the Summer 2003 blackout since the problem started far away, in the Great Lakes region – and the diversity of the fuels used in power plants. The Pennsylvania–New Jersey–Maryland (PJM) market has functioned quite well so far, both for end-users and market players.

(3) Transmission in electricity markets

In an electricity network the most identifiable points are the nodes – also called buses – where Kirchoff's laws impose constraints. Let us consider a simple network with three buses and branches and assume for simplicity no losses along the branches:

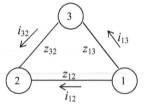

The First Kirchoff Law is related to *conservation of energy* and states that the sum of voltage drop around a closed loop *is zero*.

In our diagram, following the loop 1–2–3–1, we obtain:

$$i_{12}z_{12} - i_{32}z_{32} - i_{13}z_{13} = 0$$

where z denotes the impedance of the branch.

The Second Kirchoff Law is related to *conservation of charge* and states that the sum of the current flowing into a node *is zero*:

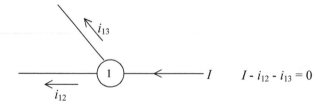

Note that the current flowing out of a node is attributed a negative sign.

Where does the power flow?

Let us consider a transfer from bus 1 to bus 2. We see it can take two different paths, direct and indirect, where the current is respectively denoted i_i and i_d:

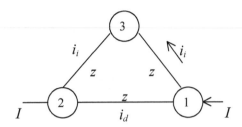

Use the two Kirchoff laws to solve for i_i and i_d:

$$I - i_i - i_d = 0$$

$$zi_d - zi_i - zi_i = 0$$

which leads to:

$$i_i = \frac{I}{3}; \qquad i_d = \frac{2I}{3}$$

What does dispatch mean?

Suppose there are two units, one at bus 1 and another at bus 3 as well as one load at bus 2:

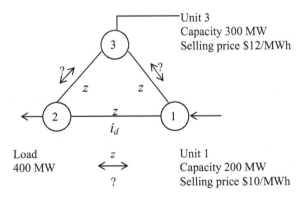

FIRST CASE: UNCONSTRAINED DISPATCH

Use the cheaper unit and recall that $\frac{2}{3}$ of a transfer flows over the direct route because of equal impedances (as calculated above):

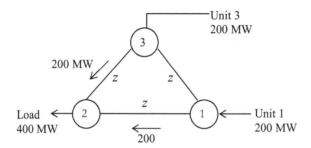

Note that the voltage difference between ① and ③ is zero since units 1 and 3 generate the same capacity.

Definition   The *Load Marginal Price* (LMP) is the price to serve an additional mega-watt at that location. In our setting, only unit 3 can provide extra capacity; hence, the LMP at:

- node 1 is \$12/MWh
- node 2 is \$12/MWh
- node 3 is \$12/MWh

since we assumed no constraints on the lines. Hence the result:

No congestion implies equal LMPs

Suppose line 1–2 has a 175-MW limit:

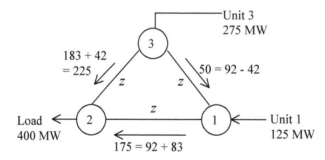

Solving the system corresponding to the Kirchoff laws and the line capacity constraint, we obtain the results indicated in the above diagram (note that $92 \approx \frac{1}{3} 275$ and $183 \approx \frac{2}{3} 275$).

- Node 1 – we can use unit 1, hence the price is \$10/MWh.
- Node 3 – we cannot use unit 1, since line 1–2 is at the limit; we use unit 3, so the price is \$12/MWh.

- Node 2 – we cannot use unit 1 or unit 3 exclusively and must increase 2 MW from unit 3 when we decrease 1 MW from unit 1; hence, the price is $14/MWh:

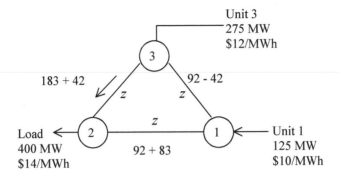

Congestion charges

LMP differences imply congestion charges. The operator pays for injections of electricity and charges for withdrawals of electricity, as shown below:

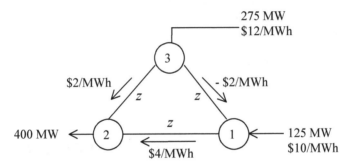

Desirable features of transmission pricing

Given its importance in ensuring liquidity in trading and safety of supply, transmission pricing in restructured electricity markets should be:

- Non-discriminatory.
- Reflect the "fair" value of transmission.
- Facilitate utilization by all potential participants.
- Encourage investments and improvement of the network.

Note that the last feature will not be achieved without the active participation of states and regulatory bodies.

Blackouts

"Advanced mathematical modeling suggests that big blackouts are inevitable" was the title of the paper written by P. Farley in the August 2004 issue of *IEEE Spectrum*, one year after the major blackout that affected southern Canada and the northern states of the US, spreading from the Great Lakes to the Atlantic Ocean. Politicians, regulators and wishful thinkers may say otherwise, but we will modestly concur with the mathematical diagnosis: the physics of electricity, the hard-to-control flow of electrons under the double constraint of the two Kirchoff laws and the cascading effect of a collapse in the network lead to the same conclusion. Investments meant to enhance and strengthen the network are certainly desirable and necessary but the capital to invest in order to obtain a network with a so-called "zero risk of blackout" would be immense. A worst case scenario analysis is not possible since "crash-testing" a grid with thousands of generators and tens of thousands of power lines and transformers is obviously not feasible.

The fact that electricity supply may be interrupted has more to do with the complexity of a network than with deregulation of electricity markets. We should keep in mind that 1 month after the major blackout that affected New York in August 2003, a similar blackout struck Switzerland and Italy, two countries which were still at that time functioning in the decade-old regulated framework.

We conclude this section by humbly paraphrasing Paul Samuelson when he was questioned by a journalist on his view of the stock market. The great economist's answer was "Stock markets will fluctuate." In like manner, we can safely predict that *power blackouts will occur*. It is the duty of the regulators and the various market players to make the probability of an occurrence very low. It is the responsibility of engineers and system builders to introduce devices preventing spillovers across wide regions. In the meantime, consumers should be grateful for the daily miracle of successfully switching on electricity: let there be light!

11.4 THE ADJUSTMENT MARKET AND RESERVES CAPACITY

Whether it is a pool or a PX, the spot market is most generally organized as a day-ahead market: by 1 : 00 p.m. the system operator has finalized the balance of supply and demand for each hour of the following day. In doing so, he has designated which bids have been accepted in the price merit order procedure and the corresponding generation units.

Suppose that in the afternoon there is a sudden surge in demand or, more frequently, that a plant outage is declared. The system operator has only a few minutes to find a solution and needs to turn to the adjustment market to find substitute electricity at a time when prices are likely to be very high. In order to avoid spikes of the order of thousands of dollars per megawatt-hour, reserve capacity has to be organized in advance:

- Either plants with a lower efficiency are maintained as reserves and rewarded by very high prices during short periods.
- Or each generator is requested to constantly keep 10 or 20% on top of the capacity already bid to the pool available. This issue of reserves is a crucial one in any

deregulated electricity market; regulators and operators need to organize beforehand solutions to an emergency situation.

Reserve commitment

A generation unit is said to be "committed" if it can be turned on, brought up to the desirable speed and connected to the system in order to deliver power to the network, all these steps taking place in a very short amount of time. The general principle, which used to prevail prior to deregulation – and still applies today, is that enough units must be committed to supply the load. But, what springs immediately to mind on further analysis of the problem is that:

- The load may vary unexpectedly, in particular in relation to weather conditions.
- A unit which was committed may face an unexpected outage.

Hence, for the general principle to be applied, *reserves* must be made available and their production rewarded.

Spinning reserve is the term used to describe the total amount of power available from all units "spinning" in the system minus the load that is supplied and losses that take place inevitably along the lines. Spinning reserves must be carried so that the outage of a unit does not create too great a drop in the system frequency. Spinning reserves are allocated so that they obey certain rules, set by regional reliability councils in the US or the likes in other countries, that specify how the reserve is to be allocated to various units. Reserves should represent a given percentage of forecast peak demand, generally 10–20%; or it must be capable of making up the loss of the most heavily loaded unit in a given period of time. Another way of calculating the reserve requirement is to define it as a *quantile of outage-related loss distribution*: choose the reserve in such a way that the probability of not having sufficient generation is smaller than 0.01, in much the same way as in finance for a bank capital requirement.

Besides spinning reserves, units are posted as "scheduled reserves" or "off-line" reserves. They include quick-start diesel or gas turbine units as well as hydroplants that can be brought into the system, synchronized and brought to full capacity quickly.

Lastly, reserves must be spread around the power system to allow various parts of the system to run in an autonomous manner, should they become disconnected.

Hence, electricity as a commodity leads to a situation where the spot, adjustment and forward markets uniquely overlap. Denoting as usual the current date (or hour) of analysis as t and the time of delivery of physical electricity as T, we have the diagram:

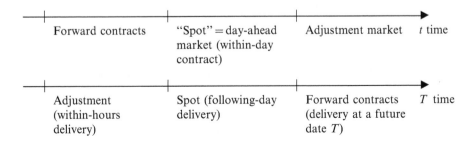

Moreover, there is *no continuity* between these markets, in the sense that the price of a forward contract $F^T(t)$ does not converge smoothly to the spot (day-ahead) price. And the day-ahead price, represented, for instance, by the average of the hourly prices for the following day, is quite different from the prices in the adjustment market, the latter being much higher and more volatile. These features will be all the more accentuated if the country (or region) under analysis is structurally short of electricity (i.e., a net importer).

Lastly, because of the collapse of the spot–forward relationship and the absence of smooth convergence of forward prices to spot prices when reaching maturity, electricity behaves like a "dual" commodity (or has a "split personality", to quote Pilipovic, 1998). We need to model, on the one hand, the dynamics of the spot price process $(S(t))_{t \geq 0}$ and, on the other hand, the dynamics of the forward curve $\{F^T(t), T > t\}_{t \geq 0}$. This discussion will be continued in the following sections.

In the case of Nord Pool, for instance, the involved entities are as described in Table 11.2.

Table 11.2 Nord Pool entities

National Grid Company	The Nordic Power Exchange	
Within the hour	The next day	New week up to 3 years
Regulating service	Spot market	Futures/forwards market
Balance between production and consumption	Physical delivery Hourly contracts	Risk management Financial agreements Weeks, blocks and seasons

On the demand side, we may represent the situation of an industrial firm in the following diagram:

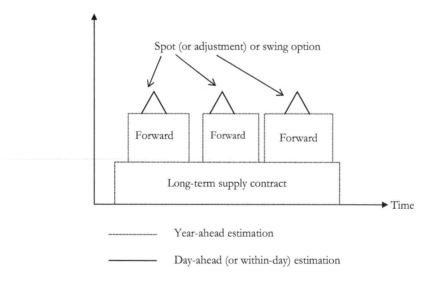

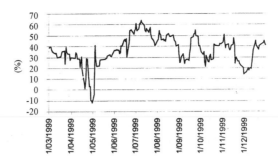

Figure 11.5 Correlation spot–first nearby Futures (Nord Pool).

Figure 11.5 shows that, even in a "quiet" market like the Nord Pool which benefits from a large fraction of hydroelectricity, the correlation coefficient between electricity spot prices and first nearby Futures prices is quite disappointing: equal to 0.62 in the best case, to −0.01 in the worst case. Note that the correlation coefficient was computed through a rollover of first nearby Futures, as discussed in detail in Chapter 14.

11.5 ELECTRICITY DERIVATIVES MARKETS

(a) Forward contracts

Given the non-storable nature of electricity, forward contracts are the most natural vehicles to trade electricity; in fact, the day-ahead spot market discussed in the previous sections may be viewed as a single-day maturity forward contract. Obviously, all electricity forward contracts carry the usual credit risk attached to forward contracts. Another difficulty in the case of electricity is the clause of "force majeure" that allows suppliers to forgo their obligation to supply in extreme circumstances, such as a political crisis, a war or strikes that disturb production, adding to delivery uncertainty.

Many authors have analyzed the prediction capability of forward prices relative to future spot prices. Geman and Vasicek (2001) demonstrate, on a US database that includes the PJM market, that *short-term* forward contracts are upward-biased estimators of spot prices observed at later dates, in agreement with the high volatility – hence, risk and, in turn, risk premium – attached to US spot markets. Bessembinder and Lemon (2002) establish the same type of results; namely, forward prices are downward-biased estimators of future spot prices if expected demand is low and demand risk is moderate; in contrast, the forward premium increases when either expected demand or demand risk is high, because of positive skewness in the power spot price distribution. Consequently, when writing:

$$F^T(t) = E_p[S(T)/F_t] + \text{Risk premium} \tag{11.1}$$

our suggestion is that the risk premium $\pi(t, T)$ is positive when $T - t$ is small (short-term forward) and T corresponds to a winter month, and even more so a summer month in the US. When $T - t$ is of the order of several years, the risk premium $\pi(t, T)$ may be negative since long-term forward contracts sold by the generator are meant to finance the acquisition of the power plant; this is particularly necessary in the absence of flexibility in production, such as in the case of a nuclear plant.

In Chapter 2 we extensively analyzed the spot–forward relationship in the general context of commodity markets. This was established through a "cash and carry" argument under the assumption of no-arbitrage: buy the commodity at date t in the cash market and "carry" it until maturity T to honor delivery of the forward contract you sold at date t and derive:

$$F^T(t) = S(t)\, e^{(r-y)(T-t)} \tag{11.2}$$

where y is the convenience yield representing the benefit of owning the physical commodity net of storage cost. As mentioned before, this convenience yield may be viewed as a *timing option*.

We have argued before that the convenience yield, with its economic representation proposed by major economists, cannot be extended to electricity. Electricity cannot be stored, hence there is no possibility of "carrying" it over the interval (t, T) and the timing option does not exist (except for hydroelectricity). One can state that equation (11.2) can always be solved to derive y from forward and spot prices. Our claim, based on the data collected over the last 7 years on spot and forward prices in restructured markets worldwide, is that the mathematical representation itself is not even appropriate: the exponential function is continuously differentiable everywhere on the real line and at the origin in particular. Hence, when t goes to T, the forward price $F^T(t)$ should converge smoothly to the spot price $S(T)$. This certainly does *not* happen during price spikes: the observed forward curves exhibit seasonality and upward moves, but there is no spike similar to the sharp ones regularly observed in power spot markets around the world.

To summarize this discussion, our view is that, in the case of electricity, we should not think in terms of:

Forward price = Spot price + Cost of carry

but in terms of:

Forward price = Spot price + Risk premium $\pi(t, T)$

where $\pi(t, T)$ varies over time t with maturity T and may have a different sign for different values of $T - t$.

Lastly, we represent in Table 11.3 the differences that should be kept in mind between the economic forecast of future spot prices and the current forward curve.

Table 11.3   Differences between forward curves and economic forecasts

Forward curve	Economic forecast
A term structure of prices at which market participants are willing to make purchase and delivery commitments today.	A prediction (possibly accurate) of future spot prices.
Market prices that include current spot prices and their dynamics, future spot prices of fuels and *risk aversion*.	Based on an economic analysis of future supply and demand, regulatory, technological and sociological trends.
The market is right.	The forecast may be wrong.
Must be used for *marking positions to market* and determining liquidation value.	Should not be used for marking to market purposes.

(b) Futures contracts

The first North American electricity Futures were introduced in 1996 by the New York Mercantile Exchange (NYMEX) for delivery in two locations: the California–Oregon Border (COB) and Palo Verde; the corresponding indexes are still today, along with PJM and ECAR, the most representative electricity indexes in the US. Later on, Futures contracts with various delivery locations across the US were introduced by NYMEX, the Chicago Board of Trade (CBOT) and the Minnesota Grain Exchange (MGEX). Following the reversal of fortunes of Enron and other energy companies in the US, NYMEX delisted electricity Futures in March 2002, and soon after CBOT did the same. Today, the only Futures contract on electricity trades on the MGEX and, specifically, for delivery in the "Twin Cities" (Saint Paul/Minneapolis).

Twin Cities' electricity on-peak and off-peak Futures contracts

- Volume: 736 MWh
- Price quotation: $/MWh
- Delivery location: Twin Cities
- Delivery period: From the first day to the last day of the delivery month
- Delivery rate: 2 MWh during consecutive on-peak (respectively off-peak) hours of the delivery month
- Last trading day: The sixth business day preceding the first delivery day.

In Europe, Nord Pool was the first exchange to start operating (in the 1990s) and by 2000 was already experiencing good liquidity on forward and Futures contracts.

Following NYMEX, in 2002 the International Petroleum Exchange (IPE) delisted the electricity Futures contracts it introduced in 1999. Today, the EEX in Leipzig has launched its own Futures contracts since many European actors trade electricity in Germany, bringing liquidity to the EEX.

In 2003 Spectron, a US-based broker, established a trading platform in Europe allowing transactions based on:

- The German day-ahead baseload and peak indexes.
- The day-ahead index for the Dutch power market.
- The day-ahead index for the French market.

Darkspreads (options to exchange coal for electricity, see Chapter 13) are traded online for the UK and Germany.

Examples of Nord Pool instruments

FUTURES WEEK CONTRACTS

- Spot reference price   Nordic system price

- Quoted currency   NOK

- Settlements   Daily cash settlement and spot reference cash settlement

- Load   Base load
- Tick size   Tick size is NOK 0.25 per MWh
- Contract volume   1 MWh
- Settlement date   Every clearing day after an opening trade until end of the delivery period

CfD SEASON CONTRACTS

- Spot reference price   Difference between an area price and the system price
  - SYARH   Area price Arhus – Nordic system price
  - SYHEL   Area price Helsinki – Nordic system price
  - SYOSL   Area price Oslo – Nordic system price
  - SYSTO   Area price Stockholm – Nordic System Price
  - SYSCPH   Area price Copenhagen – Nordic System Price
- Quoted currency   NOK
- Settlements   Expiry market settlement and spot reference cash settlement
- Load   Base load
- Tick size   Tick size is NOK 0.05 per MWh for season and year contracts and 0.25 per MWh for month contracts
- Contract volume   1 MWh
- Settlement date   Every clearing day in the delivery period

FORWARD MONTH CONTRACTS

- Spot reference price   Nordic system price
- Quoted currency   NOK/EUR from 2006
- Settlements   Expiry market settlement and spot reference cash settlement
- Load   Base load
- Tick size   Tick size is NOK 0.25 per MWh/EUR 0.01 per MWh
- Contract volume   1 MWh
- Settlement date   Every clearing day in the delivery period

It is worth noting that, on the Nord Pool, the locational price spreads between the system price and different points in this wide region may be hedged using Contracts for Differences: by holding such a CfD and a regular Futures written on the system price, one manufactures for himself a "regional Futures".

Another interesting feature of the Nord Pool is that it provides clearing for forward contracts. After two parties have signed a bilateral agreement, the clearing house takes over. In order to avoid a credit event, forward contracts are subject to margin calls but:

- The losing party can put a bank guarantee instead of cash for the margin calls.
- The winning party does not get cash before maturity of the forward contract.

European Energy Exchange (EEX)

The EEX is based in Leipzig and results from the merger in 2002 of the Leipzig Power Exchange (LPX), located in Leipzig and the European Energy Exchange (EEX) located in Frankfurt. The objective of the EEX is to become the leading energy exchange in central Europe. The electricity price is an equilibrium price resulting from a bilateral auction process involving suppliers and consumers, with physical fulfillment on the following trading day. The auction market allows market participants to place purchase and sales bids for single hours, base load blocks and peak load blocks.

As described below, the product range includes monthly, quarterly and yearly Futures based on the Phelix® (Physical Electricity Index) as the underlying price.

Phelix® Base is the average of the prices of each of the 24 individual hours on the EEX auction market. Phelix® is the average of all prices of the hours between 8 a.m. and 8 p.m. on the EEX auction market. Phelix® hourly prices on 15 December 2004 were:

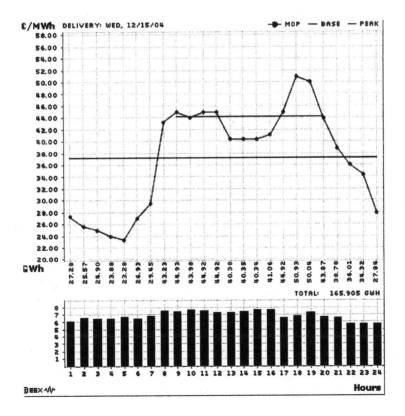

EEX FUTURES SPECIFICATIONS

Fulfillment   EEX Futures contracts are not physically settled. EEX quarter and year contracts are fulfilled by cascading; month contracts are fulfilled by cash settlement. Cascading means the automatic splitting of long-term contracts into contracts with the next shortest period of validity on the last trading day (this procedure is also used for some instruments on the Nord Pool). For example, two trading days before the start of the delivery period of a year contract, it is divided into the month contract January, February and March and three quarter contracts for the second, third and fourth quarter which together equal in sum the contract volume of the year contract. A quarter contract is divided into three month contracts of the respective quarter contract two trading days before the beginning of the delivery period, which together again equal the sum of the contract volumes of the quarter contract.

Final settlement   Final settlement is carried out at the end of the trading period. The final settlement price of quarter and year contracts defines the position value for the cascading process. For monthly Futures, the final settlement price is the basis for the calculation of the cash settlement for the delivery period.

Additional margin (or initial margin)   As happens on any exchange, when opening a position a so-called "additional margin" must be deposited. It is meant to cover the maximum overnight risk of closing all open positions for a participant under the precondition of worst price development.

Margin call (variation margin)   As usual, the difference between two consecutive days' settlement prices multiplied by the contract volume and number of contracts needs to be paid in a daily manner by the losing party for the position not to be terminated. Profit and loss will be credited or debited from participants' accounts: this is the mark-to-market procedure.

Intra-day margin   EEX AG may demand an intra-day margin to be deposited during the course of a trading day in extraordinary volatile market situations. We can observe that this clause reflects the unique features of electricity markets.

Tick size   The prices are given in euro/MWh to two decimal points, so that the smallest price change is 0.01 euro/MWh.

Delivery   Delivery periods are month, quarter and year.

Maturity   Maturity defines the point in time at which the contract shifts into delivery period. Year and quarter contracts are cascaded on the penultimate exchange trading day before the beginning of the delivery period whereas month contracts mature on the last exchange trading day before the beginning of the delivery period.

Load types   The contracts are divided into load types: base load and peak load. Base load includes the delivery days from Monday to Sunday for all 24 hours of the day. With base load, all delivery periods – month, quarter, year – can be combined. Peak load includes all days from Monday to Friday including national holidays but only between the hours of 8 : 00 to 20 : 00 (CET). All delivery periods can be combined using peak load.

Contract volume   This denotes the delivery rate of electricity per hour which underlies the settlement payment. The delivery rate per contract is 1 MW during each delivery hour of the delivery period. For instance, for a base load monthly Futures for September, this amounts to:

$$24 \times 30 \times 1\,\text{MW} = 720\,\text{MWh}$$

Monthly Futures settlement   We mentioned earlier that monthly Futures are financially settled. The settlement price for monthly Futures on the last trading day is called the "final settlement price". The final settlement price fundamentally differs from all previous daily settlement prices, as it is the daily weighted average (arithmetical monthly mean) of Phelix® Base (respectively, Phelix® Peak) for the delivery month.

As already mentioned, Phelix® Base is the average of the prices of all 24 single hours on the EEX auction market. Phelix® Peak is the average of all prices of the hours between 8 a.m. to 8 p.m. on the EEX auction market.

Physical settlement of month contracts   The EEX spot market allows the participants to combine the financial fulfillment of their Futures positions with the physical delivery of the amount of electricity as defined by contract for the duration of the delivery period. For this, the participant must only once send a fax with the order to place a bid corresponding to the Futures position on the EEX Auction Market. Doing so, he instructs the EEX market supervision with the execution until 4 : 00 p.m. of the penultimate trading day before the beginning of the delivery period. Orders can only be made for Transmission System Operator (TSO) areas the participant is activated for in the Sapri system. The market supervision will check the plausibility of the fax bid with the corresponding Futures positions. Bids can be placed for base load and peak load.

In order to guarantee the highest possible probability of execution, the bids are entered as price-independent hourly bids[1] during the entire delivery period. In the case of transmission constraints between the TSO areas, the execution of transactions takes place at the respective area price on that day.

(c) Options

Options on electricity Futures or spot prices have nearly disappeared from the US market after the bankruptcies that followed the ECAR 1998 huge spike, on the one hand, and the Enron demise, on the other hand. In Europe, some liquidity exists in options traded on Nord Pool (Eloption) and in OTC contracts. Options on the power spot price itself are in most cases arithmetic average options which smooth out spikes and make the risk acceptable to the seller. In all cases, the ownership of a generating facility or the right to it through a tolling agreement (*virtual power plant*) is the proper

---

[1] An interesting discussion of this issue can be found in Hansen and Jensen (2004).

way of hedging short positions in options. The Black–Scholes founding assumption of continuous trading in the underlying asset, making possible the dynamic adjustment of hedging strategy, collapses in the case of electricity. Except for the case of hydro-electricity, there is no *dynamic hedging* (see Taleb, 1998) since the hedging portfolio built at date t vanishes a few seconds later.

11.6   MODELING ELECTRICITY SPOT PRICES: FROM MEAN-REVERSION AND JUMP-DIFFUSION TO JUMP-REVERSION

Figure 11.6 depicts the price trajectories registered between January 1997 and December 1999 in the ECAR market that covers several Midwestern states in the US. It is interesting to note that all studies ordered by FERC into the ECAR spike during June 1998 – which cost several thousand dollars for 2 consecutive days – concluded there was no wrongdoing on the part of market participants, but was the consequence of a conjunction of catastrophic events: a long heatwave, a nuclear plant outage and congestion in the transmission of hydroelectricity imported from Canada explains this spike which bankrupted some companies holding unhedged short positions in options.

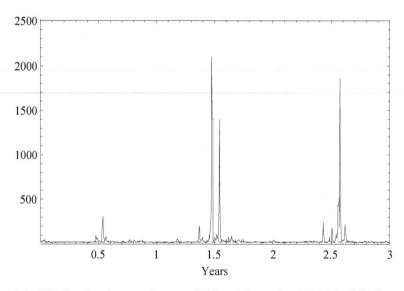

Figure 11.6   ECAR prices between January 1997 and December 1999 (the ECAR market price path).

Electricity prices definitely exhibit patterns corresponding to:

- Different times of the day translated into on-peak and off-peak prices, where on-peak prices typically cover the period 8 a.m. to 8 p.m.
- Seasons, since electricity is one of the key providers of heating in winter in all countries. Summer is a much higher consumption season for air-conditioning

purposes in countries like the US. We will not discuss intra-day differences and will refer to the electricity spot price $S(t)$ as the average of the price quoted in the day-ahead market for date t. Our view is that, starting from a good understanding of the day-ahead price process $S(t)$, we can infer the price process in the adjustment market or on-peak hours.

We can make the following observations on the existing literature concerning electricity spot prices:

- Nearly all authors recognize the seasonality effect, with two periods of high consumption in the US and, arguably, a single period in Europe; however, summers are becoming very warm in Europe as well.
- Some authors prefer to keep a continuous process for the spot price $S(t)$, exhibiting seasonality and mean-reversion:

$$dS(t) = \mu(S_t, t)\, dt + \sigma S(t)\, dW_t$$

where (W_t) is Brownian motion under the real measure P and σ is a constant or, deterministically varying volatility.

In this representation, the view is that the excursions of Brownian motion multiplied by a high σ may create violent upward moves, the mean-reversion incorporated in $\mu(S(t), t)$ bringing prices back to normal. Sometimes, a second equation accounting for stochastic volatility is added to the above equation (see Chapter 3).

- Other authors (Eydeland and Geman, 1998; Deng, 1999) introduce mean-reversion in the Merton (1976) equation and propose a process of the type:

$$dS = \mu(S_t, t)\, dt + \sigma S_t\, dW_t + S_t U_t\, dN_t$$

where:

  ○ $\mu(S_t, t)$ is the drift term accounting for seasonality and mean-reversion;
  ○ N_t is a Poisson process with intensity λ describing jump arrival;
  ○ U_t is a real-valued random variable representing jump magnitude.

From these dynamics, the jump component may definitely generate price spikes from \$40 to \$2,000 as observed in the ECAR market in June 1998. However, a possible limit to this modeling is that the force of mean-reversion necessary to bring this peak to normal values may be so high that standard daily moves following shocks in the supply or weather disappear altogether.

- Villaplana (2003) proposes the introduction of two sources of risk X and Y representing, respectively, short-term and long-term shocks and describes the spot price $S(t)$ in the following form:

$$\begin{cases} \ln S(t) = f(t) + X(t) + Y(t) \\ dX(t) = [\alpha - kX(t)]\, dt + \sigma_1\, dW^1(t) + J(t)\, dN(t) \\ dY(t) = [\beta - Y(t)]\, dt + \sigma_2\, dW_2(t) \end{cases}$$

where:

  ○ $dW^1(t) \cdot dW^2(t) = \rho\, dt$;
  ○ $f(t)$ represents the deterministic component of $\ln S(t)$;

○ the parameter of mean-reversion k is meant to be high enough to bring high prices generated by extreme weather conditions or a plant outage back to a standard level.

- Geman and Vasicek (2001) as well as Barone-Adesi and Gigli (2002) suggest a regime-switching model where the spot price switches from a "normal" state to an "extreme" state. This representation has the merit of preserving the Markov property, important for option pricing. However, the calibration of regime-switching models is known to be a delicate exercise and, as discussed in Chapter 3, proper values of the parameters are as important as the mathematical process itself.

Pure jump Lévy processes for electricity prices

A number of authors have recently exhibited both the necessary introduction of jumps to properly represent prices in the stock market and some undesirable features of jump-diffusion models. They propose instead pure jump processes: the stock price moves by jumps, most of them being very small, upward or downward and large jumps occur once in a while. Among the class of pure jump processes, Lévy processes have the merit of being well known from a mathematical standpoint. They are fully characterized by their Lévy density $k(x)$, where, for any positive or negative x, $k(x)$ represents the probability of occurrence of jumps of size x in a unit time interval. Carr, Geman, Madan and Yor (2002) propose the so-called CGMY model in which the Lévy density is defined as:

$$k_{CGMY}(x) = \begin{cases} C \dfrac{e^{-G|x|}}{|x|^{1+Y}} & \text{for } x < 0 \\[2mm] C \dfrac{e^{-M|x|}}{|x|^{1+Y}} & \text{for } x > 0 \end{cases}$$

where $C > 0$, $G \geq 0$, $M \geq 0$ and $Y < 2$.

This model is currently implemented in a number of financial institutions in the US and Europe for stock and equity index spot prices and options (see Geman, 2002). Among other properties of the model, there exist simple relationships between the four parameters C, G, M and Y and the first four moments of the price distribution.

The idea of using pure jump Lévy processes for electricity prices then appears natural. Our view, however, is that the independent increments of these processes do not permit the fine structure of a spike to be captured and that, at the very least, stochastic volatility should be incorporated in the Lévy process (see Carr, Geman, Madan and Yor, 2003). However, with the objective of making Value at Risk computations, Eberlein and Stahl (2003) show that generalized hyperbolic distributions – which are attached to another pure jump Lévy process – allow the volatility of the German electricity market, as described by the Leipzig-based EEX index, to be accurately reproduced.

Geman and Roncoroni (2002) introduce a *jump-reversion model* for electricity spot prices, namely the representation of $S(t)$, by:

$$\begin{cases} E(t) = \ln S(t) \\ dE(t) = f(t) + \theta[\mu(t) - E(t^-)]\, dt + \sigma\, dW_t + h(t^-)\, dJ(t) \end{cases} \tag{11.3}$$

where:

- $E(t^-)$ stands for the left-hand limit of f at time t.
- The deterministic function $f(t)$ accounts for seasonality.
- The second term insures that any shift away from the trend generates smooth reversion to the standard level $\mu(t)$ at mean-reversion speed θ.
- The discontinuous part reproduces spike occurrence.

Jumps are characterized by their time of occurrence, size and *direction*, in contrast to the classical Merton jump-diffusion model; more specifically:

$$J(t) = \sum_{i=1}^{N(t)} J_i$$

where:

- $N(t)$ is a Poisson process with *time-varying* intensity.
- The J_i are independent and identically distributed random variables with exponential distribution.
- The function h in equation (11.4) defines the algebraic effect of a jump J_i:

$$h(E(t)) = \begin{cases} +1 & \text{if } E(t) < \tau \\ -1 & \text{if } E(t) \geq \tau \end{cases} \tag{11.4}$$

where the threshold τ is calibrated to market data.

In summary, we should keep in mind that two series of criteria must be satisfied by a good model of commodity prices:

- *Trajectorial* properties: after calibration of the parameters, the model should generate trajectories fairly similar to those observed in the markets.
- *Statistical* properties in the sense that the first *four* empirical moments should be consistent with the model: not only should the mean and variance be well captured, but also skewness and kurtosis. Skewness captures in particular the properties of upward versus downward moves; kurtosis characterizes the tails which, in the case of electricity, are particularly important since they may represent bankruptcy or windfall profits.

Calibrating their model to a database comprising US markets with different ways of generating electricity and different climates, Geman and Roncoroni obtain very satisfactory trajectories (as depicted in Figures 11.6–11.8). Table 11.4 shows that there is an excellent fit of moments of order 1, 2 and 4, which were the first targets of calibration because of the focus on extreme events in power markets, hence of kurtosis. The skewness numbers, however, are not very good. Details of the difficult issues involved in the calibration of the process can be found in Geman and Roncoroni (2002).

Table 11.4 Observed and simulated moments of electricity prices

	ECAR		PJM		COB	
	EMP	SIMUL	EMP	SIMUL	EMP	SIMUL
Average	−0.0002	−0.0001	−0.0006	0.0000	0.0009	0.0002
Standard deviation	0.3531	0.3702	0.2364	0.2120	0.1586	0.1593
Skewness	−0.5575	1.9520	0.3949	1.2384	0.1587	0.3894
Kurtosis	21.3833	21.9810	13.1507	13.2345	6.7706	6.3280

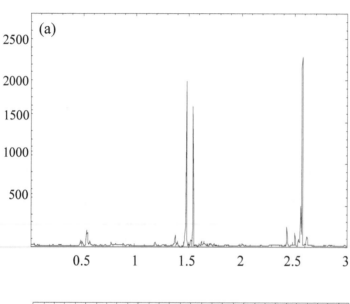

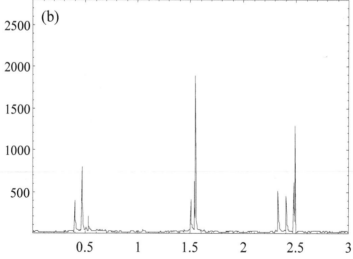

Figure 11.7 (a) MAIN – market price path; (b) MAIN – simulated price path.

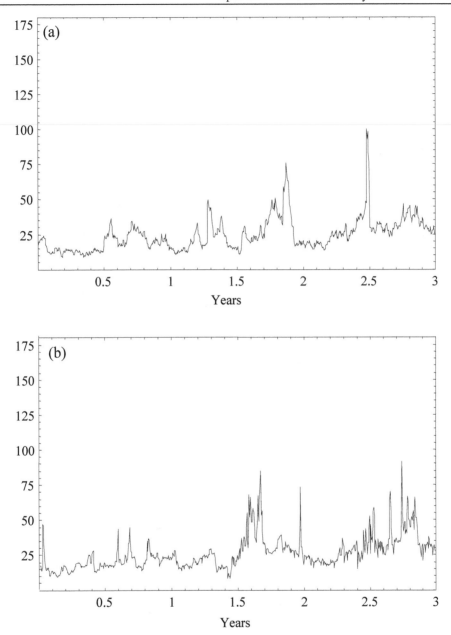

Figure 11.8   (a) COB – simulated price path; (b) COB – market price path.

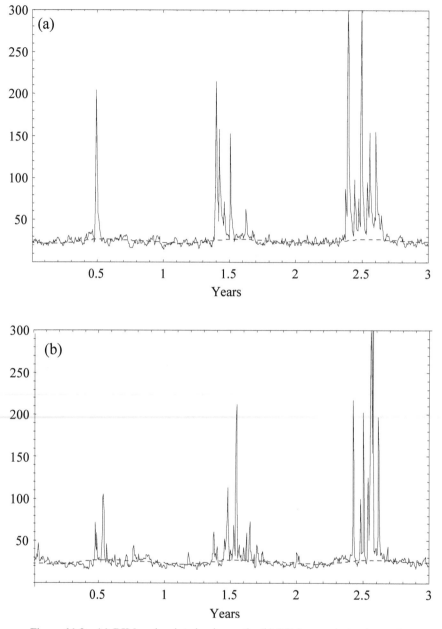

Figure 11.9   (a) PJM – simulated price path; (b) PJM – market price path.

— 12 —

Commodity Swaptions, Swing Contracts and Real Options in the Energy Industry

This chapter presents options that are particularly important in the energy industry, either in a real option approach to the valuation of physical assets or as financial instruments in their own right.

12.1 COMMODITY SWAP AND SWAPTIONS

Swaps and swaptions

Swaps in commodity markets have the same definition as in interest-rate markets and are a generalization of forward contracts.

As usual, we denote the current date as t and the period covered by the swap by $(H, H + n$ years$)$ where H is a future date $(H > t)$ and n is typically an integer but may be a fraction of a year:

On the dates $t_1, t_2, \ldots, t_q = H + n$ years, which are usually equally spaced (e.g., quarterly, monthly), the buyer of the swap pays a fixed amount of G dollars – G is the guaranteed price of the swap – corresponding to a well-defined quantity Q of the commodity underlying the swap contract:

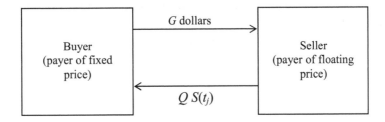

On the same dates t_j, the seller of the swap pays the amount $QS(t_j)$, where Q is the number of barrels in the case of oil (or the number of tons in the case of wheat) and $S(t_j)$ denotes the spot price on dates t_j of a unit quantity of this commodity as reflected by a major index (e.g., Platts index) in the case of gas in the UK; hence, the importance of reliable and liquid indexes in commodity markets discussed in Chapter 2.

It is clear that, if the number of cash flow exchanges reduces to one date ($q = 1$), the swap reduces to a forward contract where the price G paid by the buyer was defined at the outset of the contract and where the seller has to deliver the promised quantity. Note that commodity swaps are financially settled and do not involve any physical delivery. They are Over The Counter (OTC), customized transactions and perfectly suited for hedging activities. Again, the existence of a reliable index is crucial for the determination of each payment of the floating leg. Unsurprisingly, following the colossal development of interest-rate swaps, the swap market has exploded for such commodities as gas, oil and electricity.

As already done in the case of forward and Futures contracts, we are going to analyze the market value $V_p(t)$ of, say, a long position in a commodity swap.

At the outset of the contract:

$$V_p(t) = 0$$

since nobody makes any upfront payment and it is a fair zero-sum game between the two parties. After that date, the value of the position will change on the arrival of news and we can write:

$$V_p(t') = \sum_{j=1}^{q} V_{p_j}(t')$$

where the position p_j corresponds to the exchange of cash flows at date j. These elementary positions are, as observed before, forward contracts (with maturities $t_1, t_2, \ldots, t_q$) which have the property to involve the same *price G* of a forward contract. We saw in Chapter 2 that the price at date $t < t_j$ of a t_j maturity forward contract signed at date 0 is:

$$V_{p_j}(t) = e^{-r(t_j - t)}[F^{t_j}(t) - G]Q$$

Hence the value of the swap at date t is:

$$V_{\text{swap}}(t) = \sum_{j=1}^{q} e^{-r(t_j - t)} Q[F^{t_j}(t) - G] \qquad (12.1)$$

We can now see that G, the guaranteed price of the swap, is simply obtained by stating that $V_{\text{swap}}(t) = 0$:

$$G = \frac{\sum_{j=1}^{q} e^{-r(t_j - t)} F^{t_j}(t)}{\sum_{j=1}^{q} e^{-r(t_j - t)}} \qquad (12.2)$$

This number G is also called the *swap price* at date t. In the case of oil and gas, the swap market is fairly liquid (very liquid for oil) and the swap price, for a given hedging period and frequency of cash flows, is given by the market. Any deviation between this market price and formula (12.2) would in principle allow an arbitrage opportunity to be uncovered; liquidity issues in the swap and forward market obviously put limits on this statement.

Swaptions

In interest-rate markets, where swaps experienced huge growth in the 1990s, swaptions have become over the last few years a very popular instrument. They are experiencing the same success in commodity markets for the same reason (namely, the great liquidity of commodity swaps).

Definition   A swaption, as indicated by its name, is an option on a swap, i.e., grants its holder the right to enter at a future date T a swap relative to the period (T, T_1) at a guaranteed price G fixed at the outset of the swaption:

As we explained before, the value of the swap at date T has no reason to be zero since the guaranteed price of swap G was fixed at the date t when the swaption was purchased by the buyer, and not at date T, the beginning of the swap period. Obviously, the buyer of the swaption will only exercise his right if the swap market value at date T is strictly positive.

Consequently, pay-off of the swaption at maturity T can be written as:

$$C_{swap}(T) = \max(0, V_{swap}(T))$$

As usual, the price of the swaption at date t can be derived accordingly:

$$C_{swap}(t) = e^{-r(T-t)} E_Q[\max(0, V_{swap}(T))/F_t]$$

Hence, an assumption needs to be made about the dynamics involved in the pricing measure Q of the market value of the swap. Since that quantity can take positive or negative values, one simple solution consists in representing it as an arithmetic Brownian motion (see Section 12.3), which will lead to an explicit solution for the swaption price. A much better approach is to use the forward curve and formula (12.2) to represent the dynamics of the swap value. As usual, the key quantity to assess will be the volatility of the swap price – analogous to the volatility of the swap rate in the case of swaptions on interest rates. This volatility can be found in *forward start options* (discussed in Section 12.3(b)), which are also becoming increasingly liquid in commodity markets. To help picture the common features between swaptions and forward start options, let us represent the different dates as:

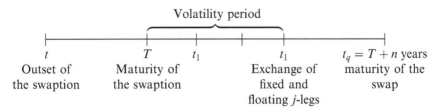

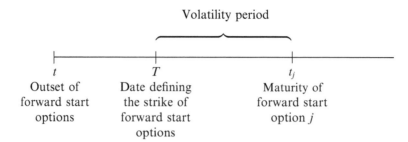

Volatility period

t	T	t_j
Outset of forward start options	Date defining the strike of forward start options	Maturity of forward start option j

12.2   EXCHANGE OPTIONS

These have existed in equity markets for a long time: by holding the stock S_2 and an option to exchange the stock S_2 for another S_1, an investor gets at maturity the *best of* the two stocks S_1 and S_2, obviously a desirable position for all investors.

The pay-off at maturity T of an exchange option is:

$$C(T) = \max(0, S_1(T) - S_2(T))$$

Margrabe (1978) provided, in the Black–Scholes–Merton setting, an exact pricing formula that has the remarkably symmetric form:

$$C(t) = S_1(t)N(d_1) - S_2(t)N(d_2) \tag{12.3}$$

where:

$$
\begin{cases}
d_1 = \dfrac{\ln\left(\dfrac{S_1(t)}{S_2(t)}\right) + \frac{1}{2}\Sigma^2(T - t)}{\Sigma\sqrt{T - t}} \\[4mm]
d_2 = d_1 - \Sigma\sqrt{T - t} \\[2mm]
\Sigma = \text{Vol}\dfrac{S_1(t)}{S_2(t)} = \sqrt{\sigma_1^2 + \sigma_2^2 - 2\rho\sigma_1\sigma_2} \\[2mm]
\rho = \text{Correl}(S_1, S_2)
\end{cases}
$$

The proof can be obtained through a partial differential equation analogous to the Black–Scholes equation or by computing the discounted expectation under the pricing measure of the final pay-off.

Turning to commodities and assuming the dynamics of their prices driven by geometric Brownian motions, we have seen that, under the pricing measure Q, $(S_1(t))$ and $(S_2(t))$ satisfy the following stochastic differential equations:

$$
\begin{cases}
\dfrac{dS_1(t)}{S_1(t)} = (r - y_1)\,dt + \sigma_1\,d\hat{W}_t^1 \\[3mm]
\dfrac{dS_2(t)}{S_2(t)} = (r - y_2)\,dt + \sigma_2\,d\hat{W}_t^2 \\[3mm]
\text{Cov}(d\hat{W}_t^1, d\hat{W}_t^2) = \rho\,dt
\end{cases}
$$

The resulting price of the option to exchange one unit of the commodity S_2 for one unit of the commodity S_1 is given by the same formula as Margrabe's, with the addition of convenience yields y_1 and y_2 – assumed to be constant in our representation:

$$C(t) = S_1(t) e^{-y_1(T-t)} N(d_1) - S_2(t) e^{-y_2(T-t)} N(d_2) \qquad (12.4)$$

where:

$$
\begin{cases}
d_1 = \dfrac{\ln\left(\dfrac{S_1(t) e^{-g_1(T-t)}}{S_2(t) e^{-g_2(T-t)}}\right) + \frac{1}{2}\Sigma^2(T-t)}{\Sigma\sqrt{(T-t)}} \\[2mm]
d_2 = d_1 - \Sigma\sqrt{(T-t)} \\[2mm]
\Sigma = \mathrm{Vol}\left(\dfrac{S_1}{S_2}\right) = \sqrt{\sigma_1^2 + \sigma_2^2 - 2\rho\sigma_1\sigma_2}
\end{cases}
$$

Note that:

1. Σ is the *volatility of S_2 relative to S_1* (i.e., of the price of S_1 expressed in the numéraire S_2).
2. The sensitivity of the value of the exchange option to the volatility of S_1 (respectively, S_2) is not necessarily positive, in contrast to the vega of a plain-vanilla European call. This is readily shown by observing that:

$$\frac{\partial C}{\partial \sigma_1} = \frac{\partial C}{\partial \Sigma} \frac{\partial \Sigma}{\partial \sigma_1}$$

The first quantity $\partial C/\partial \Sigma$ is a classical vega and, hence, positive; the second quantity $\partial \Sigma/\partial \sigma_1 = 1/\Sigma(\sigma_1 - \rho\sigma_2)$ depends on the sign of $(\sigma_1 - \rho\sigma_2)$ which may be negative if the correlation ρ is non-zero and the volatility σ_2 fairly high, which does happen in the case of natural gas. This situation does not occur in equity markets since the standard volatility there is around 18% and high volatilities around 30%. Hence, we need to be careful as the volatilities of energy commodities can lead to counter-intuitive situations (e.g., a negative vega in one of the two underlyings). In practice, this means that when we have a high correlation, the great variability of the price of gas may create a negative exposure to the volatility of the electricity price.

Lastly, let us note that, if we wish to introduce mean-reversion in the dynamics of S_1 and/or S_2, the price of the exchange option as an explicit formula given in equation (12.4) no longer holds; however, Monte Carlo methods or trees can easily provide an approximation of the option price.
3. Using the spot–forward relationship, formula (12.4) can be rewritten as:

$$C(t) = e^{-r(T-t)}[F_1^T(t)N(d_1) - kF_2^T(t)N(d_2)] \qquad (12.4')$$

where F_1^T and F_2^T denote the Futures prices for delivery at date T of commodities S_1 and S_2. These numbers can be read in the market and avoid the explicit computation of the two convenience yields.

12.3 COMMODITY SPREAD OPTIONS

These are particularly popular in *all* commodity markets, e.g., soy crush in the soybean market, and can be encountered under the several forms that are described below.

(a) The importance of spread options in commodity markets

The spread between two quantities is probably the most traded instrument in the world of commodities and energy commodities, in particular. Spread options come into play in the valuation of power plants, oil refineries, storage facilities and transmission lines, i.e., all the fundamental physical assets in the energy industry. Unsurprisingly, financial spread options are also traded as financial instruments in their own right as part of commodity portfolios.

Spreads can be broadly categorized in two ways.

(1) Spreads between two commodities

In the domain of agricultural commodities, this spread represents a "quality" spread; the same applies for different types of crude oil. This quality spread is generally rewarded by a premium (respectively, rebate) paid (received) by the buyer of a Futures contract when the physical commodity that is delivered is of a higher grade (respectively, lower). In the energy industry, this spread is often between a fuel input, such as coal, oil, gas, and an output which is either a refined product (e.g., petro-chemicals) or electricity.

The standard terminology is given in the following subsections.

CRACKSPREAD

This is the differential between the prices of refined products and the price of crude oil input. Unleaded gasoline and heating oil are the most profitable ones, consuming 80% of the crude. Unsurprisingly, options written on these two products are heavily traded (their volatility smiles were discussed in Chapter 6). Crackspreads are traded on the New York Mercantile Exchange (NYMEX) or in OTC transactions. They allow the real option representation of a refinery to be built, namely a short position in crude oil and a long position in refined products.

SPARKSPREAD

This spread represents the difference between the price of electricity (output) and the price of the corresponding quantity of primary fuel (input), taking into account the conversion rate or "heat rate". Primary fuels are essentially natural gas, coal and residual fuel oil. When coal is the primary fuel, the spread option is often called a *darkspread*. Sparkspreads are traded OTC and represent very popular instruments, particularly in Europe, where the spread is between electricity and natural gas (or coal). The use of sparkspreads in a real option valuation of gas-fired turbines will be developed in Section 12.5.

(2) Calendar spreads

These are very popular in commodity markets for another reason, namely seasonality. A typical pay-off at maturity T is of the form:

$$C(T) = \max(0, F^{T_1}(T) - F^{T_2}(T))$$

where $T < T_1 < T_2$, meaning that the option is in fact a Futures calendar spread. Unsurprisingly, this option arises in the valuation of storage facilities, such as silos and gas storage caverns and even water reservoirs, since hydroelectricity is the only form of storable electricity. There are fundamentally two ways of pricing calendar spread options:

1. Either, the Futures contracts of different maturities are perceived as the prices of two different commodities, in particular because of the seasonal effect. Under the pricing measure Q, the two Futures contracts will then be written as martingales with different volatilities. A simple example of such a representation has been seen before: in the case of a geometric Brownian motion there is no drift term in the stochastic differential equation driving the Futures price:

$$\begin{cases} \dfrac{dF^{T_1}(t)}{F^{T_1}(t)} = \sigma_1 \, dW^1(t) \\[2mm] \dfrac{dF^{T_2}(t)}{F^{T_2}(t)} = \sigma_2 \, dW^2(t) \\[2mm] dW^1(t) \cdot dW^2(t) = \rho \, dt \end{cases}$$

For a valuation of this spread see Section 12.3(c).
2. Or, one incorporates all the relevant properties of the commodity under analysis in a single stochastic process $(F^T(t))$ featuring a term structure of volatilities $\sigma(t, T)$ and the spread option at time 0 is priced as the expectation of the discounted pay-off $\max(0, F^{T_1}(T) - F^{T_2}(T))$.

In general, it is the first approach that is adopted since the calendar spread is mostly perceived by market participants as built upon two different instruments: natural gas in spring is viewed as a different commodity from natural gas in winter.

We will start the technical discussion with a third type of spread options; namely, calendar spreads on the spot price of the commodity in the sense that at the outset of the option contract the strike is defined as the price of the underlying at a future date (prior to maturity of the option). These *forward start* options are very popular in all equity markets and commodity markets as well, since they allow the buyer and seller of the option to take a view on the behavior of the underlying and its volatility over a time period starting at a future date.

(b) Forward start options

These involve a single commodity S and allow traders at date t to take a view on (or hedge against) the evolution of S over a future period $[T_1, T]$, where $t < T_1 < T$ and t is the current date. The pay-off of a forward start call option is defined as:

$$C^{\text{fs}}(T) = \max(0, S(T) - S(T_1)) \tag{12.5}$$

whereby the fixed strike k of the plain-vanilla call option defined in Chapter 4 is here replaced by the value of the commodity spot price at a future date T_1:

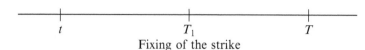

Fixing of the strike

Typically, the buyer of such a call wishes to hedge against a possible rise in the under-lying price of the commodity between dates T_1 and T (e.g., the current date t is 1 March and the buyer seeks protection against an increase in electricity prices between 1 June and 1 July). Assuming for simplicity that the commodity price is driven under the pricing measure Q by a geometric Brownian motion:

$$\frac{dS_t}{S_t} = (r - y)\,dt + \sigma\,d\hat{W}_t \tag{12.6}$$

it is clear that integrating between dates T_1 and T gives a simple expression of $S(T)$ in terms of $S(T_1)$, namely:

$$S(T) = S(T_1)\exp\left\{\left(r - y - \frac{\sigma^2}{2}\right)(T - T_1) + \sigma\hat{W}(T - T_1)\right\} = S(T_1)\exp U$$

where:

$$U = \left(r - y - \frac{\sigma^2}{2}\right)(T - T_1) + \sigma\hat{W}(T - T_1)$$

Hence, we can extract $S(T_1)$ in the pay-off of the forward start option:

$$C^{\mathrm{fs}}(T) = S(T_1)\max(0, \exp U - 1)$$

and

$$C^{\mathrm{fs}}(t) = e^{-r(T-t)}E_Q[S(T_1)(\exp U - 1)\mathbf{1}_{\mathcal{E}}/\mathcal{F}_t] \tag{12.7}$$

where $\mathcal{E} = \{$States of nature where $S(T) \geq S(T_1)\}$.[1]

Note that because the increments of the Brownian motion are *independent*, the quantities $S(T_1)$ and U (which are random variables viewed from date t) are indepen-dent and the computation involved in equation (12.7) is of the same type as the one developed in the second proof of the Black–Scholes formula in Chapter 5. Moreover, we can use the fact that the T_1-maturity forward price is constant on average under the pricing measure Q. Observing that $F^{T_1}(T_1) = S(T_1)$, we obtain:

$$E_Q[S(T_1)/\mathcal{F}_t] = E_Q[F^{T_1}(T_1)/\mathcal{F}_t] = F^{T_1}(t)$$

Pulling this quantity out of the expectation in equation (12.7) and repeating for the product $(\exp U - 1)\mathbf{1}_{\mathcal{E}}$ the computations conducted in Chapter 5, we obtain for the price at date t of the forward start option:

$$C^{\mathrm{fs}}(t) = S(t)\,e^{-y(T-t)}N(d_1) - F^{T_1}(t)\,e^{-r(T-t)}N(d_2) \tag{12.8}$$

where:

$$\begin{cases} d_1 = \dfrac{\ln\left(\dfrac{S(t)\,e^{-y(T-t)}}{F^{T_1}(t)\,e^{-r(T-t)}}\right) + \frac{1}{2}\sigma^2(T - T_1)}{\sigma\sqrt{T - T_1}} \\[4mm] d_2 = d_1 - \sigma\sqrt{T - T_1} \end{cases}$$

---

[1] The mathematical formalism is kept to an acceptable minimum.

This interesting formula is the same as the Black–Scholes formula, except that the fixed strike k has been replaced by the *forward price* of the commodity prevailing at date t for maturity T_1, the date at which the option "really" starts. Equation (12.8) shows that, even though we assumed a constant volatility σ over the whole period $[0, T]$ in equation (12.6), the only volatility which matters in the problem is the one prevailing during the period $[T_1, T]$. This is the implied volatility embedded in this forward start option which gives the market view of volatility for the future time period (T_1, T).

For example, in electricity markets a forward start call option traded in January (date t) for the period (T_1, T) (where $T_1 = 1$ June and $T = 1$ July) will convey the market risk aversion in its price, translated into implied volatility, to the possible price spikes during the month of June. Forward-start options have become quite liquid in equity and commodity markets and traders are today looking for models which not only explain the volatility smile for plain-vanilla options at some chosen maturities T but also the "forward smiles".

(c) Spread options

A spread option between two commodities S_1 and S_2 has the same type of pay-off as a standard call option, except that now the underlying is the difference $S_1 - S_2$ (or $Q_1S_1 - Q_2S_2$, where Q_1 and Q_2 are the quantities of commodities S_1 and S_2) and the strike k is non-zero. Typically, the pay-off of the spread option takes the form:

$$C(T) = \max(0, Q_1S_1(T) - Q_2S_2(T) - k) \qquad (12.9)$$

where:

- Q_1 and Q_2 are positive constants (representing quantities).
- The strike k is strictly positive.

Whether the dynamics of $(S_1(t))$ and $(S_2(t))$ are driven under the pricing measure Q by geometric Brownian motions or by diffusion processes including mean-reversion and time-varying volatilities, there is no longer an explicit formula for the option price at date t. Again, Monte Carlo *simulations of the bidimensional process* (S_1, S_2) provide an easy-to-implement pricing approach.

We saw in Chapter 6 how to build Monte Carlo simulations of the trajectories of a single commodity price $(S(t))$ by discretization of process S over the lifetime $[0, T]$ of the option. The same procedure applies here, except that consistency in the construction of the trajectories for S_1 and S_2 needs to be insured given the crucial importance of the *dependence structure* between the two price processes $(S_1(t))$ and $(S_2(t))$. To make things simple, let us suppose that both processes follow mean-reverting diffusions; for instance, driven under the pricing measure Q by the stochastic differential equations:

$$\begin{cases} dS_1(t) = a(b - \ln S_1(t)S_1(t))\,dt + \sigma_1 S_1(t)\,dW_t^1 \\ dS_2(t) = c(e - \ln S_2(t)S_2(t))\,dt + \sigma_2 S_2(t)\,dW_t^2 \qquad (12.10) \\ dW_t^1 \cdot dW_t^2 = \rho\,dt \end{cases}$$

We can immediately see that non-constant volatility parameters σ_1 and σ_2 can be incorporated in what follows. This may be readily done if:

- σ_1 and σ_2 are deterministic functions of time (e.g., exhibiting seasonality).
- σ_1 (respectively, σ_2) is a deterministic function of the commodity spot price S_1 (respectively, S_2), e.g., increasing when the commodity price rises according to the inverse leverage effect characteristic of energy commodity prices.

Returning to equation (12.10), we see that simulation of the trajectories from the equation driving $S_1(t)$ alone takes us back to Chapter 6. But we need to make sure that the correlation property is correctly represented. In order to do this, let us write the second Brownian motion W_2 as:

$$W^2(t) = \rho W^1(t) + (1 - \rho)W^3(t) \qquad (12.11)$$

where $W^3(t)$ is a Brownian motion independent of $W^1(t)$:

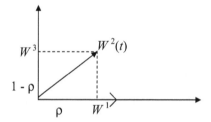

This geometric decomposition of W^2 is often referred to as the Cholesky decomposition, in particular in the Value at Risk literature where correlations need to be reflected in the analysis of the change in value of a position depending on several sources of risk $S_1, S_2, \ldots, S_q$. Figures 12.1 and 12.2 show the clouds of points generated by a bidimensional Brownian motion (W_1, W_2). In Figure 12.1 the correlation coefficient is equal to zero; in Figure 12.2, $\rho = 0.6$.

In order to build a first pair of trajectories $(\mathcal{Z}_1^{(1)}, \mathcal{Z}_2^{(1)})$ for S_1 and S_2 over the interval $[0, T]$, we first discretize it into n subintervals. The changes in S_1 and S_2 over the first subinterval of length T/n are fully defined by the draws of the Brownian increments:

$$H_1 = W_1\left(0 + \frac{T}{n}\right) - W_1(0) \quad \text{and} \quad H_2 = W_2\left(0 + \frac{T}{n}\right) - W_2(0)$$

since we remember that the discretization of equation (12.10) leads to:

$$S_1\left(\frac{T}{n}\right) = a(b - \ln S_1(0))S_1(0)\frac{T}{n} + \sigma_1 S_1(0)H_1$$

$$S_2\left(\frac{T}{n}\right) = c(e - \ln S_2(0))S_2(0)\frac{T}{n} + \sigma_2 S_2(0)H_2$$

For the quantity H_1 that is normally distributed with mean 0 and variance T/n, a random draw $\hat{H}_1$ is easy to obtain. To build a random draw denoted $\hat{H}_2$ of H_2, we need first to create a random draw $\hat{H}_3$ of the change over the same interval of an

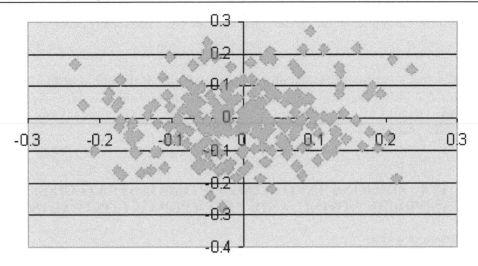

Figure 12.1 Simulations of pairs (W_1, W_2) in the case of zero-correlation.

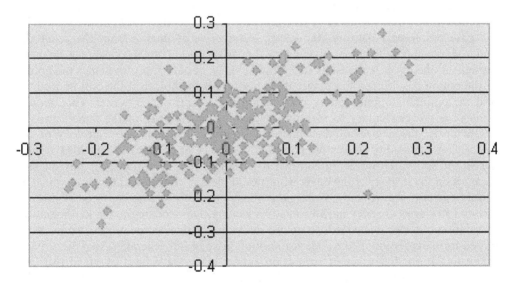

Figure 12.2 Simulations of pairs (W_1, W_2) when $\rho = 0.6$.

independent Brownian motion W_3 (same drift 0 and variance T/n) and define:

$$\hat{H}_2 = \rho\hat{H}_1 + (1 - \rho)\hat{H}_3$$

in order to satisfy the correlation property.

Constructing 1,000 pairs of trajectories for S_1 and S_2 in this manner, we obtain the corresponding terminal values $S_1(T)$ and $S_2(T)$ and, hence, 1,000 simulated pay-offs $u_1, u_2, \ldots, u_{1000}$ by plugging these numbers into equation (12.9):

$$C(T) = \max(0, Q_1 S_1(T) - Q_2 S_2(T) - k)$$

The Monte Carlo price of the spread option at date 0 is consequently equal to:

$$C^{MC}(0) = e^{-rT} \frac{u_1 + u_2 + \cdots + u_{1000}}{1000}$$

and is a very good approximation of the exact price $C(0)$ of the spread option.

Note that the methodology described above would readily allow us to handle *path-dependent* options written on S_1 and S_2 since *full trajectories* over the interval $[0, T]$ have been generated.

12.4   OPTIONS INVOLVING OPTIMAL STRATEGIES: AMERICAN, SWING AND TAKE-OR-PAY CONTRACTS

(a) American options

In the 1960s and 1970s, the first options traded on stocks were European and American options. European options were discussed in detail in Chapter 4. An American call option has the same characteristics as a European call option, except that it may be exercised at any date τ chosen by the buyer during the lifetime $[0, T]$ of the option. In the case of physical delivery, the buyer will receive at date τ from the seller the underlying commodity upon payment of the strike price k. In the case of a financial settlement, the buyer receives the cash flow $S(\tau) - k$ at date τ, positive since the holder of the option has decided to exercise it. In both cases the holder of the option needs to find the optimal stopping time τ maximizing the payout of the option. This *optimal strategy* is not elementary to identify; neither is the *fair price* of the American call.

Obviously, the pay-off of the American option depends on the trajectory of the underlying commodity S over the period $[0, T]$; hence, it deserves being called a *path-dependent* option. However, in contrast to Asian or barrier options, the pay-off also depends on the *strategy* of the buyer who tries to identify the optimal time τ at which he should exercise. As we know from game theory or decision-making in corporations, optimal strategies are very hard to uncover exactly. Unsurprisingly, the mathematical translation of the problem leads to unique difficulties and, even today, we do not have a closed-form expression of the American option price in full generality. However, many interesting properties together with approximate prices have been obtained over the decades on this challenging problem. McKean (1965) found an explicit form of the American option price in the case of infinite maturity T; an analogous expression does not exist yet for an American option with finite maturity. It is important to observe that, in the case of a European call option, the buyer plays no role over the interval $(0, T)$ and needs only to observe the cash market at maturity to decide whether he should exercise the option. The seller, on the contrary, needs to *dynamically hedge* his position by allocating the premium received at date 0 between the underlying commodity S bought in quantity Δ and the money market account M; the hedge will be adjusted when time elapses and S_t moves up or down.

In the case of an American option, the seller continues to need to actively manage his hedging portfolio in a situation which is different since exercise may occur at any time. But the buyer of the American option cannot any longer dismiss it until maturity: the question "Is it optimal to exercise the option?" is posed on each day. Knowing the future would obviously help in answering this question, but only the past is known, i.e., statistics on the observed prices of the underlying. We can however make some simple observations:

- The exercise will take place if S_τ is very high and, hence, the exercise region contains the very upper part of the quadrant (t, S_t).
- The exercise should not take place if S_τ is very low.
- The difficulty lies in identification of the *exercise boundary*.

Regarding the valuation of an American option, it is worth noting that:

- A lower bound is given by the European option with the same characteristics and underlying.
- Another lower bound is the *intrinsic value* of the American option, i.e., the value $S_\tau - k$ obtained if exercising the option immediately.
- An upper bound for the price at date t of the American option is provided by the spot price of the underlying stock or commodity S; the proof is given by an elementary arbitrage argument.
- The value of an American option on a possible exercise date is the greater of the pay-off in case of immediate exercise and the continuation value of the option.

This applies, for instance, to a *Bermudan* option which, by definition, can be exercised on any of a pre-specified finite set of dates during the lifetime $[0, T]$ of the option. A simple and efficient method to price Bermudan and American options is to use a tree approach (see Chapter 5):

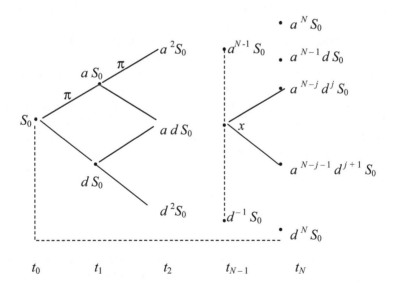

At maturity $t_N = T$, the American option either has already been exercised and no longer exists, or its value is equal to the intrinsic value; hence, the problem of its exercise and value is solved. At date $t_N - 1$ we look at a node $x = a^{N-j-1}d^j S_0$, since we have registered a total of $(N-1)$ up and down moves. The price of the American option is then equal to the greater number of the intrinsic value and the *continuation value*,[2] namely at date t_{N-1} at the node $a^{N-j-1}d^j S_0$:

$$V(t_{N-1}, a^{N-j-1}d^j S_0)$$

$$= \max\left(a^{N-j-1}d^j S_0 - k, \frac{\pi(a^{N-j}d^j S_0 - k)^+}{1+r} + \frac{(1-\pi)(a^{N-j-1}d^{j+1} S_0 - k)^+}{1+r}\right)$$

since the continuation value is the discounted expectation of the pay-off at date t_N which, conditional on the starting point, can only take two values.

Using a *backward recursive approach*, the American option price at any node may be obtained by the same reasoning and the value at the base node S_0 is the price we were searching for. Moreover, if we take a finely meshed tree and mark the nodes according to whether exercise occurs or not, we find that the plane (t, S) is divided into two regions: the domain where exercise would occur is called the exercise region and the dividing line is called the exercise boundary or *Snell envelope*. This latter terminology is usually used in a continuous time approach to this optimal stopping problem (we mentioned earlier that the binomial tree is a discretization of a geometric Brownian motion).

Swing options

Swing options have unique features that make them characteristic of the gas and electricity industry; they have existed as an embedded and very useful flexibility in contracts that have been traded for decades. Depending on weather conditions, residential consumers wish to adjust their gas consumption; depending on their current production, industrial consumers need to have access to more electricity. In all cases, *volume flexibility is an essential feature of energy contracts*. Note that, conversely, utilities or energy companies which hold long-term gas supply contracts with producing countries have incorporated this optionality with respect to the quantity they may request during each period. And the producing countries have protected themselves through Take Or Pay (TOP) provisions included in the contract.

In order to incorporate both features, we will define a swing option as follows: let us suppose that the exercise period is $[0, T]$ (e.g., a year), and the strike price k is expressed in pence per therm or dollars per megawatt-hour. Then, on each day t in the interval $[0, T]$, the buyer of the option has the right to recall from the buyer a quantity q_t such that:

$$m \le q_t \le M$$

and

$$A \le \sum_t q_t \le B$$

If m is equal to zero, there is no minimal daily withdrawal in the contract; M represents the maximal quantity recalled on day t, compatible with the generation capacity constraint of the seller.

---

[2] Recent methods introduced by Carriere (1996) and Longstaff-Schwartz (2001) propose an expression of the continuation value of the option as a simple function (quadratic or other) of the underlying asset price.

Regarding the total amount recalled $(\sum_t q_t)$, its lower bound A represents the minimal take of the buyer over the period below which the buyer may incur penalties (TOP specification). The particular case $A = B$ expresses the total take across the year as being exactly constrained.

We can see that the swing option gives *flexibility with respect to time and quantity*, a feature that is never encountered with options traded in stock and bond markets where the quantity of the underlying asset is always specified. Volume risk has always been a major attribute of commodity markets, prior to or after deregulation.

Valuation of the swing option and hedging strategy

At any date t, both buyer and seller are interested in the market value $C(t)$ of the swing option. Moreover, the buyer needs to design his optimal strategy; namely, the quantity q_t of gas or electricity he should recall (with a few hours' notice) from the seller of the option. As for the latter, he has to have a hedge built at any time, in other words, be prepared to deliver the maximal amount either from his own resources or by purchasing it on the spot market. Note that:

1. A number of authors suggest that the optimal strategy in a swing option is "all or nothing", sometimes called ruthless. This view would be correct in a world where the spot price $S(t)$ is deterministic, since the optimal solution is then essentially a "corner solution". In the situation of competitive markets, even if spot prices are at the level of $1,000/MWh, they could be at $1,500 tomorrow (see the ECAR prices in June 1998 discussed in Chapter 11) and it may be wise to recall a lower $q(t)$ today in order to ask tomorrow for a higher $q(t + 1)$ (and still satisfy the global constraint M).

   Mathematically, the simplification induced by this "all or nothing" representation is significant: we are back to a setting analogous to that of the American option where we need to identify the critical value $S^*(t)$ of the underlying commodity price above which maximal exercise should take place.
2. In fact, the problem posed in full generality is more complex since the optimal solution q_t may be an interior solution. We see that, as in the case of the American option, backward-solving is one way to proceed; placing ourselves on the last day of the lifetime of the option, the situation is clear both in terms of the value of the option and the quantity to recall. Both are defined by the global constraint and the current value of the underlying spot price.

   Working backward, we see that even by day $(T - 1)$ the strategy is non-trivial. Besides the current value of the spot price and its possible moves over the period $(T - 1, T)$, a key quantity appears in the discussion, namely the quantity of gas or electricity already taken:

$$Q(T - 1) = \sum_{t \leq T-2} q_t$$

In the spirit of Chapter 4, the value of the swing option at any date t should be written as $C(t, S_t, Q_t; r, \sigma, k, T)$ and the optimal strategy $B(t, S_t, Q_t; r, \sigma, k, T)$.

Coming back to the tree approach we discussed for the American option, we see that it may be extended to the swing option by introducing a *deep tree* in order to incorporate the development along the tree of the *two* state variables S_t and Q_t. The second dimension of the tree will exhibit the variable Q_t that starts at 0 at the beginning of the life of the option; a reasonable representation of Q_t over time at the different nodes of the tree may be at the start a discrete set of subintervals of $[0, B]$. A stochastic optimization procedure should then be implemented and performed along the tree[3] where each node contains a pair (S, Q):

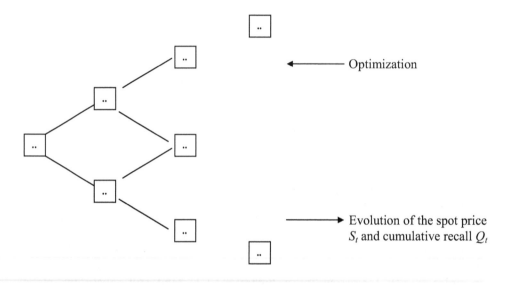

12.5 DISCOUNTED CASH FLOWS VERSUS REAL OPTIONS FOR THE VALUATION OF PHYSICAL ASSETS: THE EXAMPLE OF A FUEL-FIRED PLANT

(a) The characteristics of a power plant

Let us consider a coal-fired plant or a modern Combined Cycle Gas Turbine (CCGT) which transforms natural gas into electricity. This plant is characterized by a number of factors, which are outlined in the following subsections.

Capacity

Capacity is the maximum power output of the plant and is expressed in megawatts (MW, or 10^6 watts). This number can change with seasons and temperature (particularly so in the case of nuclear plants because of the necessary refrigeration of reactors). Typical ranges for different technologies are:

---

[3] Note that we can build a trinomial tree for the upper "layer" (i.e., the price of gas) to better represent a mean-reversion feature. The transition probabilities between nodes of the trinomial tree at different dates should reflect the choice of the underlying price process, e.g., Ornstein–Uhlenbeck for the log-price.

- Nuclear: Over 1,000 MW
- Coal: Over 500 MW
- Gas or oil baseload: 200–800 MW
- Gas or oil peaker: 50–200 MW

Minimum and maximum generation level

The maximum generation level is the plant's total capacity; the minimum level is the technically feasible minimum output (without shutting down the plant). The latter quantity has obviously a major impact on the plant's flexibility, hence value.

Ramp rate

This is the rate at which generation output can be changed and is expressed in megawatts per minute. Newer units may have rates of around 5 MW/min. This quantity also has a major impact on the flexibility of the plant, hence its ability to capture hourly or even more short-term optionality.

Maximum online, minimum offline time

For technical reasons, restrictions exist on the maximum amount (respectively, minimum) of time a plant can operate (respectively, stay offline).

Heat rate

This is a measure of the efficiency of the plant in terms of converting a given fuel into electricity. Electricity is typically expressed in kilowatt-hours (KWh). Gas is expressed in British thermal units (Btu) and other fuels can be converted into Btu equivalent. Unsurprisingly, the heat rate depends on the generation level. Examples of heat rate at maximum generation are:

- Baseload coal: 9,500 Btu/KWh or equivalently 9.5 million Btu/MWh
- Combined cycle: 7,000 Btu/KWh

Startup/Shutdown costs

These represent the costs of starting up or shutting down a plant, including the cost of extra fuel consumed during this operation.

O&M costs

Operational and Maintenance (O&M) costs are usually expressed per unit of generation.

Scheduled outages

These represent the planned downtime for maintenance of the plants. Typically, this downtime is of the order of 2–4 weeks annually.

Forced outages

These represent unplanned downtime caused by a technical failure of the unit. Power producers are very concerned by the Equivalent Forced Outage Rate (EFOR) which is defined as the number of outage hours in a given period divided by the number of generation hours in the same period. Outage rates depend on the type of unit (nuclear versus thermal versus gas) and can vary from 3% to 20%. Outage rates impact heavily on the value of the plant because they prevent the profitable production of electricity at times when prices are generally very high because of weather conditions (e.g., a protracted heatwave forcing a nuclear plant to be stopped momentarily and sending electricity prices skyrocketing, as in the ECAR region in June 1998). Conversely, an outage occurring during a spike while the generator has heavy commitments to its customers may result in a heavy loss since he will have to buy electricity at a high price in the spot market to honor his contracts.

(b) DCF approach to the valuation of a power plant

Let us now turn to valuation of the power plant; one way to proceed is to return to the fundamental lessons of corporate finance and use the Discounted Cash Flow (DCF) approach, which leads to our writing the plant value V at date 0 of analysis as:

$$V(0) = \frac{E(\tilde{\phi}_1)}{1 + r^a} + \cdots + \frac{E(\tilde{\phi}_n)}{(1 + r^a)^n} \tag{12.12}$$

where:

- n is the number of years the plant is supposed to be operating in the future before being obsolete.
- $E(\tilde{\phi}_j)$ denotes the estimated profits to be made from operating the plant in year j: revenues from selling the electricity minus the cost of fuel and the payment of O&M costs.
- r^a is a key quantity – namely, the proper *discount rate* to apply to the project.

The merit of the DCF approach is that its interpretation is easy and understood by everyone in a firm. Its limits, however, are the following:

1. The estimated value $E(\tilde{\phi}_j)$ for $j = 1, \ldots, n$ of the random cash flows $\tilde{\phi}_1, \ldots, \tilde{\phi}_n$ to be received may be difficult to assess for distant years:

$$\tilde{\phi}_j = Q_j \tilde{S}_1(j) - Q'_j \tilde{S}_2(j) - (\text{O\&M costs})_j$$

where:

- Q_j is the production of electricity in year j (e.g., in MWh);
- Q'_j is the quantity of gas fired for that output (e.g., in million Btu);
- $\tilde{S}_1(j)$ is the average selling price of electricity in year j (per MWh);
- $\tilde{S}_2(j)$ is the average purchase price of gas (per million Btu);
- $(\text{O\&M costs})_j$ denotes the operation and maintenance costs of year j.

2. More complex and crucial is the assessment of the discount factor r^a: taking $r^a = 5\%$ when it should be 7% or 8% is going to drastically shift the estimation of the power plant price by millions of dollars or euros given the magnitude of the numerators $E(\tilde{\phi}_1) \cdots E(\tilde{\phi}_n)$ in equation (12.12).

   The different answers we may want to keep in mind are the following:

   ○ identify projects of the same risk and revenue profile in order to infer r^a from their realized return;
   ○ use the cost of capital of the acquiring firm for r^a; however, this choice has the undesirable feature of not reflecting the riskiness of the acquired plant, in terms of the debt-to-equity ratio or its physical features (such as heat rate, amount of emitted particles);
   ○ maintain a sector perspective and estimate the expected return in the energy industry through the Capital Asset Pricing Model (CAPM):

$$r^a = r_f + \beta(E(\tilde{r}_m) - r_f)$$

   where r_f is the risk-free rate; β denotes the beta of the industry sector with the stock market; and $\tilde{r}_m$ is market return.

3. A better solution is possible if there exist liquid forward markets both for electricity output and fuel input. Since O&M costs do not vary too much over time and can be adjusted in a deterministic manner (particularly to cover inflation), we can write the revenues in year j as:

$$\phi_j = Q_1 F_1^j(0) - Q_2 F_2^j(0) - (\text{O\&M costs})_j$$

where the prices of electricity and gas $F_1^j(0)$ and $F_2^j(0)$ can now be *locked in* forward markets (if the difference is positive). Hence, the cash flows ϕ_j attached to the power plant are no longer random – as long as there is no counterparty risk – and the discount factor r^a can be reasonably approximated by the cost of capital of the acquiring company.

(c) Valuation of a power plant using a real option approach

In the following subsections we will start with some general considerations on the use of real options.

Validity of the real options approach

There are a few conditions that need to be satisfied for the real options approach to be legitimate:

1. The option must have a starting date and a maturity T, where T may be infinite.
2. The underlying source of risk S (or sources of risk S_1, S_2) must be clearly identified.
3. S_1 (and S_2) must be traded in continuous time in liquid markets, in order to allow for dynamic hedging, the cornerstone of valuation by arbitrage.
4. We should be able to exhibit appropriate stochastic processes for the evolution over time of $S_1(t)$ and $S_2(t)$, in particular because data series of past values are available.

5. The type of option must be recognized: European versus American versus compound,[4] since it will obviously impact the price obtained for the physical asset. In practice, this choice is rarely unique and one will make a compromise between the tractability and accuracy of the representation.
6. The processes identified for S_1 and S_2 should lead to a situation of *market completeness*, otherwise there will not be unicity of the valuation, which is quite problematic when one is paying tens of millions of dollars to acquire a physical asset.

In practice, if a real life valuation problem fails to meet conditions 3 and 4, the real option approach is highly questionable.

Let us observe that in the developments made in Section 12.5(b), the volatilities of the spot prices of electricity and gas, $S_1(t)$ and $S_2(t)$, appear nowhere in the valuation. In practice, a company which wants to purchase a *peaker* (a small and flexible gas-fired turbine) clearly plans to benefit from spikes in electricity prices and possibly make all its revenues on days when prices are above \$100 per megawatt-hour. Obviously, the volatility of power prices is present in the bid quoted for the power plant; hence, this volatility should be present in the valuation procedure.

Keeping in mind that a modern peaker has a very high ramp rate, one has the *option* to adjust production over very short time periods. This flexibility is fully captured by the *real option approach* to the valuation of a power plant and the grid of the time horizon should reflect the corresponding granularity.

Valuation of a flexible CCGT

The power plant may be switched on/off with very short notice and can be replicated by a strip of *sparkspread options*:

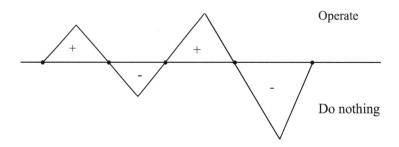

When the price of electricity is high and the pay-off of the sparkspread positive, the peaker is switched on; otherwise, it is turned off. By replication arguments, we can state that the value of the gas turbine at time 0 is:

$$V(0) = \sum_{j=1}^{N} C^j(0)$$

---

[4] A compound option is an option written on an option.

where the number N depends on the granularity associated with the ramp rate and the estimated lifetime of the peaker. Each sparkspread j has a pay-off:

$$C^j(j) = \max(0, Q_1 S_1(j) - Q_2 S_2(j) - O\&M_j)$$

Assuming for the sake of argument that O&M costs are negligible, the sparkspread reduces to an exchange option. We saw in Section 12.2 that the price at date 0 (or t prior to maturity) of a commodity exchange option does *not* (like Margrabe's formula) include any interest rate, risk-free or not. The value of the option – and the gas turbine – resides in the *relative price of electricity versus gas and its volatility*. Interest rates, which are usually present everywhere in finance since they convey the time value of money, play no role here. The right *numéraire* (see Geman, El Karoui and Rochet, 1995) is the price of gas or this price times the million Btu of gas fired in the plant.

As said before, the higher the flexibility of the peaker, the greater the number of such options and the resulting value of the power plant. By incorporating O&M costs, the different sparkspreads attached to the successive periods may be priced through Monte Carlo simulations of the bi-dimensional process (S_1, S_2). We can now see from equation (12.4) that, in the current period of fast-growing energy prices, the value of the gas turbine increases accordingly since the price at date 0 of the sparkspread is a homogeneous function of degree 1 of S_1 and S_2:

$$C(\alpha S_1(t), \alpha S_2(t)) = \alpha C(S_1(t), S_2(t)) \quad \text{for any positive } \alpha$$

In practice, the valuation of the power plant will involve a mixture of positions in forward contracts to secure future revenues while keeping a fraction of the capacity available for peak hours and days where prices spike.

The value of asset optionality: An elementary case study

We can do this by considering two gas-fired plants in California with heat rates of 8,000 and 10,000 Btu and studying their values (in $ millions) during April (shoulder month) and August (peak month):

	April		August	
Heat rate	8,000	10,000	8,000	10,000
"Forward-type" valuation (no optionality) ($m)	1.0	−0.3	10.4	9
Monthly optionality ($m)	1.3	0.6	10.4	9
Daily optionality ($m)	1.7	1.2	10.4	9
Peak/offpeak optionality ($m)	1.9	1.3	10.4	9

Kyoto pricing of a coal-fired plant

We can use the same sparkspread representation but need now to incorporate the cost of emissions. The pay-off at maturity of such a *darkspread* has the following form:

$$C(j) = \max(0, Q_1 S_1(j) - Q_2 S_2(j) - Q_3 E(j) - O\&M_j)$$

Figure 12.3   Kyoto pricing of a coal plant.

where:

- S_2 denotes the price of coal.
- $E(j)$ is the price of a ton of carbon at date j.
- Q_3 is the number of tons of carbons emitted by the coal-fired plant to produce Q_1 megawatt-hours of electricity.

12.6   VALUATION OF A GAS STORAGE FACILITY

(a) Introduction

There are different types of underground natural gas storage:

- Depleted natural gasfields and oilfields with sufficient porosity, permeability and retention characteristics.
- Aquifers – water can go up or down depending on the type of gas injected. The geology of aquifers is similar to that of depleted production fields, essentially consisting of water-bearing sedimentary rock covered with impermeable cap rock.
- Salt caverns – storage is developed by injecting water into a salt formation, the water dissolving the salt and creating a storage cavern.

Depleted fields as storage reservoirs

Some general features can be noticed:

1. Depleted gasfields, oilfields and aquifer fields are characterized by a low turnover rate. The injection season for gas typically lasts from March/April until October/November; the reservoir is emptied during winter – the period of high gas consumption.
2. During an occasional upward spike in prices during summer, injections can be suspended and gas earmarked for injections can be diverted to the spot market.
3. These reservoirs primarily take advantage of the *summer/winter spread*.

4. Injection and withdrawal programs are associated with the purchase and sale of gas in the Futures/forwards markets in order to lock in the seasonal spread.
5. The optionality consists in the ability to time hedging decisions and to occasionally suspend injections or withdrawals that were planned.

Salt dome storage

1. Salt domes offer high deliverability compared with other types of underground storage. A salt formation storage facility can be turned over several times during the heating season. During summer in the US, salt dome storage is used to satisfy cooling load of electricity.
2. As in the case of aquifers, injection and withdrawal rates depend on the amount of gas in storage, which makes optimal management of the facility more difficult:

   ○ high pressure in storage slows down injections and accelerates withdrawals;
   ○ low pressure has the opposite effect.

3. Storage for peaking operations is dedicated to swing demand.

Note that whatever its form the storage facility is all the more valuable, as it is located next to various pipelines. Conversely, facilities are crucial to the development of hubs or Liquefied Natural Gas (LNG) terminals.

Storage optionality

To motivate the mathematical formulation provided in Section 12.6(b), we can already observe the following properties:

- Depleted oilfield or aquifer storage is an *option on a seasonal spread*, with the price of natural gas as the underlying of the option.
- Additional optionality is related to:

   ○ the option to switch from injection to withdrawal mode or vice versa, when justified by market conditions;
   ○ the option to adjust the timing of hedges in the forward market;
   ○ the option to deliver to multiple pipelines, depending on the location of the storage facility.

- Optionality is limited by *operational constraints*:

   ○ the rate of injections and withdrawals changes with the level of gas in storage, as stated before;
   ○ gas may have to be injected into storage due to contractual obligations even when it is unprofitable to do so under the current seasonal spread (e.g., because of take-or-pay provisions in the supply contract).

The following diagram represents the activity of a gas company:

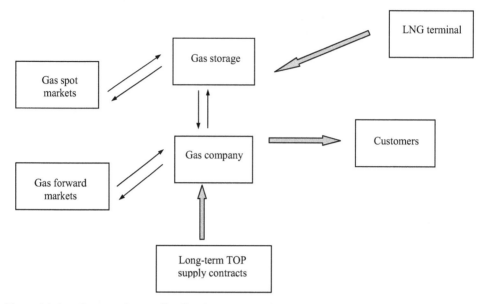

Two-thirds of natural gas distribution companies in the US use storage as a hedge, according to a study published in the journal *RISK* in September 2004.

In Europe, a number of countries which are net importers of natural gas have strategic storage: Germany's gas storage represents 21% of the annual demand; this fraction is 23% in Italy and 24% in France while it is less than 4% in the UK.

(b) Valuation of gas storage

Like inventory for other commodies, storage serves as a buffer against unexpected changes in demand or supply. In the gas industry, storage has other benefits:

- To exploit deterministic seasonality in the market price of gas.
- To honor swing optionalities embedded in contracts sold to customers.
- To provide balancing services and peak availability.

The value of gas storage is the sum of discounted expected revenues under an optimal strategy over all possible future trajectories of the gas price process:

$$V(0) = \max_{\mathcal{C}} E\left[\sum_{t=1}^{T}(L_t - L_{t+1})S(t)\,e^{-rt}\right] \tag{12.13}$$

where:

- L_t denotes the inventory level.
- $L_t - L_{t+1}$ represents the change in inventory between dates t and $t+1$.
- $S(t)$ is the market price of gas at date t.
- $\mathcal{C}$ denotes constraints related to storage capacity and volume at the beginning and at

the end of the operating period, such as a non-negative volume at any time and a half-full (or empty) storage at the end.

Moreover, the withdrawal and injection rates constrain the possible values for $(L_t - L_{t+1})$.

The seasonality of gas prices and changes in the shape over time of the forward curve are crucial to the value of a storage facility.

Parallel shifts of the gas forward curve are, on the contrary, irrelevant:

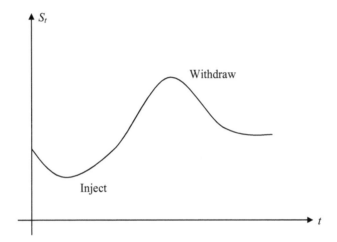

Returning to equation (12.13), several methods can be envisioned to solve the corresponding optimization problem:

- The most elementary one consists in using the current forward curve to find the optimal portfolio of long and short forward contracts attached to injections and withdrawals of gas. The corresponding value is the *intrinsic value* of the storage facility.
- The second approach is to find an optimal portfolio of calendar spread options. Each of them involves a variable quantity of the underlying gas. Hence, it is not straightforward but looks quite similar to the methodology discussed in the context of swing options.
- Stochastic optimization on a tree or through Monte Carlo simulations: the quantity of cumulative withdrawal denoted Q_t in the case of swing options is now replaced by the current level of inventory L_t and we can again work back in time to solve the optimization problem.

Coal, Emissions and Weather

13.1 THE COAL MARKET

Between the controversy around nuclear power and the uncertainties about oil production worldwide, coal is not about to disappear yet from the energy picture. Nuclear energy may be gradually creeping back into favor in European countries, such as France and Finland, but the talk is also about coal. Some groups in Germany want to persuade the government to revive Germany's coal industry, deemed uneconomic and due to be run down over the next decade. Coal has also made a comeback in the US amid concerns with gas and expectations of sustained strong demand from countries such as China and India. Some 92 coal power plants, representing $69bn of investment, are planned in the next few years. Over the last year, coal prices rose incredibly, reaching over $75 per tonne in 2004 while the previous high point ($45) was reached three times in the previous decade. As for coke, a form of processed coal used to fire steelmakers' furnaces, its price has increased over the past 3 years from $70 a tonne to a high of $450 in 2004. The price has since settled to numbers between $250 and $300 a tonne (the latter in October 2004). There are many reasons for this phenomenon: the sharp increase in shipping costs, the management of supply (which is getting more short-term-oriented), the difficulties of nuclear plants during long heatwaves and the desire of coal-producing companies to return to profitability.

The year 2003 started on a bullish note accentuated by the problems faced by a number of nuclear reactors in Japan and the threats of strikes in Polish mines. But, at the same time, there was fierce competition against producers in South Africa selling coal Free On Board (FOB) for delivery in the second quarter of 2003 at the price of $28 and against those in Colombia who could match these prices and still make profits because of the difference in shipping costs to Europe. During this time, the China National Coal Import and Export Company (CNCIEC) was selling coal of equivalent quality at the price of $26.5, Australia at $24.5 for FOB Newcastle coal and stocks were piling up in Richards Bay (South Africa). At the same time, demand from steelmakers was consistently very strong in Japan as traditional thermoelectric production of electricity had to make up for the occasional failure of some nuclear reactors.

The conjunction of these events resulted in the rise in coal prices which started in the Atlantic market, where CIF prices in Rotterdam went from $33 in August to more than $50 at the end of 2003 and over $70 in summer 2004, as depicted in Figure 13.1.

Freight costs have been skyrocketing everywhere, impacting all coal prices, but particularly Atlantic ones because of long itineraries. For example, on the route Richards Bay to Rotterdam, prices for a capsize of 150,000 tonnes went from $4.85 per tonne early in 2002 to $10.50 by the end of the same year. After a quiet period at the beginning of 2003, prices one again started to rise, reaching $14 in September and $27 at the end of October 2003. The other Atlantic itineraries followed the same

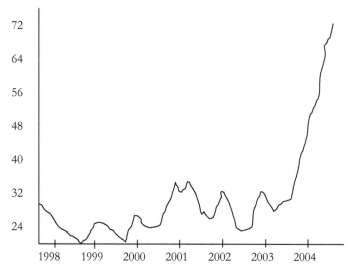

Figure 13.1   Coal spot price on the Asian market.

pattern: freight from Colombia to Amsterdam went from $8.10 at the beginning of January 2003 to more than $20 some 10 months later. In the Pacific, the freight cost from Queensland to Japan rose from $6.50 in August to $18.10 in October. And, finally, the route between New South Wales and northern Europe, which already cost $12.95 for a Panamax[1] of 120,000 tonnes at the beginning of 2003, went to $42 in November, making access to European markets impossible for those Australian producers un- willing to push their prices lower than $20. The only winners in the game were Russian and Polish companies which exported to western Europe over the first 9 months of 2003, respectively, 8.7 and 6.6 million tonnes (i.e., an increase of 28.5% and 10% compared with the same period of the previous year).

As discussed in Chapter 1, the rise of freight costs over the last 2 years has not been primarily due to coal transactions but to the massive imports of iron ore by the big Asian steelmakers, who increased their production by 12.5% over the first 10 months of 2003. Among them was China, which beat all records by producing 180 million tons, representing a rise of 22% over 2002. The congestion of Chinese harbors – a queue of 10 ships was reported in the Chinese port of Qinhuangdao during 2003 – consumed an important part of freight capacity. Moreover, bad harvests in Europe forced grain importers to recourse to new producers located in very distant regions.

Returning to coal, the sharp increase in shipping costs is not the only explanation for the rise of 70% on average of CIF prices during 2003. Higher FOB prices (15% in Indonesia, 39% in South Africa, 45% in Australia, 48% in Colombia) also played their part. In particular, FOB prices of coke departing from Richards Bay in South Africa continued to increase, from $24 at the beginning of 2003 to $40 in November 2003. Among the various other reasons, dry weather conditions as a result of a long heatwave that started in June 2003 and progressively got worse over the summer were responsible for a shortage of hydroelectric power in Finland, Denmark, Spain and Portugal,

---

[1] A ship capable of passing through the Panama Canal.

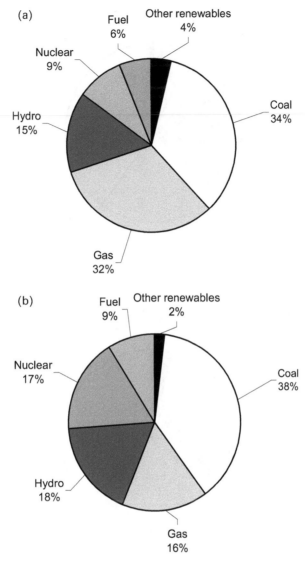

Figure 13.2   (a) Distribution of worldwide electricity production – 2000; (b) distribution of worldwide electricity production – 2020.
Source: IEA.

leading these countries to complement the production of hydroelectricity. At the same time, a number of nuclear power plants in Europe (particularly in France, the first producer of nuclear electricity) were momentarily out of order because of the insufficient cooling capacity of river water. Newly deregulated companies had as a first goal to continue to serve their customers and bought coal in the spot market, contributing to the rise of prices, itself accentuated by speculators anticipating even higher prices – keeping in mind that, in sharp contrast to electricity, coal may be stored. By the end of 2003, the strikes in Poland and the skyrocketing cost of freight over long distances for

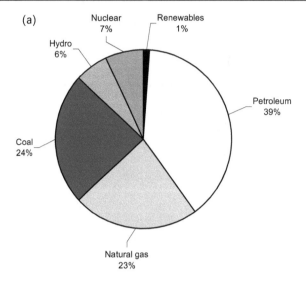

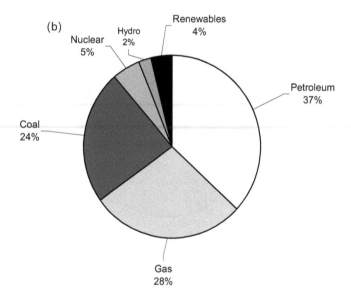

Figure 13.3   (a) World energy outlook – 2002; (b) world energy outlook – 2030.
Source: IEA.

Australian coke led to prices of \$70/ton for CIF coal in Brazil and Central Europe, representing an estimated FOB price of over \$50.

The sharp rise in coal prices in 2003 and 2004 also affected the rest of the world. China's steel production,[2] which went from 18.9 million tons in August 2003 compared with 15.4 during the same month of 2002, was accompanied by a total import of

---

[2] Coal as a raw material underpins some 70% of the world's steel industry.

between 2 and 3 million tonnes of coal in 2003, up from only 0.2 million tonnes in 2002. Hence, the FOB prices of \$47/tonne of coal departing from Australia at the end of 2003 did not represent a maximal point. Moreover, for Australian producers, the US dollar-denominated price was not the one they expected for their output, considering the drop of more than 18% of the US dollar against the Australian dollar over the year 2003.

Regarding thermal coal, the future is also unclear. From January to September 2003, the increase in exports of CNCIEC has continued to those countries with which China has not only signed long-term low FOB price supply contracts, such as Japan (24%), South Korea (23.5%), Taiwan (17.6%), Malaysia, the Philippines, but also with Turkey where coke imports from China have soared from 37,400 tonnes in 2002 to 844,600 tonnes in 2003. At the same time, China is increasingly importing coke – 1.8 million tonnes in 2001, 7.7 in 2002 and more than 10 in 2003, some estimates mentioning a level of more than 100 million tonnes of imported coke for 2005.

Outlook for the future

The year 2003 ended with FOB prices around \$35 to \$40 for thermal coke, \$45 to \$50 for coke and CIF prices between \$60 and \$70; it seems likely that 2004 may end as a record year for the coal market. At the international level, the stream of mergers and acquisitions continues: the Australian company Xstrata (itself controlled at 40% by the Swiss trading group Glencore) has recently bought MIM Holdings, the most important of the stand-alone producers, next to the multinational giants BHP Billiton, Anglo Coal and Rio Tinto. In Canada, the companies Fording, Teck Cominco and Luscar Coal have merged to form Fording Coal Partnership, while, in Indonesia, PT Bumi Resources is in the process of acquiring Kattim Prima, which used to belong to BP and Rio Tinto.

Regarding spot prices in the near future, it seems that high oil prices are going to maintain the desirability of thermal coal while growth in the Asian steel industry should sustain coke prices at a high level. Although the demand profile is fairly clear, there is still uncertainty on the supply side. Will the competitiviness of Poland and Russia be restored? A comeback by Russia would impact in particular the thermal coal market, for which large reserves also exist in Australia, South Africa, Indonesia and Colombia. In order to meet its commitment to reduce emissions by 14.3% under the Kyoto Protocol, Finland recently decided to build a major nuclear plant.

Regarding the US and Asia, the situations seems fairly clear:

- Gas-fired generation will be consolidated, with 175 GW of new gas turbines.
- Coal will play a predominant role:
  - 50% of the power stations in the US are currently fueled by coal;
  - 59 GW will be provided by new coal stations, costing \$68bn;
  - the US has more coal than Saudi Arabia has oil;
  - the US government predicts that 50% of world energy consumption will be coal by 2015.
- Asia needs at least 1,000 new coal stations, one-third of them for China.

Figure 13.2 shows that estimations of the International Energy Agency place at 38% the share of coal in world electricity production in 2020, up from 34% in 2000, while the share of coal remains at a constant level of 24% in the world energy picture during the same time period. The share of global coal reserves is shown in the following diagram (*source*: Global Energy Advisory (2004):

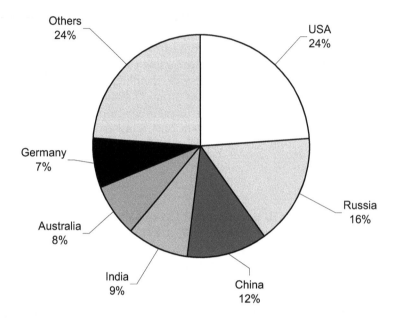

The National Coal Price Index (NCPI) is an aggregation of prices across the major reported coal types, weighted by volume and type of transaction. It is interesting to compare this graph with the Coal Stock Price Index (CSPI) defined by Platts Research and Consulting as a weighted average stock price of seven publicly traded coal producers:

Figure 13.4   National Coal Price Index (NCPI).
Source: Platts.

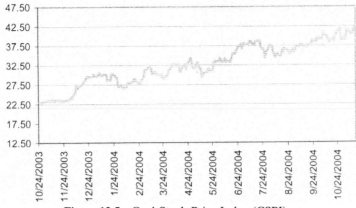

Figure 13.5   Coal Stock Price Index (CSPI).
Source: Platts.

The sharp rise in coal price during this period is shown in Figure 13.4. Interestingly, coal-related company share prices have been increasing at the same if not higher rate. As we will discuss in Chapter 14, this is in contrast to the situation classically encountered in commodity markets, where positive covariance with the stock market as a whole is an important explanatory factor of resource-related companies' share prices. As illustrated by the examples of oil and coal in the recent past, it seems that the commodity price's impact becomes predominant during periods of a sharp rise, possibly also nourished by the higher number of shares traded by speculators and hedge fund managers.

Coal Futures contracts

The Commodity Futures Trading Commission (CFTC) approved in May 1998 the launch by the New York Mercantile Exchange (NYMEX) of coal Futures and options. In response to dramatic changes in the electricity and coal industries, NYMEX began (in July 2001) trading coal Futures written on the Central Appalachian Index, the most liquid US coal index – the Appalachian Mountains are one of the main sources of coal within the US. This index reflects the price for coal transfer at docks along specified stretches of the Ohio River or Kanawha River in West Virginia. It is important to keep in mind that US coal exports – chiefly Central Appalachian bituminous coal – account for a significant percentage of the world export market and, hence, are a relevant factor in world coal prices. As mentioned before, another important component of these world prices is transportation since coal is a bulk commodity.

NYMEX coal Futures contract

The terms and conditions of the Futures contract include:

- Contract unit: 1,550 tons of coal.[3]
- Delivery location: A delivery facility on the Big Sandy River or on the Ohio River (with a discount for delivery on the Sandy River).

---

[3] Note that the US ton represents 2,000 lb or 907 kg, while a metric tonne equals 1,000 kg.

- Delivery period: Beginning no earlier than the delivery month and at least 7 days before the end of the month, to be completed by the last day of the month.
- Termination of trading: Trading in the delivery month ceases 4 days before the last business day of the month prior to the delivery month.
- Btu content: Minimum 12,000 gross calorific value per pound (lb), with a tolerance of 250 Btu/lb.
- Ash content: Maximum 13.5%; sulfur content: maximum 1%; moisture: maximum 10%; sizing: 3-in. topsize.
- Prices and fluctuations: Prices are quoted in dollars and cents/MBtu. The minimum price fluctuation is $0.001/MBtu and the maximum daily fluctuation is $0.100/MBtu above or below the preceding day's settlement price. In the nearest 2 months of trading, the maximum daily price fluctuation goes up to $1.00.

In April 2003, NYMEX moved its coal Futures contract division from open outcry trading to its ClearPort^{sm} electronic platform, trading over the same hours as other commodities. Trade on ClearPort^{sm} starts at 7.00 p.m. Sunday until 2.30 p.m. the following day and at 3.15 p.m. Monday through Thursday to 2.30 p.m. the following day.

Risk-management through NYMEX coal Futures

Coal is today the largest power-generating fuel in the US, because of the closure of some nuclear plants and the cost of building new Combined Cycle Generation Turbines (CCGTs). More precisely, coal-generated electricity in the US accounts for approximately 55% of total electricity output. The US has more high-quality coal than any other country, with nearly 30% of the world's bituminous and anthracite reserves. Hence, the once relatively sedate cash markets for coal have become all the more volatile as electric utilities are no longer eager to enter into long-term coal supply contracts that once were the industry norm. Instead, they prefer short-term more flexible contracts and try to reduce their inventory holding levels.

Coal Futures now provide the electric power industry as well as the coal industry with new risk-management tools:

- Coal producers can sell Futures contracts to lock in specific sales prices for the volume of coal they intend to produce in the coming months.
- Electric utilities can buy coal Futures to hedge against rising prices for their *baseload fuel*.
- Power marketers who have exposure to both the generating and selling sides use coal Futures to hedge their vulnerability to generation price risk and electricity Futures (when they exist) and control their delivery price risk.
- Non-utility industrial coal users, such as steel mills, can use Futures to lock in their own coal supply costs.
- International coal-trading companies can use Futures to hedge their export or import prices.

- Power-generating companies that use both coal and natural gas to produce electricity can use coal Futures in conjunction with natural gas Futures to offset seasonal cost variations and take advantage of the differential between the *crackspread* and *sparkspread* (i.e., the relative value of the electricity generated by each of the two fuels, coal and gas – see Chapter 12).

Coal indexes worldwide

As has been mentioned several times in this book, the existence of a reliable index is necessary for the construction of financially settled options and Futures contracts; it also allows the growth of Over The Counter (OTC) transactions tied to this index.

The international market for coal is characterized by producers and traders selling either FOB of suitable size contracted by the purchaser, or on a CIF basis, with the seller arranging sea freight. In either case, coal and shipping costs are usually denominated in US dollars, which means a currency adjustment for countries like the UK where many power plants use coal as fuel. Accordingly, London is a major center for coal financial transactions.

International spot coal indexes

The three international indexes are related to the three major coal-trading locations, with different CIF versus FOB specifications:

- CIF ARA where ARA denotes the Antwerp–Rotterdam–Amsterdam basin. CIF ARA coal must provide 6,000 kilocalories per kilo and contain no more than 1% sulfur.
- FOB Richards Bay requires the same physical characteristics for the underlying coal and represents the South African region.
- FOB Puerto Bolivar in Colombia is characterized by calorific content of 11,300 Btu/lb and again up to 1% sulfur.

All three international indexes are quoted in $/metric tonne. Obviously, the recent decline of the dollar is a contributory factor to the sharp rise in coal indexes.

Regarding the US, the most popular daily spot coal indexes are:

- Central Appalachian (underlying NYMEX contract).
- Powder River Basin.
- Illinois Basin.
- Pittsburgh Seam.
- Colorado Utah

In all cases, the calorific content is expressed in Btu/lb.

The key coal information providers

(a) The MCIS (McCloskey Coal Information Services) NWE Steam Coal Marker

This is a long-established price indicator, first quoted in January 1991. The price is a spot price delivered CIF to northwest European ports, in $/tonne for 6,000-kcal/kg

(25.13-Gigajoules/tonne) coal below 1% sulfur content, on a CIF and Net As Received (NAR) basis. To ensure that no one business sector is dominant in the survey, a wide variety of major buyers, sellers, traders and brokers are contacted before the index is produced. Prices that are quoted on a FOB basis are converted to CIF using freight rates provided by the London ship-broking community servicing the relevant routes for delivery.

The coals monitored are all steam coals for power stations and general industrial use purchased from single barge cargoes to large-capsize vessel cargoes into ARA, France, Belgium, the North Sea, Ireland and the UK. The index excludes high-sulfur coals.

(b) Energy Argus's COAL Daily Index

In December 1998 *COAL Daily*, a Washington-based publication, launched the *International Index* to track coal shipments to northwest Europe. Sources are asked to give their best price estimates for spot coal, shipped on a CIF basis to ARA ports with 6,000 kcal/kg at 1% sulfur. The index reflects the current price of both direct and OTC spot coal market transactions. Input is collected up to 3 p.m. on the last business day prior to publication from contacts with most major buyers, sellers and traders, while discarding the top and bottom 10% of responses. Energy Argus's *COAL Daily* also quotes the other international indexes (FOB Richards Bay and FOB Puerto Bolivar) as well as the US indexes (Central Appalachian, Illinois Basin) mentioned before.

(c) Tradition Financial Services API Coal Indexes

Tradition Financial Services (TFS) is a broker for OTC physical and derivative products that has been instrumental in developing transactions in coal from offices in London, Singapore and Sydney. The first TFS API index (#1) was launched in February 1998 as a monthly index for the ARA coal price. This index no longer functions and has been replaced by TFS API #2. In December 2001, an accord was reached with *McCloskey Coal Report*, Energy Argus's *COAL Daily* and *South African Coal Report* to formalize methodology guidelines for creation of the new indexes – TFS #2, #3, #4 – in consultation with the major coal information providers.[4]

(1) THE TFS API #2

TFS API #2 is a weekly basket index for the ARA coal price on the basis of 6,000 kcal/kg, CIF and NAR. It is calculated and published on a weekly basis by means of:

- The weekly MCIS NWE Steam Coal Marker published each Friday in the *McCloskey Coal Report*.
- The International Index compiled each week in *COAL Daily* by Energy Argus and published the following Monday.

TFS API # 2 is the arithmetic average of these two numbers.

---

[4] Note that the numbers of these indexes are not related to the major freight routes discussed in Chapter 1 and are defined as follows: Route 4 goes from Richards Bay (South Africa) to ARA; Route 6 from Newcastle (Australia) to ARA; Route 7 from Puerto Bolivar (Colombia) to ARA.

(2) THE TFS API #3

TFS API #3 is a weekly (every Friday) basket index price with a basis of 6,700 kcal/kg, FOB Newcastle. The index is the arithmetic average of two prices:

- The FOB Newcastle price as published every Friday by *McCloskey Coal Report*.
- The Barlow Jonker Index (BJI) as published every Thursday in Barlow Jonder's *COALFAX*.

(3) THE TFS API #4

This is a weekly (published every Friday) basket index price on the basis of 6,000 kcal/kg, FOB, NAR at Richards Bay. The index is the arithmetic average of three quantities:

- The FOB Richards Bay price as published every Friday in *McCloskey's Fax*.
- The Spot Coal Price Index (SCPI) as published every Friday in the *South African Coal Report*.
- The FOB Richards Bay price as published every Friday in Energy Argus's *COAL Daily*.

(d) The Standard European Coal Agreement (SECA) Index

The SECA contract was launched in late 1999. It is a standardized FOB barge ARA contract with a quality specification of 6,000 kcal/kg, which reflects the average steam coal grade used in Europe. The contract is for physical delivery with payment due in 5 days. It has also led to OTC financial transactions and forward contracts. Hence, tracking the contract may provide valuable information on the northwest European market. Table 13.1 shows some reference spot coal prices and Table 13.2 shows European OTC forward prices on 15 September 2004 (Q4 denotes the fourth quarter and Cal the whole calendar year).

Table 13.1 Some reference spot coal prices

	August 2003	**July 2004**	**August 2004**
MCIS Europe steam coal	41.15	78.70	77.85
Richards Bay FOB	31.43	66.24	61.69
MCIS Asian steam coal	33.94	78.85	73.94
MCIS Japan CIF	36.47	81.11	75.05
Newcastle FOB	25.44	62.18	57.54

Source: McCloskey Group.

Table 13.2 European OTC forward prices on 15 September 2004

	Bid	**Offer**
TFS API #2 Q4 04	73.00	73.25
TFS API #2 Cal 05	71.50	72.00

Source: TFS, London.

The UK-based company globalCoal has developed an electronic platform for coal based on standardized qualities and a Standard Coal Trading Agreement (SCoTA); SCoTA has created standards for:

- FOB barge deliveries at ARA.
- FOB deliveries at Newcastle, Australia.
- FOB deliveries at Puerto Bolivar, Colombia.
- FOB deliveries at Richards Bay, South Africa.

The SCoTA forward curve for FOB delivery at Richards Bay, South Africa, prevailing on 15 September 2004 is shown in Table 13.3.

Table 13.3 The SCoTA forward curve for FOB delivery at Richards Bay, South Africa on 15 September 2004

	Bid	Offer	Average
Oct-04	50.50		
Nov-04	53.25	54.95	54.10
Dec-04	52.00	55.00	53.50
Jan-05	49.50	56.00	52.75
Feb-05	49.50	56.00	52.75
Mar-05	49.50	56.00	52.75
Apr-05	49.50	55.00	52.75
May-05	49.50	56.00	52.75
Jun-05	49.50	56.00	52.75
Jul-05	49.50	56.00	52.75

Source: globalCoal.

13.2 EMISSIONS

According to the World Energy Outlook (WEO) 2002, carbon dioxide (CO_2) emissions will increase by 1.8% per year between 2000 and 2030. From 12,369 million tonnes (Mt) of CO_2 equivalent in 2000, emissions will reach 16,397 Mt in 2030 for OECD (Organization for Economic Cooperation and Development) countries, representing an average increase of 0.9% per year. The power generation sector will contribute almost one-half of the increase in global emissions between 2000 and 2003 and will remain the largest source of CO_2 emissions in 2030. In OECD countries, its share will rise from 38% in 2000 (4,725 Mt of CO_2) to 40% in 2030 (6,254 Mt of CO_2). The global atmospheric concentration of CO_2 is shown in Figure 13.6.

Today, power generation is responsible for 65% of industrial emissions of CO_2 in OECD countries. The EU has decided to introduce a CO_2 emission trading scheme in two phases (2005–2007 and 2008–2012) to coincide with the first Kyoto Protocol commitment period. The scheme will cover CO_2 emissions from all combustion plants with a rated thermal input of more than 20 MW capacity, as well as from the metals, minerals and paper/pulp industries.

Even in the US, which has not signed the Kyoto Protocol, New York Attorney General Eliot Spitzer demanded in July 2004 that the nation's largest utilities significantly reduce greenhouse gas emissions. The US Intergovernmental Panel on Climate Change (IPCC) has concluded that the Earth is warming: "There is no dispute that the temperature will rise; the disagreement is how much." Warning of flooded coasts and crippled industries, the state of Massachusetts unveiled in May 2004 a plan to cut emissions by 10% by 2020. In June 2004, California proposed 30% cuts in car emissions by 2015; many other US states are weighing similar actions. US energy companies are also planning for the future. American Electric Power, the number one coal-burning utility, is trying to accumulate credits for cutting carbon dioxide. It is investing in renewable energy projects in Chile, renovating school buildings in Bulgaria and exploring ways to burn coal more cleanly in the US. Du Pont has cut its greenhouse gas emission by 65% since 1990 while Alcoa Inc. is aiming at a 25% cut by 2010. General Electric is anticipating growing markets for its wind power division and for more energy-efficient appliances; General Motors is spending millions of dollars to develop hydrogen-powered cars that would not emit CO_2.

The introduction of emission allowances will obviously modify operating costs in the power generation sector, which is experiencing at the same time numerous regulatory changes and market restructuring. In particular, if the price of CO_2 reaches a certain level, coal plants – which produce twice the amount of CO_2 as CCGTs – will become less competitive. The stack merit order discussed in Chapter 11 may be changed between coal and gas. Some estimates place the level at which the switch in competitiveness may take place at €19/tonne of CO_2. The impact may affect the whole power sector and its investment decisions, and will lead to an increasing amount of trading of emission rights or green certificates. The development of such a market is viewed by some human rights groups as a new device for developed countries to continue to exploit the resources of the planet for their own benefit (Figures 13.6 and 13.7 depict the increased atmospheric concentration in CO_2 and world global warming).

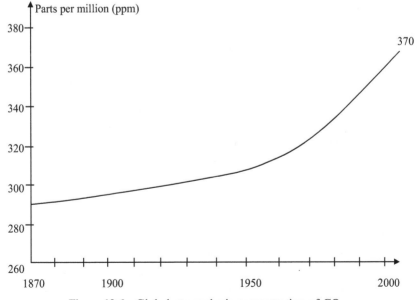

Figure 13.6   Global atmospheric concentration of CO_2

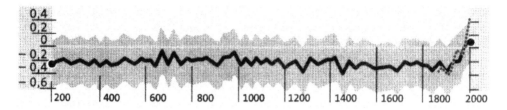

Figure 13.7 Climate over past millennia.
Source: Jones and Mann, *Review of Geophysics*, 2004.

Green certificates

Green certificates are also known as Green Tickets, Tradable Green Certificates (TGCs) or Renewable Energy Credits (RECs). A green certificate is a piece of paper (or more generally, an electronic record in an official database) which states that 1 unit of electricity (e.g., 1 MWh) has been generated by a renewable energy power plant, such as a wind turbine, a solar cell or a small hydro power plant.

The countries or US states in which green certificate systems exist have slightly different procedures, but all lead to the same principle: after production of an amount of renewable electricity over a certain period (e.g., 1 month) has been measured by a qualified metering device, the organization responsible for this metering provides the information to a so-called "issuing body". The issuing body then issues a number of green certificates corresponding to the amount of renewable electricity generated and puts them on the "certificate account" of the owner of the renewable electricity production installation. The producer can sell these certificates, creating for himself an additional source of income.

Trading of green certificates

Green certificates can be bought and sold just like any other good or commodity. The first owner of a green certificate is the producer of the renewable electricity. The certificate then travels to the accounts of successive buyers. In some systems, there is a time limit to the validity of green certificates (e.g., in the Netherlands green certificates are only valid 1 year after they have been issued).

Procedures to consume certificates roughly amount to the following: if an owner of a certificate wishes to consume that certificate, he transfers the certificate from his certificate account to a "retirement account". This is a unique account, usually held by the issuing body or the tax service – a certificate transferred to this account can no longer be traded. Consumption of certificates can take place on behalf of the owner, or a client of the owner.

Governmental and private green certificate systems

There are two sorts of green certificate systems. Some have been issued by governments, as part of their renewable energy policy. This is the case, for instance, in Australia, Texas and the Netherlands. In other cases, the construction of green certificate systems has been a private initiative. In California, for instance, the system has been defined by

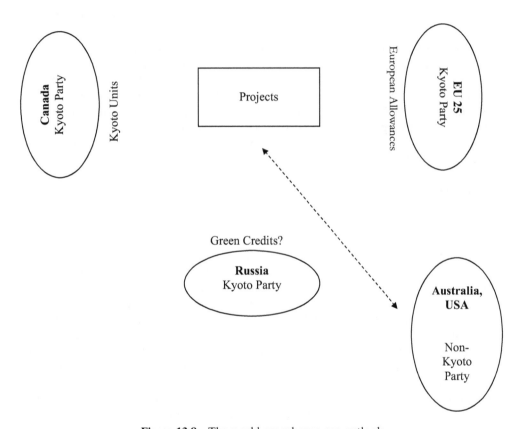

Figure 13.8   The world greenhouse gas outlook.

the manager of the California Power Exchange. The largest private green certificate system has been built in Europe. Companies from 16 European countries have organized the Renewable Energy Certificate System (RECS), whose main aim is to facilitate trade in green electricity in a trustworthy manner.

Green certificates and green electricity

Today, we can buy "green electricity" in a growing number of countries. In Europe, this is the case in Germany, the UK, the Netherlands, Switzerland, Sweden, Norway and

Finland, among others. In the US and Canada, there are a number of green electricity programs as well.

A customer of green electricity is very unlikely to get his electricity directly from a wind farm or solar panel; he gets it like everyone else from the national grid, since there are no physical differences between green and non-green electricity. A green electricity consumer buys from his electricity supplier the *guarantee* that the amount of electricity he consumes on an annual basis is produced or purchased by the supplier from renewable energy sources. In countries or US states with green certificate systems, evidence of green production is provided by green certificates. A supplier just has to show that he has acquired and retired at least the same amount of green certificates as he has sold green electricity to his consumers. A consumer wanting to make his electricity green can do so by matching his consumption to acquisition of a corresponding number of green certificates. These may be acquired either from the same supplier, or from a company that specializes in selling green certificates, such as World Wide Green. Such exchanges as the International Petroleum Exchange (IPE), the European Energy Exchange (EEX), Nord Pool or Energy Exchange Austria (EXAA) also allow the trading of these certificates. In November 2004, the Commodity Futures Trading Commission (CFTC) awarded the Chicago Climate Exchange a license to offer Futures on emission allowances. This exchange plans to launch in December 2004 Futures on sulfur dioxide emission allowances.

The EU-ETS scheme

From 1 January 2005, companies that are part of the EU's Emission Trading Scheme (EU-ETS) will need allowances to emit CO_2. The scheme is mainly intended for large industrial emitters during its first trial period (2005–2007); a few countries (e.g., Sweden) have however chosen to include smaller operations, mainly smaller district heating power plants. Sanctions will be severe if companies decide not to comply with the regulation. If a firm does not deliver a sufficient amount of allowances on time, it will have to pay a penalty of €40/tonne of CO_2 and €100 as of 2008; the firm will have to deliver the missing EU allowances the following year. Emission allowances cannot be saved, though, from the trial period to the next period, this being the first Kyoto commitment period (2008–2012). Moreover, a list of non-complying companies will be published. Through the EU-ETS scheme, companies in the trading sector should adopt a CO_2 strategy which also involves accounting for CO_2 emission management. The EC believes the introduction of EU-ETS will make it 35% cheaper to cut emissions than where reductions had to be made within each member state, as long as free trading of emissions develops within the EU. This should lead to efficient pricing of emission allowances.

Many member states were quite generous in their National Allocation Plans (NAPs) for the trial period, which caused a dramatic fall in price in the emissions market. In October 2004, prices had gone back to normal levels and a tonne of CO_2 traded at a price between €8 and €9. The Swedish government, however, has taken a different view from most other member states. The country's NAP includes a reduction of 20% for many companies, such as power producers, even though Sweden is allowed to increase its emissions under the Kyoto Protocol. The EC has unconditionally accepted Sweden's NAP. The EU-ETS can be visualized as:

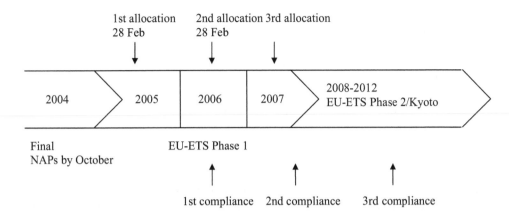

If allowances in the EU-ETS are considered to be financial instruments, financial institutions would have access to this market and improve liquidity and, in turn, efficient trading. Swedish regulators have recently decided that emission allowances should be considered financial instruments in Sweden, which implies that transactions in Sweden not made directly through bilateral agreements may only be brokered through securities companies authorized by the Swedish Financial Supervisory Authority.

Preparations for trading are being made and transactions have been taking place for some time. In July 2004 the International Emissions Trading Association (IETA) introduced separate EU-ETS contracts as well as a simplified version of its Emissions Trading Master Agreement.

13.3 WEATHER AND COMMODITY MARKETS

(a) Introduction

Weather plays a key role in all commodity markets, with the exception of metals. It has been consistently the prime factor in explaining the yield and quality of agricultural commodities.[5] We have seen in electricity markets how a protracted heatwave can send power prices to thousands of dollars; a dry winter in the northern countries of Europe, where most of the electricity is hydro, can be readily identified in a database of power prices.

Turning now to agricultural markets, prices follow seasonal patterns where periods of extreme volatility coincide with harvests that are most exposed to extreme weather. Late frosts can decimate the Brazilian coffee crop and this translates into the high volatility observed on coffee Futures prices during summer in the northern hemisphere. Frosts can also damage orange juice production in Florida: in the subtle paper "Orange juice and weather", Roll (1984) examines whether the prices of orange juice Futures contracts could be identified as the best predictors of the weather in Florida. In a

---

[5] Film-lovers may remember from the movie *Trading Places* the crucial role early information on weather played in building and destroying fortunes in orange juice Futures contracts.

multi-year database of soybean Futures prices Geman and Nguyen (2002) exhibit that volatility is highest at pre-harvest times and then goes down when the crop is known. The seasonal nature of agriculture implies that the supply side is inelastic or "sticky" and any shock in production has a major impact on prices.

Besides temperature, rain is another major element in agricultural commodity markets. Too little rain can cripple the crop during the growth phase; too much rain can cause crop failure or damage crop quality at harvest. An example of an extreme weather event is drought, which still affects on a regular basis many arid parts of the world, such as India or Ethiopia. Even in a highly sophisticated production environment, such as Australia, the drought of 2002 caused wheat production to plummet from 20 million metric tonnes in 2001 to 9 million tonnes. In India, low rainfall is the most dangerous factor in monsoon season crop production. During the 2002–2003 season, India received the lowest ever recorded amount of rain in July, the crucial month for crops; the drought caused a drop of 19% in the food grain production and a 3.1% decline in GDP. The 2002 report by the Wisconsin Agricultural Statistical Services notes that corn and soybean farmers reduce their planting volume if they anticipate lower than normal rainfall; high rainfall, however, implies a higher probability that crops will incur disease.

In the case of Australian wine, Gladstone (1992) argues that temperature, sunshine, humidity and rainfall are the dominant weather risks that affect the wine industry. Given the rapid growth of Australian wine production between 1998 and 2003, with export volumes increasing by 170% to AU$2.4bn in value, there is an increasing demand for financial instruments that allow winegrape producers to hedge against weather risks. The 1998 report into the Australian wine and grape industry established that weather risks account for 42% of the loss in Australian Chardonnay grape production.

Prior to the introduction of weather derivatives, agricultural companies essentially had two ways of hedging the volatility of their revenues: get crop insurance from the state or a private insurance company; or take positions in Futures markets.

In the case of France, over the last 15 years champagne growers have built up reserves of wine from those years when the vintage is excellent both in quality and quantity. These reserves are made up of grapes that are transformed into wine, but do not go through the second fermentation procedure that leads to champagne. They can be kept for 10 years. In April 2003 a frost destroyed many young buds, resulting in a yield of 8,250 kg/ha in October 2003 compared with the average yield of 10,400 kg/ha and leading to the use of reserves. In 2004 the vintage was excellent and reserves have been replenished (see Declerck, 2004).

(b) Weather derivatives

Most of the weather derivatives traded on exchanges or contracted in OTC transactions as of today have been tied to temperature and appeared in the course of deregulation of the electricity and gas industry worldwide as a valuable hedging instrument. Utilities have for a long time been facing *volume risk* in the form of lower demand in the case of a warm winter or cool summer, but gas and electricity prices used to be regulated. Utilities now facing demand risk and *price risk* have in most cases chosen to buy hedging instruments against variability of demand, a risk they have learned to quantify in terms of missing dollar revenues. Consequently, they can have at least a *business pricing* approach to the valuation of weather derivatives for which the Black–Scholes formula or some extension of it are not appropriate since the underlying asset, temperature, is not traded (see, e.g., Geman and Leonardi, 2005, for a general discussion of this valuation). Figures 13.9 and 13.10 depict the evolution of electricity prices together with temperature in two major regions of the US, Pennsylvania–New Jersey–Maryland and Cinergy (Midwest).

Weather derivatives are traded on the Chicago Mercantile Exchange (CME) for monthly and seasonal contracts at 21 locations: 15 in the US, 5 in Europe and 1 in Japan. In Japan, the monthly or seasonal index defining the pay-off at maturity is formed as the average temperature across the period of the contract. In the case of the US and Europe, the index is expressed in terms of *degree days*. In meteorological terms, a degree day is the difference between a reference temperature, typically 65°F or 18°C, and the mean temperature on a given day defined as the arithmetic average of daily maximal and minimal temperatures. During winter, meteorologists calculate heating degree days by subtracting the mean daily temperature from the reference 65°F; if this difference is negative, it means that no heating fuel nor electricity is consumed and the number of Heating Degree Days (HDD) is set to zero. Put in other terms:

$$(\text{HDD})_{\text{day}\,j} = \max(0, 65°\text{F} - \text{Average temperature}_j)$$

Cooling Degree Days (CDD), typically attached to summer, are symmetrically defined on day j as:

$$(\text{CDD})_{\text{day}\,j} = \max(0, \text{Average temperature}_j - 65°\text{F})$$

Degree days closely track the extent to which consumers use their heating systems or air conditioners. Figures 13.11 and 13.12 show the high correlation between HDD and gas and power use in the case of two US utilities.

In both cases, the R^2 are highly significant (see Clemmons, Kaminski and Hrgovcic, 1999).

Consequently, a utility wishing to hedge its revenues against a warm winter will buy a *put option* written on *cumulative degree days*. If we define winter as the period covering the months of December, January and February, the cumulative degree days attached to that season will be defined as:

$$\text{Cum HDD} = \sum_{j=1}^{90} (\text{HDD})_j$$

where $(\text{HDD})_j$ denotes HDD on day j.

The utility will identify the number k of total HDD over winter below which its revenues will be severely damaged and buy a put option whose pay-off at maturity $T = 28$ February is defined as:

$$P(T) = \text{Nominal amount} \times \max(0, k - \text{Cum HDD}(T))$$

where nominal amount A represents the extra loss in revenues per missing HDD. Symmetrically, a construction company which cannot operate in the case of a very cold winter will buy a call option written on cumulative degree days providing at maturity:

$$C(T) = A \max(0, \text{Cum HDD}(T) - k)$$

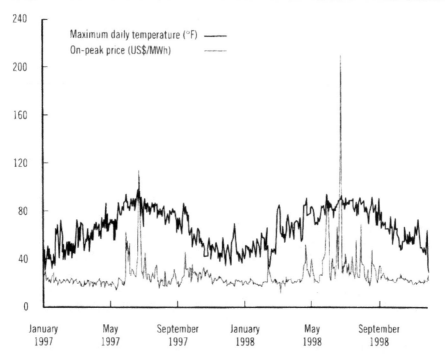

Figure 13.9 Pennsylvania–New Jersey–Maryland power price versus maximum temperature.

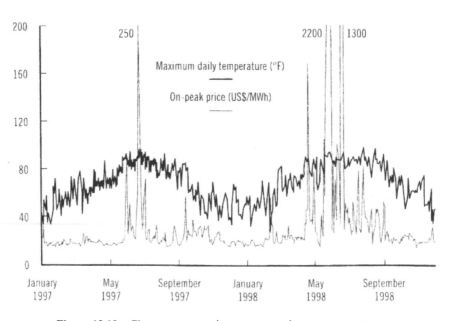

Figure 13.10 Cinergy power price versus maximum temperature.

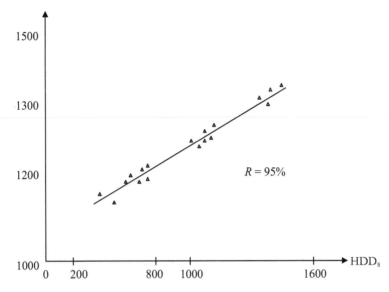

Figure 13.11 Correlation between monthly power consumption and heating degree days.

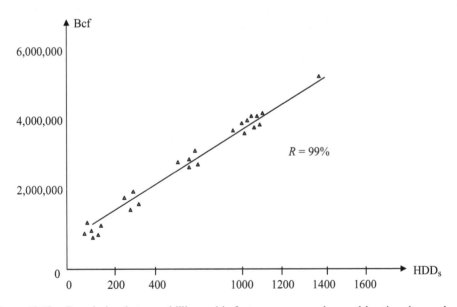

Figure 13.12 Correlation between billion cubic feet gas consumption and heating degree days.

In order to diminish the outflow at date T for the seller of the option and increase the liquidity of this new market, the weather derivative pay-off is capped in practice. In the case of a capped call, in which the dollar cap is denoted as B, the pay-off becomes:

$$C^s(T) = \min(B, A \max(0, \text{Cum HDD}(T) - k))$$

Here we can recognize a *call spread* (defined in Chapter 4) that provides at maturity the following algebraic gain profile:

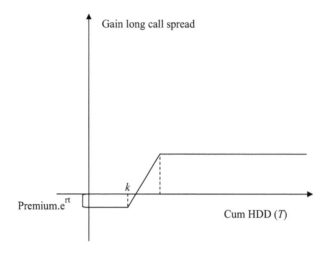

This is also the type of gain profile attached to the purchase of a layer of reinsurance for claims in excess of Ak dollars up to B dollars. Unsurprisingly, in the absence of dynamic hedging and replicating portfolio, weather derivatives are often held by the seller until maturity and evaluated at date 0 according to *actuarial pricing*.

Another approach to the valuation of weather derivatives mentioned earlier is "business pricing", which utilities with their experience of the market and historical database on demand and revenues may implement.

For instance, in Figure 13.13, Dischel (1999) uses official US data to build the curves of residential electricity sales as a function of temperature.

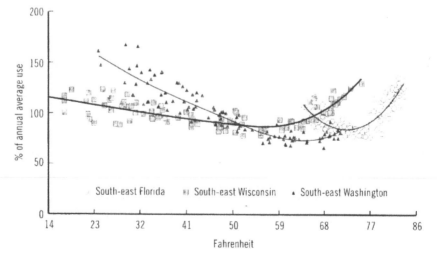

Figure 13.13   Residential electricity sales.
Source: Dischel (1999).

Regions as different as southeast Wisconsin and southeast Washington have in common the property of exhibiting a high use of residential electricity for low temperatures (below 45°F) and high temperatures (above 68°F). The range of temperatures is much narrower in Florida where it seldom gets very cold. Assuming that the demand for power can be represented as a second-degree polynomial of the temperature index, one or the other root of this polynomial depending on the season allows one to express temperature as a function of demand. Using the power stack function, one can in turn express the price of power as a function of demand, hence of temperature. From all these elements, the utility may infer an "acceptable" price for a weather derivative it can buy on the CME or from a bank. This approach does not have the precision of the Black–Scholes formula but provides a reasonable way of addressing the serious *incompleteness* of weather markets. Geman (2000) proposes a "Bermuda triangle" including electricity, insurance and weather derivatives to reduce in a combined position the incompleteness of each of the three markets.

Commodities as a New Asset Class

14.1 INTRODUCTION

Commodities used to be viewed as a separate asset class – which they are – because they cannot be priced by arguments of net present value. A bond, whether a Treasury or a defaultable corporate bond, is priced as the discounted expectation (under the risk-neutral measure) of future coupon and principal payments. The same type of reasoning may apply to the pricing of a stock, with dividend payments as future cash flows. Along the same lines, we note that other founding pricing results – such as the Capital Asset Pricing Model (CAPM) which states the investor is rewarded for the time value of the money put upfront to purchase the stock *and* for the risk he is holding – cannot arguably be extended to commodities. As we have repeated several times in this book, commodities are priced by *supply*, *demand* and *inventory*.

Besides the above differences in the methodological approach, commodities are perceived as a distinct asset class because of their counter-cyclic nature: over the last 45 years, both commodity spot prices and commodity Futures have outpaced inflation. Moreover, in the current period of historically low interest rates worldwide and sluggish stock markets, commodity-related investments perform remarkably well. Hedge funds, which used to be profitable through such strategies as buying and selling volatility while remaining neutral to the stock market, are looking for new styles as well as new assets, including real assets and commodities. While they used to be viewed essentially as a protection against inflation, commodities are now recognized as an asset class in its own right, providing high returns on top of the diversification benefits they bring to a portfolio of stocks and bonds. Both in relative and absolute terms, commodities have been performing remarkably well. For a non-dollar-based investor, recent results are somewhat mitigated by the decline of the US dollar against the euro or the Japanese yen since most commodity markets are dollar-denominated. For a US investor, however, commodity returns over the last 5 years have been extremely high, as shown in Figure 14.2. A number of experts think the commodity sector remains undervalued, particularly when compared with the financial markets, and that prices will continue to rise.

In all cases the diversification effect brought by commodities is excellent: for instance, we can see in Table 14.1 a correlation of −0.16 computed over the period 1990–1999 between the S&P 500 and New York Mercantile Exchange (NYMEX) crude oil.

We should not be surprised to find in the correlation coefficient the negative effect on the stock market of a rise in oil prices. Interestingly, the correlation between the FTSE 100 (UK) stock index and the London Brent is quite close, at −0.17. These numbers compare with a correlation of 0.63 between the two major UK and US stock indexes

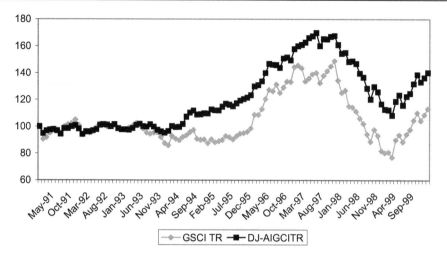

Figure 14.1   Growth of $100: 1991–1999.

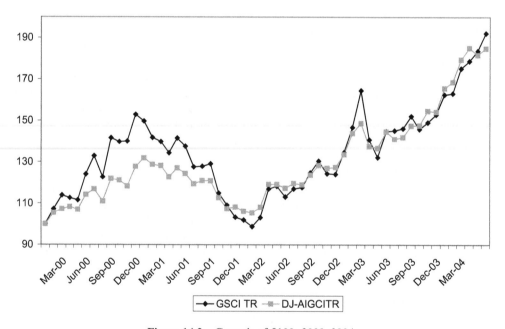

Figure 14.2   Growth of $100: 2000–2004.

Table 14.1   Correlation coefficients over the period 1990–1999

	S&P 500	**FTSE 100**	**NYMEX crude oil**	**IPE crude oil**
S&P 500	1	0.63	−0.16	−0.17
FTSE 100	0.63	1	−0.19	−0.17
NYMEX crude oil	−0.16	−0.19	1	0.98
IPE crude oil	−0.17	−0.17	0.98	1

and of 0.98 between the price changes of the crude oil listed on NYMEX and the International Petroleum Exchange (IPE) in London.[1]

Consider an investor who holds a portfolio of stocks and bonds. If he decides to add commodities, in the form of commodities Futures or index Futures to his position, the diversification effect will shift his Markowitz frontier upward. The following diagram shows the improvement of an efficient frontier:

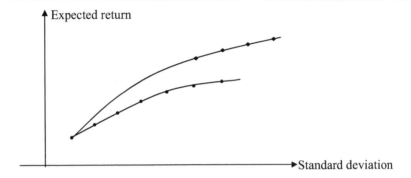

If the expected return on the commodity index is equal to that of financial instruments, the overall risk of the portfolio, as measured by standard deviation, is strictly reduced with no change to anticipated return. In the current period of bullish commodity markets, the gain will be at the same time in the form of a lower σ and a higher expected return $E(\tilde{r}_p)$ and the classical performance measure defined by the *Sharpe ratio*:

$$\frac{E(\tilde{r}_p) - r_f}{\sigma(\tilde{r}_p)}$$

will be much higher.

Turning now to metals, research on the London Metal Exchange (LME) and precious metals also reflects the benefits of metal indexes as an alternative means of capturing commodity returns not found through direct investment in the underlying production firms, as well as the benefits of rolling a position in Futures contracts (see Schneeweis and Spurgin, 1997). In fact, as we will discuss throughout this chapter, Futures contracts-based commodity investments have two separate sources of return: *price* and *roll*. Price return is obviously derived from changes in commodity Futures prices. Roll return arises from rolling long positions in forward or Futures contracts through time, which may be performed in a discerning manner. For instance, an experienced investor may capture a premium due to an increased convenience yield in periods of high volatility and tight supply – recall the spot–forward relationship established in Chapter 2:

$$F^T(t) = S(t)\, e^{(r-y)(T-t)}$$

it appears that if y is very high at date t the commodity can be bought in the Futures market at a discount to the spot market. The position in Futures will be optimally

---

[1] The number 0.98 was obtained after converting sterling-denominated IPE prices into US dollars, in order for the comparison to have economic validity; the correlation between the S&P 500 and the FTSE was computed through the same procedure.

liquidated at times when the convenience yield y is lower, and not necessarily at maturity of the Futures contract.

We conclude this introduction by stating that the question today is no longer whether commodities constitute a new *asset class*, but how we can design the best position for a given investor.

14.2 THE DIFFERENT WAYS OF INVESTING IN COMMODITIES

We can identify several ways of getting exposed to commodity price changes, and will discuss whenever appropriate *passive* versus *active* strategies.

(a) Purchase of the physical commodity in the cash market

An investor or a hedge fund can in principle buy any commodity in the spot market, either by a direct transaction with the producer or through an intermediary. Let us suppose the transaction is conducted by a Dutch fund with a coffee grower in Vietnam and involves 1 million coffee bags. Even if shipping is organized by an intermediary, the fund manager will have to deal with the storage issues related to these coffee bags: space, humidity level, perishability. With a commodity such as natural gas the situation gets worse since a salt cavern or the like is necessary to store the gas; with electricity, as already explained, storage is in general not feasible. An exception to the major difficulties attached to the purchase of the physical commodity is provided by precious metals, which do not require much space nor care; they cannot, however, constitute the bulk of the diversified commodity portfolio an investor wishes to hold.

(b) Purchase of the stock of commodity-related companies

Buying the shares of natural resource companies has been a traditional way of benefiting from an anticipated rise in the price of a commodity. To be exposed to oil prices, one buys the stock of major oil firms since most of the revenues of these companies come from the exploration, refinery and sales of petroleum products; in order to avoid currency risk, US investors will buy Exxon or Texaco shares while UK investors will choose BP shares. However, it is clear that in all cases oil companies' stock prices have positive betas (i.e., they covary positively with the stock market as a whole). Moreover, decisions on the capital structure of the firm or idiosyncratic corporate governance issues, such as dividend policy or merger decisions, have a major impact on the stock price.

The non-existence of risk management activities meant to smooth out earnings over time, or even a firm's poor communication with its shareholders, can also have disastrous consequences. This is illustrated by the recent example of Royal Dutch Shell, where a reduction of the company's estimated oil reserves was accompanied by poor performance in terms of timely release of information to the public. Charts in Chapter 2 (see pp. 30–31) depict how the stock price of the oil company spiraled down at a time oil prices were skyrocketing. At the same time, other major oil companies, such as Total or Exxon, were experiencing a significant increase in their stock prices.

In summary, one must keep in mind that buying the shares of a natural resource company certainly introduces a noise component in the desired exposure to the commodity.

(c) Purchase of commodity Futures

A direct way to build targeted exposure to a given commodity is to take a long or short position in Futures written on that commodity. We gather here some properties collected from previous chapters:

- Futures contracts are traded on an exchange that provides the transparency and integrity of the clearing house. Hence, the investor only needs to build an account with a broker holding a seat on the exchange. Note that Futures accounts can only be opened with licensed Futures Commission Merchants (FCMs) who are registered with the Commodity Futures Trading Commission (CFTC).
- Only a fraction of the Futures contract face value – the margin deposit or initial margin – needs to be paid upfront. It represents in general a small percentage of the contract dollar amount and is often paid as Treasury bills or other types of collateral.
- As mentioned before, the Futures contract may be financially settled by design or the position closed prior to maturity by a symmetric position in Futures with the same maturity. In both cases, the investor does not need to worry about physical delivery and related concerns.
- Hence, the only real issue is a proper *roll* of the Futures position if the investment horizon of the investor is farther away than the most deferred liquidity maturity. This part of the strategy deserves a lot of care and attention, as discussed in Section 14.3 dedicated to commodity Futures indexes.

(d) Purchase of commodity options

In Chapter 4 we observed the leverage effect provided by an investment in options, namely that:

$$\frac{\delta C}{C} > \frac{\delta S}{S}$$

if there is a rise in the price of the underlying S. Consequently, in order to get 100% dollar-for-dollar exposure to commodity price S, a fund manager will invest two-thirds (or a fraction of this order) of the fund's assets in high-quality short-term Government securities, playing the role of the riskless asset, and only one-third in derivative instruments written on the commodity. Such a position can be represented by:

$$C(t) + k \, e^{-r(T-t)}$$

which, as shown in the put call parity of Chapter 4, is equal to:

$$S(t) + P(t)$$

i.e., an *insured portfolio* where the stock price is replaced by the commodity price.

In principle, the option may be written on the commodity spot price. For liquidity considerations, the investor will buy an option written on the Futures price. In both cases, a *buy-and-hold* strategy provides at maturity of the option the wealth:

$$V(T) = \max(S(T), k)$$

where k is the strike chosen for the option.

In the few instances where the investor is an option trader, he may conduct an *active* strategy and not hold the option until its maturity T. Instead, recalling the Taylor expansion of the call price:

$$C(t + \delta t, S_t + \delta S_t) - C(t, S_t) = \underbrace{\frac{\partial C}{\partial t} \delta t}_{\text{"time decay"}} + \underbrace{\frac{\partial C}{\partial S} \delta S_t}_{\text{positive if } \delta S_t > 0} + \underbrace{\frac{1}{2} \frac{\partial^2 C}{\partial S^2} (\delta S_t)^2}_{\text{positive convexity}} \quad (14.1)$$

the investor chooses to liquidate the option after a significant move in $(\delta S_t)^2$ in order to "cash in" the positive convexity term.[2] This will more than offset the negative time decay. Lastly, the second term is positive if the anticipation of a rise in the commodity price is realized. Such a roll of options may also be used in long-term portfolio insurance perspective, particularly in the context of stochastic volatility where equation (14.1) has an additional term. This interesting issue is discussed in the context of stocks in Bick (1995).

(e) Commodity indexes and commodity-related notes

Today, commodity indexes represent the easiest way of getting exposure to commodities or to a given sector since the most popular commodity indexes exist under several forms. Decades and centuries ago, an analogous form of investment was offered by commodity-linked notes, such as the 20-year bond issued in 1863 by the US Confederation of the South denominated in both sterling and French francs (see Anson, 2002) and containing an option to convert the bond into bales of cotton: a beautiful example of a structured security! More recently, commodity-linked notes have been tied to major commodity indices, such as the DJ-AIG or GSCI, leading to a return that is a *linear* function of the index value, or to commodity index options, in which case the upfront payment is higher but the pay-off profile exhibits the desirable *convexity* feature.

For practical purposes, the issuers of such notes may be investment banks, financial institutions or individual commodity producers raising capital to extend their operations while providing investors with exposure to the commodity. As a side remark, it should be noted that an insurance company or another entity that wishes to carry such an exposure, without being allowed by its regulatory body to hold

---

[2] The ratio gamma/theta, sometimes called the psi (ψ), is carefully monitored by option traders.

commodity-related funds in its assets, may do so by entering a *total return swap* with a bank that will do the purchase in its place. We then have the classical exchange of cash flows:

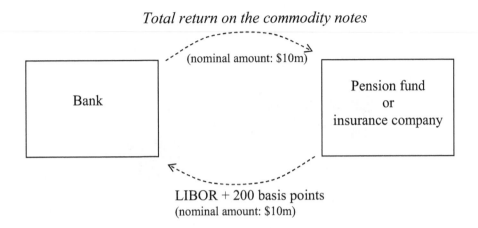

Total return on the commodity notes

(nominal amount: $10m)

Bank

Pension fund
or
insurance company

LIBOR + 200 basis points
(nominal amount: $10m)

14.3   COMMODITY INDEXES AND COMMODITY-RELATED FUNDS

One of the most attractive aspects of commodity investment today is that there exist a number of indexes that allow passive strategies that can in turn be enhanced into active strategies. Most alternative asset classes (e.g., real estate) do not have passive indexes[3] and, hence, require the investor to select active managers. Moreover, commodity indexes can be reconstructed over a vast time period, providing in turn a historical track record that is useful in developing asset allocation strategies.

(a) The Commodity Research Bureau (CRB) Index

The Reuters/CRB Futures Index was first calculated by the CRB in 1957 and made its inaugural appearance in the 1958 *CRB Commodity Year Book*. Since 1957, there have been nine revisions to the index's components, the latest in December 1995. The CRB Futures Index was designed to provide a dynamic representation of broad trends in overall commodity prices, hence the periodic adjustments in order to reflect changes in market structure and activity.

The Reuters/CRB Futures Index is comprised today of the 17 commodities depicted below, with an equal weight of 6%:

---

[3] In fact, some real estate indexes are being constructed but are not well established yet and cannot have the breadth of commodity indexes because of location, type of building, etc.

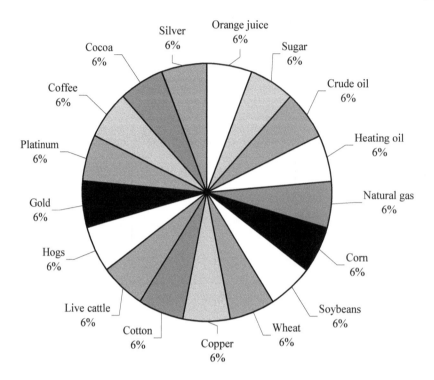

A *double-averaging* procedure takes place for computation of the index: first, across time and, second, across commodities:

1. To start, each of the index's 17 components is *arithmetically* averaged using the prices of all the designated contract months that expire on or before the end of the sixth calendar month from the current date but subject to the following rules:

   o no contract will be included in the calculation while in delivery;
   o there will be a minimum of two contract months for each component commodity (adding contracts beyond the 6-month window if necessary);
   o there will be a maximum of five contract months for each commodity (dropping the most deferred contracts to remain at five if necessary).

2. These 17 component averages are then *geometrically* averaged:

   Geometric average $= \sqrt[17]{\text{Crude average} \times \text{Heating average} \times \text{Sugar average} \times \cdots}$

3. The resulting average is then divided by 30.7766, the 1967 base year average for these 17 commodities. The result is then multiplied by an adjustment factor of 0.8486, necessitated by the nine revisions to the index since its inception in 1957. Finally, that result is multiplied by 100 in order to convert the index into percentage terms. Put in other terms:

   $$\text{Reuters/CRB Futures Index} = \frac{\text{Current geometric average}}{\text{1967 Geometric average}} \times 0.8486 \times 100$$

Table 14.2 Contract months eligible for inclusion in the index

Commodity (symbol)	Exchange	Contract months
Corn (C)	CBOT	Mar, May, Jul, Sep, Dec
Soybeans (S)	CBOT	Jan, Mar, May, Jul, Aug, Nov
Wheat (W)	CBOT	Mar, May, Jul, Sep, Dec
Cattle (Live) (LC)	CME	Feb, Apr, Jun, Aug, Oct, Dec
Hogs (Lean) (LH)	CME	Feb, Apr, Jun, Jul, Aug, Oct, Dec
Gold (GC)	COMEX	Feb, Apr, Jun, Aug, Dec

The CRB Futures Index is widely viewed as a broad measure of overall commodity products because of the diverse nature of the 17 commodities of which it is comprised and serves as a very good measure of macroeconomic trends. No single month or commodity has an undue impact on the index. The many averaging procedures make the index hard to manipulate and also less sensitive to discontinuities associated with temporary supply and demand imbalances in a given month or commodity. Table 14.3 shows the different commodity sectors covered by the index.

Table 14.3 Commodity sectors covered by the index

Group	Components
Energy	Crude Oil (CL), Heating Oil (HO), Natural Gas (NG) (17.6%)
Grains	Corn (C), Soybeans (S), Wheat (W) (17.6%)
Industrials	Copper (HG), Cotton (CT) (11.8/%)
Livestock	Live Cattle (LC), Lean Hogs (LH) (11.8%)
Precious metals	Gold (GC), Platinum (PL), Silver (SI) (17.6%)
Softs	Cocoa (CC), Coffee (KC), Orange Juice (JO), Sugar (SB) (23.5%)

The CRB Futures index has been recognized for years as the main barometer of commodity prices and is closely followed by the financial press. This explains why the index price level creates an immediate impact on other markets. In order to have protection against inflation and benefit from potential returns from commodity prices, investors may take long positions in the CRB Futures Index Futures contracts traded on NYMEX since 1986.

Reuters – CRB Futures Index Futures Contract Specification

Contract quote	Index points (e.g., 240.00 or 240.05)
Trading symbol	CR
Contract size	$500. Index
Trading hours	9:40 a.m. to 2:45 p.m. New York Time
Tick size (minimum price fluctuation)	0.05 (5 basis points) or $25
Daily price limits	None
Position limits	5,000 contracts net long or short
Last trading day	Second Friday of the expiration month
Contract settlement	Settlement at maturity by cash payment

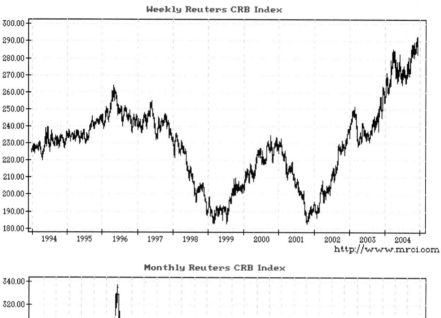

(b) The Goldman Sachs Commodity Index (GSCI)

The GSCI is a measure of the performance of actively traded, dollar-denominated nearby commodity Futures contracts. The weights assigned to the individual commodities are based on a *5-year moving average of world production*. As already mentioned, the weights used in an index play a key role in structuring the properties of the index and, in turn, the instruments and investment returns related to it. It is well known that the major equity indexes (S&P 500, Dow Jones, Eurostoxx 50) are weighted averages of current values of company stocks, where the weights are equal to the *market capitalization* of the companies entering the index. World production is usually perceived as analogous to these quantities in the case of commodities, but there may be other choices (e.g., traded volume), as we have argued a few times in the book.

Currently, the GSCI contains 24 commodities from all commodity sectors: 6 from energy and 11 agricultural products. This diversity minimizes the effects of the arguably idiosyncratic features of some individual commodity markets. Together, the number of its constituent commodities and their economic weighting allow the GSCI to respond to economic growth: when world economies fare well, the metals sector of the GSCI responds better than agricultural components. Agricultural and petroleum-based commodities, however, generally respond best of all. Note that individual commodities are screened by liquidity for inclusion in the GSCI. The eligibility requirements are effective implementation and true inevitability.

GSCI components and weights

Currently, 24 commodities meet the eligibility requirements of the GSCI. A list of these components and their weights is presented in Table 14.4 and Figure 14.3.

Table 14.4   GSCI components and dollar weights (%) on 30 July 2004

Energy 68%	Industrial metals 7%	Precious metals 2%	Grains and softs 17%
Crude Oil	Aluminum	Gold	Wheat
Brent Crude Oil	Copper	Silver	Red Wheat
Unleaded Gas	Lead		Corn
Heating Oil	Nickel		Soybeans
Gas Oil	Zinc		Cotton
Natural Gas			Sugar
			Coffee
			Cocoa

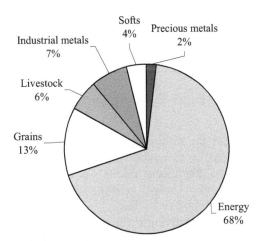

Figure 14.3   Goldman Sachs Commodity Index.

Note that for practical purposes, the GSCI Spot Index measures the price levels of commodities, not the returns available to investors. Two other indexes are available for investment purposes: the GSCI Excess Return Index and the GSCI Total Return Index.

The GSCI Excess Return Index

By design, the GSCI reflects a *passive portfolio* of long positions in *commodity Futures*. However, unlike a passive equity portfolio, a passive Futures portfolio requires regular transactions since Futures contracts expire. In this respect, the Futures portfolio represented by the GSCI can be compared with a bond portfolio of specific duration. The maturity chosen is the nearby contract; it obviously needs to be *rolled forward* at the beginning of the expiration month. Many commodities, like those in the energy and industrial metals sectors, have liquid Futures contracts that may be rolled every month. Other commodities, such as those in the agricultural sector, have only a few contract months each year that trade with sufficient liquidity, and they are the ones that are included in the GSCI Excess Return Index. Table 14.5 shows a listing of the expiration months included in the GSCI Excess Return Index.

Table 14.5   Expiration months in the GSCI Excess Return Index

Crude Oil, Brent Crude Oil, Heating Oil, Gasoil, Unleaded Gas, Natural Gas	All
Wheat, Hard Red Winter Wheat	Mar, May, Jul, Sep, Dec
Cotton	Mar, May, Jul, Dec
Aluminum, Copper, Nickel, Zinc, Lead, Tin	All
Corn, Cocoa, Coffee	Mar, May, Jul, Sep, Dec
Sugar	Mar, May, Jul, Oct
Soybeans	Jan, Mar, May, Jul, Nov
Gold	Feb, Apr, Jun, Aug, Dec
Silver	Mar, May, Jul, Sep, Dec
Platinum	Jan, Apr, Jul, Oct

The roll procedure

We have already stated that the roll procedure is a key component of investment in Futures contracts conducted by Commodity Trading Advisors (CTAs), hedge fund managers and other investors. Significant amounts of money may be made by avoiding liquidity shortage and capturing *changes in shape of the forward curve* – a key component of the expertise in commodity trading.

The rolling forward of the underlying Futures contract in the GSCI Excess Return Index may be thought of as rolling from one basket of nearby Futures to a second nearby basket. In the case of the GSCI, it is calculated at the end of each day during the roll period at daily settlement prices. The portfolio is shifted from the first to the second nearby basket at a rate of 20% per day during the 5 days before the end of the 5th business day. It is adjusted so that 20% of the contracts held are in those second nearby basket of contracts that are further from maturity, with 80% remaining in the roll process; it continues on the 6th, 7th and 8th business days with relative weights of first to second of 40%/60% and 20%/80%. At the end of the 9th business day, the last of the old first nearby baskets is exchanged, leaving the entire portfolio in the second nearby basket – which becomes the new first nearby basket. Note that from the end of the 5th business day to the end of the 9th business day, the portfolio is a mixture of two baskets and can contain more than one Futures maturity per commodity.

The last thing to emphasize in the roll process is that roll percentages refer to the *quantities* of contracts, not their values. The dollar value of the portfolio is redistributed at the end of the 6th business day in such a way that the *number* of contracts of the first nearby basket is 80% of the total. The world production weighting of the GSCI is accomplished by keeping the quantity weights of the individual components of the basket proportional to world production weights. In summary, the GSCI Excess Return Index captures the returns from a passive, world production-weighted mix of Futures contracts written on the 24 commodities composing the GSCI Spot Index.

The GSCI Total Return Index

The GSCI Total Return Index is constructed to be comparable with a simple investment in traditional assets. To make Futures investments comparable with typical long positions in equities and bonds, the Futures contract needs to be *fully collateralized*. In a fully collateralized Futures purchase, the investor pays the face value of the Futures contract as collateral at the time the Futures position is opened. Hence, the investor receives the Treasury bill (T-bill) rate on this collateral as well as the return for holding the Futures contract.

In other words, the investor receives the excess return described above plus the T-bill return on the collateral. This fully collateralized return is called the "total return" and is the basis for the GSCI Total Return Index.

The GSCI Spot Index

The GSCI Spot Index measures the price levels of commodities, not the returns available to investors. At the end of every business day, the GSCI is composed of the same proportions (by weights) of the underlying commodities and expirations as the portfolio represented by the GSCI Excess Return Index.

(c) The Dow Jones–American International Group Commodity Index (DJ-AIGCI)

Like the other indexes, the DJ-AIGCI is designed to be a liquid benchmark for commodity investments:

1. To that end, the DJ-AIGCI relies on 5-year averaging of both liquidity data and dollar-adjusted production data in order to determine the relative quantities of included commodities. We have seen that liquidity is an important indicator of the value placed on a commodity by financial and physical market participants. Production data, on the other hand, are a useful measure of economic importance but may underestimate the economic significance of storable commodities (e.g., gold) at the expense of relatively non-storable commodities (e.g., live cattle). This is why the DJ-

AIGCI relies on *production*, a quantity exogenous to the Futures markets, and *liquidity*, a quantity endogenous to these markets, to define the relative weightings.

2. To ensure that no single commodity or commodity sector dominates the index, the DJ-AIGCI relies on several diversification rules. Among these rules are:

   ○ no related group of commodities (e.g., energy, or metals, or livestock and grains) may constitute more than 33% of the index;
   ○ no single commodity may constitute less than 2% of the index.

   Diversification rules will be applied each year, when the DJ-AIGCI is reweighted and rebalanced on a price–percentage basis. An oversight committee meets annually in June to determine the changes in the index composition effective the following January.

3. Index composition: The DJ-AIGCI is composed of Futures contracts on 20 physical commodities. In the same way as discussed for the other indexes, a long Futures position is maintained by selling nearby contracts and purchasing contracts that have not yet reached the delivery period. In that sense, the DJ-AIGCI is a "rolling index". The DJ-AIGCI is composed of commodities traded on US exchanges, with the exception of aluminum, nickel and zinc which trade on the LME. Trading hours for the US commodity exchanges are between 8.00 a.m. and 3.00 p.m. Eastern time and a daily settlement price for the index is published at approximately 5.00 p.m.

The DJ-AIGCI is calculated on an excess return basis and reflects the return on underlying commodity price movements. The total return index based on the DJ-AIGCI, the DJ-AIGCITR, reflects the return on a fully collateralized investment in the index. In addition, there are seven subindexes representing the major commodity sectors within the index: Energy (including petroleum and natural gas), Petroleum (including crude oil, heating oil and unleaded gasoline), Precious Metals, Industrial Metals, Grains, Livestock and Softs (see Figure 14.4 and Tables 14.6–14.10).

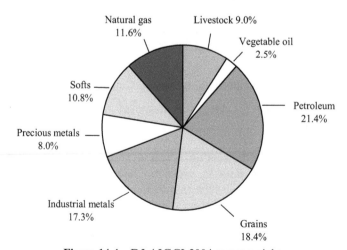

Figure 14.4   DJ-AIGCI 2004 target weights.

Table 14.6 DJ-AIGCI weightings (as of July 2004)

Name	Exchange	Weight
Aluminum	London Metal Exchange (LME)	7.10
Soybean Oil	Chicago Board of Trade (CBOT)	1.72
Corn	Chicago Board of Trade (CBOT)	5.09
Coffee	Coffee, Sugar, Cocoa Exchange (CSCE)	2.78
Crude Oil	New York Mercantile Exchange (NYMEX)	16.66
Cocoa	Coffee, Sugar, Cocoa Exchange (CSCE)	1.99
Cotton	New York Cotton Exchange (NYCE)	1.82
Gold	Commodity Exchange Inc. (New York) (COMEX)	5.31
Copper	Commodity Exchange Inc. (New York) (COMEX)	6.67
Heating Oil	New York Mercantile Exchange (NYMEX)	4.71
Unleaded Gas	New York Mercantile Exchange (NYMEX)	5.37
Live Cattle	Chicago Mercantile Exchange (CME)	6.73
Lean Hogs	Chicago Mercantile Exchange (CME)	5.12
Natural Gas	New York Mercantile Exchange (NYMEX)	9.92
Nickel	London Metal Exchange (LME)	1.86
Soybeans	Chicago Board of Trade (CBOT)	5.14
Sugar	Coffee, Sugar, Cocoa Exchange (CSCE)	3.80
Silver	Commodity Exchange Inc. (New York) (COMEX)	2.18
Wheat	Chicago Board of Trade (CBOT)	3.76
Zinc	London Metal Exchange (LME)	2.27

Table 14.7 CBOT DJ-AIG Futures Price Index

Index quote	Underlying index for each corresponding CBOT DJ-AIGCI Futures contract
Minimum tick size	0.1 point
Frequency	15 seconds
Contract months	Jan, Feb, Apr, Jun, Aug, Oct, Dec (first 3 months listed at all times)
Last day calculated	The 11th business day of the contract month
Settlement	Last-day calculation used for cash settlement of the corresponding DJ- AIGCI Futures contract
Quotation hours	8.15 a.m.–2.15 p.m. Chicago time
Ticker symbol	AIF

Table 14.8 Exchange-traded instruments related to the DJ-AIG indexes: (a) CBOT DJ-AIGCI Futures contracts

Trading unit	$100 × the DJ-AIG Futures Price Index
Price quote	Points ($100)
Tick size	0.1 points ($10 per contract)
Daily price limit	No limit
Contract months	Jan, Feb, Apr, Jun, Aug, Oct, Dec (first 3months listed at all times)
Last trading day	The 11th business day of the contract month
Final settlement day	The 11th business day of the contract month
Settlement	Cash settlement on the final settlement day. The final settlement price is $100 × the DJ-AIG Futures Price Index
Trading hours	8.15 a.m.–2.15 p.m. Chicago time
Ticker symbol	Al

Table 14.9 Exchange-traded instruments related to the DJ-AIG indexes: (b) CBOT DJ-AIGCI Futures options

Trading unit	One CBOT DJ-AIGCI Futures contract
Price quote	Points ($100 per point)
Tick size	0.05 points ($5.00 per contract)
Strike price interval	In five-point intervals: one with the strike price closest to the previous day's settlement price on the underlying CBOT DJ-AIGCI Futures contract and the next ten consecutive higher and the next ten consecutive lower strike prices, called the "first tier". In ten-point intervals: the next ten consecutive higher and the next ten consecutive lower strike prices above and below the first-tier strike price band, called the "second tier".
Daily price limit	No limit
Contract months	Jan, Feb, Apr, Jun, Aug, Oct, Dec. Serial months will be added such that three consecutive contract months will be listed
Last trading day	The 11th business day of the contract month
Exercise	Any business day the option is traded
Expiration	Unexercised options expire at 7.00 p.m. on the last trading day
Trading hours	8.15 a.m.–2.15 p.m. Chicago time
Ticker symbol	OAI

Table 14.10 Exchange-traded instruments related to the DJ-AIG indexes: (c) Commodity TRAKRS Index Futures[4]

Ticker symbol	CCC
Underlying index	The DJ-AIGCI Total Return (or the "Index")
Contract size	$1 × the product of the value of the index and the multiplier.
Contract months	One (1) listing with contract expiration date
Trading hours	8.30 a.m.–3.00 p.m. (Chicago time) Mondays through Fridays
Minimum fluctuation	0.01 index points of $0.01 per contract
Position limits	22,000,000 contracts
Final settlement date	Commodity TRAKRS Futures will be settled on 28 June 2006
Last trading day	Trading in an expiring contract concludes on the final settlement date
Final settlement price	$1 × the product of the closing value of the index on 28 June 2006 and the multiplier

(d) The S&P Commodity Index (SPCI)

The SPCI measures price changes in a cross section of agricultural and industrial commodities that have actively traded US Futures contracts. The index, launched in August 2001, tracks 17 commodities in 6 sectors – energy, fibers, grains, meat and livestocks, metals and softs.

As already mentioned, commodity-linked investments as part of an overall asset allocation have gained acceptance in recent years. They add proven diversification benefits to a traditional equity and fixed income portfolio. SPCI Futures and options on Futures based on the SPCI were launched in late 2001.

Notable features of SPCI

1. Geometric average weighting: Geometric averages have often been adopted in price index computations and underpin such well-known indexes as the US Consumer Price Index (CPI) and Producer Price Index (PPI). Besides the choice of the average, the index adopted implies that each included commodity has a constant value share in the index at all times. The index portfolio is rebalanced over time according to this rule, which forces the index to buy individual commodities when they are low and sell them when they are high, leading effectively to the portfolio insurance strategy discussed before. This rebalancing leads to "arbitrage" opportunities between index Futures and Futures in underlying components, in the spirit of trading dispersion between an equity index and its individual stock components. This enables the Futures contract to often trade at a discount to fair value, which further ensures

---

[4] TRAKRS (Total Return Asset Contracts) are non-traditional Futures designed to enable investors to track a broad-based index of commodities (or other asset classes). They are cash-settled, electronically traded Futures contracts.

liquidity in the index Futures contract. In addition, geometric averaging is more consistent with the computation of compounded returns and, therefore, may be preferred by investors from the point of view of risk minimization.[5] Let us observe that a leading stock index, the Value Line Geometric Index, introduced in 1961 was already using a geometric average of the prices of the stocks included in the index and an equal dollar amount invested in each and every stock.

2. Individual commodity weights are based on open interest in Futures markets. An index-weighting structure based on the dollar value of the open interest for individual commodities ensures that a commodity's share in the index is a function of the size of the underlying Futures market.

3. Commodity weights are adjusted for implicit double-counting between upstream and downstream commodities.

For example, crude oil is used as input to the production of unleaded gasoline, both of which are index components. Downstream commodities (e.g., gasoline) are included at full weight and the index weight of upstream commodities (e.g., crude oil) is reduced to the extent that these are embodied in derived products.

INDEX CALCULATION

As mentioned before, SPCI is a generalized geometric index meant to reflect the price performance of a basket of US-traded commodity Futures contracts. The formula for the index at date t takes the following expression:

$$I(t) = K \prod_{i=1}^{n} (P_i(t))^{w(i)}$$

where:

- $P_i(t)$ is the price of commodity i at time t.
- $w(i)$ is the weight of commodity i, normalized in such a way that $\sum_{i=1}^{n} w(i) = 1$.

More precisely, $P_i(t)$ is the average price of the two nearest active contracts for each component commodity that are not yet in the delivery month when the front month SPCI Futures contract expires. Hence, on 2 February 2004, for instance, the index price for wheat would be the average of the March and May Futures prices for CBOT wheat. The index is calculated every 15 seconds starting with the opening of trading of any of the component commodity Futures markets and continuing until the final settlement price for each component commodity's Futures contract.

The base number for SPCI was 1,000 on 31 December 1997 and index history is available from 31 December 1987.

Two additional indexes can be calculated from the SPCI:

1. The Continuous Contract Index reflects the actual dollar amount invested in the underlying commodity basket. It erases the "profit or loss" associated with contract rolls.

---

[5] For some probability distributions, including the log-normal one, the variance of the geometric average is smaller than the variance of the arithmetic average.

2. The Total Return Index is the percentage change of the continuous contract value plus T-bill interest on an unleveraged position. The T-bill rate is added quarterly to the closing value of the previous quarter's total return value.

Commodity weights

Commodity weights are determined by the value of the Commercial Open Interest (COI) in Futures of a particular commodity, relative to the aggregated value of COIs for all included commodities. Data for COIs are taken from the weekly *Commitment of Trader Report*, as published on the website of the CFTC. The value of the weekly COI for each commodity is calculated by multiplying the value of each contract as determined by the daily closing price averaged across the two most active contract months and the trading days in the week.

Note that some index components are primary commodities that are used as inputs for processed commodities that are also index components. In such cases, downstream commodities are included at full component weight and upstream commodities are entered at a reduced weight. The reduction is based on the extent to which the primary commodity is embodied in one or more downstream commodities on the basis of industry common practice translation formulas (e.g., crusher's margin for soybeans). The diagram below shows the upstream/downstream commodities that constitute index components:

Upstream		Downstream
Crude oil	⇒	Heating oil, unleaded gasoline
Soybeans	⇒	Soybean meal, soybean oil
Soybean meal	⇒	Live cattle, hogs
Corn	⇒	Live cattle, hogs

Index weights are fixed for 1-year periods; weights for individual commodities are calculated using the average value of COIs for the 104 weeks prior to the last Friday in October of each year. To be considered for inclusion in the SPCI, a commodity's total (*long plus short*) COI must have a 2-year average value of at least $500m and its prospective index weight must be greater than 1%.

In all cases, the final authority for index composition, weighting and rebalancing rests with the SPCI Committee.

SPCI FUTURES AND OPTIONS

These are traded on the New York Board of Trade (NYBOT). The contract settlement is in cash and the maturities are January, February, April, June, August, November.

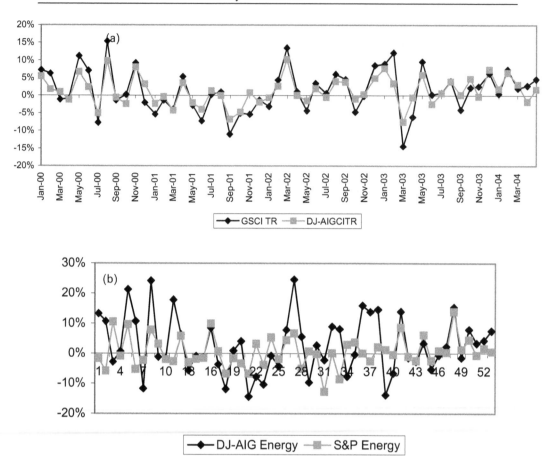

Figure 14.5 (a) Monthly commodity index total returns: 2000–2004; (b) monthly energy sub-index returns: 2000–2004.
Source: CISDM.

(e) Deutsche Bank commodity indexes

The Deutsche Bank Liquid Commodity Index (DBLCI) and the Deutsche Bank Liquid Commodity Index–Mean Reversion (DBLCI-MR) track the performance of investments in a small set of liquid commodities. These indexes, like the other indexes reviewed so far, allow us to gain exposure to commodities while avoiding the purchase of the physical commodities. Both indexes are quoted in total return terms both on commodities and the cash sum invested. In contrast to the GSCI and S&P commodity indexes, Deutsche Bank indexes are quoted in a *variety of currencies*.

The DBLCI is the base index. It is composed of six commodities: Sweet Light Crude Oil (WTI), Heating Oil, Aluminum, Gold, Wheat and Corn. These cover the biggest commodity sectors and are held in fixed notional amounts that reflect world production and inventories in these sectors. Notional weights refer to the US dollar weights of the various assets at the inception of the index in 1988, as shown in Table 14.11.

Table 14.11 Notional weights at index inception in 1988

Commodity	Symbol	Exchange	Notional weight (%)
Sweet Light Crude Oil (WTI)	CL	NYMEX	35
Heating Oil	HO	NYMEX	20
Gold	GC	COMEX	10
Aluminum	AL	LME	12.5
Corn	C	CBOT	11.25
Wheat	W	CBOT	11.25

The index value is calculated daily using the closing prices of listed instruments on each of the commodities; these instruments are traded on some of the largest and most transparent exchanges in the world. Each commodity is also among the most liquid ones in its sector. During the course of a year, weights calculated in US dollar terms can vary from notional weights as prices move. However, each December, rebalancing is performed to reset the weights back to fixed levels.

The maturities of the listed instruments and the way in which the money invested in them is transferred to longer dated instruments as they expire (the "roll") have been chosen to enhance returns on the index and to be as close to a cash index as possible. At each roll, the USD value of the instrument that is being rolled is transferred to the new contract.

The DBLCI-MR

The DBLCI-MR comprises the same underlying assets as the DBLCI with the same initial notional weights set in 1988. Listed instruments are rolled using the same mechanism as the DBLCI. However, in contrast to the DBLCI, weights are reset every time one of the commodities undergoes a "trigger event", defined as the 1-year moving average that is a multiple of 5% away from the 5-year moving average. When this happens, the weights of all commodities are rebalanced: "expensive" commodities have their weights reduced, while "cheap" commodities have their weights increased according to a simple formula.

The weights can never be negative since the index is long only. When all commodities are within 5% of their 5-year averages, the weights revert to the weights of the base index, the DBLCI.

COMMODITIES AND MEAN-REVERSION

Researchers and experienced commodity investors are aware that most commodities trade within defined ranges. As discussed previously in this book, the reasons for this feature are numerous. For instance, when prices of commodities rise:

- New production capacity is brought online to benefit from the high prices while stocks are liquidated (as long as this capacity exists).
- More supply becomes available from alternative sources previously considered uneconomic.

- Quota systems that attempt to control supply are eventually suspended.
- Demand for the commodity falls as it faces competition from cheaper sources.

Opposite arguments come into play when prices are low. The net effect is to keep commodity prices bounded along a long-run average price. The DBLCI-MR builds on this persistent characteristic of commodities while aiming at extracting extra returns from holding a diverse portfolio of commodities. Again, the construction of a commodity index has crucial implications for the returns of index long-investment strategies.

(f) The London Metal Exchange (LME) Index

In January 1999 the LME announced that it would be launching a *dollar-denominated* index, called LMEX, comprising the six LME primary metals: aluminum, copper, lead, nickel, tin and zinc. The goal was to provide a single liquid reference that would track the performance of the world's most traded non-ferrous, base metal contracts.

As in all cases, LMEX Futures and traded option contracts provide investors and fund managers with instruments allowing them to position the risk/return profile of a metals-exposed investment portfolio without facing the issues related to physical delivery. Given the notoriety of the exchange where it is traded, the LMEX offers transparency of index price changes as well as the security of a clearing house.

Construction of the LMEX

Key to the integrity of the index is insuring that the weighting of its components provides a true representative value of the overall non-ferrous, base metal market. The index, with a face value of 1,000 at its inception and denominated in US dollars, incorporates in the weighting of each metal a combination of *world production* and *LME trading volume*; the goal is to take into account world economic relevance and the ability to trade metals. By applying this rationale, the current index weighting:

- Uses a 5-year arithmetic average of each metal.
- Sources production data from the World Bureau of Metal Statistics.
- Sources LME volume data from the LME clearing house.
- Incorporates an arithmetic average of production volume in tons and LME trading volume in tons.

INDEX VALUE

The index incorporates the price of each the six primary metals across three maturities, taking the third Wednesday closing prices for each of the first three qualifying months. It is calculated according to the formula:

$$\text{Index value} = [W_{Al}(Al\ 1\ \text{month} + Al\ 2\ \text{months} + Al\ 3\ \text{months})$$

$$+ \text{Other metals analogous terms}] \times K$$

where:

- W_{Al} = % weighting of aluminum.
- Al 1 month = 1st month 3rd Wednesday aluminum price.
- K = constant such that index value (4 January 1999) = 1,000.

Table 14.12 shows the contract's current weighting.

Table 14.12 Current index weightings

	Weighting to nearest number of lots	Weighting in tonnage	Volume weighting (%)
Aluminum	25	625	41.8
Copper	20	500	33.4
Lead	5	125	8.4
Nickel	5	30	2.0
Tin	3	15	1.0
Zinc	8	200	13.4
Total	*86*	*1,495*	*100.00*

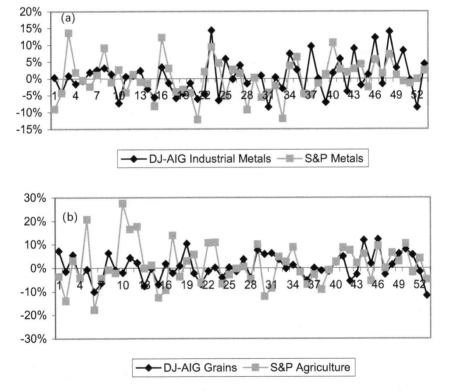

Figure 14.6 (a) Monthly industrial metals subindex returns: 2000–2004; (b) monthly grains subindex returns: 2000–2004.
Source: CISDM.

The derivatives pegged to the LME index are described in Tables 14.13 and 14.14.

Table 14.13 Futures contract specification

Contract size	$10 per index point
Initial LMEX value	1,000 on 4 January 1999
Maturity months	Monthly for 12 months
Last trading day and time	17.00 GMT second Wednesday of settlement month
Settlement basis	Cash settlement based on the index value at close of the last trading day
Cash settlement	Day following the last trading day
Quotation	Index points
Minimum price move	0.1 index point
Clearing	Cash cleared through the London clearing house, with margin offset to underlying metals

Table 14.14 Options contract specification

Contract size	Valued at $10 per index point
Exercise day and time	19.15 GMT, second Wednesday of settlement month
Last trading day and time	16.35 GMT on exercise date
Settlement basis	Cash settlement based on the index value
Cash settlement	Day after exercise day
Maturity months	Monthly for the front three months
Option premium	Paid on the 1st business day following trade date
Tick size	$0.01

An investor who anticipates a rise in metals prices will take a long position in LMEX Futures or buy call options; if he has the opposite view, he will short the Futures and buy puts (or sell calls). In all cases, the management of the position will require a proper modeling of the underlying index dynamics. We have already mentioned at several places in this book that this modeling could incorporate economic insights about the behavior of the commodity price in the short to medium term: for instance, a positive drift in a geometric Brownian motion or an increasing trend in the level of mean-reversion could translate the view of a cycle of upward-moving prices.

14.4 CONCLUSION

The vibrant interest in commodity-related funds seems likely to stay for some time. In July 2004 Barclays Global Investors, a unit of Barclays PLC of London, launched a pooled commodity fund meant to provide European investors with an opportunity to track the performance of a benchmark index, the Goldman Sachs Total Return Commodity Index discussed in this chapter. Other commodity-related funds have been established for some while and have performed very well in recent years: the Merrill Lynch Gold General Fund achieved a return of 121% over the past three years. Its strategies included buying the shares of companies that mine gold or even small quantities of securities backed by a fixed amount of bullion. State Street Global Advisors offers strategies linked to the GSCI and the DJ-AIG commodity indexes to institutional investors worldwide and is exploring launching active commodity strategies internationally. Pacific Investment Management launched a fund in June 2002 that aims to enhance overall returns of the DJ-AIGCI through investments in inflation-linked fixed income securities. The recent introduction of index-tracking instruments allows an increasing number of investors to match the performance of well-established commodity indexes in the same way structured securities have been financially engineered in equity markets for two decades.

Other categories of investors, such as pension funds, insurance companies and university endowments – even Harvard's, are pouring more money into commodities. These long-term institutional investors hold, on average, investments in energy, industrial and precious metals, livestock, agriculture and other commodities which are estimated to be twice those of hedge funds. Many analysts conservatively figure that roughly 150 institutions have passive investments pegged to the GSCI, up from fewer than 50 in 2000. Goldman Sachs estimates that more than $25bn are tied up in the index, compared with $8bn just 4 years ago. AIG estimates that an additional $8bn to $10bn of investments are pegged to the DJ-AIGCI, up from about $200m a few years ago.

More than 6% of the Ontario Teachers' Pension Plan CAN$79bn are invested in commodity-related investments. Its largest equity investment is in Nexen Inc., a Canadian oil and gas concern; its second largest is in Fording Canadian Coal Trust. Ontario Teachers now owns 85% of Canada's coal reserves. Early this year, the fund also acquired a 50% stake in 25 US power generation facilities. Harvard University has been investing in commodities for more than a decade and its internal benchmark calls for allocating 13% of the university's $19.3bn endowment to oil, gas and other commodities. This is two percentage points less than the weighting assigned to US stock and two points more than the allocation to US bonds. Unlike many pension funds that passively follow a benchmark, Harvard *actively* manages its commodity investments and 10 percentage points of the 13 allocated to commodities are invested in timber. During the 5 years ended 30 June 2004, the S&P 500 stocks index averaged −2.2% a year. Over the same period, Harvard's average annual return from commodities was roughly 16%.

Last but not least, the fact that commodity prices tend to rise with inflation is a very desirable feature for pension funds which sometimes pay annuities pegged to an inflation index.

Appendix

Glossary

American-style option
An option that may be exercised at any date during its lifetime.

Amsterdam Power Exchange
The Amsterdam Power Exchange launched a day-ahead spot market for Dutch electricity in May 1999. It publishes a daily index of all trading volumes.

Annual Contract Quantity (ACQ)
The amount of gas specified in a buyer's nomination purchase contract for one year. Some rights and obligations, such as swing and take-or-pay, may need to be taken into account depending on the amount of gas taken versus the amount contracted for.

Arbitrage-free model
Any model that excludes the possibility of making money with no risk and a null investment.

Asian option
Asian (or average rate) options have pay-offs that depend on the arithmetic average of prices of the underlying commodity over a period of time; the averaging period may correspond to the entire life of the option or be a subperiod. Asian options are one of the most popular exotic options in the energy markets.

Ask
The level at which sellers are willing to sell. *See* **Bid/ask**.

At the beach
In the UK, when gas has been brought ashore to a terminal by producers but is not yet in the national transmission system, the gas is call "at the beach".

At-the-money
1. At-the-money spot: an option whose strike is the current market price of the underlying asset.
2. At-the-money forward: an option whose strike is the current market price of the forward contract with the same maturity as the option under analysis.

Average rate option
See **Asian option**.

Backwardation
A forward curve is backwardated when forward prices are decreasing with maturity. Market participants except the spot price to go down. *Contrast with* **Contango**.

Balancing mechanism
In an electricity grid or natural gas pipeline network, the means of ensuring that supply and demand are matched.

Barge
Vessel used to carry oil products, coal or other commodities, often along a river; barges vary in capacity, usually from 1,000 to 5,000 tonnes.

Barrel
Standard measure of quantity for crude oil and petroleum products. Barrel, US barrel and standard barrel are all equal to 42 US gallons or 159 litres.

Barrel of Oil Equivalent (BOE)
Volume of natural gas expressed in terms of its energy equivalent to oil. About 6,000 cubic feet of gas equal one barrel of oil equivalent, or 5.8 million British thermal units (Btu).

Barrier option
Barrier options (knock-out, knock-in) are exotic options that are (de)activated if the underlying commodity price touches a pre-specified barrier during the lifetime of the option.

Baseload or load
The minimum expected power consumption at a given time. Baseload power is generally supplied from larger plants, which cannot be ramped up and down as quickly as peaking generation plants. As baseload demand is generally predictable and steady, it is less expensive than peak power.

Basis
The differential that exists at any time between the spot price of a given commodity and the price of the nearest Futures contract. The basis may reflect different time periods, product forms, qualities, locations.

Basis risk
Basis risk is the risk that the value of a Futures contract will not move in line with that of the underlying exposure. Alternatively, it is the risk that the cash–Futures spread will widen or narrow between the dates at which a hedge position is implemented and liquidated. Basis risk may be related to location, quality, type or calendar basis.

Basis swap
Basis swaps are used to hedge exposure to basis risk, such as locational risk or time exposure risk.

Basket option
An option that enables the purchaser to buy or sell a basket of commodities. The value of a basket option depends on the volatilities of the individual commodities and the correlations between the prices of commodities in the basket. A simple example of a basket option is an exchange option.

BBL
Abbreviation for barrel.

BCF
Billion Cubic Feet (of gas).

Benchmark crude
Synonymous with reference crude or marker crude. A crude oil whose price is used as a reference against which other crudes are priced, because of its liquidity: the New York Mercantile Exchange West Texas Intermediate and International Petroleum Exchange Brent are the two world references.

Bid/ask
A measure of market liquidity, also known as bid/offer. The bid is the price level at which buyers are willing to buy, and the ask is the price level at which sellers are willing to sell. The thinner the spread, the higher the liquidity.

Bilateral contract
A contract signed between two parties without the necessary intermediation of any exchange. *See also* **OTC contracts**.

Bill of Lading (B/L)
A shipowner's receipt for its cargo, which documents all cargo details.

Biomass energy
Energy produced by the combustion of plants and agricultural waste.

Blackout
A total loss of power caused by the failure of the generation or transmission system.

Book
The set of forward or option positions held by a trader or company.

Bottleneck
Caused when the flow of electricity is greater than the system capacity between two connected grids. Bottlenecks can lead to the isolation of an area.

Brent blend crude oil
UK Brent blend is a blend of crude oil from various fields in the east Shetland basin. The crude is landed at the Sullom Voe terminal and is used as a benchmark for the pricing of a large proportion of the world's crude oil production.

British thermal unit (Btu)
The amount of heat required to raise the temperature of one pound of water by $1°$ Fahrenheit (technically from $60°F$ to $61°F$). It is used to compare the heat-producing value of different fuels.

Bushel
There are 60 pounds in a bushel.

Buy-back price
The price that an oil company pays to a state for oil that the company has produced but which is owned by the state.

Butterfly spread
The simultaneous purchase of an out-of-the-money strangle and sale of an at-the-money straddle. The buyer profits if the underlying remains stable, and has limited risk in the event of a large move in either direction.

Calendar or time spread
The price differential between different maturities forward contracts.

California–Oregon Border (COB)
The name of a US electricity index and of Futures contracts that used to be traded on NYMEX.

Call spread
A position formed by the purchase of a call option at one strike and the sale of another call option at a higher strike. The premium received by selling one option reduces the cost of buying the other but the call spread still has a positive price at date 0.

Cap
A supply contract between a buyer and seller, whereby the buyer is assured that he will not have to pay more than a given maximum price. In the case of an option, the existence of a cap (e.g., capped call) means that the seller of the option will not pay more than this cap if the option is exercised at maturity; this feature makes the option market more liquid.

Capacity
Electricity: the capability of electrical equipment, such as generators or transmission lines, typically expressed in megawatts or megavoltamperes.
Gas: the transportation volume of natural gas pipelines, typically expressed in millions of cubic feet per day.

Carbon dioxide (CO_2)
A gas produced by the burning of fuel. Most scientists believe it is a major contributor to the greenhouse effect.

Carbon dioxide equivalent
The accepted measurement unit for greenhouse gases under the Kyoto Protocol.

Carriage, Insurance and Freight (CIF)
A CIF shipping means the cost of cargo, insurance and travel/freight to a named destination are all included in the price paid by the seller of the good. The buyer, however, must assume the additional charges of getting the good into his warehouse. *Contrast with* **FOB**.

Cash-and-carry arbitrage
A strategy whereby a trader generates a riskless profit by selling a Futures contract and buying the underlying to deliver at maturity of the Futures. The Futures contract must be expensive relative to the underlying. If the Futures is theoretically cheap compared with the cash commodity, the trader can sell the underlying and buy the Futures, building a reverse cash-and-carry arbitrage.

Chicago Mercantile Exchange (CME)
Established in 1898 as the Chicago Butter and Egg Board, it became incorporated as the CME in 1919. The CME offers, among other products, Futures and options cumulative Heating Degree-Days (HDDs) and Cooling Degree-Days (CDDs) for selected cities in the US.

CIF
See **Carriage, Insurance and Freight**.

Clearing house
An exchange clearing house settles transactions executed on the floor, collects the margin deposits and oversees the delivery procedures for positions not liquidated prior to maturity.

Combined-Cycle Gas Turbine (CCGT)
An energy-efficient gas turbine system, where the first turbine generates electricity from the gas produced during fuel combustion. The hot gases pass through a boiler and then into the atmosphere. The steam from the boiler drives the second electricity-generating turbine.

Commodity swap
Commodity swaps enable both producers and consumers to hedge commodity prices. The consumer usually pays the fixed price and the producer the floating price. If the floating-rate price of the commodity is higher than the fixed price, the difference is paid by the floating payer, and vice versa. Usually, only the payment streams, not the principal, are exchanged, although physical delivery is becoming increasingly common. Swaps are sometimes used to hedge risks that cannot readily be hedged with Futures contracts, such as geographical or quality basis risk.

Contango
A commodity market is in contango when the forward curve is increasing with maturity. Market participants expect the price to go up.

Contract for Differences
A short-dated swap agreement used to minimize the basis risk between a reference index (e.g., the daily published *Platt's* quote for dated Brent) and the forward price quote for a specific month. The settlement of a CfD is based on the published price difference at a designated time. In the UK, CfDs are used by generators and suppliers to manage their risks and may involve the payment of a fee by the buyer of the CfD.

Convenience yield
This describes the yield that accrues to the owner of a physical inventory but not to the owner of a contract for future delivery. It represents the benefit of having the physical product immediately available and offers a theoretical explanation for backwardated forward curves.

Conversion factors

1 tonne of crude	= 7.5 barrels
1 barrel of crude	= 5,604 cubic feet of natural gas or 0.996 barrels of gas oil
1 US barrel	= 42 US gallons = 158.978 litres
1 million barrels of crude a day	= 50 million tonnes a year
1 megajoule	= 947.81 Btu = 238.85 kcal
1 cubic foot	= 0.0283 cubic metres

Cracking
The technological process used in petroleum refineries to break heavier molecules of hydrocarbons into lighter ones.

Crack spread
Calculation of the worth of a barrel of crude oil in terms of the value of its refined products, such as gasoline and heating oil. Crack spreads may be based on a variety of refinery models and also depend on the type of crude input. They are usually expressed in dollars and cents per barrel of crude.

Crude oil
The most commonly traded crudes are North Sea Brent, the US West Texas Intermediate and Dubai.

Cubic foot
Standard unit for measuring gas; 1 cubic foot $= 0.0283$ cubic meters.

Cumulative degree-days
The sum of heating degree-days or cooling degree-days over a specified period.

Degree-day
The difference between an average daily temperature and a reference level, typically 65° Fahrenheit (18° Celsius). Degree-days are used as a basis for temperature-related weather derivative deals.

Delivery month
The month in which a Futures contract matures and can be settled by physical delivery. Also known as the contract month.

Delta
Sensitivity of an option price to changes in the price of the underlying asset; or partial derivative of the option price with respect to the underlying price.

Derivative
A financial instrument derived from a cash market commodity or a Futures contract. Derivatives can be traded on regulated exchanges or over-the-counter. The fundamental examples of derivatives written on the spot commodity are Futures and options.

Digital
Or binary. Option that pays a fixed sum or zero depending on the occurrence of a specific event.

Dynamic hedging
Hedging an option position by buying or selling the underlying in an amount equal to the option delta and monitoring the hedge over time.

E&P
Denotes exploration and production in the oil and gas market.

ECAR
East Central Area Reliability Co-ordination Agreement – a North American Electric Reliability Council region.

Electricity Forward Agreement (EFA)
A standardized swap-like instrument used in electricity markets to hedge or trade pool prices.

Electricity utility
An enterprise engaged in the generation, transmission and/or distribution of electricity within a designated service area.

Embedded option
Embedded options are included in physical commodity contracts and may be beneficial to the buyer or seller of the contract.

European Energy Exchange (EEX)
The EEX was founded in August 2000 and merged with its rival, the Leipzig Power Exchange (LPX), in early 2002. As of early 2003, it offered Futures and spot markets in electricity.

European option
An option that may only be exercised on its expiration date, in contrast to an American option.

European Union Electricity Directive
The European parliament and council directive concerning common rules for the internal market in electricity and aiming at ensuring the free movement of electricity across EU member countries.

Exchange of Futures for Physical (EFP)
The conversion of a Futures position into a physical position via simultaneous buy/sell transactions.

Exchange option
An option giving the buyer the right to exchange a given quantity of a commodity for another quantity of another commodity at maturity.

Exchange-traded option
An option traded and cleared on an organized exchange. Such options are usually standardized by strike, maturity and underlying.

Exotic option
An option whose payout structure is more complicated than a plain-vanilla put or call option. Examples of exotic options include Asian options, barrier options, digital options and spread options.

Federal Energy Regulating Commission (FERC)
The US government agency charged with regulating electricity and natural gas industries.

Feedstock
Raw material used by any processing unit. For instance, crude oil is a feedstock of oil refineries and petrochemical plants.

FOB
See **Free On Board**.

Force majeure
The legal term describing the contract clause that allows the supplier to forgo his obligation to supply in extreme circumstances, such as a political crisis, war or strikes that disturb production. It also applies to a buyer who is unable to take delivery of the commodity.

Forward contract
A supply contract between a buyer and seller, whereby the buyer is obligated to take delivery and the seller is obligated to provide delivery of a fixed amount of a commodity at a predetermined price on a specified future date. Payment in full is due at the time of delivery.

Forward Freight Agreement (FFA)
FFAs are derivatives instruments used to hedge risk in the shipping and freight sector.

Forward start option
An option whose strike is equal to the underlying price observed at a future pre-specified date prior to the maturity of the option.

Free-On-Board (FOB)
Under an FOB contract, the seller provides the commodity at a lifting installation and the buyer takes responsibility for shipping and freight insurance.

Freight derivatives
Derivatives instruments used to hedge risk in the freight markets. Freight derivatives, such as swaps or forward freight agreements, can be used to protect shipowners against changes in freight rates.

Futures contract
An exchange-traded contract between a buyer and a seller whereby the buyer is obligated to take delivery and the seller is obligated to provide delivery of a fixed amount of a commodity at a predetermined price at a specified location. Futures contracts are traded exclusively on regulated exchanges and are settled daily through margin calls.

Gas
Natural gas is composed mainly of methane (CH_4) and ethane (C_2H_6). In North America "gas" is the abbreviation for gasoline.

Gas oil
A middle distillate and form of heating oil used primarily in heating and air-conditioning systems. One of the most actively traded oil products, gas oil is the underlying of very liquid International Petroleum Exchange and NYMEX Futures contracts. In refining terms, gas oil comes between fuel oil and lighter products, such as naphtha and gasoline.

Gigawatt (GW)
1 billion watts.

Gigawatt-hours (GWh)
1 billion watt-hours.

Grid
An electricity transmission system.

Heat rate
A measure of how efficiently a power plant converts a fuel (coal, gas or other) into electricity; it is a key determinant of the spark spread. Precisely, the heat rate is the ratio of British thermal units of fuel consumed in order to produce one kilowatt-hour of electricity. The lower the heat rate, the higher the conversion efficiency.

Hedge
The initiation of a position in Futures or options that is intended to protect the buyer (or seller) against an adverse move in the price of the actual commodity. For example, the sale of Futures

contracts in anticipation of future sales of the commodity, produced or harvested, as a protection against possible price declines.

Historical volatility
The annualised standard deviation of percentage changes in the spot price (or forward price) over a specific period. A number derived from a database of past market prices.

Hydropower
Electrical energy produced by falling or flowing water. A hydroelectric power plant uses the liberated potential energy to spin a turbine generator that produces electricity.

Implied volatility
The volatility parameter derived from option market prices by inversion of the Black–Scholes formula.

Independent Power Producer (IPP)
Non-utility power-generating company.

Independent System Operator (ISO)
In the US, an entity responsible for ensuring the efficient use and reliable operation of the transmission grid. Individual ISOs cover either a single state (e.g., the California ISO) or a region (e.g., the midwest ISO). ISO responsibilities can include co-ordinating scheduling for transmission transactions, ensuring the instantaneous balancing of generation and load, managing operating reserves and co-ordinating transmission payments. In some cases, ISOs are also responsible for managing power exchange activities (such as the GME in Italy).

Index
A reference number representing the commodity spot price in a given region and providing an indication of the market trend. The index may be the cash price registered over time, or an average of prices over a day, or an estimation quoted by a major information provider. An index may also represent a basket of commodities. In all cases, a reliable index is necessary to the existence of derivative transactions; it may be used as a benchmark in OTC transactions.

Interconnector
A gas pipeline running from Bacton in England to Zeebrugge in Belgium. It opened in October 1998 and allows the UK to export gas to, or import gas from, Continental Europe for the first time.

International Energy Agency (IEA)
A Paris-based organization of leading oil-consuming nations mainly based in the West, which co-ordinates its members' energy policies. It also compiles energy statistics, including forward supply/demand projections for countries both within and outside its membership.

International Petroleum Exchange (IPE)
London oil exchange that has Futures and options contracts in Brent blend crude oil and gas oil and a Futures contract in UK natural gas. In June 2001 the IPE became a wholly owned subsidiary of the Intercontinental Exchange.

Interruptible service
Gas or electricity sales that are subject to interruption for a specified number of days or hours during times of peak demand or in the event of system emergencies. In exchange for interruptibility, buyers pay lower prices.

In-the-money
An option whose intrinsic value is positive. The option is in-the-money if the underlying Futures price is above a call option's strike price or below a put option's strike price.

Kilowatt-hour
Unit of electricity equivalent to the power of one kilowatt operation for one hour. For example, ten 100-watt light bulbs burning for one hour would consume one kilowatt-hour of electricity.

Kyoto Protocol on Climate Change
An agreement made in Kyoto, Japan in December 1997 under which industrialized countries agreed to adopt specific goals and timelines for nationwide reductions of greenhouse gas emissions between 2008 and 2012. The two major mechanisms for achieving this goal are emissions-trading and the Clean Development Mechanism. The European Union has a target goal of 8% reduction in greenhouse gases and Japan's goal is a 6% reduction.

Light
Typically crude oil with an API gravity of more than 28 degrees.

Liquidity
A market is liquid when it has a high level of trading activity and when trades of fairly large size can be rapidly executed.

Liquidity risk
The risk that a desk or a company does not rapidly find a counterparty if it wishes to purchase or sell a commodity, in particular to hedge a derivative position.

Liquefied Natural Gas (LNG)
Natural gas (mainly methane) that has been liquefied for ease of storage and transportation. The gas is liquefied by reducing the temperature to 162°C, less often by increasing the pressure.

Load shape
The profile of the daily (or weekly) electricity needs of residential customers.

Mark-to-market
To mark-to-market is to calculate the value of an instrument or a portfolio of instruments at the current market spot and forward prices of the underlying. Marking-to-market allows the liquidation value of a position to be estimated.

Margin
Margin is a deposit, usually of money or liquid assets like Treasury bills, that secures the execution of a contract. In order to take a position in Futures traded on an exchange, both the buyer and seller need to deposit a sum called the "original margin". Additional funds called "margin calls" are required each day from the party against whom the price has moved in order for the position not to be liquidated by the clearing house.

Master agreement
The model master power purchase and sale agreement is an attempt to standardize the conditions needed to establish trading relationships in US power markets by providing standard documentation for all trading agreements.

Megawatt-hour (MWh)
1 million watt-hours.

Monte Carlo simulation
A method of pricing derivatives by simulating a great number of trajectories of the underlying variable (or vectors of variables). Averaging the outcomes of the simulation gives an approximation of the derivative's value. Monte Carlo methods are useful in the valuation of complex derivatives for which exact analytical solutions do not exist as of today, but it can be very computationally intensive.

Multi-factor model
A model in which a number of state variables (or factors) drive the dynamics of the commodity price process or forward curve evolution.

National Balancing Point (NBP)
A *notional* point in the UK National Transmission System (NTS) used as a delivery point for gas that is traded "entry paid", i.e., already in the NTS, rather than "at the beach". For accounting and balancing purposes, all gas is supposed to flow through this point.

National Grid Transco
This company owns and operates the high-voltage electricity transmission network in England and Wales and the UK's natural gas transportation system.

Natural gas
Gas consisting mainly of methane and ethane that is found in the earth's crust, often found in association with crude oil. Natural gas Futures and options contracts are traded on the New York Mercantile Exchange, International Petroleum Exchange and Kansas City Board of Trade.

Net Present Value (NPV)
The assessment of the worth of future payments by looking at the present value of those future cash flows discounted at an appropriate rate, called "cost of capital".

New Electricity Trading Arrangements (NETAs)
NETA is a system of bilateral trading between generators, suppliers and consumers on the UK market, the aim of which is to reduce wholesale electricity prices.

New York Mercantile Exchange (NYMEX)
The most important US energy Futures exchange. Along with metals Futures and options, the exchange offers trading for energy Futures and options in crude oil, heating oil, gasoline, natural gas and electricity, as well as propane Futures and options on the crude oil/gasoline and crude oil/heating oil crack spreads.

Nomination
The notification to put into effect a contract or part of a contract. For example, a gas flow nomination from a shipper is meant to notify the pipeline owner of the amount of gas he

wishes to transport or hold in storage at a given future date. In the oil industry, the buyer often has the choice of the nomination of delivery within a 2-month period.

Non-firm service
Electricity transmission service offered to customers which anticipates possible interruption of deliveries and benefit from lower prices.

Nordpool
Oslo-based electricity exchange, which listed the world's first exchange-traded electricity Futures contracts in October 1995. The exchange now lists spot market, Futures, forward and options contracts based on the combined Norwegian, Swedish, Finnish and Danish power markets and clears bilateral contracts as well.

North American Electric Reliability Council (NERC)
A group formed in 1968 by US utilities to promote adequacy of supply in the electricity utility systems of North America. The council consists of 10 regional reliability councils. NERC is the official overseer of US power grid reliability.

Open interest
Open interest refers to the number of Futures contracts outstanding at a particular moment (i.e., the number of contracts that have not been canceled by an offsetting trade). Exchanges provide information on the open interest at the close of each day's trading.

Option
A contract that gives its purchaser the right (but not the obligation) to buy or sell the underlying commodity at a certain price, the strike, on or before an agreed date, the maturity of the option.

Out-of-the-money
An option with no intrinsic value: for calls, an option with an exercise price above the spot or Futures market price; for puts, an option with an exercise price below the Futures price.

Over-the-counter (OTC)
A private transaction negotiated between two parties (or bilateral contract) as opposed to a standardized contract traded on an exchange through the intermediary of the clearing house which becomes the only counterparty. An OTC contract leaves both parties exposed to the other's default event.

Paper market
A market for contracts where delivery is settled in cash, rather than by delivery of the physical product on which the contract is based.

Path-dependent option
A path-dependent option has a payout related to the trajectory of the underlying over all or part of the life of the option. The most usual option in energy markets, the Asian option, is path-dependent, as its payout is related to the average spot (or Futures) price of the commodity.

Platt's
A major information provider, specialized in news, prices, data, analysis and research for oil and energy commodities.

Put–call parity
The relationship that links at any date European call and put option prices with same strike and maturity, the current spot price of the underlying and the discounted strike price. It only relies on the assumption of No arbitrage.

Put option
An option giving its buyer the right (but not the obligation) to sell a commodity Futures contract at a specific price within a specific period of time. It obligates the seller, or writer, of the option to buy the underlying at the designated price.

Quanto option
An option whose payout at maturity involves the spot (or Futures) price of a commodity and the value at that date of a foreign currency expressed in the domestic numéraire.

Real option
A physical asset whose profits mimic the payouts of a portfolio of options; may be valued using option pricing theory.

Repurchase agreement
A repurchase agreement (or repo) is a contract in which a party sells a commodity to another and commits himself to buy back this commodity at a later date at a stipulated price.

Reserves
Back-up power that must be set aside at all times to meet fluctuations in system demand within a given range and to replace a plant momentarily out of order.

Risk management
Control and limitation of the risks faced by a desk or an organization due to its exposure to changes in financial market variables, such as foreign exchange, interest rates, commodity prices and counterparty creditworthiness. Market risks are usually managed by hedging with financial instruments, although a firm may also reduce risk by adjusting its business practices.

Seasonality
Most commodity markets, spot and forward, are affected to some extent by an annual seasonal cycle or "seasonality" that is translated into the observed prices and volatility.

Shipper
A company that transports gas along a pipeline system. Shippers need to be registered with the local regulatory body. In UK gas market terms, a shipper is a company that buys gas "at the beach" and pays Transco to transport the gas along the pipeline system.

SO_2 allowance trading
Allowance trading is the centerpiece of the US Environmental Protection Agency's acid rain program. Allowances are the "numéraire" with which compliance with SO_2 emission requirements is achieved. They authorize a unit within a utility or industrial source to emit one US ton of SO_2 during a given year or any year thereafter.

Spark spread
The difference between the price of electricity produced by a power plant and the price of the fuel used to generate it, adjusted for equivalent units. To express it in $/MWh, the spread is calculated

by multiplying the price of gas (in dollars per million Btu), by the heat rate (in Btu/KWh), dividing by 1,000 and subtracting this quantity from the electricity price (in $/MWh).

Speculator
In commodity markets, the term "speculator" refers to any actor who does not handle the physical commodity but takes financial positions and expects to profit from movements in prices.

Spinning reserves
Power plants that are on line but not operating at their maximum capacity. In the case of the sudden failure of another generation unit, the system operator must be able to call some of the remaining units to quickly ramp up and provide some extra capacity. In principle, the combined spinning reserves must be at least equal to the production of the largest single generator.

Spot
The term spot (or cash) refers to a good that is available for immediate delivery, at a price called the "spot price".

Spot market
In the energy sector, the spot market is the physical/cash crude, refined product, gas or electricity market. The market for immediate delivery rather than future delivery.

Spot price
The price of a security or commodity in the cash market.

Spread option
An option written on the differential between the prices of two commodities. Spread options may be based on the price differences between prices of the same commodity at two different locations (location spreads); prices of the same commodity at two different points in time (calendar spreads); prices of inputs to, or outputs from, a production process (processing spreads); and prices of different grades of the same commodity (quality spreads). The NYMEX and the IPE offer exchange-traded options on energy spreads: heating oil/crude oil, gasoline/crude oil crack spread options, etc.

Standard deviation
The most popular measure of the dispersion of a random variable around its mean, defined as the square root of a second-order mean-centered moment.

Storage capacity
The amount of gas that can be stored to cover peak demand. The main types of storage are salt cavers, aquifers and depleted gas fields. LNG is stored in insulated metal tanks.

Storage gas
Gas kept in storage in order to balance supply and demand over time.

Supply stack
The supply stack describes the various generating units available to produce power within a given region and ranked by merit order (i.e., from the lowest price of electricity output to the highest). Usually, the stack curve starts with cheap-to-run hydro and nuclear plants that supply the baseload. Coal- and oil-fired plants are in the middle of the supply stack and gas units act as peakers when demand and power prices are high.

Swap
A contract whereby, at regular intervals, a floating price (spot market price of the commodity on that date) is exchanged for a fixed price over a specified period. The agreement defines the volume, duration and fixed reference price. Differences are settled in cash for specific periods – monthly, quarterly or 6-monthly. In energy, swaps are also known as contracts for differences or fixed-for-floating contracts.

Swing option
The right to take more or less of a specified commodity on each day of the lifetime of the option under a daily (capacity) constraint and a global constraint. Swing options are most commonly used in the gas market and naturally appear in standard electricity contracts.

Swiss Electricity Price Index (SWEP)
Launched in 1998, SWEP was the first electricity index in Continental Europe. It is based in the Swiss town of Laufenburg, a major hub for power exchange between Switzerland and Germany.

Take-or-pay contract
Under this clause – a standard one in the gas industry – the buyer is obliged to pay for a specified amount of natural gas whether he takes it or not.

Theta
Partial derivative of the option price with respect to time; measures the speed of the time decay of the option price.

Third-Party Access (TPA)
Defines a situation where the owner of a pipeline or electricity network is obliged to transport gas, crude or electricity in a nondiscriminatory way for any third party at the same rate as all users. Third-party access can either be regulated by a separate agency or law, or negotiated between the incumbent and the new entrant.

Time value
Part of the option premium that reflects the excess over the option's intrinsic value, or the entire premium, if there is no intrinsic value. The option time value declines until expiration.

Ton
A unit of weight used in the US and Canada and equal to 2,000 pounds, or 907 kilograms.

Tonne
A metric unit of mass equal to 1,000 kilograms or 2,204 pounds.

Transco
US industry jargon for transmission facilities, or for a company engaged almost exclusively in the provision of transmission service.

UK Power Exchange (UKPX)
Electronic exchange that launched electricity Futures in June 2000. Trading is open to companies active in the UK power market.

Unbundling
The separating of the various components of electricity production, supply and service functions, in order to introduce greater elements of competition in these segments of the industry.

Value-at-risk
The Value-at-Risk (VaR) of a portfolio is the worst loss expected to be suffered over a given period of time with a given probability. The time period is known as the holding period, and the probability is typically 95% or 99%. The corresponding VaR is the 5% or 1% quantile of the P&L distribution.

Vanilla option
A standard European call or put option. A plain-vanilla option pays out the difference between the strike price of the option and the spot price of the underlying at the time of exercise.

Vega
Partial derivative of the option price with respect to the volatility of the underlying commodity.

Volatility
A measure of the variability of a market factor, most often the price of the underlying instrument. Volatility is defined mathematically as the annualized standard deviation of the natural log of the ratio of two successive prices. The actual volatility realized over a period of time (i.e., historical volatility) is calculated from recorded spot data. The implied volatility is derived from the market prices of options by inverting the Black–Scholes formula.

Volatility skew
The difference in implied volatility between out-of-the-money puts and calls, as expressed by the difference between the 90-implied volatility and the 110 one, the current ATM.

Volatility smile
The curve obtained by plotting the implied volatilities of options with the same underlying and maturity against their strikes. It is usually shaped as a smile with a minimal value for a strike equal to the current spot price.

Weather derivatives
Financial instruments whose pay-offs at maturity are defined by a weather-related index. Most instruments are based on degree-days, but rainfall or wind power are becoming increasingly popular underlyings.

West Texas Intermediate (WTI)
US crude oil used as a benchmark for pricing much of world crude oil production.

Wholesale
Energy supplied in usually large quantities by a producer or marketer to another for eventual resale to consumers.

References

Abramovitz, M. and I. Stegun (1972) *Handbook of Mathematical Functions* (Applied Mathematics Series, 55). Springer-Verlag, Berlin.

Ané T. and H. Geman (2000) "Order flow, transaction clock and normality of asset returns", *Journal of Finance*, **55**, 2259–2285

Anson, M. (2002) *The Handbook of Alternative Assets* (Wiley Finance Series). John Wiley & Sons, Chichester, UK.

Bachelier, L. (1900) "Théorie de la spéculation". *Annales Scientifiques de l'Ecole Normale Supérieure*, **17**, 21–86.

Barone-Adesi, G. and A. Gigli (2002) "Electricity derivatives" (Working paper). National Center of Competence and Research, Università della Svizzera Italiana.

Bates, D.S. (2000) "Post-87 crash fears in the S&P futures option market". *Journal of Econometrics*, **94**, 181–238.

Bessembinder, H. and Lemon (2002) "Equilibrium pricing and optimal hedging in equilibrium electricity forward markets". *Journal of Finance*, **57**, 1347–1382.

Bessembinder, H., J.F. Coughenour, P.J. Seguin and S.M. Smoller. (1995) "Mean reversion in equilibrium asset prices: Evidence from the Futures term structure". *Journal of Finance*, **50**(1), 361–375.

Bick, A. (1995) "Quadratic Variation Based Strategies". *Journal of Financial and Quantitative Analysis*.

Black, F. (1975) "Fact and fantasy in the use of options and corporate liabilities". *Financial Analyst Journal*, **31**, 36–41.

Black, F. (1976) "Studies of stock price volatility changes". *Proceedings of the 1976 Meetings of the American Statistical Association, Business and Economic Statistic Section* (pp. 177–181).

Black, F. (1976) "The pricing of commodity contracts". *Journal of Financial Economics*, **3**, 167–180.

Black, F. and M. Scholes (1973) "The pricing of options and corporate liabilities". *Journal of Political Economy*, **81**, 637–659.

Borovkova, S. and H. Geman (2004) "Seasonal and stochastic effects in energy commodity forward curves". *Third World Congress of the Bachelier Finance Society, Chicago*.

Brennan, M.J. (1958) "The supply of storage". *American Economic Review*, **48**, 50–72.

Brennan, M.J. (1959) "A model of seasonal inventories". *Econometrica*, **27**, 228–244.

Bühler, W., O. Korn and R. Schöbel (2001) "Pricing and hedging of oil futures: A unifying approach" (Working paper). Tübingen University.

Carr, P., H. Geman and D. Madan (2001) "Pricing and hedging in incomplete markets". *Journal of Financial Economics*, **62**, 131–169.

Carr, P., H. Geman, D. Madan and M. Yor (2002) "The fine structure of asset returns: An empirical investigation". *Journal of Business*, **75**, 305–332.

Carr, P., H. Geman, D. Madan and M. Yor (2003) "Stochastic volatility for Lévy processes". *Mathematical Finance*, **13**, 345–382.

Carrière, J. (1996) "Valuation of the early-exercise price for options using simulations and non-parametric regression". *Insurance: Mathematics and Economics*, **19**, 19–30.

Chalmin, P. (2004) *Cyclope*. Editions Economica, Paris.

Chambers, M.J. and R.E. Bailey (1996) "A theory of commodity price fluctuations". *Journal of Political Economy*, **104**(5), 924–957.

Clemmons, L., V. Kaminski and J. Hrgovcic (1999) "Weather derivatives: Hedging Mother Nature". In: *Insurance and Weather Derivatives*. RISK Books.

Clewlow, L. and C. Strickland (2000) *Energy Derivatives*. Lacima Publications.

Cootner, P. (1960) "Returns to speculators: Telser versus Keynes". *Journal of Political Economy*.

Cox, J.C., S. Ross and M. Rubinstein (1979) "Option pricing: A simplified approach". *Journal of Financial Economics*, **7**, 229–264.

Cox, J.C., J.E. Ingersoll and S.A. Ross (1981) "The relation between forward prices and futures prices". *Journal of Financial Economics*, **9**, 321–346.

Cox, J.C., J.E. Ingersoll and S.A. Ross (1985) "A theory of the term structure of interest rates". *Econometrica*, **53**, 385–408.

Deaton, A. and G. Laroque (1992) "On the behaviour of commodity prices". *Review of Economic Studies*, **59**, 1–23.

Declerck, F. (2004) *Où va le Cycle du Champagne*. Ed. Ceressec.

Deng, S. (1999) "Stochastic models of energy commodity prices and their applications: Mean reversion with jumps and spikes" (Working paper). Georgia Institute of Technology.

Deng, S., B. Johnson and A. Sogomonian (2001) "Exotic electricity options and the valuation of electricity generation and transmission assets". *Decision Support Systems*, **30**, 383–393.

Derman, E. and I. Kani (1994) "Riding on a Smile". *RISK*, January.

Dishel, R. (1999) "A weather risk management choice: Hedging with degree-day derivatives". In: *Insurance and Weather Derivatives*. RISK Books.

Duffie, D. (1989) *Futures Markets*. Prentice Hall.

Duffie, D. and R. Kan (1996) "A yield-factor model of interest rates". *Mathematical Finance*, **6**(4), 379–406.

Dupire, B. (1994) "Pricing with a smile". *RISK*, January

Eberlein, E. and G. Stahl (2003) "Both sides of a fence: A statistical and regulatory view of electricity risk". *RISK*, **8**, 34–38.

Edwards, F. and C. Ma (1992) *Futures and Options*. McGraw-Hill.

El Karoui, N., H. Geman and V. Lacoste, (2000) "On the role of state variables in interest rates models". *Applied Stochastic Models in Business and Industry*, **16**, 197–217.

Eydeland, A. and H. Geman (1995) "Asian options revisited: Inverting the Laplace Transform". *RISK*, March.

Eydeland, A. and H. Geman (1998) "Pricing power derivatives". *RISK*, September

Eydeland, A. and K. Wolyniec (2003) *Energy and Power Risk Management: New Developments in Modeling, Pricing and Hedging* (Wiley Finance Series). John Wiley & Sons, Chichester, UK.

Fama, E.F. and K.R. French (1987) "Commodity futures prices: Some evidence on forecast power, premiums and the theory of storage". *Journal of Business*, **60**, 55–73.

Fama, E.F. and K.R. French (1988) "Business cycles and the behavior of metals prices". *Journal of Finance*, **43**(5), 1075–1093.

Fusai, G. and A. Roncoroni (2005) *Implementing Models in Quantitative Finance: Methods and Cases*. Springer-Verlag, Berlin.

Gabillon, J. (1991) "The term structure of oil futures prices" (Working Paper 17). Oxford Institute for Energy Studies.

Gay, G. and S. Manaster (1986) "Implicit delivery options and optimal delivery strategies for financial futures contracts". *Journal of Financial Economics*, **16**, 41–73.

Geman, H. (1989) "The importance of the forward neutral probability measure for stochastic interest rates" (Working paper). ESSEC.

Geman, H. (1999) *Insurance and Weather Derivatives*. RISK Books.

Geman, H. (2000) "Scarcity and Price Volatility in Oil Markets" (EDF Trading Technical Report).

Geman, H. (2002) "Pure jump Lévy processes for asset price modelling". *Journal of Banking and Finance*, 1297–1316.

Geman, H. and M.P. Leonardi (2005) "Alternative approaches to weather derivatives valuation". *Managerial Finance*, **31**.

Geman, H. and V.N. Nguyen (2002) "Soybean inventory and forward curves dynamics" (ESSEC working paper). *Management Science* (forthcoming).

Geman, H. and V.N. Nguyen (2003) "Analysing volatility surfaces for energy commodities" (Working paper). ESSEC.

Geman, H. and A. Roncoroni (2002) "Understanding the fine structure of electricity prices". *Journal of Business*, forthcoming in 2005.

Geman, H. and O. Vasicek (2001) "Forwards and futures on non storable commodities: The case of electricity". *RISK*, August.

Geman, H. and M. Yor (1992) "Processus de Bessel, options asiatiques et fonctions confluentes hypergéométriques" (Note). *Comptes Rendus de l'Académie des Sciences*.

Geman, H. and M. Yor (1993) "Bessel processes, Asian options and perpetuities". *Mathematical Finance*, **4**(3), 349–375.

Geman, H, N. El Karoui and J.-C. Rochet (1995) "Changes of numéraire, changes of probability measure and option pricing". *Journal of Applied Probability*, **32**, 443–458.

Ghosh, S., C.L. Gilbert and A.J. Hughes Hallett (1987) *Stabilizing Speculative Commodity Markets*. Clarendon Press, Oxford, UK.

Gibson, R. and E.S. Schwartz, (1990) "Stochastic convenience yield and the pricing of oil contingent claims". *Journal of Finance*, **45**, 959–976.

Gladstone, J. (1965) "The climates and soils of south-western Australia in relation to grape-growing". *Journal of Australian Institutional Agricultural Science*, **31**.

Glasserman, P. (2000) *Monte Carlo Methods in Financial Engineering*. Springer-Verlag.

Grandmill, W. (1991) *Investing in Wheat, Corn and Soybeans*. Probus Financial Publishing.

Grossman, S.J. (1977) "The existence of futures markets, noisy rational expectations and informational externalities". *Review of Economic Studies*, **44**.

Halvorse, R. and T.R. Smith (1991) "A test of the theory of exhaustible resources". *Quarterly Jounal of Economics*, 123–163.

Hansen, T. and B. Jensen (2004) "Energy option in a HJM framework" (Working paper). Copenhagen Business School.

Harrison, J.M. and D. Kreps (1979) "Martingales and arbitrage in multiperiod securities market". *Journal of Economy Theory*, **20**, 381–408.

Harrison, J.M. and S. Pliska (1981) "Martingales and stochastic integrals in the theory of continuous trading". *Stochastic Processes and Their Applications*, **11**, 381–408.

Harvey, A.C. (1989) *Forecasting, Structural Time Series Models and the Kalman Filter*. Cambridge University Press.

Heston, S.L. (1993) "A closed-form solution for options with stochastic volatility with applications to bond and currency options". *Review of Financial Studies*, **6**(2), 327–343.

Hilliard, R. and J. Reis (1998) "Valuation of commodity Futures and options under stochastic convenience yields, interest rates, and jump diffusions in the spot". *Journal of Financial and Quantitative Analysis*, **33**(1), 61–86.

Hobbs, B.F., C.B. Metzler and J.S. Pang (2000) "Strategic gaming analysis for electric power systems: An MPEC approach". *IEEE Transactions on Power Systems*, **15**(2), 638–645.

Hotelling, H. (1931) "The economics of exhaustible resources". *Journal of Political Economy*, **39**, 137–212.

Ilic, M. and J. Zaborszky (2000) *Dynamics and Control of Large Electric Power Systems*. John Wiley & Sons.

Jarrow, R. (1987) "The pricing of commodity options with stochastic interest rates". *Advances in Options and Futures Research*, **2**.

Kaldor, N. (1939) "Speculation and economic stability". *The Review of Economic Studies*, **7**, 1–27

Kavussanos, M. and N. Nomikos (2001) "Price discovery, causality and forecasting in the freight futures market". *Journal of Banking and Finance* (forthcoming).

Kemna, A. and T. Vorst (1990) "A pricing method for options based on average asset values". *Journal of Banking and Finance*, **14**, 113–130.

Keynes, J.M (1930) *The Applied Theory of Money*. Macmillan & Co., London.

Kleinman, G. (2001) *Commodity Futures and Options: A Step-by-step Guide to Successful Trading*. Prentice Hall.

Koekebakker, S. and F. Ollmar (2005) "Forward curves dynamics in the Nordic electricity market". *Managerial Finance*, **31**.

Litterman, R. and J. Scheinkman (1991) "Common factors affecting bond returns". *Journal of Fixed Income*, 54–61.

Litzenberger, R.H. and N. Rabinowitz (1995) "Backwardation in oil Futures markets: Theory and empirical evidence". *Journal of Finance*, **50**(5), 1517–1545.

Lowry, M., J. Glauber, M. Miranda and P. Helmberger (1987) "Pricing and storage of field crops: A quarterly model applied to soybeans". *Journal of Agricultural Economics*, **69**, 740–749.

Madden, M. and N. White (2001) *Liberalising Gas Markets in Europe*. The Petroleum Economist Ltd, London.

Margrabe, W. (1978) "The value of an option to exchange one asset for another". *Journal of Finance*, **33**, 177–187.

McKean, H. (1965) "Appendix: A free boundary problem for the heat equation arising from a problem in mathematical economics". *Industrial Management Review*, **6**(Spring), 32–39.

Merton, R. (1973) "The theory of rational option pricing". *Bell Journal of Economics and Management Science*, **4**, 141–183.

Merton, R. (1976) "Option pricing when underlying stock returns are discontinuous". *Journal of Financial Economics*, **3**, 125–144.

Merton, R. (1990) *Continuous-time Finance*. B. Blackwell.

Metropolis, N., A. Rosenbluth, M. Rosenbluth, A. Teller and E. Teller (1953) "Equation of state calculations by fast computing machines". *Journal of Chem. Phys.*, **21**, 1087–1092.

Miltersen, K. and E. Schwartz (1998) "Pricing of options on commodity futures with stochastic term structures of convenience yields and interest rates". *Journal of Financial and Quantitative Analysis*, **33**, 33–60.

Ng, V.K. and S.C. Pirrong (1994) "Fundamentals and volatility: Storage, spreads, and the dynamics of metals prices". *Journal of Business*, **67**(2), 203–230.

Perfetti, P. (1997) *Analyses Techniques*. Economica Ed., Paris.

Pilipovic, D. (1997) *Energy Risk: Valuing and Managing Energy Derivatives*. McGraw-Hill.

Pindyck, R. (2001) "The dynamics of commodity spot and futures markets: A primer". *Energy Journal*, **22**(3), 1–29.

Reagan, P.B. (1982) "Inventory and price behavior". *Review of Economic Studies*, **49**, 137–142.

Reagan, P.B. and M.L. Weitzman (1982) "Asymmetries in price and quantity adjustments by the competitive firm". *Journal of Economics Theory*, **27**, 410–420.

Richter, M.C. and C. Sorensen (2002) "Stochastic volatility and seasonality in commodity Futures and options: the case of soybeans" (Working paper). Copenhagen Business School.

Routledge, B.R., D.J. Seppi and C.S. Spatt. (2000) "Equilibrium forward curves for commodities". *Journal of Finance*, **55**(3), 1297–1338.

Samuelson, P. (1965) "Proof that properly anticipated prices fluctuate randomly". *Industrial Management Review*, **6**(Spring), 41–49.

Samuelson, P. (1965) "Rational theory of warrant pricing". *Industrial Management Review*, **6**(Spring), 13–31.

Scheinkman, J. and J. Schechtman (1983) "A simple competitive model with production and storage". *Review of Economics Studies*, **50**, 427–441.

Schneeweis, T. and R. Spurgin (1997) "Comparisons of commodity and managed futures benchmark indexes". *Journal of Derivatives*, **4**, 33–51.

Schwartz, E.S. (1997) "The stochastic behavior of commodity prices: Implications for valuation and hedging". *Journal of Finance*, **52**(3), 923–973.

Simon, Y. (1986) *Bourses de Commerce et Marchés de Marchandises*. Dalloz, Paris.

Slade, M.E. (1982) "Trends in natural-resource commodity prices: An analysis in the time domain". *Journal of Environmental Economics and Management*, **9**, 122–159.

Taleb, N. (1998) *Dynamic Hedging* (Wiley Finance Series). John Wiley & Sons, Chichester, UK.

Telser, L.G. (1958) "Futures trading and the storage of cotton and wheat". *Journal of Political Economy*, **66**, 233–255.

Vasicek, O. (1977) "An equilibrium characterization of the term structure". *Journal of Financial Economics*, **5**(3), 177–188.

Villaplana, P. (2004) "A two-state variables model for electricity prices". *Third World Congress of the Bachelier Finance Society, Chicago*.

Williams, J.C. (1986) *The Economic Function of Futures Markets*. Cambridge University Press.

Williams, J.C. and B.D. Wright (1991) *Storage and Commodity Markets*. Cambridge University Press.

Wood, A. and B. Wollenberg (1996) *Power Generation, Operation and Control*. Wiley Interscience.

Working, H. (1948) "Theory of the inverse carrying charge in Futures markets". *Journal Farm Economics*, **30**, 1–28.

Working, H. (1949) "The theory of the price of storage". *American Economic Review*, **39**, 1254–1262.

Working, H. (1953) "Futures trading and hedging". *American Economic Review*, **43**, 314–343.

Index

Lightning Source UK Ltd.
Milton Keynes UK
UKHW031941250819
348506UK00002B/2/P